Adobe Audition: Soundtracks for Digital Video

LIMITED WARRANTY AND DISCLAIMER OF LIABILITY

THE CD-ROM THAT ACCOMPANIES THE BOOK MAY BE USED ON A SINGLE PC ONLY. THE LICENSE DOES NOT PERMIT THE USE ON A NETWORK (OF ANY KIND). YOU FURTHER AGREE THAT THIS LICENSE GRANTS PERMISSION TO USE THE PRODUCTS CONTAINED HEREIN, BUT DOES NOT GIVE YOU RIGHT OF OWNERSHIP TO ANY OF THE CONTENT OR PRODUCT CONTAINED ON THIS CD-ROM. USE OF THIRD-PARTY SOFTWARE CONTAINED ON THIS CD-ROM IS LIMITED TO AND SUBJECT TO LICENSING TERMS FOR THE RESPECTIVE PRODUCTS.

FIREWALL MEDIA (AN IMPRINT OF LAXMI PUBLICATIONS PVT. LTD.) AND/OR ANYONE WHO HAS BEEN INVOLVED IN THE WRITING, CREATION, OR PRODUCTION OF THE ACCOMPANYING CODE ("THE SOFTWARE") OR THE THIRD-PARTY PRODUCTS CONTAINED ON THE CD-ROM OR TEXTUAL MATERIAL IN THE BOOK, CANNOT AND DO NOT WARRANT THE PERFORMANCE OR RESULTS THAT MAY BE OBTAINED BY USING THE SOFTWARE OR CONTENTS OF THE BOOK. THE AUTHOR AND PUBLISHER HAVE USED THEIR BEST EFFORTS TO ENSURE THE ACCURACY AND FUNCTIONALITY OF THE TEXTUAL MATERIAL AND PROGRAMS CONTAINED HEREIN. WE HOWEVER, MAKE NO WARRANTY OF ANY KIND, EXPRESS OR IMPLIED, REGARDING THE PERFORMANCE OF THESE PROGRAMS OR CONTENTS. THE SOFTWARE IS SOLD "AS IS" WITHOUT WARRANTY (EXCEPT FOR DEFECTIVE MATERIALS USED IN MANUFACTURING THE DISK OR DUE TO FAULTY WORKMANSHIP).

THE AUTHOR, THE PUBLISHER, DEVELOPERS OF THIRD-PARTY SOFTWARE, AND ANYONE INVOLVED IN THE PRODUCTION AND MANUFACTURING OF THIS WORK SHALL NOT BE LIABLE FOR DAMAGES OF ANY KIND ARISING OUT OF THE USE OF (OR THE INABILITY TO USE) THE PROGRAMS, SOURCE CODE, OR TEXTUAL MATERIAL CONTAINED IN THIS PUBLICATION. THIS INCLUDES, BUT IS NOT LIMITED TO, LOSS OF REVENUE OR PROFIT, OR OTHER INCIDENTAL OR CONSEQUENTIAL DAMAGES ARISING OUT OF THE USE OF THE PRODUCT.

THE SOLE REMEDY IN THE EVENT OF A CLAIM OF ANY KIND IS EXPRESSLY LIMITED TO REPLACEMENT OF THE BOOK AND/OR CD-ROM, AND ONLY AT THE DISCRETION OF FIREWALL MEDIA (AN IMPRINT OF LAXMI PUBLICATIONS PVT. LTD.).

THE USE OF "IMPLIED WARRANTY" AND CERTAIN "EXCLUSIONS" VARIES FROM STATE TO STATE, AND MAY NOT APPLY TO THE PURCHASER OF THIS PRODUCT.

Adobe Audition: Soundtracks for Digital Video

Roman Petelin
Yury Petelin

FIREWAL MEDIA
(An Imprint of Laxmi Publications Pvt. Ltd.)
BANGALORE • CHENNAI • COCHIN • GUWAHATI • HYDERABAD
JALANDHAR • KOLKATA • LUCKNOW • MUMBAI • RANCHI
NEW DELHI

Published by :
FIREWAL MEDIA
(*An Imprint of Laxmi Publications Pvt. Ltd.*)
113, Golden House, Daryaganj,
New Delhi-110002

Phone : 011-43 53 25 00
Fax : 011-43 53 25 28

www.laxmipublications.com
info@laxmipublications.com

Economy Edition Price : **Rs. 250.00** *Only.* *Edition* : 2010

OFFICES

© **Bangalore**	080-26 61 15 61	© **Chennai**	044-24 34 47 26
© **Cochin**	0484-237 70 04, 405 13 03	© **Guwahati**	0361-254 36 69, 251 38 81
© **Hyderabad**	040-24 65 23 33	© **Jalandhar**	0181-222 12 72
© **Kolkata**	033-22 27 43 84	© **Lucknow**	0522-220 95 78
© **Mumbai**	022-24 91 54 15, 24 92 78 69	© **Ranchi**	0651-221 47 64

FAD-2835-250-ADOBE AUDI:SOUNDTR DIGI-PET **C—818/09/11**

Printed at : Sanjeev Offset Printers, Delhi.

Contents

To our beloved daughter
and granddaughter Anna

Introduction

This book is about Adobe Audition, one of the most powerful sound editors available today. In it, we look at how the application can be used to record and process a high-quality sound track for digital video.

The predecessors of Adobe Audition are Cool Edit and Cool Edit Pro. The best features of these applications have been retained in Adobe Audition, and new tools for sound processing have also appeared.

Some time ago, we wrote book [3], which contains a comprehensive description of Cool Edit Pro 2 interface and techniques for using the application. The print run sold out, and we began to prepare the second edition. We were planning to add a description of new features in the latest version, Cool Edit Pro 2.1, but it turned out that the application had changed its name and owner. It is now called Adobe Audition, and the rights to it belong to Adobe Systems Incorporated (**http://www.adobe.com**).

Thus, the rights to a powerful sound editor were purchased by a company well known for its applications for working with images. In our opinion, this indicates that professional and amateur movie directors are concerned with improving the quality of the sound that accompanies digital video.

This is a book about the latest version (at the time of writing) of an application that, under its new name, is likely to become even more popular.

In this book, we describe the application's features while working on a particular project. For the project, we chose to create a video clip with a sound track. We recorded sound in two ways: with a video camera (speech synchronous with video) and directly to an Adobe Audition file (a narrator's voice accompanying an independent video image). Each chapter, in turn, describes and demonstrates with examples how this original material can be improved by using processing and effects available in the application. All the important intermediate results of the conversions are saved in files on the disc that accompanies this book.

The book isn't a comprehensive description of Adobe Audition. Readers who wish to know all the features of the application should refer to [3].

Features to Keep in Mind

To get the most out of Adobe Audition in your creative work, you should keep in mind some of its important features. Let's look at them more closely.

Adobe Audition is intended for work with digital audio. This means that analog sound waves must be first converted to a series of binary digital samples (this process is called sampling). Conversion is done using an analog-to-digital converter (ADC). As a result, a digital image of the sound is obtained that is called a waveform.

Waveforms are stored on the hard disk as files of various formats. Most often, these are WAV files. Thus, when you are "assembling" an audio composition in Adobe Audition, you are using the WAV files as building blocks.

Adobe Audition has two principally different working modes: editing individual waveforms and multitrack editing a set of waveforms. Each mode has a main menu and main window: **Edit Waveform View** and **Multitrack View**. In fact, there are two sound editors that have different purposes and are combined in one functional whole. You should be aware that editing operations done in **Edit Waveform View** (such as cut, paste, and processing with effects) are destructive by nature. When you save a file, the changes are introduced directly into the waveform. Editing done in **Multitrack View** (such as moving and joining waveforms, changing the volume and panorama, adjusting the parameters of real-time effects, etc.) is non-destructive.

The **Undo** function gives you freedom when working with waveforms. You need not worry that an interesting result in your creative work might be lost. However, freedom has its cost. The ability to repeatedly undo operations requires memory space. Although all automatically created copies will be automatically deleted from the hard disk after you close the file or exit the application, you need a lot of free space on your hard disk when working with Adobe Audition. However, you can decrease the number of **Undo** levels or disable this function completely if you are short of memory.

Many musical editors with audio data processing tools offer two ways to use effects: applying an effect in real time and recomputing audio data. The first is more convenient, because you can adjust the parameters of the effect and hear the result immediately. However, you need a powerful computer to do this. Using an effect in the recomputing mode allows you to process audio data with a relatively "weak" computer, but the process can take a long time. This might discourage you from experimentation or introducing improvements.

The best strategy of using effects could be the following. First, turn on the loop playback of a waveform and find the effect parameters that fit best to your intentions. Then, recompute the waveform once by applying the effect with the found parameters to it.

In Adobe Audition, you can use both its native, built-in effects and those connected using DirectX.

An important feature of Adobe Audition is support for real-time effects in the **Multitrack View** mode.

The main use of effects in the **Edit Waveform View** mode is recomputation of audio data. A full-featured real-time mode is not provided in **Edit Waveform View**. However, there is a substitute for the real-time mode. The **Preview** button is available in the effect dialog box, so you can try the parameters of the effect. Any changes to the parameters that you make in the effect dialog box using its controls are heard immediately. However, to use this feature effectively, you should have a powerful computer. Unlike the "true" real-time mode, the preview mode only lets you use one effect at a time.

We already mentioned that Adobe Audition is a multitrack environment that allows a user to put any number of waveforms (blocks) on different tracks to play them simultaneously or combine all the tracks into one later. Mixing involves combining all waveforms on the tracks into two (or more) output channels. You can edit, add, or remove blocks, and Adobe Audition will continually monitor the changes (such as moving or deleting a block, changing the volume, etc.) made during this multichannel session. As soon as you change something, Adobe Audition computes the changes and corrects the mix sent to the application's output. These corrections are done by the application in the background mode, i.e., background mixing directed to a pair of output devices (a single stereo sound card) or to several output devices (a few stereo sound cards, or one multichannel sound card). Adobe Audition generates mixes for any set of the output devices used. If you use one stereo sound card, Adobe Audition generates only one stereo mix. If your computer is connected to a multichannel system, a separate mix must be created for each output device. The multichannel output requires a lot of processing, meaning that mixing becomes slower. The sound card and the computer should match each other, and it is pointless to install an expensive sound-digitizing device in a cheap computer.

In addition to audio files of various formats, such as WAV, Adobe Audition allows you to use 'session files' (with the extension SES). Earlier, we called WAV files the building blocks, using which any audio composition, such as a song, can be assembled. Now we can say that a session file is a song proper, although an SES file does not actually contain any audio data. It is very small in size, and it contains only instructions for Adobe Audition in the following form:

- ❐ Paths to the WAV files used
- ❐ Track names
- ❐ Playback start/stop times of particular WAV files

- ❒ Volume level and panorama set before playing each file, and how these parameters should change during the playback
- ❒ Connected real-time effects, and how their parameters should change

You could compare an SES file to a conductor, and WAV files to the members of an orchestra. The conductor instructs each performer when he or she must start playing and how the part should be played. The conductor needs the orchestra. Similarly, an SES file is meaningful only when it and the session WAV files are located in certain folders. You cannot just copy an SES file onto a diskette and insert the diskette into another computer, and you cannot rename a session WAV file or move it to another folder. If you do, and then try to open the SES file to play the composition, it will not work. The conductor won't find the musicians at the appropriate places, and the concert won't take place. This doesn't mean it is impossible to move SES files and the related WAV files from one folder to another. For this purpose, Adobe Audition includes special file-saving operations.

In Adobe Audition, it is possible to extract audio data from AVI files and tracks of audio CDs. In the multitrack mode, MIDI and AVI files can be used in addition to audio files. The ability to work with video is most important.

The multitrack mode implements modern editing technologies using automation envelopes. Real-time effects can be applied not only to individual tracks, but also to track groups that make up buses. Using a mixer, you can route signals between effects connected to a bus. Also available are operations related to creating and using loops and grooves.

The application recognizes DX effects installed in the system, and decides whether they are compatible with it.

In addition to the tools for analyzing the processed sound properties that were already available in earlier versions of Cool Edit Pro (such as the current and instantaneous spectrum analyzers and the histogram of audio signal level distribution), Adobe Audition has a virtual stereo goniometer that allows the user to judge the quality of the stereo field (in particular, the mono compatibility of a composition) from the appearance of Lissajous figures.

Adobe Audition also has a built-in proprietary WAV-to-MP3 converter.

The Structure of the Book

This book consists of twelve chapters, an introduction, two appendices, and an index. It is accompanied by a CD Extra-format disc.

Chapter 1 covers an extremely important issue: How to prepare Adobe Audition for work. The convenience of working and the quality of the results depend on making the necessary preliminary settings correctly.

The chapter describes the options of dialog boxes you'll be using when preparing the application for work. The following issues are considered:

- General and system settings
- Selecting audio data processing parameters and multitrack editing parameters
- Editing lists of recording/playback devices

We recommend that you return periodically to the first chapter as you master new techniques. This will allow you to better understand the goals of the preparation operations and their influence on the result.

Chapter 2 covers working with files and waveforms. It looks at how to open, save, and close files, control the waveform view, and play audio. In addition, we'll examine how to collect a waveform sequence on one track, allow other applications to use the opened file, clear the disk space from unwanted files, and extract audio data from a digital audio CD to Adobe Audition.

In *Chapter 3*, we'll look at how to record sound with a microphone. This involves choosing and connecting a microphone, creating a new project, setting a record level, starting recording, and monitoring its course.

This chapter also contains a plan for creating a video clip using recorded sound. The following chapters will demonstrate the main techniques of analysis and processing audio data that are recorded from a microphone and intended to be a component of the asynchronous audio accompaniment of the video clip.

The source material consists of a few takes with a narrator's voice (the file EX03_02.WAV located in the EXAMPLES folder on the CD accompanying the book). This is a "raw" recording that was intentionally made under conditions unfavorable for work with a microphone.

Chapter 4 demonstrates the tools that should be used for analyzing a recording, and how this should be done. The essence of analysis is clarified, and the following techniques are described:

- Monitoring the recording
- Qualitative (visual) and quantitative (with meters) analysis of the waveform and the level of the recorded audio signal
- Spectral analysis of instantaneous (**Spectral View**) and classical (**Frequency Analysis**) spectrum

This chapter also includes a clarification of the file statistics contained in a level distribution histogram and examples of using the histogram for choosing the parameters of dynamic range processing.

The use of the analytical tools is illustrated with examples (the files EX04_01.WAV and EX04_02.WAV, located in the EXAMPLES folder on the CD accompanying the book).

Finally, the chapter presents a signal processing strategy (including montage, noise reduction, filtration, dynamic processing, and processing with effects) that is implemented in the subsequent chapters.

In *Chapter 5*, we look at how to get rid of flaws, noise, and distortions that are present in the recording. This involves deleting unwanted fragments, montage of the recording, waveform normalization, and many other operations.

In this chapter, we also discuss the techniques of using tools that help to struggle against distortions: **Clip Restoration** and **Noise Reduction** (the latter is based on analysis of a noise sample).

All intermediate operations are illustrated with the files from EX05_01.WAV to EX05_03.WAV, and the final result is saved in the EX05_04.WAV file (all the files are located in the EXAMPLES folder on the CD accompanying the book).

In *Chapter 6*, we discuss frequency filtration and examine filters built into the application:

- **Dynamic EQ** — an equalizer with the dynamic control of the adjustment frequency, gain, and bandwidth
- **FFT Filter** — a filter based on the Fast Fourier Transform
- **Graphic Equalizer** — a universal graphic equalizer
- **Notch Filter** — a multiband notch filter
- **Parametric Equalizer** — a seven-band parametric equalizer
- **Quick Filter** — an eight-band graphic equalizer
- **Scientific Filters** — Bessel, Butterworth, and Chebyshev filters

Continuing our work on the project, we demonstrate how to remove the alternate-current background noise with the **Notch Filter** and, most importantly, obtain a signal (the file EX06_01.WAV), in which unwanted spectral components are attenuated with the **FFT Filter**.

In *Chapter 7*, we discuss dynamic processing and examine **Dynamics Range Processing**, one of the dynamic processing devices available in Adobe Audition.

Based on the statistical analysis described in *Chapter 4*, we select the parameters of the dynamic range processing and apply it to the signal. The result is saved in the NSINC1.WAV file.

We apply the complete set of processings to the other audio files and save the results in the file NSINC2.WAV (the second asynchronous fragment of the sound track) and in the files SINC1.WAV, SINC2.WAV, and SINC3.WAV (the synchronous fragments of the sound track). The order of these files in the project should be as follows: SINC1.WAV, NSINC1.WAV, SINC2.WAV, NSINC2.WAV, and SINC3.WAV.

In *Chapter 8*, we introduce built-in effects based on the signal delay: **Delay, Dynamic Delay, Multitap Delay, Echo, Echo Chamber, QuickVerb, Reverb**, and **Full Reverb**.

For demonstration purposes, we process the signal saved in the NSINC1.WAV file with some of the effects and save the results in the files from EX08_01.WAV to EX08_03.WAV.

In *Chapter 9*, we describe techniques for using plug-ins connected to Adobe Audition via DirectX. We introduce one of the DirectX plug-ins from the package Waves Platinum Native Bundle 4: Waves RVox, which is a gate, compressor, and limiter at the same time.

We use Waves RVox to reduce noise and amplify the level of the signal saved in the EX07_01.WAV file. The result is saved in the EX09_01.WAV file.

In *Chapter 10*, we comprehensively describe the work in the multitrack environment. Along with general principles of work in the **Multitrack View** mode, we describe in detail:

- Methods of recording audio data during a multitrack session and techniques of importing waveforms into the session
- Techniques of choosing track attributes and connecting effects to the tracks
- Working with buses and a mixer and locking tracks to free up processor resources
- Peculiarities of using the parametric equalizers connected to each track

The chapter also describes operations with blocks (such as moving, copying, splitting, deleting, grouping, and selecting fragments and groups of blocks), loops, and grooves. All available methods of tempo control and tonality transposition are described.

Much attention is paid to automation. We describe methods for creating and editing automation envelopes.

Chapter 11 covers work with the sound track of a digital video. It describes the techniques of exporting the sound track of a movie from Adobe Premiere Pro and importing it to Adobe Audition. A few tricks of working in a multitrack project are illustrated with an example of mixing a stereo sound track in Adobe Audition.

Chapter 12 considers issues of creating surround-sound projects. We present brief information about multichannel audio, discuss the peculiarities of building a 5.1 studio, and describe the **Multichannel Encoder** dialog box that allows the user to position imaginary sound sources over the surround panorama and control their movement.

The chapter also discusses passing a 5.1 sound track mixed in Adobe Audition to an Adobe Premiere Pro project.

Appendix 1 describes the contents of the CD that accompanies this book. A special feature of this disc is that it is in CD Extra format, i.e., is suitable for both playing with a CD player and reading with a computer.

Its CD-ROM partition contains example projects and files with intermediate and final results of processing, as well as some useful information and a few musical compositions. The material is arranged as an offline version of our site **www.musicalpc.com.**

The **CD Digital Audio** partition contains our musical compositions mixed down using Adobe Audition.

Appendix 2 contains a list of files with examples located in the EXAMPLES folder on the CD accompanying the book. It also contains a brief description of each file and the relations between the available files.

References

1. Petelin, Roman, and Yury Petelin. *PC Music Home Studio: Secrets, Tips, & Tricks.* Wayne: A-LIST, *2002.*
2. Petelin, Roman, and Yury Petelin. *Cakewalk SONAR: Plug-Ins & PC Music Recording, Arrangement, and Mixing.* Wayne: A-LIST, 2002.
3. Petelin, Roman, and Yury Petelin. *Cool Edit Pro 2 in Use.* Wayne: A-LIST, 2003.
4. Petelin, Roman, and Yury Petelin. *Cubase SX 2: Virtual MIDI and Audio Studio.* Wayne: A-LIST, 2004.

Chapter 1

Preparing for Work

Generally speaking, you can start working with Adobe Audition without making special settings. The demo project supplied with the application will sound properly, and you'll be able to record. However, while working with the application (or if you encounter problems), you'll have to open the **Options** menu, which contains commands and submenus that define the working modes of Adobe Audition:

- **Timed Record Mode** — switches on recording with the timer.
- **Monitor Record Level** — switches on the signal level meter (rather than select this mode, you can double-click the meter in the main window).
- **Show Levels on Play and Record** — displays the signal level not only during recording, but also during playback.
- **MIDI Trigger Enable** — enables control of the application via the MIDI interface. The parameters of this mode are set using the **Shortcuts (Keyboard&MIDI Triggers)** command.
- **Synchronize Cursor Across Windows** — enables retention of the cursor position or a selected portion of the waveform when you switch between opened files. (This can be useful when making a recording montage. For example: The mode is on, you're working with the file 1.WAV and you have selected a fragment between positions 0:01:00 and 0:02:00. If you switch the main window to the file 2.WAV, the fragment from 0:01:00 to 0:02:00 will be also selected in that waveform.)
- **Windows Recording Mixer** — opens the standard Windows mixer dialog box.

- **Start Default Windows CD Player** — starts the default Windows CD player.
- **Scripts & Batch Processing** — edits a list of signal processing operations (a script).
- **Settings** — specifies the application's parameters and working modes.
- **Device Properties** — selects playback and recording devices.
- **Device Order** — edits the lists of playback and recording devices.
- **Shortcuts (Keyboard&MIDI Triggers)** — selects shortcuts (on the computer keyboard and the MIDI keyboard).

A comprehensive description of all these commands is given in [3]. We shall look at just three of them for now: **Settings, Device Properties,** and **Device Order.** Using them, you can finely adjust the application's interaction with the hardware; set some audio data processing parameters, and customize the application interface as you want. The purpose of the options available through these commands is described in this chapter.

1.1. Selecting the Main Settings Using the *Settings* Window

Select the **Option > Settings** command. The **Settings** window will appear. It contains seven tabs: **General, System, Colors, Display, Data, Multitrack,** and **SMPTE.** Specify the main application settings by opening these tabs in turn.

1.1.1. General Settings – the General *Tab*

The **General** tab of the **Settings** dialog box (Fig. 1.1) contains options that define general application settings.

There are five checkboxes in the upper left part of the tab.

The **Show Tip of the Day** and **Use shiny look** checkboxes don't affect application operation. If the **Show Tip of the Day** checkbox is checked, a "tip of the day" will appear every time you start the application. If the **Use shiny look** checkbox is unchecked, the toolbar buttons and some other controls will look flat; if it is checked, they will appear three-dimensional. The other three checkboxes are more significant:

- **Auto-play on command-line load** — turns on auto-play mode if the user starts the application from the command line and specifies an audio file name as a parameter.
- **Live update during recording** — draws a waveform in the working area of the main window during recording.

- **Auto-scroll during playback and recording**— fixes the cursor in place during playback or recording (while the waveform will move relative to it).

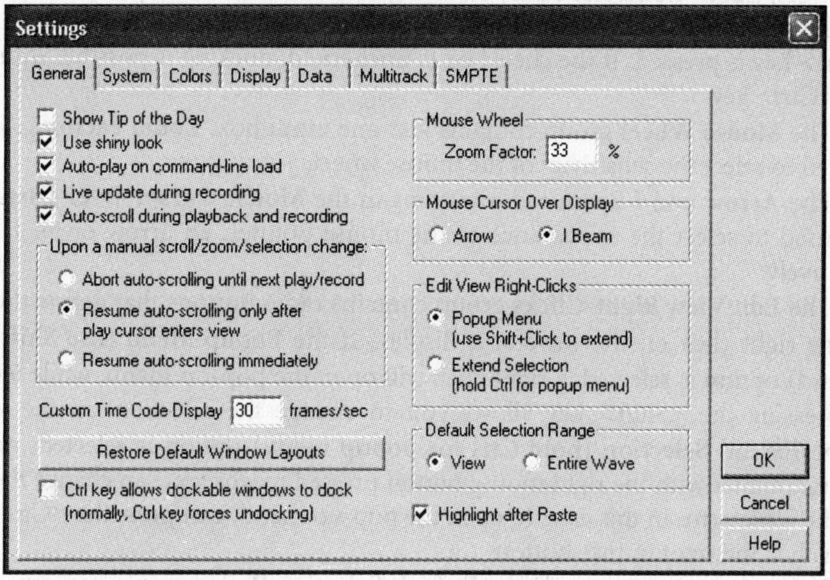

Fig. 1.1. General tab of the **Settings** dialog box

The last two modes are dependent on hardware. If you have a slow processor, failures during playback or recording are likely.

Using the **Upon a manual scroll/zoom/selection change** group, you can select the scrolling method used when you change the selection or the waveform zoom during playback or recording:

- **Abort auto-scrolling until next play/record** — stops auto scrolling; to resume it, you have to start recording or playback.
- **Resume auto-scrolling only after play cursor enters view** — resumes auto scrolling only after the cursor enters the displayed portion of the waveform.
- **Resume auto-scrolling immediately**— self-explanatory.

The **Custom Time Code Display … frames/sec** input box selects the custom time code (hours:minutes:seconds:frames), in which you can change only the frames-per-second rate.

The **Restore Default Window Layouts** button restores the default settings for all Adobe Audition windows.

If the <Ctrl> key allows dockable windows to dock (normally, <Ctrl> key forces undocking) checkbox is checked, some main window panels (including **Transport Controls, Zoom Controls, Time, Selections/View Controls, Play List,** and **Organizer**) can be docked to each other and to the borders of the main window only when the <Ctrl> key is pressed. If the checkbox is unchecked, docking is possible without using the <Ctrl> key.

The **Mouse Wheel** group contains just one input box, **Zoom Factor: ... %,** which is used to select the sensitivity of the mouse wheel.

The **Arrow** and **I Beam** radio buttons in the **Mouse Cursor Over Display** group are used to select the appearance of the mouse pointer: an arrow or an I-beam, respectively.

The **Edit View Right-Clicks** group contains radio buttons that define the function of the right click on the waveform display. If the **Popup Menu (use Shift+Click to extend)** option is selected, a right click will open the pop-up menu, while left-clicking at pressing the <Shift> key allows you to change the selection on the waveform. If the **Extend Selection (hold Ctrl for popup menu)** option is selected, moving the mouse pointer with the right mouse button pressed means you can change the selection on the waveform. In this case, to open the pop-up menu, first press the <Ctrl> key, and then click the right mouse button.

Using the radio buttons in the **Default Selection Range** group, you can change the default selection on the waveform. When the **View** option is selected, the default selection will be the fragment of the waveform displayed in the working area of the main window. If you select the **Entire Wave** option, the entire current waveform will be considered selected by default (including fragments that aren't visible due to a high zoom level). The setting selected in this group is important for processing the waveform with effects. If you don't select a waveform fragment beforehand, the effect will act on the default selection.

If the **Highlight after Paste** checkbox is checked, the audio data just inserted into the current waveform will be highlighted (the default color is white). Otherwise, it will be difficult to distinguish the inserted fragment from the data in the waveform.

1.1.2. System Settings — the System Tab

The options under the **System** tab of the **Settings** dialog box (Fig. 1.2) allow you to change the application's system settings.

First, and most important: If you don't understand the purpose of the options on this tab, don't change anything! Use the **System** tab only when you really need it, and only after reading the description given in this section.

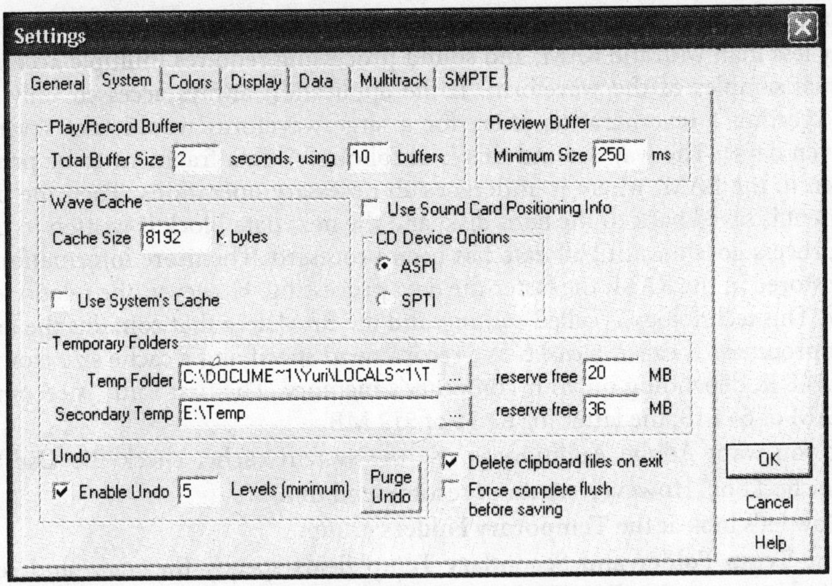

Fig. 1.2. Settings dialog box, **System** tab

Let's look at the **Play/Record Buffer** group.

The **Total Buffer Size ... seconds** field defines the total size (in seconds) of buffers that contain audio data. The greater the size of buffers containing temporary audio data during playback or recording, the more reliably the application will work. On the other hand, the more memory is occupied by the buffers, the less memory is left for other purposes.

The **using ... buffers** input box shows the number of the buffers discussed in the previous paragraph. This number also can affect sound quality: Some audio drivers don't work correctly if there are too many buffers. This leads to failures during playback or recording. If this happens, try to decrease the number of the buffers or change their total size.

The **Preview Buffer** group contains the only field, **Minimum Size ... ms.** In this field, you can specify the size of the buffer to be used when you want to listen to the tentative results of processing a waveform with an effect. When the buffer is small, any changes in the effect's settings will become apparent instantly (without a noticeable delay), but playback failures are likely. With larger buffer sizes, you're unlikely to encounter failures because the application will have enough time to process audio data, but its response to adjustments of the effect's settings will be much slower.

Now let's look at the **Wave Cache** group. Here, **Cache Size ... K bytes** shows the size of the cache memory. The application allows free operation with waveforms that last long time and are hundreds of megabytes in size. When necessary, Adobe Audition uses the free space on the hard disk. The rate of data exchange with the disk is significantly less than with the RAM, and sound processing requires multiple accesses to individual samples of the waveform. If the application always accessed only the hard disk, creating a reverberation effect for a large waveform would take several hours (or even days). The way around this is as follows. A data fragment to be processed is written to the RAM, where it undergoes all necessary operations. Then the processed fragment is saved back to the hard disk, and the next data block is written to the RAM. The process goes on until all data has been processed. The more information temporarily stored in the RAM, the faster the data processing. However, the relationship isn't linear. This technology is called *caching*, and the RAM area that contains the data block being processed is called a *cache*. We recommend specifying a cache size from 8,192 K to 32,768 K, depending on your computer's memory. The first value is recommended for RAM of 64 MB, the latter for RAM of 512 MB.

If you want Adobe Audition to use the system cache, check the **Use System's Cache** checkbox. However, we don't recommend this.

Now let's look at the **Temporary Folders** group.

The **Temp Folder** and **Secondary Temp** fields specify the main and secondary folders for temporary files. To improve the application's performance, these folders should be on different physical disks. For each of the temporary folders, you can specify the minimum space on the disk in the **reserve free ... MB** input boxes. The application won't use this space for auxiliary information. If the space becomes less than the value specified here, the application will warn you, and you'll be able to delete data that you don't need.

The **Undo** group contains options that control the Undo function:

- **Enable Undo** — turns on and off the undo mode with the number of levels specified in the **Levels (minimum)** input box.
- **Purge Undo** — deletes auxiliary information necessary for the undo operation with a level higher than the specified one.

For example, if you performed ten operations and clicked the **Purge Undo** button when the maximum number of undo levels was five, you would be able to undo only the last five operations (not ten). Sometimes, if there is little free space on the disk, it makes sense to limit the possibility of recovering very old versions of the waveform.

Now all that is left are two checkboxes on the **System** tab.

If the **Delete clipboard files on exit** checkbox is checked, the data on the clipboard will be deleted after you exit the application. Otherwise, the data will remain on the clipboard, and you'll be able to use it in other applications.

Adobe Audition makes it possible to avoid working directly with audio files. If you use the **File > Flush Virtual File** command in the **Edit Waveform View** mode, all the information from the current file will be transparently copied to one of the temporary folders, and the source file will be closed from the point of view of the operating system. Thanks to this, other applications will be able to use the file. Using MS Windows tools, you can rename or even delete files previously loaded in Adobe Audition. However, if you keep on working with this file in Adobe Audition, it will look as though nothing happened to the file. Having finished processing the file, you can save it, and the newly edited file will appear in place of the old one. This technique is called *flushing*. To avoid problems when overwriting the original version of the file with the new version, the **Force complete flush before saving** checkbox is provided. It is unchecked by default: If you check it, the **Flush Virtual File** command will be executed automatically (if it wasn't done manually) and transparently. In other words, audio data will be first copied to a temporary folder, the original file will be closed, and only then will the save command be executed. Naturally, this will slow down execution of the save command.

1.1.3. Interface Colors and Display Parameters – the Colors *and* Display *Tabs*

Using the options of the **Colors** tab in the **Settings** window (the tab contains the **Waveform**, **Spectral**, and **Controls** tabs), you can specify the colors of the interface controls. Because the colors don't influence how the application works, we will not describe the options under this tab: Their purpose is intuitive. If you need them, you can read [3].

The application can display an audio file in spectral representation (as an instantaneous spectrum diagram) and in temporal representation (as a waveform oscillogram). Using the options of the **Display** tab in the **Settings** window (Fig. 1.3), you can change the representation parameters.

The parameters of the spectral display are defined using the options of the **Spectral Display** group.

The classic algorithm of computing the spectrum assumes that the signal being analyzed is infinite in time, and any changes made to it infinitely long ago affect it to the same degree as current changes. In reality, every signal has a beginning and an end, the spectrum analyzer is turned on and off at certain moments, and physical instruments for spectrum analysis "forget" information about events that happened long ago. The **Windowing Function** drop-down list includes transformation algorithms used to display the signal spectrum. The algorithms differ in terms of functions used to take the history of the signal being analyzed into consideration.

If you aren't accustomed to a particular spectrum analysis algorithm, it doesn't matter which one you choose: The difference between them is almost unnoticeable.

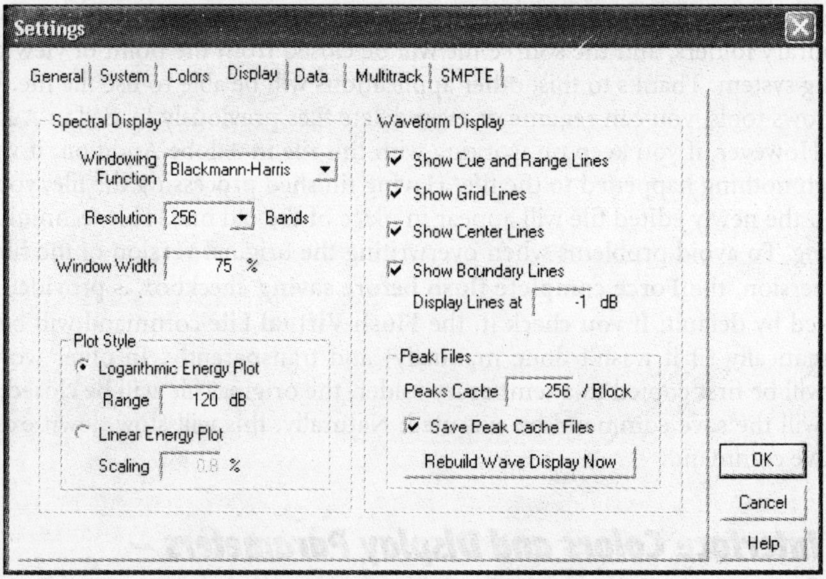

Fig. 1.3. Settings dialog box, **Display** tab

The **Resolution** … **Bands** drop-down list allows you to select the resolution for representing the signal in the spectral form. The greater the number of the bands, into which the frequency range is divided, the more accurate the analysis, but the longer the computation time. Because the *Fast Fourier Transform (FFT)* algorithm is used for spectrum analysis, the value of the **Resolution** … **Bands** parameter is the same as the sample size.

The **Window Width** … **%** input box expresses the width of the spectral window as a percentage of the sample size. We recommend that you leave it at 100%.

The **Plot Style** radio button group defines the style of the spectrum plot: **Logarithmic Energy Plot** denotes a logarithmic plot whose range is specified in decibels (**Range ... dB**), while **Linear Energy Plot** denotes a linear plot whose range is specified as percentage (**Scaling** … **%**).

The **Waveform Display** group contains controls for choosing the style and parameters of the waveform display. First of all, this involves four checkboxes:

- **Show Cue and Range Lines** — displays lines that indicate the boundaries between phrases detected with the commands of the **Edit > Auto Cue** submenu [3, *Section 4.11*].
- **Show Grid Lines** — shows the grid lines.
- **Show Center Lines** — shows the central grid line (the zero line).
- **Show Boundary Lines** — shows the boundary grid lines.

The value specified in the **Display Boundary Lines at ... dB** input box defines the positions of the horizontal boundary lines that help you visually estimate the signal level. 0 dB corresponds to the maximum possible value of the signal amplitude. When this level is exceeded, the signal is clipped. This results in noticeable sound distortions. If you specify **Display Boundary Lines at ... dB** at –1 dB and see that the waveform image doesn't cross the boundary lines, you are likely to avoid distortion.

Now let's look at the **Peak Files** group.

The **Peaks Cache ... /Block** field specifies the number of the samples in a data block when reading information from or writing it to auxiliary peak files designed to speed up the operations of loading WAV files and displaying waveforms. When working with large WAV files (dozens of megabytes), you should increase this value to 1,024.

If the **Save Peak Cache Files** checkbox is checked, Adobe Audition will save both WAV files and PK files (peak files). These files contain information that make it possible to speed up drawing the envelope of audio waves on the screen the next time the corresponding WAV file is loaded. When the space taken by peak files becomes too large, you can delete the oldest. Be careful not to delete a necessary WAV file!

By clicking the **Rebuild Wave Display Now** button, you can update (rebuild) the image of the waveform.

1.1.4. Audio Data Processing Parameters – the Data Tab

Using the **Data** tab of the **Settings** window (Fig. 1.4), you can control the parameters of audio data processing.

If the **Auto-convert all data to 32-bit upon opening** checkbox is checked, audio data will be automatically converted to 32-bit format when a file is opened.

The **Interpret 32-bit PCM .wav files as 16.8 float** checkbox enables a mode, in which 32-bit WAV files in PCM format are compatible with the data format used in earlier versions of Cool Edit Pro.

Since an audio file is represented with 16-bit samples, you might suppose that 16-bit arithmetic is used for its transformation (such as creating a reverberation effect). However, if this were the case, noticeable sound distortions would appear after a few transformations (16 bits are insufficient for this purpose). This is why contemporary sound editors such as Adobe Audition use more than 16 bits. Because of such an expansion of the dynamic range of digital signal representation, the errors accumulated when performing operations on audio data are insignificant. However, after all transformations necessary for a particular effect are completed, these data are transformed to common 16-bit format; the dynamic range of the signal is narrowed back to the standard of 96 dB. Of course, some useful information is lost after sound transformation: To compensate for this, some pseudorandom noise with very small amplitude can be added to the signal. The dynamic range will appear to remain at 105 dB, which corresponds to 24-bit representation. If you are a mathematician or a physicist, you won't believe this: A 16-bit signal cannot have such a dynamic range. Nevertheless, thanks to the peculiarities of human hearing, the addition of pseudorandom noise creates the impression that the sound quality is better than with 16-bit resolution. This approach is also used in Adobe Audition.

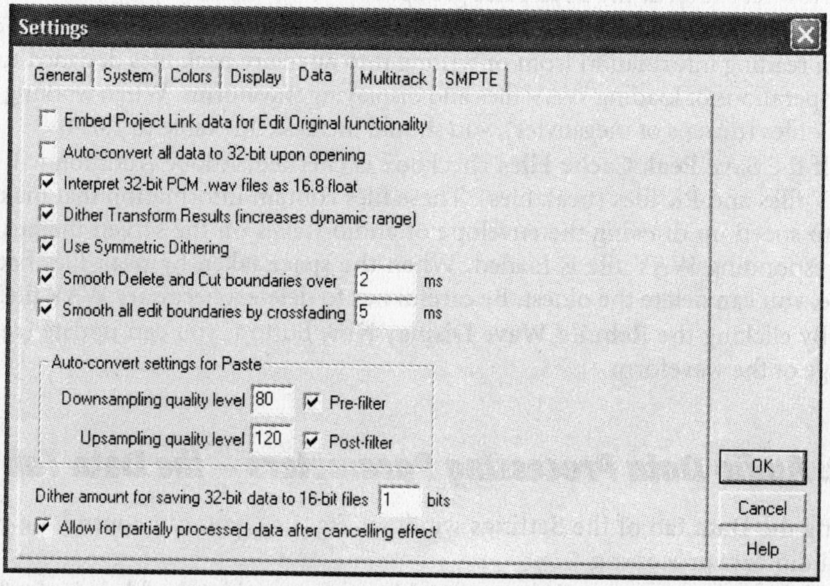

Fig. 1.4. Settings dialog box, **Data** tab

To switch the effect of seemingly increasing the dynamic range (called *dithering*) on or off, use the **Dither Transform Results (increases dynamic range)** checkbox.

The **Use Symmetric Dithering** checkbox turns on a special dithering algorithm, in which the added digital noise samples can be both positive and negative and are distributed near the zero level symmetrically on average. This algorithm makes it possible to avoid a direct component in the processed signal and, therefore, clicks at the edges of the processed fragment. This is why you should check the **Use Symmetric Dithering** checkbox, although it is difficult to hear the difference in the results of symmetric and asymmetric dithering (except the clicks that are likely in asymmetric dithering).

The **Smooth Delete and Cut boundaries over ... ms** checkbox should be checked to smooth over waveform fragments at their boundaries after the **Cut** and **Delete** operations, and to eliminate clicks. In the appropriate field, specify the length of the interval (in milliseconds), during which the previous fragment smoothly transits into the next one.

If the **Smooth all edit boundaries by crossfading ... ms** checkbox is checked, smoothing will be done at the boundaries of edited fragments. This operation is similar to *crossfade* (which decreases the amplitude of the previous fragment while simultaneously increasing the amplitude of the current fragment). The time during which crossfading takes place should be specified in the appropriate field (in milliseconds).

The **Auto-convert settings for Paste** group allows you to specify the parameters of automatic conversion during the Paste operation. Automatic conversion is done when the pasted data block is of a different format to that of the waveform being edited.

The **Downsampling quality level** and **Upsampling quality level** fields show numbers from 30 to 1,000 that specify the accuracy of downsampling and upsampling operations.

The accuracy of the algorithm is specified in numbers that have no measuring units. Users can only guess which actual parameter corresponds to these numbers. In the application, resampling isn't just reduction of samples or addition of intermediate ones: Adobe Audition also uses interpolations of various orders with various intervals and various approximation criteria.

The **Pre-filter** checkbox turns on special filtration of digitized audio data before downsampling. The **Post-filter** checkbox turns on filtration after upsampling.

In the **Dither amount for saving 32-bit data to 16-bit files ... bits** input field, specify a fractional number (between 0 and 1) that determines the amount of pseudorandom noise to be added when saving 32-bit data as 16-bit files. A value of 1 turns on addition of a pseudorandom signal, while a value of 0 turns it off. To partially add a pseudorandom signal, specify 0.5.

The **Allow for partially processed data after canceling effect** checkbox determines how the application should complete processing the waveform after you cancel it by clicking **Cancel** button in the progress-indicator window. If this checkbox is unchecked, the results of processing the waveform will be lost. If the checkbox is checked, the samples already processed by the application will remain in the waveform and in the corresponding file.

1.1.5. Parameters of Multitrack Editing — the Multitrack *Tab*; Synchronization Options — the SMPTE *Tab*

Adobe Audition is a multitrack editor. After each audio file is processed individually, you can put these files on separate tracks and start the montage using your audio program. Working in the **Multitrack View** mode is comprehensively discussed in *Chapter 10.*

Here, we will describe options of the **Multitrack** tab of the **Settings** window (Fig. 1.5) that determine some parameters of this mode.

In the **Play/Record** group, you can redefine the number and size of the memory buffers used during recording and playback:

- **Playback Buffer Size (response time) ... seconds** — determines the buffer size during playback.
- **Playback Buffers** — determines the number of the playback buffers.
- **Recording Buffer Size ... seconds** — determines the buffer size during recording.
- **Recording Buffers** — determines the number of the recording buffers.
- **Background Mixing Priority (Lower = Higher Priority)** — determines the priority of mixing relative to the other processes in a multitrack session; the lower the specified number, the higher the priority (you can enter fractions such as 0.8).

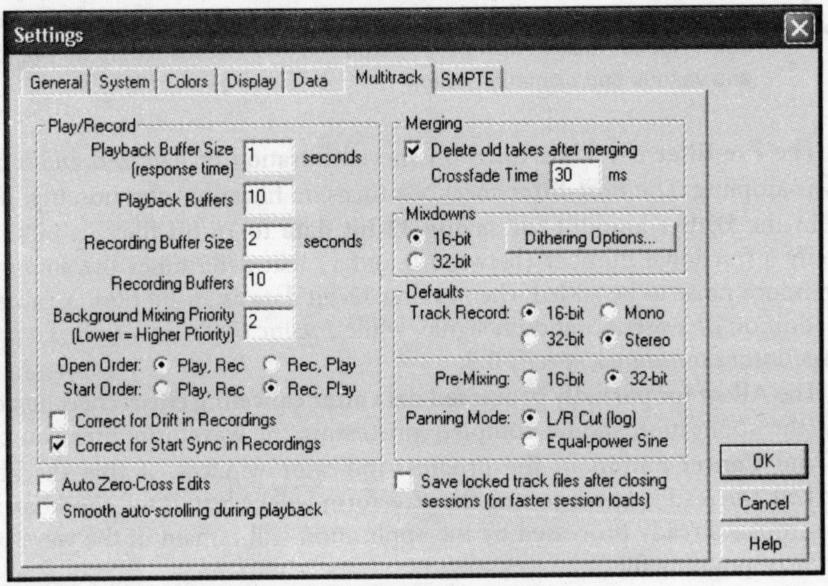

Fig. 1.5. Settings window, **Multitrack** tab

For multitrack editing, you should use sound cards that support duplexing (simultaneous playback and recording). Technically, different devices are used for recording and playback. Before you start working with these devices, the software must perform a procedure that makes it possible to use the devices: In other words, it must "open" them. For some sound cards, the order in which the devices are opened in a multichannel environment is important. This order is specified with the radio buttons of the **Open Order** group. The **Start Order** group of radio buttons specifies the order of starting the playback and recording devices in the multitrack mode. Although recording and playback are performed simultaneously, one of the devices must start first, and the other will be second. Some sound cards require a particular order. You may be wondering what will happen if a wrong order is selected: The answer is, nothing bad. Wrong settings might affect the result of your work, but few people are able to notice this; many sound editors miss such fine settings. Adobe Audition allows users to take into account the features of their equipment to make the most of it. For example, the playback and recording devices of SB Live! sound cards use different clock generators whose clock rates cannot be completely the same in principle. As a result, recording is done with one sample rate, while the sample rate of playback is different (however, insignificantly, by only a fraction of percent). The same problem is typical of a system with several sound cards. We would like to reiterate that few users can notice the difference, but Adobe Audition allows for correction.

When the **Correct for Drift in Recordings** checkbox is checked, the application will synchronize between the playback device and the device used to record the waveform. If the sample rates of these devices differ, the drift will be removed by resampling. If devices that use the same clock generator are used for recording and playback, this checkbox must be unchecked. This option is valid only for new tracks recorded during the session. Resampling will start immediately after recording finishes, and can take a noticeable amount of time.

Some sound cards have a small latency before the recording starts. This can lead to problems in the multitrack mode when the playback has started but the recording has not. The latency is small — a few milliseconds — but it can be perceived as a time disagreement between different instrumental parts if these parts were recorded with different sound cards. The **Correct for Start Sync in Recordings** option allows you to compensate for such a disagreement by introducing latency before playback starts. If this doesn't help, you can discover the latency through experimentation and enter the **Multitrack Latency** parameter manually (this procedure is described in *Section 1.2.2*).

The **Merging** group contains options for merging waveforms from different tracks to one mix:

- If the **Delete old takes after merging** checkbox is checked, the old material will be deleted after merging. This operation frees up disk space.
- The **Crossfade Time ... ms** field specifies the crossfade time when a new fragment is recorded into existing material. If two fragments were merged by abruptly switching off one of them and switching on the other, it is difficult to avoid a click. Merging is done as follows. At the end of the first fragment, its signal level is decreased gradually but quickly to zero from the rated one. Conversely, at the beginning of the next fragment, its signal level is increased from zero to the rated value. The transition is unnoticeable to the human ear. This is the essence of crossfading.

In the **Mixdowns** group, you can select the bit depth of mixing (combining several tracks into one). This can be either **16-bit** or **32-bit**. When performing intermediate operations, it makes sense to select the greatest possible bit depth. Use the 16-bit depth only when you write a finished recording to a medium.

Clicking on the **Dithering Options** button opens the **Mixdowns Dithering Options** dialog box, in which you can select the parameters of dithering that accompanies downsampling the audio data. This window is identical to the **Convert Sample Type** window whose controls are described in [3, *Section 4.15*].

In the **Defaults** group, select the parameters set by default:

- **Track Record** — the audio file record format
- **Pre-Mixing** — the bit depth of preliminary mixing
- **Panning Mode** — one of the following panning modes: **L/R Cut (log)** (logarithmic panning) or **Equal-power Sine** (sinusoidal panning with equal power)

We only need to consider three of the **Multitrack** tab's checkboxes.

If the **Auto Zero-Cross Edits** checkbox is checked, the following operation will be automatically performed prior to the editing operations (such as Cut, Delete, and Paste). The edges of the selection will be moved to the nearest points, at which the waveform crosses the zero level. This will allow clicks at the edges of the edited fragments to be avoided.

If the **Smooth auto-scrolling during playback** checkbox is unchecked, the multitrack editor will use "pagewise" scrolling that saves computer resources. If the checkbox is checked, "smooth" scrolling will be used, which is identical to that used in the waveform editor.

Adobe Audition allows the user to connect real-time effects to tracks. After the necessary effects are connected, the track can be locked. The application will actually recompute the track waveforms, taking into account the connected effects. A few new files will appear in a temporary folder, and they — not the displayed waveforms — will be read during playback. Naturally, recomputation will take some time, but it will free processor resources because the application won't have to compute effects in real time. When you need to change the effect settings, simply unlock the track. If the **Save locked track files after closing sessions (for faster session loads)** checkbox is checked, temporary files containing the waveforms of the locked tracks will be saved after you close the session (normally, all temporary files are deleted after closing a session). When you return to the session, there will be no need to compute these files, and loading will be done faster.

It only remains to consider the last tab of the **Settings** window.

The **SMPTE** tab of the **Settings** window contains options that define the parameters of synchronization through the SMPTE interface. For most computer musicians, this tab will be of no interest. In home studios, you seldom need to mix audio material recorded with several different devices. However, you should know that Adobe Audition allows you to work with the SMPTE interface, and the **SMPTE** tab makes it possible to optimize this. For details of the options of the **SMPTE** tab, see [3].

1.2. Choosing Devices for Recording and Playback Using the *Device Properties* Window

Let's carry on preparing Adobe Audition for work. Now you should choose devices for data input and output. The necessary options are located in the **Device Properties** window, which contains five tabs:

- **Wave Out** — selects a digital audio output device.
- **Wave In** — selects a digital audio input device.
- **MIDI Out** — selects a MIDI output device.
- **MIDI In** — selects a MIDI input device.
- **Ext. Controller** — selects an external controller.

1.2.1. Digital Audio Output Devices – the Wave Out *Tab*

The upper left part of the **Wave Out** tab of the **Device Properties** window (Fig. 1.6) contains a drop-down list of available audio data output devices.

All other parameters on this tab relate to the device selected in this list.

There is an information field, **Order**, to the right of the drop-down list. The number it contains is the number of the driver selected in the drop-down list. The **Change** button opens the **Device Ordering Preference** dialog box (see *Section 1.3*), which allows you to change the order of the drivers in the list.

If the **Use this device in Edit View** checkbox is checked, the selected device will be used in the waveform editor Edit View.

The right part of the tab is occupied by the **Supported Formats** table, which shows whether the selected device supports particular audio signal formats.

The left columns of the table contain sample rates from 8 to 96 kHz. The values shown are approximate (fractional parts of the numbers are omitted; for example, **11K** corresponds to 11.025 kHz). All these sample rates have been standard for a long time.

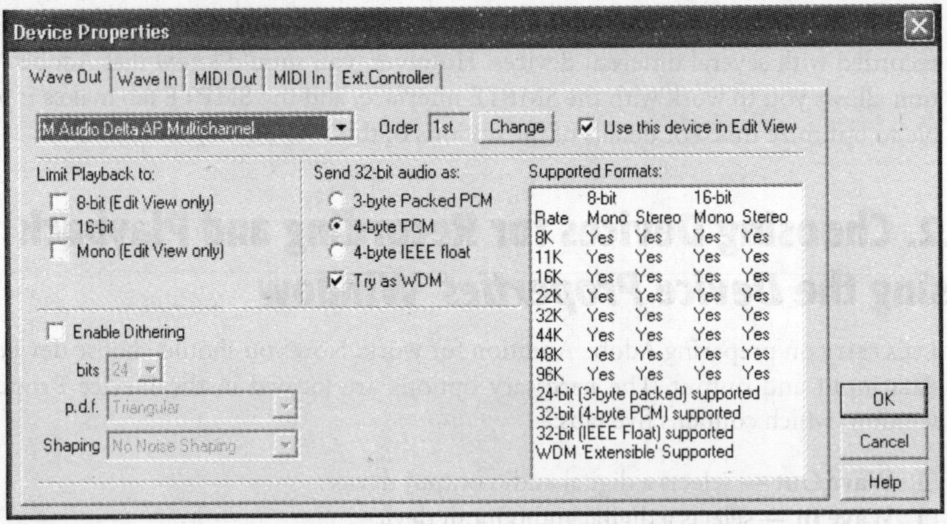

Fig. 1.6. Device Properties window, **Wave Out** tab

The top row of the table contains four possible combinations of modes: **8-bit/16-bit** (the bit depth, or signal resolution) and **Mono/Stereo**.

It is very simple to use this table. Select a row and a column that correspond to the mode you are interested in. If the sound card supports this mode, you'll see **Yes** in the appropriate cell.

The options in the **Limit Playback to** group are used to compensate for limitations inherent in your hardware. For example, if your sound card cannot process 32-bit audio and can work only with 16-bit data, you can use this group to playback 32-bit data, albeit with low quality (to do this, check the **16-bit** checkbox). If your sound card supports stereo, you shouldn't check the **Mono** checkbox.

The **Send 32-bit audio as** group contains radio buttons that determine the 32-bit audio data representation form. Before you select one of the three variants, read the manual for your sound card.

When the **Try as WDM** checkbox is checked, the WDM driver will be used if there is one on your system.

Your sound card may be 16-bit, but regardless of this you should use 32-bit representation: This will allow you to avoid the sound quality degrading after repeated transformations of waveforms, and to keep all fine changes. To some extent, it is possible to keep useful features of 32-bit audio when playing it with a 16-bit sound card. To do this, use dithering. If the **Enable Dithering** checkbox is checked, dithering noise will be mixed with the signal played through the output device. The properties of this noise are available for you.

In the **bits** field, specify a bit corresponding to the amplitude of the dithering noise. For example, if you have a 16-bit sound card, it would be reasonable to specify **16** in the **bits** field.

Below this field, there is the **p.d.f.** drop-down list (whose name stands for Probability Distribution Function), in which you can select one of several noise models. It is up to you which one is the most suitable. The models are displayed in a particular order. The first one (**Rectangular**) corresponds to the greatest harmonic distortion and the least noise (as it seems to the listener). The last (**Shaped Gaussian**) corresponds to the least harmonic distortions and the greatest noise. The developers of Adobe Audition recommend choosing the **Triangular** probability distribution function as a compromise between two features: the worsening of the Signal-to-Noise Ratio (the SNR loss) and the noise modulation.

Another method for struggling against quantization noise, *noise shaping*, uses special algorithms for rounding the values of samples during downsampling. After using this method, most of the quantization noise is concentrated in the high-frequency area, which the human ear perceives worst of all. Usually, noise shaping is applied in combination with dithering.

The bottom part of the window contains the **Shaping** drop-down list. In this list, you can select a type of noise shaping that corresponds to one of the variants of the noise spectrum distribution over the audio frequency band. If you make a good choice, it will be possible to mask the quantization noise and the noise introduced by dithering. The developers of Adobe Audition recommend the following variants:

- **Noise Shaping A** and **B** — for sample rates less than or equal to 32 kHz
- **Noise Shaping C1**, **C2**, and **C3** — for sample rates greater than or equal to 44.1 kHz
- **Noise Shaping D** — for sample rate of 48 kHz
- **Noise Shaping (44.1 KHz)** — for sample rate of 44.1 kHz
- **Noise Shaping (48 KHz)** — for sample rate of 48 kHz
- **Noise Shaping (96 KHz)** — for sample rate of 96 kHz

1.2.2. Digital Audio Input Devices – the Wave In *Tab*

Options on the **Wave In** tab of the **Device Properties** window (Fig. 1.7) are used for selecting digital audio input devices and their working modes.

Most of the controls on this tab are similar to those on the **Wave Out** tab. Only two options need an explanation: the **Multitrack Latency** field and the **Adjust to zero-DC when recording** checkbox.

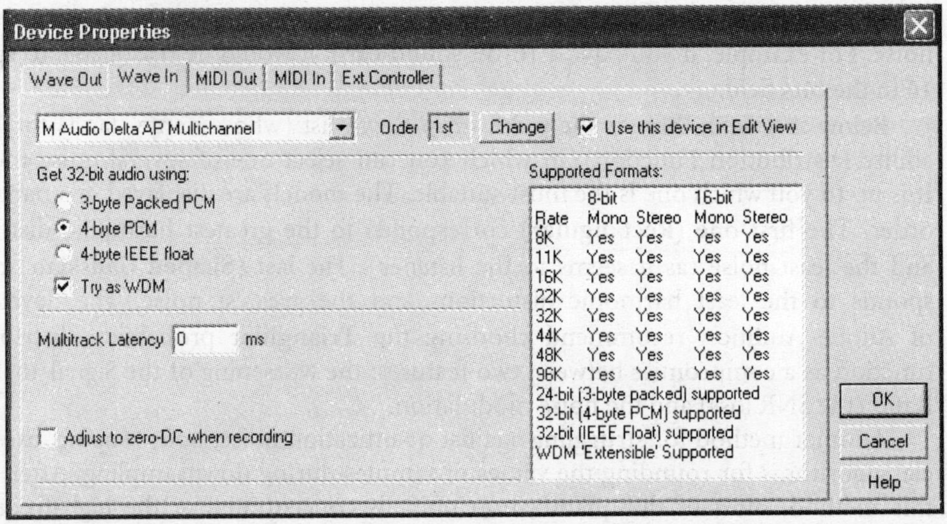

Fig. 1.7. Device Properties window, **Wave In** tab

We already mentioned that some sound cards have a small amount of latency before the recording starts. Such latency can be a problem in the multitrack mode: Playback has started but recording hasn't. Adobe Audition makes it possible to compensate for this latency by starting the playback later, so that it is synchronized with the recording. Enter the latency into the **Multitrack Latency** field. There is a simple method for finding the precise value of the latency. However, to use it you need certain skills in working with Adobe Audition. If you don't have them, you may skip the following algorithm and return to it at a later time.

Below is a procedure for finding a value for **Multitrack Latency**:

1. In the waveform editing mode, generate any signal (for example, sinusoidal) with a short duration (for example, 1 s) and a sufficiently high frequency (about 3 kHz).
2. Enter the multitrack mode and put the generated waveform at the beginning of the first track.
3. Prepare the second track for recording and put the cursor at the beginning of the tracks.
4. Adjust the sound card mixer so that the card records the signal it plays (if there is one sound card in your computer). If you have several sound cards, connect the output of the card that plays the first track to the input of the sound card used for recording. The mixer of the latter card should be adjusted to record the signal from this input.
5. Start recording in Adobe Audition and stop it in a second. This will be enough.

6. Return to the editing mode for the newly recorded waveform.
7. Change the horizontal zoom of the waveform so that the rest that precedes the front edge of the recorded signal takes up most of the window. Select the fragment of the waveform that corresponds to this rest.
8. Choose **Samples** as a unit of time measurement. The **End** field will display the number of the last sample in the selection (corresponding to the end of the rest before the recording). Remember this value; let's suppose it is 88.
9. Multiply the value by 1,000 and divide it by the sample rate in Hz. The result is the sought value in milliseconds. For example, 88 × 1,000/48,000 = 1.833...
10. Enter the obtained value into the **Multitrack Latency** field (with reasonable accuracy). In our example, it is 1.833.
11. Enter the multitrack mode, clear the second track and repeat steps 3 to 7 to make sure that there is no latency before the recorded signal.

To perform multichannel recording, some computer musicians install several multimedia cards, each of which has a good analog-to-digital converter (ADC). However, it would be wiser to spend a little more money and buy one specialized multichannel card. This will allow you to avoid many synchronization-related problems. All of the installed sound cards can be very good, but different cards (even cards of the same model) have different clock generators, which cannot be completely synchronous in principle.

The **Adjust to zero-DC when recording** checkbox enables a mode in which the DC component of the recorded signal is corrected. Some devices can pass the DC component to the ADC input. As a result, the waveform is recorded with an offset relative to zero. When performing montage of such waveforms, clicks are likely. If the **Adjust to zero-DC when recording** checkbox is checked, Adobe Audition automatically corrects the DC component so that each waveform on the track in the main window will be symmetrical about the zero level.

1.2.3. *MIDI Output and Input Devices – the* MIDI Out *and* MIDI In *Tabs*

Options of the **MIDI Out** tab of the **Device Properties** window (Fig. 1.8) are used to select digital output devices for MIDI events and synchronize signals transferred via the SMPTE interface.

In the **MIDI Output** drop-down list select a MIDI output device driver, and in the **SMPTE Output** drop-down list select a driver for synchronizing signals transferred via the SMPTE interface.

Options of the **MIDI In** tab of the **Device Properties** window (Fig. 1.9) are used to select digital input devices for MIDI events.

Select a driver of the device being synchronized in the **SMPTE Slave Device** drop-down list. If the **Use Internal Timestamps** checkbox is checked, internal timestamps will be used.

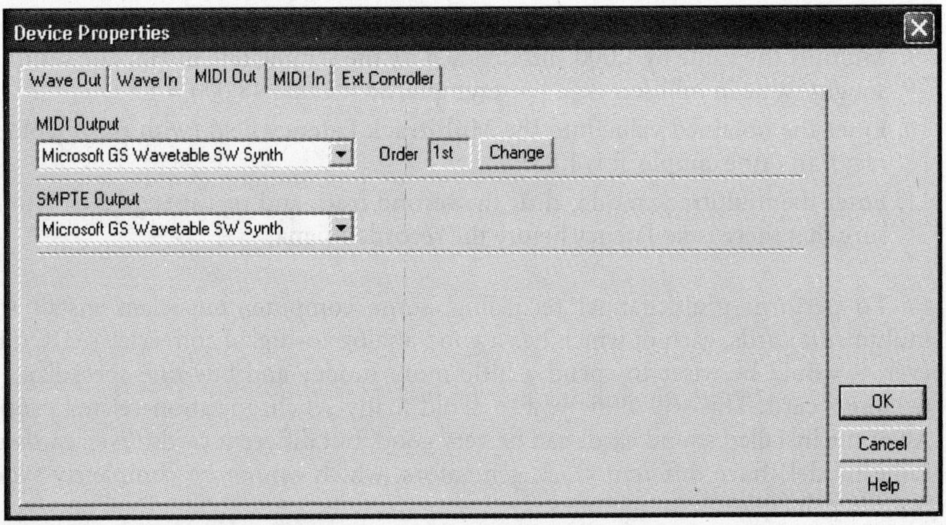

Fig. 1.8. Device Properties window, **MIDI Out** tab

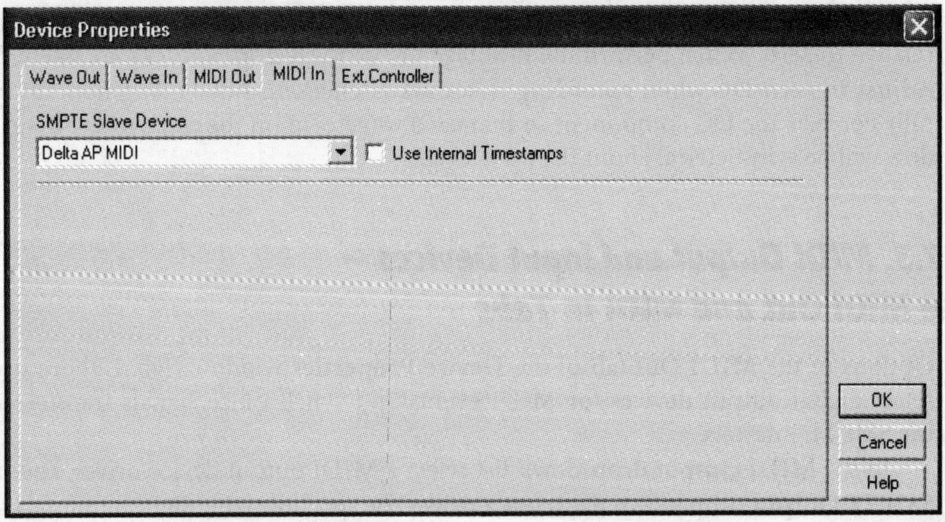

Fig. 1.9. Device Properties window, **MIDI In** tab

1.2.4. An External Controller – the Ext.Controller *Tab*

The **External Controller Device** drop-down list in the **Ext. Controller** tab of the **Device Properties** window (Fig. 1.10) is used to select an external controller out of those available in your computer and support Adobe Audition.

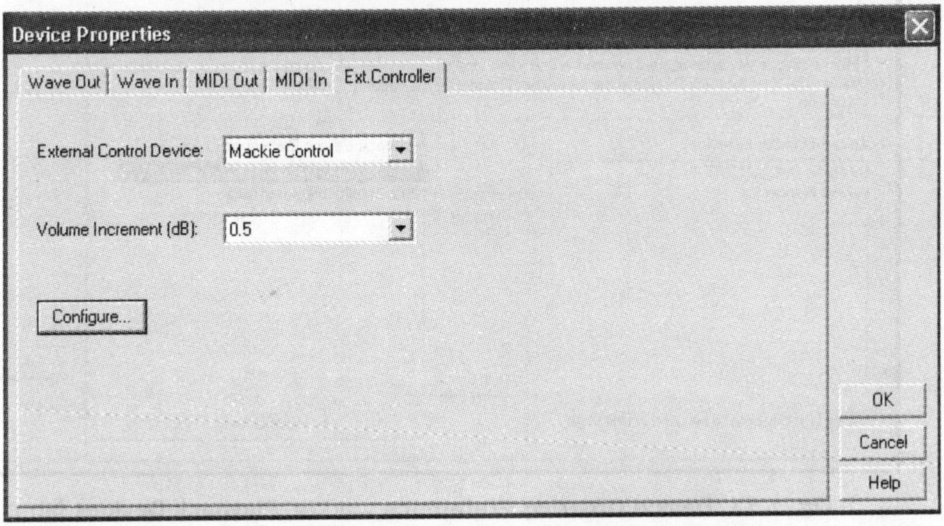

Fig. 1.10. Device Properties window, **Ext.Controller** tab

The **Volume Increment (dB)** drop-down list located on this tab allows you to select a volume increment value corresponding to an elementary signal sent from the external controller.

1.3. Editing Lists of the Playback/Recording Devices Using the *Device Ordering Preference* Window

The **Device Ordering Preference** window is used to change the order of the playback and recording devices in the lists of the **Device Properties** window, as well as to reorder the I/O track ports in the multitrack mode. The window contains four tabs:

- **Playback Devices** — edits the list of digital audio output devices.
- **Recording Devices** — edits the list of digital audio input devices.
- **MIDI Output Devices** — edits the list of MIDI output devices.
- **MIDI Input Devices** — edits the list of MIDI input devices.

We don't need to consider each of the tabs individually, because their appearance is identical. We will only describe the purpose of the **Playback Devices** tab of the **Device Ordering Preference** window (Fig. 1.11).

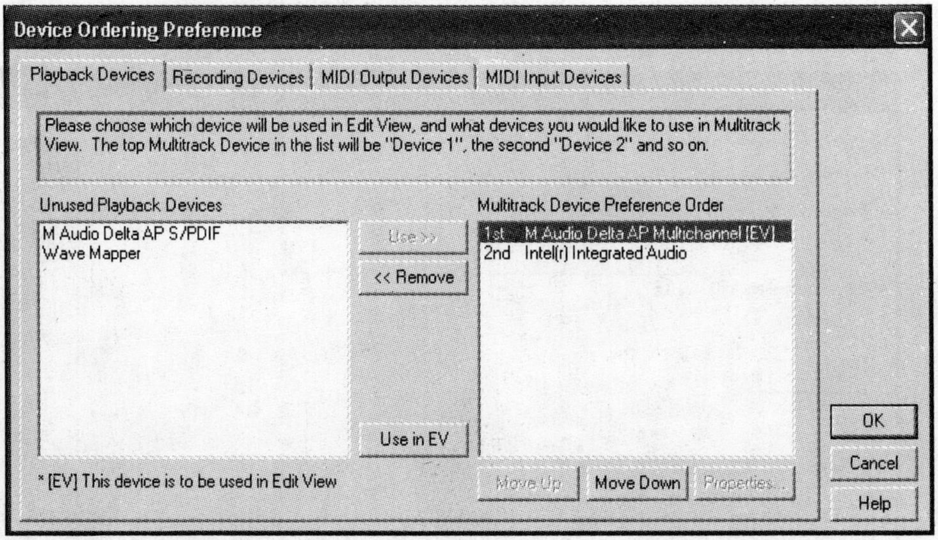

Fig. 1.11. Device Ordering Preference window, **Playback Devices** tab

The **Unused Playback Devices** list contains devices that are available in your system but unused in the multitrack mode.

The **Multitrack Device Preference Order** list contains devices that are used in the multitrack mode. To move a device selected in the **Unused Playback Devices** list to the **Multitrack Device Preference Order** list, click the **Use>>** button; to move a device in the opposite direction, click the **<<Remove** button.

To change the order of the devices in the **Multitrack Device Preference Order** list, select a device and click the **Move Up** button to move it up or the **Move Down** button to move it down.

If you click the **Use in EV** button, the selected device will be used in the waveform editor (**Edit Waveform View**).

An information field located at the top of each tab displays necessary recommendations and tips.

The **Properties** button opens the **Device Properties** dialog box described in *Section 1.2*.

Having finished the preparations, you can start working with the application. Of course, you should begin with the simplest and most common actions.

Chapter 2

Working with Files and Waveforms. Audio Playback

Adobe Audition can work in two different basic modes:

- ❒ Editing individual mono or stereo waveforms
- ❒ Multitrack editing, during which you can create a composition using individual waveforms as building blocks

Each mode has its own main menu and main window (**Edit Waveform View** and **Multitrack View**, respectively). In fact, these are two separate sound editors combined into one functional whole. Adobe Audition's main working mode is multitrack, and the application enters this mode on start-up. The technique for using Adobe Audition as a multitrack editor supporting multichannel recording can be described in general terms as follows:

- ❒ One-channel recording (using aliasing) or multichannel recording in the multi-track mode
- ❒ Editing recorded waveforms and waveforms obtained from external sources (e.g., sample libraries, digital audio CD tracks, or digital video sound tracks) in the **Edit Waveform View** mode
- ❒ Returning to the multitrack mode, doing the montage, and mixing a composition based on the edited waveforms, real-time effects, and automation

In this approach, working on a composition begins and ends in the **Multitrack View** mode, but the **Edit Waveform View** mode is a link in the technological chain.

Let's start by looking at the application's available tools when editing individual mono or stereo waveforms in the main window of **Edit Waveform View**.

2.1. Introducing the *Edit Waveform View* Window

After you start the application for the first time, it will enter the multitrack mode. To switch it to the waveform editing mode, press the <F12> key or select the **View > Edit Waveform View** command in the main menu. If you then close Adobe Audition and restart it, it will enter the mode in which it was closed.

The main window of the application in the **Edit Waveform View** mode looks as shown in Fig. 2.1.

Fig. 2.1. Main window in the **Edit Waveform View** mode

In the upper part of the main window, there is a toolbar whose appearance and toolkit can be customized. You can put various tools (buttons corresponding to the main menu commands) on the toolbar or remove them from it.

> You can select tools displayed in the main window using the **Toolbars** submenu of the **View** menu.

To find out what a particular tool does, place the mouse pointer on it and wait (for nearly one second). A tip with a list of the tool's functions will appear next to the tool. We will not describe the purpose of the tools, because they can vary, completely duplicate the main menu items, and are comprehensively described in [3].

However, we would like to look at the left button on the toolbar. This button is another way of switching between the **Edit Waveform View** and **Multitrack View** windows. The appearance of the button changes depending on which mode is current. In the **Edit Waveform View** mode, it looks like this: 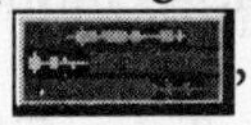, while in the **Multitrack View** mode it looks like this: 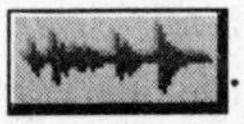.

In Fig. 2.1, you can see a working area that doesn't contain any information. It is empty because an audio file has yet to be loaded into the application's memory. If you read an audio file from disk or record audio from any of the sound card's available inputs, this area will display a waveform. We will describe this area further after going through how to obtain an audio file.

There are a few more tools and controls in the main window, but there is no point in considering them right now. First, we have to get a waveform in the main window: This can be loaded from a file, pasted from the clipboard, or recorded.

2.2. Working with Files

Commands that make it possible to work with files are contained in the **File** menu, and are as follows:

- **New** — creates a new file.
- **Open** — opens an existing file.
- **Open As** — opens a file and overrides its attributes.
- **Open Append** — opens a file and appends it to the opened one (the appended waveform is put after the waveform displayed in the editor window).

- **Extract Audio From Video** — extracts the sound track from a video file and loads it in Adobe Audition.
- **Extract Audio From CD** — extracts a track from a digital audio CD and loads it in Adobe Audition.
- **Revert to Saved** — reverts to the last saved file.
- **Close** — closes the currently edited file.
- **Close All (Waves and Session)** — closes all files and the current multitrack session.
- **Close Only Non-Session Waveforms** — closes any opened file not being used in the current multitrack session.
- **Save** — saves the file with its current name.
- **Save As** — saves the file with a name specified by the user.
- **Save Copy As** — saves a copy of the file.
- **Save Selection** — saves only the selected fragment of the waveform.
- **Save All** — saves all current waveforms and sessions.
- **Batch File Convert** — converts file formats in the batch mode.
- **Flush Virtual File** — flushes the opened file so that it can be used by another application.
- **Free Up Space in Temp Files** — opens a window that contains information about the amount of free space on the hard disk (using this window, you can free up or reserve some disk space).
- **Exit** — exits Adobe Audition.

2.2.1. Opening Files

The **File** > **Open** command allows you to open an audio file. It displays the **Open a Waveform** dialog box (Fig. 2.2).

In addition to controls traditional for file-open windows in all Windows applications, this one contains a few fields that are worth mentioning.

The **Recent Folders** drop-down list contains folders you accessed earlier when opening files. To move from one folder to another quickly, just select the appropriate line in this list.

If you don't have files suitable for exercises, you can use files from the EXAMPLES folder on the CD that accompanies this book (such as EX02_01.WAV or EX02_02.WAV). The first two digits in the file names denote the chapter, in which the example is used (or mentioned for the first time); the following two digits are the number of the example in the chapter.

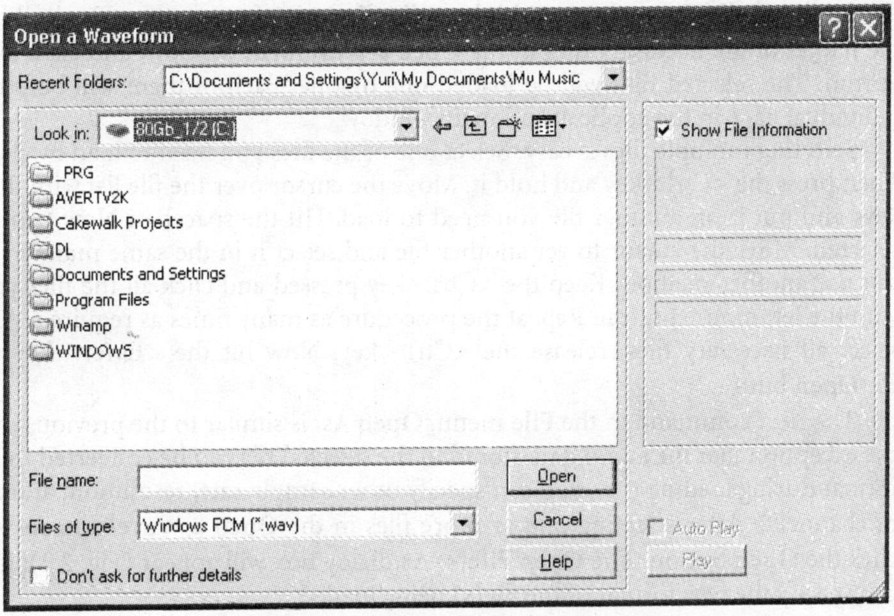

Fig. 2.2. Open a Waveform dialog box

When the **Show File Information** checkbox in the **Open a Waveform** window is checked, the information about the format of the selected file, its duration, and the amount of memory it takes up is displayed.

If the **Auto Play** checkbox is checked, the file selected in the **Recent Folders** drop-down list will be played. You can also listen to the selected file by clicking the **Play** button.

Adobe Audition supports many audio files of various formats and even allows loading files of unknown formats, assuming that they use pulse-code modulation (PCM) for sound representation. Before loading such a file (with a header unknown to Adobe Audition), the application will ask you to determine the sample rate, the number of channels (whether the file is mono or stereo), and the resolution of audio data representation. If the file sounds wrong (too slow, with noise, or only noise is heard), and you are sure it stores audio samples, you should repeatedly try to load it with different combinations of its format parameters.

Going back to the **Open a Waveform** window, if the **Don't ask for further details** checkbox is checked, Adobe Audition won't ask you for details on audio data representation in the unknown format: It will assume that the file has the same format as the previously loaded one.

In the **Files of type** drop-down list, you can select the audio file type (the default is WAV).

Adobe Audition can load multiple audio files one after another. To do this, select the names of the necessary files in the **Open a Waveform** window, and click the **Open** button. The selected files will be loaded one by one. Each of them will be put on an individual page in the application's main window.

Selecting multiple files is easy. Select one of the files you need to load by clicking it. Then press the <Ctrl> key and hold it. Move the cursor over the file list with the arrow keys and put it on another file you need to load. Hit the spacebar. Now two files are selected. Move the cursor to yet another file and select it in the same manner. Or you can use another method. Keep the <Ctrl> key pressed and click all the files you need with the left mouse button. Repeat the procedure as many times as required. After you select all necessary files, release the <Ctrl> key. Now hit the <Enter> key or click the **Open** button.

The next command in the **File** menu, **Open As**, is similar to the previous one, with the exception that the audio data stored in the selected file can be converted to another format during loading (i.e., you can specify other sample rate, resolution, and number of channels). After selecting one or more files in the **Open a Waveform As** window, click the **Open** button. The **Open File(s) As** dialog box will appear (Fig. 2.3); in it, you can specify the new format of the file(s) being loaded.

In the **Sample Rate** list, select a sample rate.

In the **Channels** group, select the **Mono** or **Stereo** mode.

In the **Resolution** group, select the resolution: **8-bit**, **16-bit**, or **32-bit (float)**.

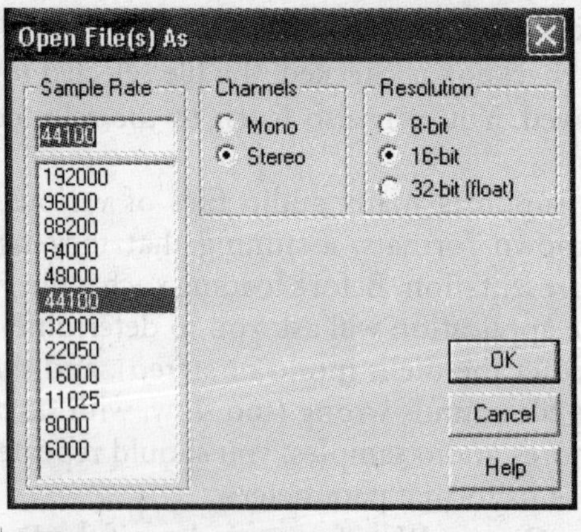

Fig. 2.3. Open File(s) As dialog box

Contrary to some users' opinion, a new format isn't selected in the **Files of type** drop-down list of the **Open a Waveform As** window. In fact, this list is just a logical filter that speeds up the search for a file whose type you know.

Audio data conversion will start after you click the **OK** button in the **Open File(s) As** dialog box. The process can take quite a long time, because it involves several operations; how many and what type depends on how the original and specified formats relate to each other. You don't need to worry about this, as the application will automatically specify the necessary set of operations and perform them all. A progress bar will inform you about the beginning and progress of each operation. After all necessary operations are completed, the converted and loaded waveform will appear in the working area of the main window.

Adobe Audition also can perform the completely automatic conversion of a previously specified file sequence. This feature is described in [3, *Section 3.8*].

We're sure you know about audio file formats (MP3, Real Audio, Microsoft ADPCM, etc.), in which various methods of audio data compression are used. Most of them use *compression with loss*: The quality of the recording decreases, but it takes less disk space.

Never use compression to store your project's intermediate audio files! Here is an example of wrong behavior:

A user records music with a microphone and saves the recording as an MP3 file. After a while, he or she opens the file to eliminate noise from it and do some dynamic processing, and again saves the file as MP3. Then he or she uses the file in a multitrack project and saves the result of mixing in an MP3 file. The sound quality in this negative example will quickly degrade with every save operation. To avoid this, use the Windows PCM format.

Now let's look at how audio samples are represented in such files. It is obvious that if recording is done with a microphone (almost always, a mono one), it is reasonable to use the mono format. However, if an originally mono recording acquires stereo properties after processing (such as effects that use delays), it should be in stereo format *before* processing. If you're not going to use effects that give a recording stereo properties in the waveform editing mode, and you want to use real-time effects when mixing your multitrack project, you shouldn't change the mono format of the waveform to stereo. The audio data stream from the outputs of the effects will be supplied to a stereo audio port or bus. This is why the sound of the stereo effects does not depend on the format, in which the original mono data is represented.

Resolution is a very important issue. We cannot imagine where 8-bit audio files could be used, and so will consider only the 16-bit and 32-bit (float) formats used for audio data representation when editing in Adobe Audition. The 16-bit format should be used when a recording originally has a low quality. Obviously, if a recording was done with a multimedia microphone connected to a sound card's microphone input, there is no point in talking about saving fine nuances obtained during processing low-quality sound.

Things are different if you have high-quality recording equipment and a special studio for audio recording. Using the 32-bit format will help you avoid error accumulation when repeatedly using various effects.

2.2.2. Saving and Closing Files

The **Save** command of the **File** menu saves the edited file with the name it had before being loaded from the disk. If the file was created with the **New** command, the **Save As** command of the **File** menu will be executed instead of the **Save** command.

The **Save As** command saves the files with the name specified by the user. After you select this command, the **Save Waveform As** dialog box will open (Fig. 2.4). It contains standard controls, but has two distinctive features.

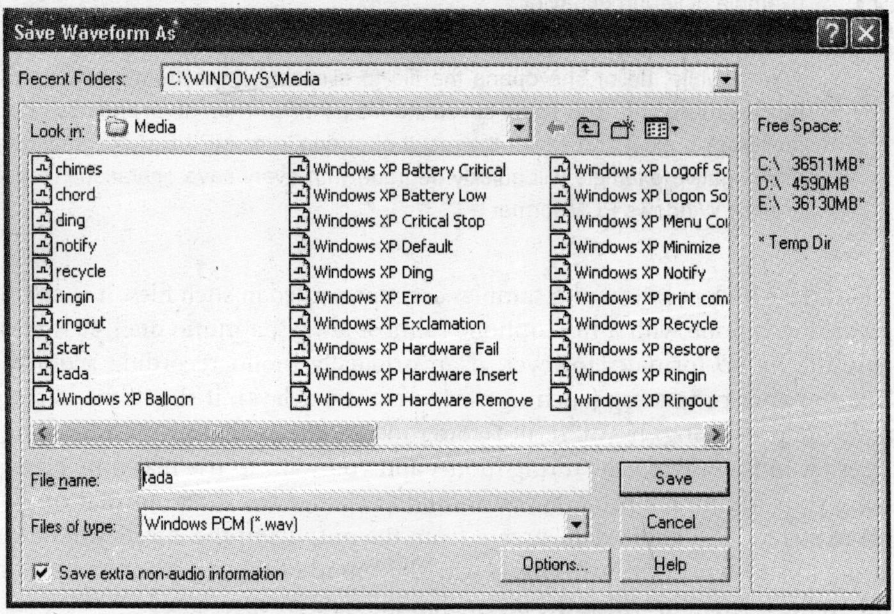

Fig. 2.4. Save Waveform As dialog box

The first one is the **Options** button. Clicking on it opens a dialog box whose appearance depends on the audio file format. For some formats, the **Options** button isn't available. The options of that dialog box can also vary. For example, they can allow you to select a method for audio data compression.

The second feature is the **Save extra non-audio information** checkbox. When it is checked, the audio file will contain extra information, such as the name of the composition, copyright, etc., in addition to the format specification and the waveform.

The next command of the **File** menu, **Save Copy As**, is similar to the **Save As** command, but the file is saved in another folder.

The **File** > **Save Selection** saves only the selected fragment of the waveform.

The **Save All** command, which also saves files, is available in the **Edit Waveform View** mode only if you have used the **Open Append** command that loads files and combines their waveforms. The **Save All** command allows you to save all combined waveforms in one file. You must be careful when using this command, as the application doesn't ask for a filename. The file containing the combined waveform will be saved with the name of the file loaded first (to which the other files were appended), leading to the possibility of the original file being overwritten. Of course, you can try to recover the lost information, but doing this will involve a lot of work cutting the appended waveforms.

The **Revert to Saved** command can be useful when you decide to abandon all changes made after the last save or the last load. In other words, the **Revert to Saved** command loads the file whose name is displayed in the main window caption. When executing this command, the application will ask you to confirm saving the current waveform in the file.

The **Close** command closes the edited file. To be more precise, it frees the application's memory of the waveform being edited. The application returns to the initial state.

The **Close All (Waves and Session)** command closes all files of all sessions.

The **Close Only Non-Session Waveforms** command closes all opened audio files not being used in the current session (not inserted into the multichannel environment).

2.3. Viewing Waveforms and Playing Files

Let's suppose you used the **File** > **Open** command to load a file with audio data (e.g., the EX02_01.WAV file from the EXAMPLES folder in the CD that accompanies this book). The view in the application's main window changed. The working area now contains a graphical image (an oscillogram) of the audio signal: a waveform. Fig. 2.5 shows how a stereo waveform could look.

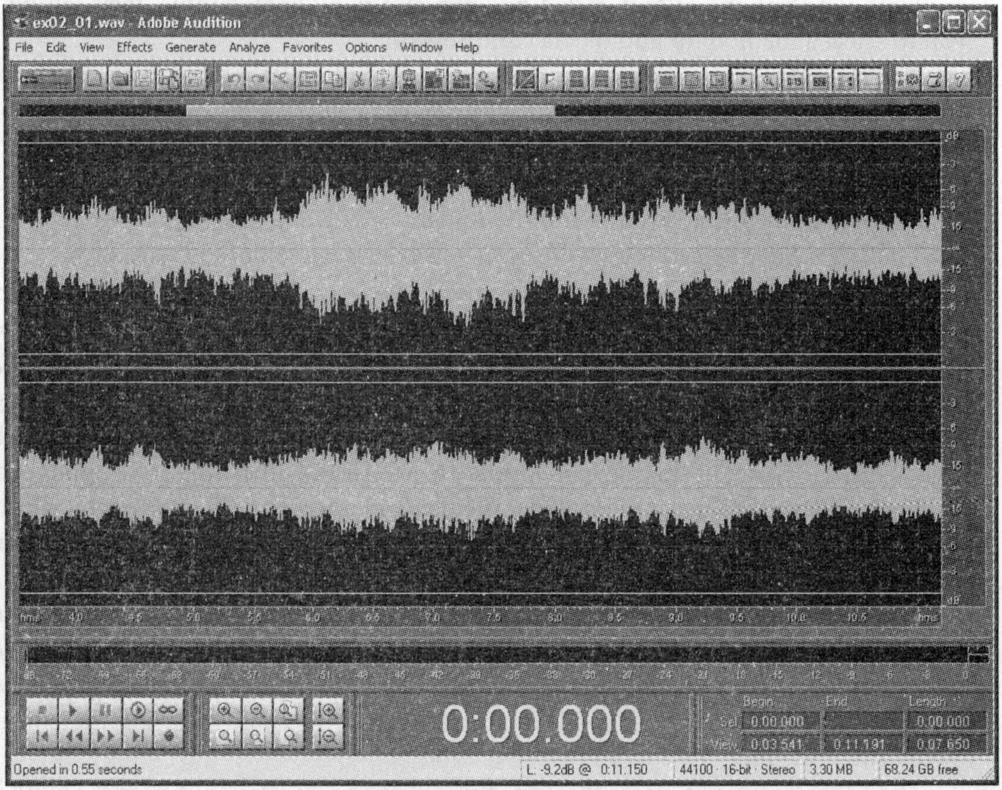

Fig. 2.5. Stereo waveform

2.3.1. Controlling the Waveform Display

Before we look at the waveform more closely, let's define two terms: a *marker* and a *cursor*. On the screen, both objects look like ordinary vertical lines. The marker is a dashed line, while the cursor is a firm one.

The marker points at a place (or, more precisely, the time) in the waveform where the recording or playback starts. The marker can be seen only in the static state, i.e., in the **Stopped** mode.

By contrast, the cursor exists and is visible only in dynamic modes, during recording or playback. In the image of the waveform, it points at the place currently played or recorded.

In Fig. 2.5, the time position is described with a sample number (this is why the numbers on the horizontal axis have a lot of zeroes).

It often happens that the image of the entire waveform doesn't fit in the working area of the main window, and only a portion of it is visible. To help you understand what portion is displayed, there is a diagram above the waveform image. A light box in the diagram denotes the displayed portion (the purpose of the diagram is similar to that of the scrollbar). By dragging the box with the mouse, you can scroll the waveform. If the entire diagram is lit, it means the entire waveform is displayed in the window. The ratio of the box width to the width of the diagram is equal to the ratio of the displayed fragment length to the length of the entire waveform. Right-click the diagram: A pop-up menu will appear that allows you to control the zoom of the waveform display (Fig. 2.6).

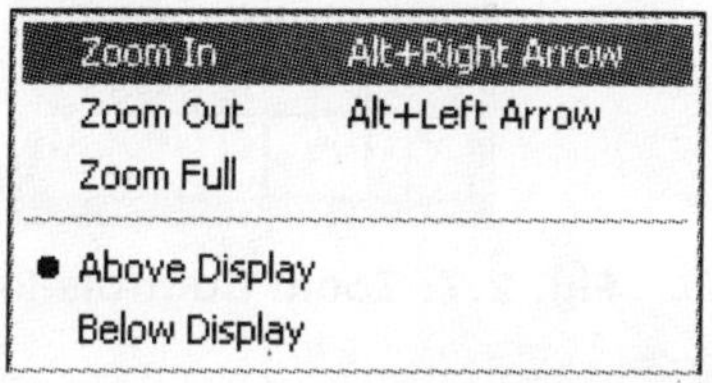

Fig. 2.6. Pop-up menu of the display diagram

If you select the **Zoom In** command, the waveform will be enlarged; if you select **Zoom Out**, it will be scaled down. The **Zoom Full** command displays the entire waveform.

The other two commands of the pop-up menu can change the position of the diagram: either above the work area of the main window (**Above Display**) or below it (**Below Display**).

If a waveform fragment is selected, its length and position within the waveform are reflected by a gray box on the diagram. This is very convenient: After any movements along the waveform, you can always return to the selected fragment by dragging the green box onto the gray.

The diagram is a convenient tool. Its width corresponds to the length of the waveform. The green movable box on the diagram is a scroll box that corresponds to the currently displayed portion of the waveform. If the entire waveform is displayed in the window, the scroll box takes up the entire diagram and cannot be moved. As soon as you zoom out the diagram horizontally (using the **Zoom Out Horizontally** command), the width of the scroll box will decrease. By dragging the scroll box, you can scroll the waveform. If you grab an edge of the scroll box and move it, the corresponding edge of the displayed portion of the waveform will also move. As a result, the horizontal zoom level of the waveform will change accordingly.

There is another method for scrolling the waveform image. Grab the horizontal coordinate scale — the ruler — located below the waveform (the mouse pointer will take the form of a hand) and move it in the desired direction. Thus you can rewind or fast-forward the waveform. The ruler has another useful feature, which allows you to zoom out the waveform horizontally. If you select a fragment of the ruler while keeping the right mouse button pressed, the selected fragment will be stretched over the screen after you release the mouse button.

The tools of the **Zoom Controls** toolbar (Fig. 2.7) allow you to change the waveform zoom level vertically and horizontally.

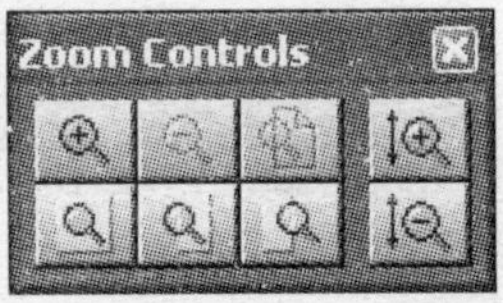

Fig. 2.7. Zoom Controls toolbar

The horizontal zoom level of the waveform is set using the following buttons:

- **Zoom In Horizontally** — enlarges the waveform.
- **Zoom Out Horizontally** — scales the waveform down.
- **Zoom Out Full Both Axis** — displays the entire waveform.
- **Zoom to Selection** — changes the zoom level so that the entire selection of the waveform is displayed.
- **Zoom In to Left Edge of Selection** — zooms in and displays the left edge of the selection.
- **Zoom In to Right Edge of Selection** — zooms in and displays the right edge of the selection.

To zoom the waveform in and out vertically, use the **Zoom In Vertically** and **Zoom Out Vertically** buttons.

In the following work, you won't be able to do without tools for selecting waveform fragments.

We'll start describing them from the simplest to the most complicated. Suppose you need to listen to a fragment not from the beginning, but from a particular moment. Move the mouse pointer to that position and click once. If the audio file is stereo, try to position the mouse pointer so that it is near the line dividing the tracks of the left and right channels (it doesn't have to be exactly on the line). A marker will appear at the point where you clicked: This is a vertical dashed line whose upper and lower ends are "fastened" to the main window with little yellow triangles. In the example shown in Fig. 2.8, this vertical line is near the position of the 350,000th sample.

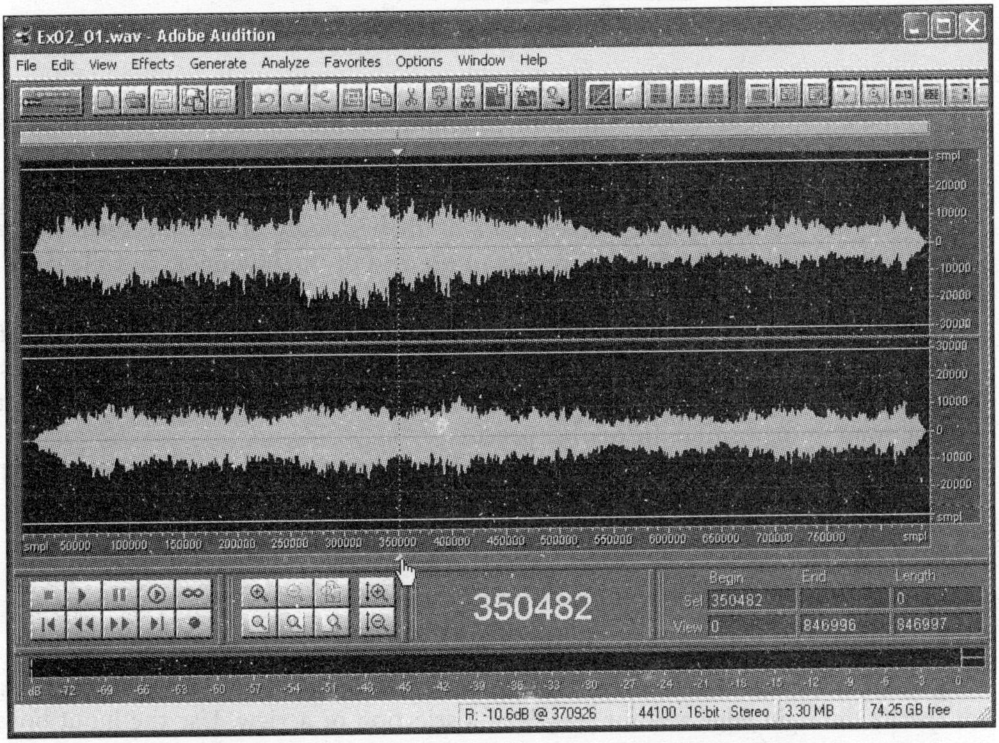

Fig. 2.8. Marker near the position of the 350,000th sample

To be more precise, the marker is at the position of sample # 350,482. This can be seen from the current position display.

If you now click the  **Play** button (or press the spacebar), playback will start from the position of the marker.

Try to put the marker exactly at the position you want; we bet you won't be able to do this first time. It is especially difficult to "hit the target" if you work with a long waveform. The accuracy of visually putting a marker will almost always be several samples or even tens of samples. Sometimes the accuracy of putting a marker is very important. In such situations, you should use one of the six input boxes on the **Selection/View Controls** panel (Fig. 2.9) located by default at the bottom of the window, to the right of the time indicator.

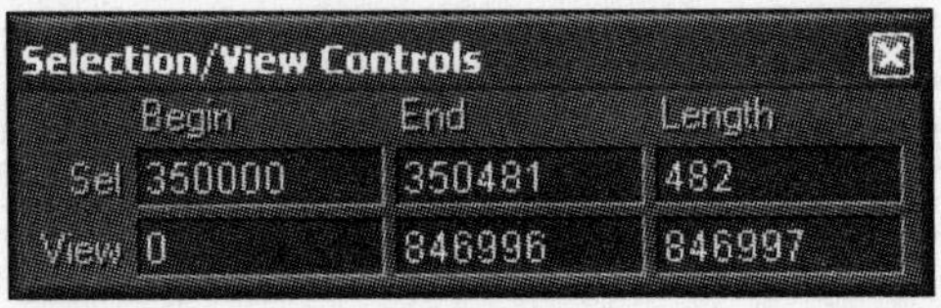

Fig. 2.9. Selection/View Controls panel

These input boxes form a table with two rows and three columns.

The top row (**Sel**) displays the time parameters of the waveform selection (and allows you to edit them), and the bottom row (**View**) displays the time parameters of the displayed fragment of the waveform.

The left column (**Begin**) corresponds to the beginning of the waveform fragment, the middle column (**End**) corresponds to the end of the fragment, and the right column (**Length**) displays the fragment length.

To specify a precise marker position, click the input box at the intersection of the **Sel** row and the **Begin** column. The box will become editable. Enter the necessary number and press the <Enter> key. Although we used a waveform selection tool, it allowed us to position the marker precisely.

To define the edges of a selection with high accuracy, specify them in the input boxes at the intersections of the **Sel** row and two following columns:

- **Begin** (for the left edge of the waveform selection)
- **End** (for the right edge of the waveform selection)

To define the edges of a selection or a displayed fragment, you can specify its beginning and end; we just covered this method. However, there is another one: You can specify the right edge and the length of a selection or a view. Use the input boxes in the **Length** column. Remember that only two of the three values of the waveform time parameters are independent. If you specify the coordinate of the right edge of the fragment, the application will automatically compute its length and display it in the appropriate input box, and vice versa.

Specifying fragment edges by entering numeric values is more precise than the graphical method, but it isn't always convenient, and can slow your work with the waveform. The graphical method is simpler and quicker.

As already mentioned, to place a marker you should click the working area of the main window once. If you make a double click, the displayed fragment of the waveform will become selected. If you want to select a part of this fragment (i.e., a shorter portion of the recording), use the following procedure.

Move the mouse pointer to the beginning (or the end) of the fragment and click the left button. Keeping the button pressed, move the mouse pointer to the end (or the beginning) of the fragment. The result will look similar to that shown in Fig. 2.10.

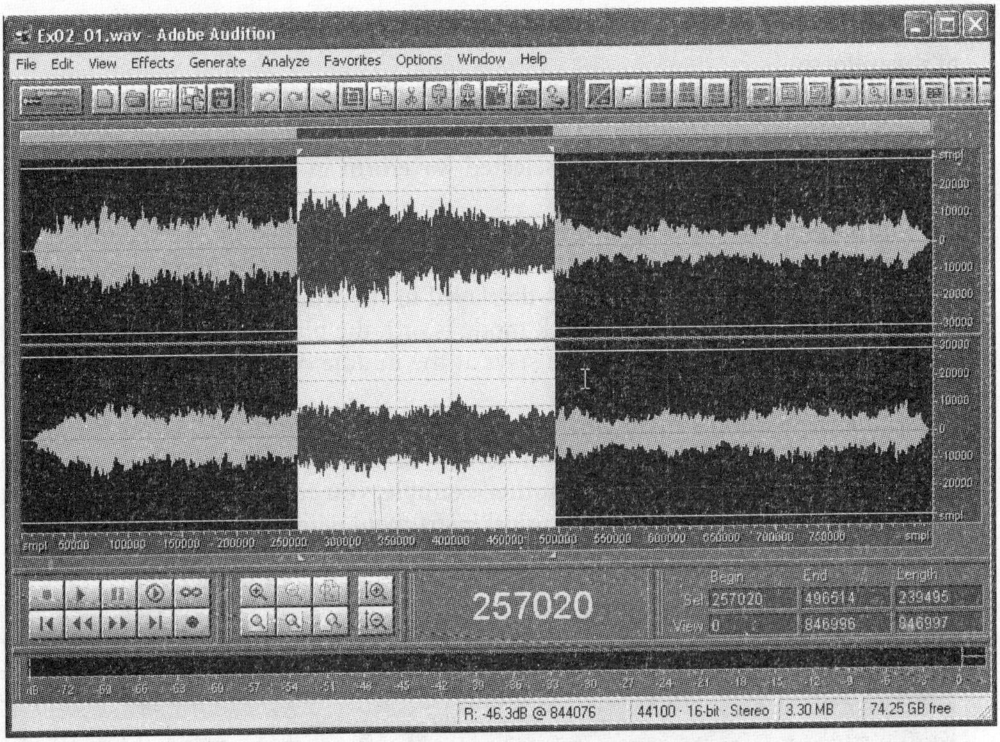

Fig. 2.10. Selection of a stereo waveform

If you need to resize the selection, you don't have to repeat the above procedure. As soon as you click the waveform, all your previous work on selecting the audio fragment will be lost. To avoid this, resize the selection either with the left mouse button in combination with the <Shift> key, or with the right mouse button (depending on which settings you chose in the **Edit View Right-Clicks** group on the **General** tab of the **Settings** dialog box).

So now you have selected a fragment of the waveform. If you now click the  **Play** button, only this selection will be played. Playing a fragment isn't the only reason for selecting it. The application performs all operations only with selected fragments.

Adobe Audition allows you to work with each stereo channel separately. For this purpose, you should select fragments in a special way. Doing this is easy. Move the mouse pointer to the upper or lower track (to work with the left or right channel, respectively), and not to the line dividing the tracks. When the mouse pointer is at the appropriate place, it will change its appearance: **L** (Left) or **R** (Right) will appear next to the arrow. After that, you can work with the audio data of the individual channels in the same way as with a whole waveform. Fig. 2.11 shows selection of the left channel of a waveform.

The **Edit > Select Entire Wave** command (or the <Ctrl>+<A> shortcut) selects the entire waveform. Waveforms loaded in the application but placed on non-active pages aren't selected. If you put a selected waveform in the multitrack environment, it will remain selected.

You might have noticed a firm vertical line moving along the waveform image during playback. This is a cursor that points at the fragment being played. Under certain conditions (when the fragment displayed in the window is significantly less than the waveform and a special playback mode is on), the played fragment is displayed in an interesting way: The vertical line stays at the middle of the window, and the waveform image moves.

In the application's main window, you can edit the waveform at the sample level (the microlevel). Sometimes, this can be very useful, for example, when you need to delete a short pulse (a click). For another example, you can draw a sound wave manually and use it to create your own musical instrument with a unique timbre.

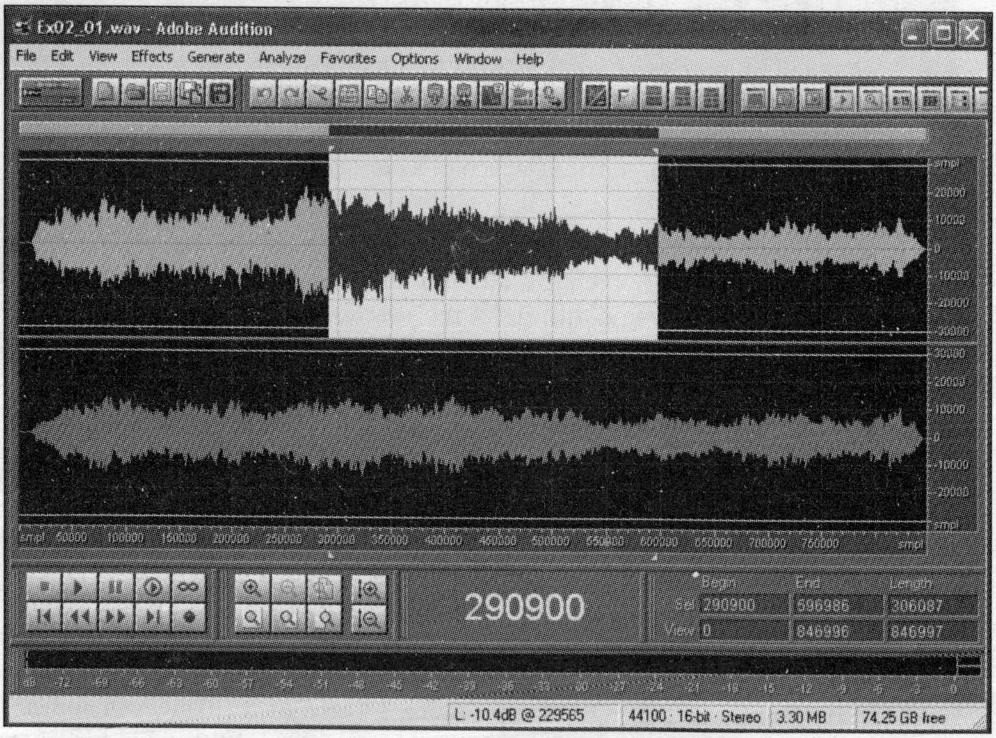

Fig. 2.11. Left channel of a waveform

Let's look at this editing mode in practice. To edit a waveform at the microlevel, set the appropriate zoom level. By repeatedly clicking the **Zoom In Horizontally** button, get to the zoom level, at which individual samples are visible and can be grabbed with the mouse (the mouse pointer will take the form of a hand with the index finger straightened out). In this mode, the sound samples are displayed as little squares connected with thin lines (Fig. 2.12).

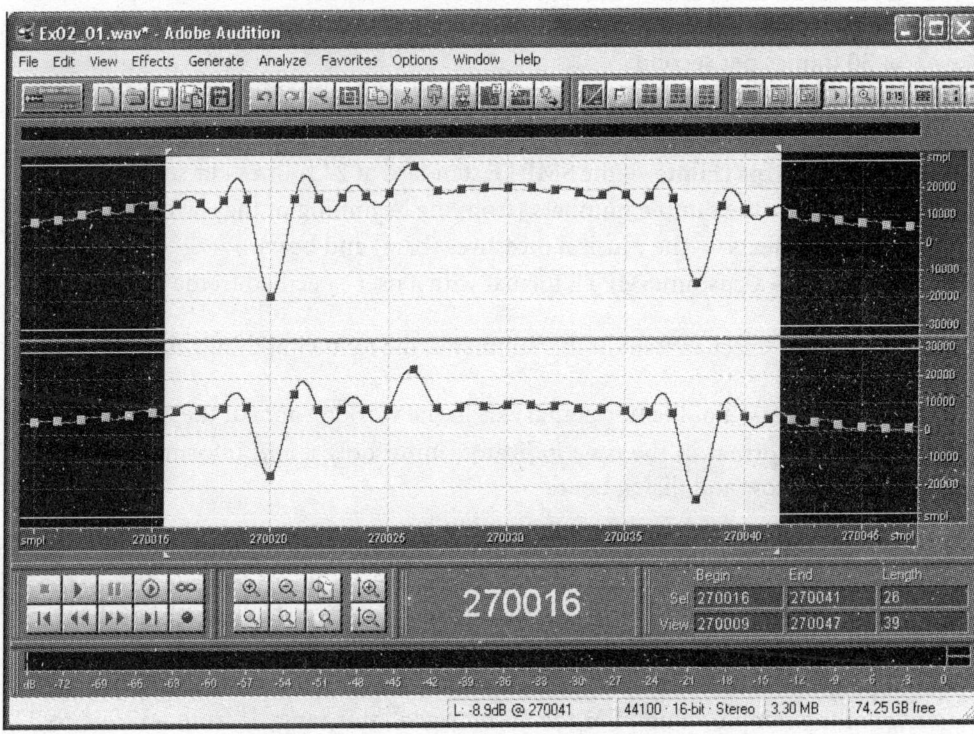

Fig. 2.12. Editing individual audio samples

These lines help you to make assumptions of what the signal will look like after it passes through the sound card's digital-to-analog converter (DAC) (including the low-pass filter, see [1]). You might have guessed that these squares can be dragged up or down. This is how the shape of the signal is edited at the microlevel. You can return to the normal zoom level (to edit at the amplitude envelope level rather than at the sample level) by repeatedly clicking the **Zoom Out Horizontally** button or by clicking the **Zoom Out Full Both Axis** button once.

The working area of the main window, in which the waveform is displayed, is a coordinate plane.

The time coordinates are plotted on the horizontal axis. You can choose the units, in which it is measured. To do this, use the **View > Display Time Format** submenu. The following time formats are available:

- **Decimal (mm:ss:ddd)** — the common format (minutes:seconds:milliseconds)
- **Compact Disc 75 fps** — the digital audio CD standard at 75 frames per second
- **SMPTE 30 fps** — the SMPTE standard (hours:minutes:seconds:frames) at 30 frames per second
- **SMPTE Drop(29.97 fps)** — the SMPTE standard at 29.97 frames per second
- **SMPTE 25 fps (EBU)** — the SMPTE standard at 25 frames per second
- **SMPTE 24 fps (Film)** — the SMPTE standard at 24 frames per second
- **Samples** — the sample numbers (from the beginning of the waveform)
- **Bars and Beats** — the musical measures (bars) and beats
- **Custom** — a custom SMPTE format with a user-specified frame rate

When you select an item in this submenu, the following things change:

- The graduation of the horizontal axis in the working area of the main window
- The time format in the time indicator, input boxes, and information fields of the main window and dialog boxes

If the mono format is selected for the waveform, the working area will display only one track. For the stereo format, two tracks will be displayed one below the other. More precisely, the track corresponding to the left channel will be above the track corresponding to the right channel.

The graduation of the vertical axis (individual for each track) corresponds to the range of the sample values. For the 16-bit signal, this range is from –32,768 to 32,767, and for the 8-bit signal, it is from –0 to 255. For users' convenience, three more graduation variants are provided:

- As percentages of the maximum valid sample value of 100%
- Normalized graduation: as decimal fractions (1 corresponds to the maximum valid sample value)
- In decibels

The units of measurements of the waveform span are selected using the commands of the **View > Vertical Scale Format** submenu.

Now let's look at the application's main window in the waveform view mode. The window can display the current waveform spectrum instead of the waveform itself. In this case, the vertical axis is graduated by frequency rather than by sample value.

There is a status bar at the bottom of the main window. Its fields display information about the recorded sound. To the left of it, the current application mode is displayed (**Stopped, Playing**, or **Recording**).

The **Data Under Cursor** field displays the current coordinates of the mouse pointer. This field is convenient for estimating the signal level at characteristic points. To do this, put the mouse pointer at one of the points.

The next field, **Sample Format**, displays the format selected when creating the waveform (e.g., **44100 16-bit Stereo** denotes 44.1 kHz, 16 bits, stereo).

The next fields display the following (from left to right):

- Disk space taken by the audio file (the **File Size** field)
- Total length of the waveform (the **File Size [time]** field)
- Amount of free space on the logical disks containing temporary folders for copies of the audio file created by the application during the current session (the fields **Free Space[K]** and **Free Space[time]**)

The right field, **Keyboard Modifiers**, displays the keyboard state.

During recording or playback, the contents of the fields change, informing you about the status of the application.

If digits appearing in the fields of the status bar distract you, turn off some or all of these fields. Right-click the status bar, and in the pop-up menu, uncheck the fields you don't want to view.

Now you know how to control the waveform display in the application's main window.

2.3.2. Playing a File and Rewinding/Fast-Forwarding a Waveform

By default, the lower left part of the main window contains a panel with buttons similar to those on a tape recorder. This is the *transport panel* (Fig. 2.13). Like some other panels of the main window, it can be undocked from the other panels and the main window borders. After that, it becomes moveable, and its name, **Transport Controls**, appears on it. You can dock it back to the other panels. Remember, the options for dockable panels are selected on the **General** tab, and their color layout is selected on the **Controls** page of the **Colors** tab of the **Settings** dialog box.

Fig. 2.13. Transport Controls panel

Using the buttons of the **Transport Controls** panel, you can control recording, playback, and displaying waveforms. Let's look at what they do.

 **Stop** — stops recording or playback. After you click it, the cursor will return to the marker. The next recording or playback will start from the marker position.

 **Play** — starts playback. If you right-click it, you open a menu that presents four variants of how the application reacts to clicking this button.

- **Play View** — only the displayed portion of the waveform is played. When the cursor reaches the right edge of the visible portion of the waveform, the playback will stop, and the cursor will return to the right edge of the waveform portion.
- **Play from Cursor to End of View** — playback starts from the marker and stops when the right edge of the visible portion of the waveform is reached. If a fragment of the waveform is selected, only this fragment will be played. After playback stops, the cursor will return to the beginning of the selection.
- **Play from Cursor to End of File** — the playback starts from the marker and stops at the end of the waveform.
- **Play Entire File** — the entire waveform is played.

 **Pause** — pauses during recording or playback. The cursor stops where it was caught by clicking this button. Another click on the button resumes recording (or playback).

 **Play to End** — another button for starting playback. By default, the entire waveform and not only the displayed portion or a selection can be played. During playback, the waveform image is scrolled so that the cursor always remains at the center of the screen. After playback finishes, or the **Stop** button is clicked, the portion of the waveform around the marker (i.e., the area, at which the playback started) will be displayed. Right-clicking on this button opens a pop-up menu similar to the pop-up menu of the **Play** button.

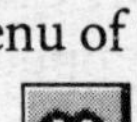 **Play Looped** — turns on looped playback. Playback will start from the marker position. When the cursor reaches the right edge of the displayed waveform

fragment, playback does not stop, but continues from its left edge. If a waveform fragment is selected, only the selection will be played cyclically.

Go to Beginning or Previous Cue — this button moves the marker to the beginning of the waveform or the previous cue position [3, *Section 4.11*].

Rewind — the rewind button. If the application is in the **Stopped** state, clicking this button will move the marker towards the beginning of the waveform. If you click the button once, the marker will move one step. If you click and keep the mouse button pressed, the marker will keep moving until it reaches the beginning of the waveform or until you release the **Rewind** button.

Right-clicking on the **Rewind** button opens a menu, in which you can select rewind speed. The upper two items of the menu correspond to a variable rewind speed. The longer you keep the **Rewind** button pressed, the faster the rewind. If you select any other item, a fixed rewind speed will be set.

If you click the **Rewind** button during waveform playback, the cursor and not the marker will move backwards. This will sound like an actual tape recorder rewinding a tape. When you release the button, the playback will resume from the point to which the cursor has moved.

Fast Forward — the fast-forward button. It differs from the **Rewind** button only in the direction of tape movement.

Go to End or Next Cue — this button moves the marker to the end of the waveform or to the next cue position.

Record — the button that starts recording.

Load an audio file from the CD that accompanies the book (e.g., EX02_01.WAV from the EXAMPLES folder) and use it to test these buttons in different situations and modes; refrain from recording (the **Record** button) for now.

2.4. Collecting a Waveform Sequence on One Track

Like the **File > Open** command, the command **File > Open Append** is used to open files. However, when loading one or more files with the **Open Append** command, the waveforms will be put in a sequence on one track (if the audio data is mono) or on one pair of tracks (for stereo data). In other words, this command is used for combining several waveforms from different files to one resulting file.

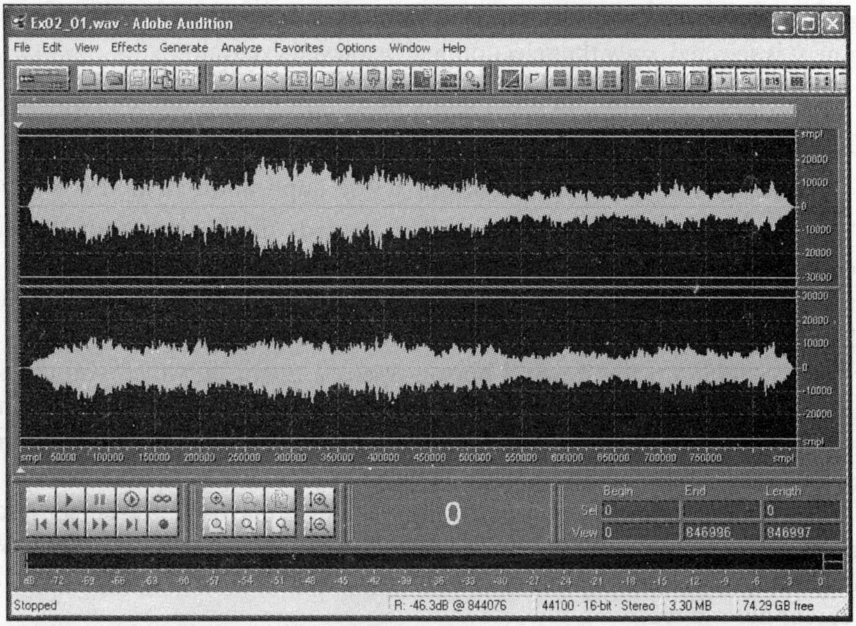

Fig. 2.14. Main window page with the waveform from EX02_01.WAV

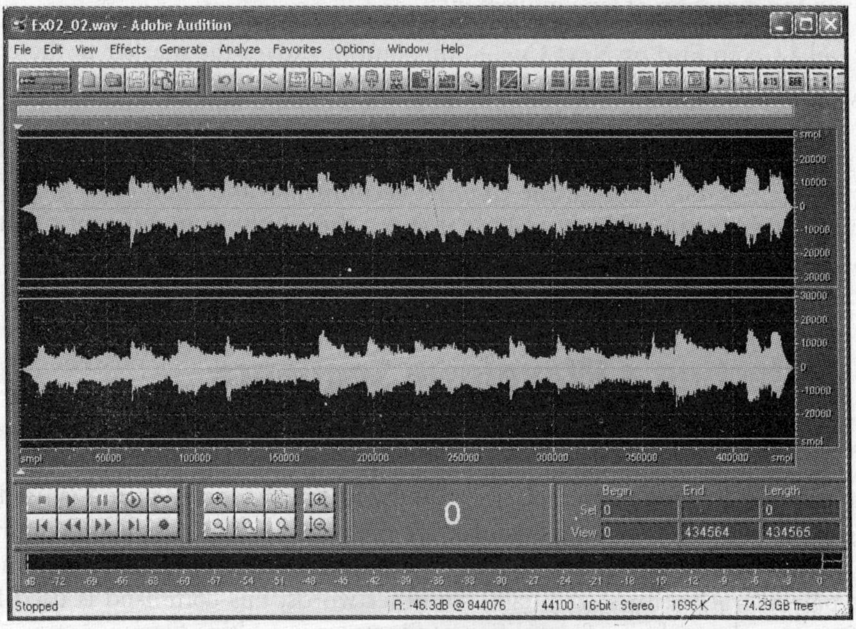

Fig. 2.15. Main window page with the waveform from EX02_02.WAV

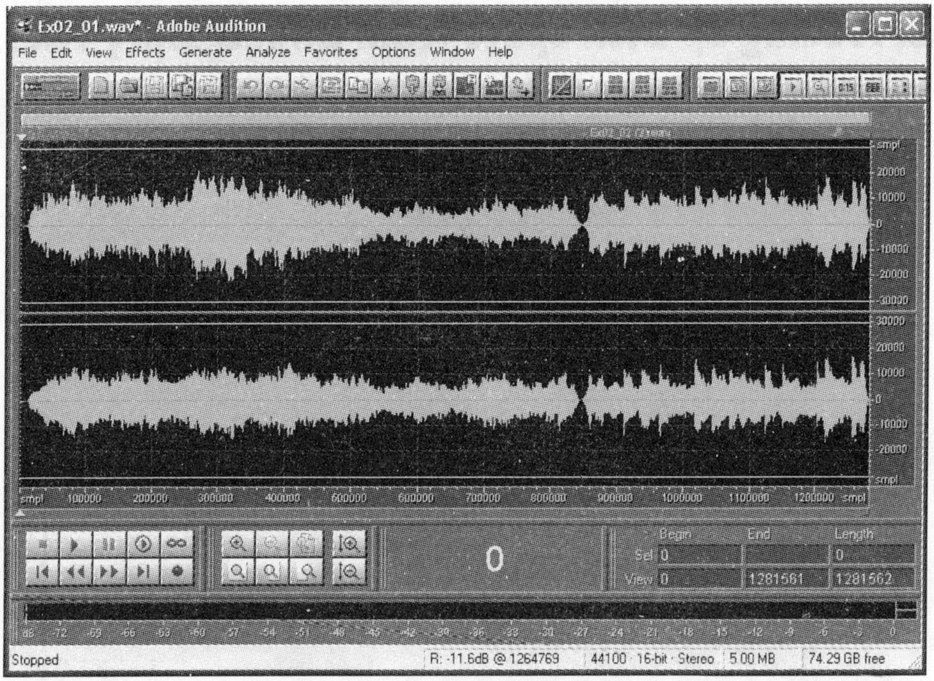

Fig. 2.16. Two waveforms combined using the **Open Append** command

Fig. 2.14 and 2.15 show the contents of two pages of the main window after loading files EX02_01.WAV and EX02_02.WAV from the EXAMPLES folder with two **Open** commands. Fig. 2.16 shows the result of applying the **Open Append** command to EX02_02.WAV (EX02_01.WAV was loaded earlier).

The position at which the waveform starts is marked with a red vertical dashed line and the file name.

2.5. Making the Opened File Available to Other Applications

When working with Windows applications, you have probably encountered situations when a file opened in one application was needed in another application. However, Windows doesn't always allow this. For example, a document file opened in Microsoft Word cannot be moved to another folder with Windows Commander.

The **File > Flush Virtual File** command frees a file opened in Adobe Audition so that it can be used by another Windows application.

2.6. Freeing up Disk Space from Unnecessary Files

The **File > Free Up Space in Temp Files** command opens the dialog box of the same name (Fig. 2.17) that is used for freeing up and reserving disk space.

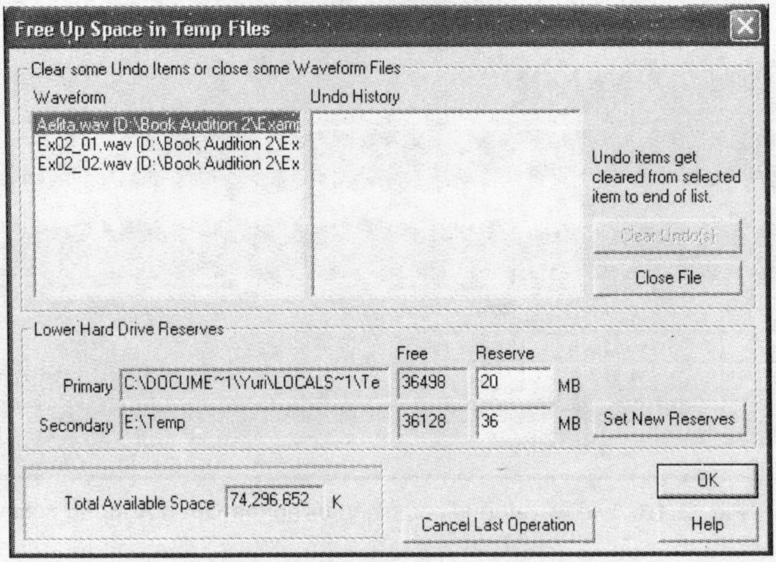

Fig. 2.17. Free Up Space in Temp Files dialog box

The **Clear some Undo Items or close some Waveform Files** group contains two drop-down lists:

- **Waveform** — a list of opened audio files. Select a file you don't need at the moment and click the **Close File** button.
- **Undo History** — the history of the **Undo** function (related to the file selected in the **Waveform** list). Select an operation you no longer need and click the **Clear Undo(s)** button.

The **Lower Hard Drive Reserves** group allows you to specify a minimum amount of free space on the first (**Primary**) and the second (**Secondary**) disks. These values in megabytes should be entered into the corresponding **Reserve** input boxes. By clicking the **Set New Reserves** button, tell the application to set new parameters for the reserved space.

The **Total Available Space** field shows how much disk space is available.

When Adobe Audition becomes short of free disk space, it will automatically open the **Free Up Space in Temp Files** dialog box, in which you should click the **Cancel Last Operation** button to cancel an operation that cannot be completed because of shortage of disk space. Then you should free up some disk space with the controls of this dialog box or operating system tools to continue working with Adobe Audition.

2.7. Extracting Audio Data from a Digital Audio CD to Adobe Audition

The **File > Extract Audio From CD** command opens a dialog box of the same name (Fig. 2.18) that is used for extracting audio data from a digital audio CD to Adobe Audition.

In fact, the **Extract Audio From CD** command performs a task similar to the task of numerous "grabbers," applications that make it possible to copy a CD track by converting it into a WAV file that can be used in a computer. Many musicians use such applications to create remixes.

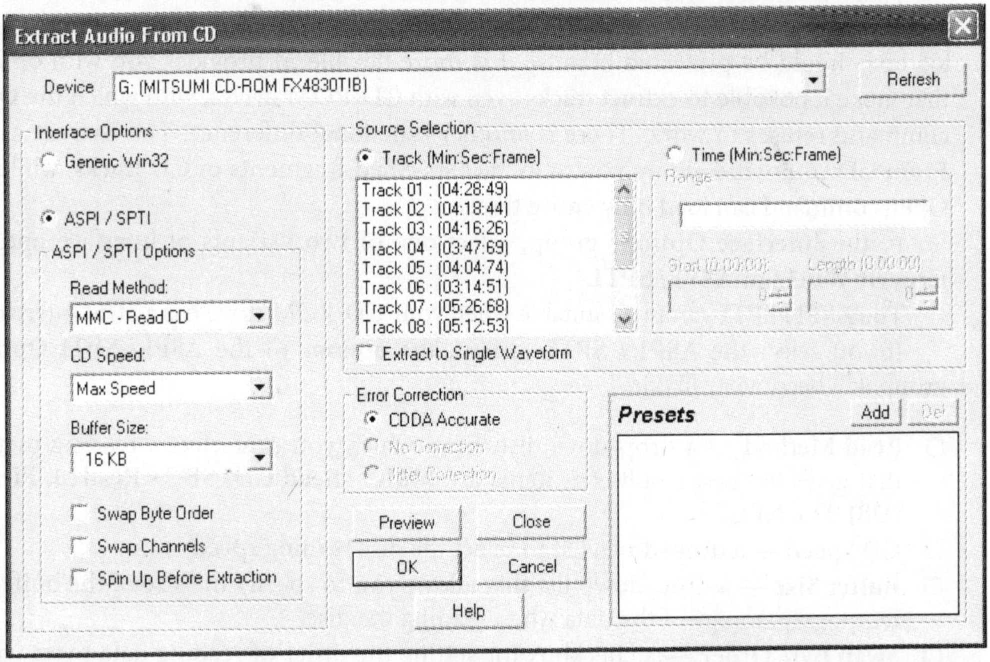

Fig. 2.18. Extract Audio From CD dialog box

Sometimes, musicians extract fragments from CDs to create *loops* (short fragments of drum parts used in loop modes) and *grooves* (fragments of melodic parts). Sometimes, they extract a very short fragment, such as a single note played with a particular instrument. Based on this fragment, they use special programs to create all the other notes. The instrument obtained like this can be then loaded into a sampler and used in compositions.

Of course, you should be extremely careful when converting other people's compositions recorded on CDs to editable WAV files: You must not infringe copyright.

Let's look at the controls of the **Extract Audio From CD** dialog box.

The **Device** drop-down list contains all CD players available in your system. Select the device, in which the CD is inserted.

Not all CD-ROM drives support ripping (extracting audio data from the tracks of a digital audio CD). Therefore, if you failed to extract audio with the **Extract Audio From CD** command, don't rush to blame Adobe Audition. More likely, this was because of your CD-ROM drive.

There is another way of extracting tracks from CDs. Use the **Open** command to load them as if they were CDA files. However, using the **Extract Audio From CD** dialog box should be preferred because it is more flexible. It provides you with options that make it possible to extract tracks even with CD-ROM drives, with which the **Open** command refuses to work. There is another functional difference. The **Extract Audio From CD** command allows you to extract specified fragments of CD tracks, while the **Open** command can load only entire tracks.

In the **Interface Options** group, select one of two variants of interface options: **Generic Win32** or **ASPI / SPTI**.

The **ASPI / SPTI** variant is suitable when your CD-ROM drive has a SCSI interface.

If you select the **ASPI / SPTI** variant, the options of the **ASPI / SPTI Options** group will become available:

- **Read Method** — a drop-down list, from which you can select a reading method that gives the best results (its items are **MMC - Read CD**, **SBC - Read10**, **Plextor (D8)**, **D5**, **NEC**)
- **CD Speed** — a drop-down list to select the disc reading speed
- **Buffer Size** — a drop-down list that allows you to specify the size of the buffer for temporary storage of the data when reading the disc
- **Swap Byte Order** — a checkbox for setting the order of reading data bytes typical to DEC and Macintosh (it must be unchecked when you work on a PC)

- **Swap Channels** — a checkbox for turning on the channel swapping mode, in which the right channel of the digital audio CD track will be output to the left channel of Adobe Audition, and the left channel of the digital audio CD track will be output to the right channel of Adobe Audition
- **Spin Up Before Extraction** — a checkbox for spinning up the CD-ROM drive before data reading starts

The **Generic Win32** option in the **Interface Options** group should be chosen if the **ASPI / SPTI** variant does not produce positive results.

The **Source Selection** group provides two variants of data loading: **Track (Min:Sec:Frame)** and **Time (Min:Sec:Frame)**.

If you select the **Track (Min:Sec:Frame)** radio button, you'll have to select one or more tracks in the appropriate list. If the **Extract to Single Waveform** checkbox is checked, all audio tracks, regardless of their number, will be represented as one waveform (in Adobe Audition, they will be recorded sequentially, one after another).

If the **Time (Min:Sec:Frame)** radio button is selected in the **Source Selection** group, Adobe Audition will extract a fragment that has the length specified in the **Length** field of the **Range** group and starts at the moment specified in the **Start** field of the **Range** group.

Both the start moment and length of the fragment being extracted are specified in the *minute:second:frame* format (remember that in a digital audio CD, there are 75 frames in one second).

The diagram located above the **Start** and **Length** fields is a visual indicator of where the fragment being extracted is positioned on the audio track.

In comparison to a CD-ROM, the data on a digital audio CD has weaker protection against reading errors caused by low quality of recording, failures of phase synchronization, defects on the disc's surface, etc. Under the normal work of a CD-ROM driver when it plays digital audio discs, correcting algorithms are performed directly by the drive's hardware. When CD tracks are extracted via the IDE or SCSI interface, software correction might be required.

Adobe Audition provides use of correcting algorithms during extracting tracks from a Digital Audio CD. The **Error Correction** group contains options for data correction when reading it from a disc:

- **CDDA Accurate** — the CD-ROM drive supports hardware error correction when extracting CD-DA tracks via the IDE and SCSI interfaces (no software correction is required).
- **No Correction** — turns off software correction.

- **Jitter Correction** — turns on software correction for reading errors cause by jitter (occasional changes of the relative phase shift of reference oscillators in different digital devices [1]).

If you have a modern CD-ROM drive, most likely the first variant will be selected automatically. The last variant, which is appropriate for older CD-ROM drives, should be selected when there are clicks and sample dropouts in the extracted audio data.

The selected track fragment or a list of tracks to be extracted can be saved as a preset. To add a preset to the **Presets** list, click the **Add** button. A very simple dialog box will open, in which you should only specify a name for the preset you create. To delete a preset from the list, click the **Del** button.

If you want to listen preliminarily to the extracted audio material in Adobe Audition, click the **Preview** button (its name will change to **Stop**; clicking this modified button will stop the preliminary listening).

To activate extraction of audio data from a digital audio CD to Adobe Audition, click the **OK** button.

Chapter 3

Recording Audio with a Microphone

Electronic music written by a talented person is interesting in itself and doesn't need any additional "enlivening". At the same time, remarkable results can be obtained by combining synthesized sound with the sound of actual acoustic instruments. In addition, songs are a significant part of music. A video movie must contain not only a picture, but also sounds. In these cases, a microphone is essential.

It is very easy to start recording in Adobe Audition. Just click the **Record** button on the transport panel. However, before you do this, you must:

- Connect a microphone to your sound card
- Make sure that an appropriate audio data input device is selected
- Select a format for the file that will contain the recorded audio data
- Set a recorded signal level so that any distortions are unlikely

These points are the subject of this chapter.

3.1. Selecting and Connecting a Microphone

There are several different types of microphones that differ in terms of their construction and the principles by which they convert audio oscillations to electric ones. We'll concentrate only on electrodynamic and electrostatic microphones, because microphones of other types don't provide the necessary quality. Electrodynamic microphones can be moving-coil or band type. Electrostatic microphones are capacitor and electret type (the latter being a special kind of the former).

The working principles of an electrodynamic microphone are as follows. The pressure of sound waves moves a membrane and an inductance coil (in moving-coil microphones) or a band (in band microphones) connected to the membrane. The movement of these components in a constant magnetic field causes an electromotive force at the ends of the coil or band. Changes in the force carry certain information.

A capacitor microphone needs an external power supply. A stretched membrane oscillates relative to a static electrode under the influence of sound waves. These two components form a capacitor, acting as its plates. When the membrane oscillates, the capacity of the capacitor changes. Alternate electric current proportional to the sound pressure appears in the electric circuit. Electret microphones have the same working principles as capacitor microphones, but voltage on the capacitor plates is provided not by an external source, but by the electric charge on the membrane or static electrode. The material of which they are made is electret, in other words, can keep charge for a long time.

The main features and parameters of microphones that determine their quality are the following:

- *Sensitivity.* A microphone must catch weak sounds without masking them with its internal noise. You should preferably choose microphones with high sensitivity. The best models are equipped with sensitivity switches.
- *Dynamic range.* A microphone must "hear" quiet sounds without being overloaded by loud ones.
- *Frequency-response curve.* If you don't know the frequency characteristics of the sound source in advance (for example, you have never heard the singer's voice before), you should go for a microphone with a uniform frequency response that will perceive sound oscillations of all frequencies equally well. However, to record a particular person's voice or the sound of a particular musical instrument, it would be better to use a microphone that emphasizes the features determining the beauty of the sound.
- *Internal noise level.* The lower, the better.
- *Directional characteristics* (that determine how the sensitivity of a microphone depends on the direction to the sound source). There are three main types of microphones, according to their directional characteristics:
  - Omnidirectional (circular directional characteristics; suitable for recording groups of singers or instruments)
  - Bidirectional (figure-of-eight directional characteristics curve; used for recording dialogues or duets)
  - Unidirectional (cardioidal and supercardioidal); heart-shaped directional characteristics curve; used under complex acoustic conditions; perceive almost no sounds from any direction except the main one

The best microphones are equipped with switches to change directional characteristics, so they can be used under any conditions.

A microphone is not something you can skimp on. The quality of the recorded sound and, therefore, your success depends on the microphone. This is why you should be very careful when purchasing a microphone.

When equipping a studio and choosing between dynamic and capacitor microphones, many sound producers prefer the latter. High sensitivity, wide frequency and dynamic ranges, and the capability to catch the finest nuances of a voice are pros when such microphone is used in a studio. There is only one con: An average capacitor microphone is more expensive than its dynamic "cousin."

In addition to their undoubted advantages, any capacitor microphones have a few disadvantages. First, they endure bad weather worse than dynamic microphones. Second, they require an external power supply. This is why it is difficult, if not impossible, to connect a capacitor microphone directly to a sound card. When working with a capacitor microphone, you need a special adapting device combined with a power supply. These can be components of a mixer.

To decrease the influence of various acoustic interference sources, secure your microphone to a rack with special anti-shock suspension.

Thus, there are a few variants for connecting a microphone to a sound card:

- A *dynamic microphone* is connected either directly to the sound card input or to the microphone input of a mixer whose output is connected to the linear input of the sound card. The second variant should be preferred because it diminishes the noise level.
- A *capacitor microphone* is connected to the microphone input of a mixer (or a mixer amplifier) that has a phantom voltage source. The output of the mixer or mixer amplifier is connected to the linear input of the sound card.

You should be careful when using a dynamic microphone with a mixer (or a mixer amplifier) that has a phantom voltage source necessary for capacitor microphones. Make sure that the phantom voltage source is off! Otherwise, under certain conditions, the dynamic microphone can be damaged.

Choose the most suitable variant and connect your microphone to your sound card.

Make sure the appropriate digital audio input device is selected on the **Wave In** tab of the **Device Properties** window (see *Section 1.2.2*, Fig. 1.7).

3.2. Creating a New Project

Before you start recording sound with the microphone, you must tell the application that you are going to do this. In other words, you must create a new project. To create a new project, to which a new waveform will be recorded, use the **File** > **New** command. If another waveform has been edited before selecting this command, it won't be lost. That waveform will be retained on another page, and you'll be able to move to that page using the **Window** menu.

The **File** > **New** command opens the **New Waveform** dialog box, which is an exact copy of the **Open File(s) As** window discussed in *Section 2.2.1* (Fig. 2.3).

Select the sample rate in the **Sample Rate** list. It is best to select the maximum sample rate of those supported by your sound card. If your computer isn't powerful enough, you'll have to abandon a high sample rate. However, in any case you should select a value of at least 44.1 kHz. Otherwise, the recording quality will be very low.

In the **Channels** group, select the **Mono** or **Stereo** mode. When recording with a mono microphone, it makes sense to select **Mono**. Selecting **Stereo** in this case will result in duplicating the memory space necessary to store the file. You'll be able to impart stereo features to the sound later when you process it with effects.

In the **Resolution** group, select a resolution. It makes no sense to select the **8-bit** option, because the sound quality in this case will be beneath all criticism. In fact, you should choose between the **16-bit** and **32-bit (float)** options. If disk space isn't a critical resource, select **32-bit (float)**. This will allow you to process the audio repeatedly with various effects without fear that the accumulating errors could become noticeable to the ear.

If you select the **File** > **New** command before recording and specify the format of the future waveform, the application won't open the **New Waveform** window again after you click the **Record** button in the main window. Rather, it will start recording immediately.

3.3. Setting a Recording Level

Before you click the **Record** button, make sure that the signal from the sound source (microphone, CD player, sound card's internal synthesizer, or any other source connected, for example, to the sound card's linear input) is supplied to the input of the analog-to-digital converter (ADC). Doing this is very simple: Minimize the main window of the application and start the mixer program of your sound card. In the window that will open, select the sound source and set a recording level so that there are no non-linear distortions when the volume is at maximum. We don't show the mixer window here because its appearance depends on your sound card and which of its drivers are installed in your system.

You can check the presence of the sound and roughly estimate its quality by ear.

If you don't hear the sound through the acoustic systems or headphones connected to the output of the sound card, and the indicators of the sound card's mixer program don't respond when you speak to the microphone, there could be several reasons. First, there may be a wrong switching or a break in the microphone-cable-mixer-cable-audio card input chain. Second, the digital audio input device may be wrongly selected. Third, the input of the mixer program might be muted.

Adobe Audition provides a very convenient tool for precisely adjusting the recording level. By default, there are signal meters and a graduated strip (the **Level Meters** panel, Fig. 3.1) in the lower part of the window. The default range of the strip is from 0 to –72 dB (numbers from 0 to –69). The level range is editable. To change it, right-click the strip and select a range of displayed levels in the pop-up menu (from 24 to 120 dB).

The notion of a signal level is thoroughly explained in [1], so here we'll give only a brief definition. The *level* of an audio signal describes the signal at a particular moment, and is a rectified and averaged audio signal voltage (in decibels) measured at the specified preceding interval and divided by a certain conventional value. The signal level is directly related to the volume.

Double-click the strip or select the **Options > Monitor Record Level** command of the main menu. The strip will become active. If the stereo format has been selected for audio data, the strip will indicate the signal levels of the left and right audio channels: Two bright bands will be shorter or longer in accordance with the changing values of the signal levels in the right and left channels. To make it easier for you to watch the peak values of the levels, the indicators remember them for a short time. If the format of audio data is mono, you'll see only one shifting band instead of two.

In essence, the double click you've just made on the level meters is an "idle" start of the analog-to-digital converter (ADC), during which audio samples aren't stored in the computer memory but just the current signal level is indicated.

Your main goal is not to allow the signal level to reach 0 dB, but it shouldn't be very low (Fig. 3.1).

There are two small squares one above the other to the right of the zero mark. These are indicators of overload (signal clipping) of the left and right channels. They light up if the signal amplitude reaches or exceeds the maximum allowable value. A level of 0 dB corresponds to the maximum allowable value of a digital audio signal sample. If the signal being recorded exceeds this value, an overflow of the ADC will happen. This will be heard as a noticeable signal distortion, especially when the overflow happens often or within a long time interval. This is why the overload indicators warn you with a red color. The recording session is in danger!

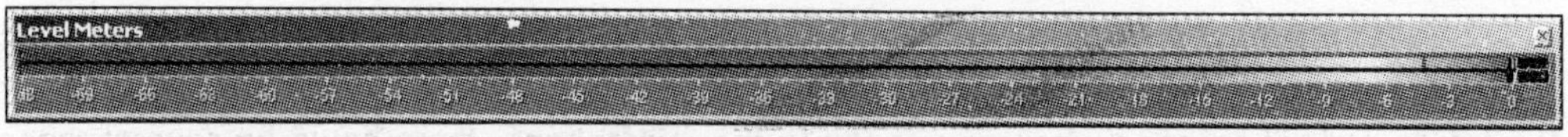

Fig. 3.1. Level meters. Signal level is rather high, but doesn't exceed 0 dB

If the sound source allows you to repeat the recording (for example, when recording from a CD), it would be wise to listen to all of the material first. Every time the overload indicators light up, go through the following procedure:

1. Stop the playback.
2. Decrease the signal level a little by making adjustments on the sound card mixer (with the virtual mixer).
3. Reset the overload indicator (put out the virtual LEDs by clicking them).
4. Rewind the recording (set a marker before the point in the waveform at which the overload took place).
5. Listen to the problematic fragment of the recording once more.

While recording with a microphone, it is impossible to predict how the sound volume will be changing. Nevertheless, you should rehearse what you're going to record (a speech, a vocal part, or playing a musical instrument). During the rehearsal, you may vary the distance from the sound source to the microphone, their positions, and the sound volume. In addition, it would be wise to direct the microphone so that it doesn't perceive noise (if there is a noise source in the room).

After you find the necessary level with the mixer, don't forget to stop the idle work of the ADC. Double click the level indicators again or click the **Stop** button.

To conclude the topic of the signal meter, we'll consider the commands of the pop-up menu opened with a right click on the meter:

- **Monitor Record Level** — turns on the signal meter (also done with a double click on the meter).
- **Show on Play and Record** — displays the signal level both during recording and playback.
- **Clear Clip Indicators** — resets overload indicators (also done with a click on the indicators).

- **Adjust for DC** — corrects the measured signal level, taking into account the presence of the direct component.
- **Show Valleys** — displays current minimum values of the signal level (valleys).
- **120 dB Range...24 dB Range** — allows the user to select the range of the measured level values.
- **Dynamic Peaks** — dynamically displays the maximum values of the signal level (peaks): The dashes denoting the peaks will change their positions after a certain delay.
- **Static Peaks** — statically displays the peaks; the dashes denoting the peaks will change their positions only if their levels are exceeded. In other words, after you stop recording or playback, the highest level value of the whole session will be marked on the meter.

Like some other panels of the main window, the **Level Meters** panel can be dragged with the mouse. You might find it more convenient to place the **Level Meters** panel vertically and dock it to the right side of the main window as shown in Fig. 3.2.

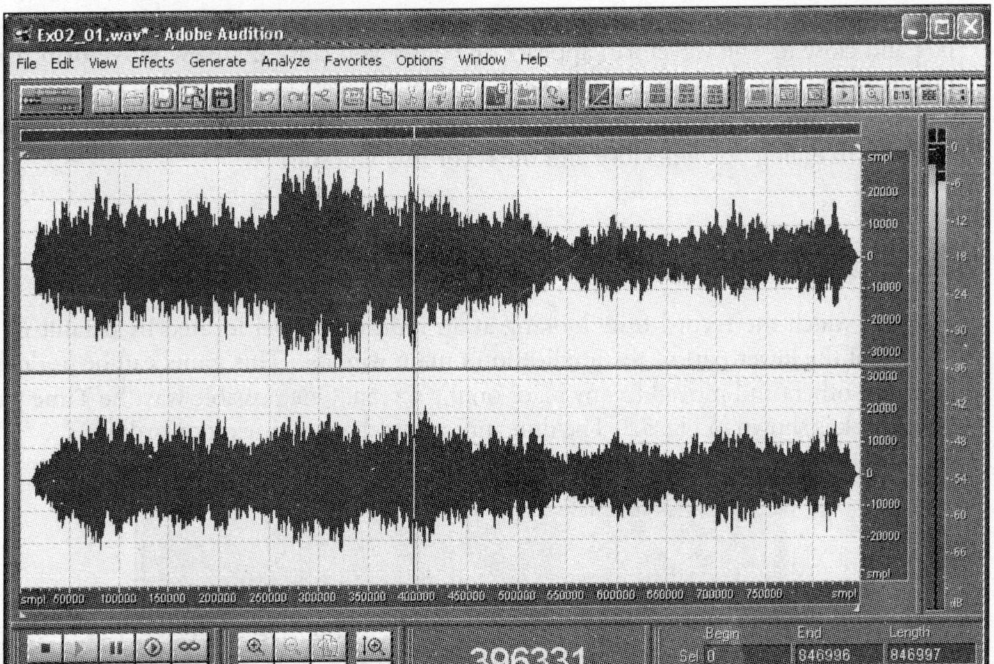

Fig. 3.2. Level meter placed vertically

3.4. Starting Recording

Now you have to select one of two possible recording modes. Right-click the **Record** button. A menu for mode selection will appear. It contains two items, **Instant Record** and **Timed Record.**

If you select the **Instant Record** mode, the recording will start as soon as you click the **Record** button.

The **Timed Record** mode allows you to specify the start time and the length of a recording session. This procedure is described in [3, *Section 2.2*].

Select **Instant Record**. You can click the **Record** button at last! Most likely, the recording will start instantly.

However, if you skipped the stage of creating a new project (if you did not execute the **File > New** command), another scenario is likely: The **New Waveform** dialog box will open. Thus the application will suggest that you decide what format must be used for recording. The appearance of the dialog box can be perceived from another point of view: A waveform doesn't exist until you specify necessary parameters in the dialog box and close it. The waveform appears only after you close the **New Waveform** dialog box. However, this waveform doesn't contain a sample until the recording session starts.

Immediately after you click the **OK** button or press the <Enter> key, the **New Waveform** dialog box will close and the recording will start.

3.5. Watching the Record Time

You can watch the record time looking at an indicator panel located by default in the middle of the lower part of the application's main window. This panel can be undocked from the others and moved to any place on the screen. One possible way the **Time** panel could look is shown in Fig. 3.3. The time indication changes during recording.

Fig. 3.3. Time indicator

In our example, the numbers **0:06.938** indicate that zero minutes, six seconds, and 938 milliseconds have elapsed from the start of recording. In this case, time is displayed in the decimal format.

You can select another display format in the submenu of the **View > Display Time Format** command.

3.6. Done... What Next?

Here we have seen how to record audio data in the **Instant Record** mode. In this mode, recording starts immediately after you click the **Record** button and specify the waveform parameters.

So you started recording by clicking the **Record** button. If your computer is powerful enough, the recording will go on smoothly. No failures will happen, and the values of the time parameters and the amount of memory will change monotonously in the indication fields.

If you need to interrupt recording temporarily, click the **Pause** button.

You can consider that you have a waveform at your disposal only after you click the **Stop** button. The recording is finished. To be on the safe side, save it in a file.

So is that it? Nothing of the kind: The main work is yet to start. The amount and contents of this main work depend on the product you're planning to create. Adobe Audition has features that allow you to recover an old recording stored on a magnetic tape or a vinyl record, record a musical composition or a song from scratch, or create a commercial or a jingle. In addition, if you use Adobe Audition in combination with Adobe Premiere Pro and Adobe After Effects, you'll be able to process a soundtrack for a digital video. To some extent, this book will help familiarize you with these features of Adobe Audition, but we'll concentrate mainly on a step-by-step description of work on a project whose goal is creating a video clip.

The role of the sound in a video clip is dual:

- On screen — as speech, music, or a vocal part synchronized with the picture
- Off screen — as asynchronous musical, speech, or noise accompaniment for the picture

If you're going to process sound that must be synchronized with the picture, the general procedure will be the following:

1. Record the sound simultaneously with the picture with a video recorder.
2. Extract audio from the digital stream of audio and video data to a separate track.

3. Process the audio track (suppress the noise, filter the sound, convert the dynamic range, apply effects, mix the track with other sound tracks, etc.), but don't disrupt its synchronicity with the picture (in particular, don't move, shorten, or lengthen any audio fragments independently of the video).
4. Export the processed audio track to a video file.

Implementation of these operations in Adobe Audition involves working in the multitrack mode (see *Chapters 10* and *11*).

When it comes to asynchronous audio, things are both simpler and more complex. This audio can be recorded independently of video (in the waveform editing mode or in the multitrack mode). Then you can process it as you like (for example, you can cut out fragments containing errors). All necessary operations should be done in the waveform editing mode. However, to perform montage and mixing of the sound track, and to synchronize roughly it with video, you'll eventually have to switch to the multitrack mode.

In the following chapters, we'll show you the main techniques for analysing and processing audio data recorded from a microphone and intended to be part of asynchronous audio accompaniment of a short video clip. As a source material, we'll use the files from EX03_01.WAV to EX03_05.WAV from the EXAMPLES folder on the CD-ROM that comes with this book. These are "raw" recordings intentionally made under conditions unsuitable for working with a microphone. They contain a few typical errors that will subsequently be eliminated or at least masked during editing. When describing the main features of the application, we'll apply them to this original file, and we'll save all intermediate results in other files (their versions are contained on the accompanying CD-ROM). Therefore, you'll be able not only to read about one operation or another, but also to compare your resulting files with ours.

Chapter 4

Analyzing the Recording and Elaborating a Signal-Processing Strategy

So the sound is recorded with a microphone, and the recording is saved in a file. As you already know, when working on this book, we created example files named EX03_01.WAV to EX03_05.WAV and saved them in the EXAMPLES folder on the accompanying CD-ROM. These files are components of a project whose goal is to record a short video clip with an audio track.

We chose such a goal deliberately. We believe that this is the most frequent practical goal. We think that many readers use (or would like to use) their computers to create a presentation or advertising video and audio material.

We hope that the contents of the video clip we are going to create are interesting and useful for our readers. This is why the clip is devoted to books on computer technology and to A-LIST publishing house, which specializes in such books.

According to our plan, the video clip should consist of five parts. In the first part (EX03_01.WAV), an on-screen narrator greets the viewers and says a few words about the publishing house. Here, the sound is recorded simultaneously with the video image and is synchronized with it. This feature must be retained after all processing. In the second part (EX03_02.WAV), the narrator (off screen) talks about A-LIST's main categories of books; his voice accompanies a series of digital photos. In the third part (EX03_03.WAV), the narrator (on screen) continues his story about the publishing house and picks out some of its bestsellers. As in the first part, here the sound must be synchronized with video. In the fourth part (EX03_04.WAV), the narrator (off screen) talks about the bestsellers while the book covers are displayed on the screen. Finally (EX03_05.WAV), the narrator (on screen) invites you to visit the publishing house's site.

Methods for processing synchronous and asynchronous audio differ. In the next few chapters, we'll mainly discuss processing non-video-dependent sound (EX03_02.WAV and EX03_04.WAV). We'll take the file EX03_02.WAV as an example, assuming that EX03_04.WAV should be processed in a similar fashion.

We are still a long way from fulfilling our plan. Now, we must take the next step, which is to analyze the obtained recording, estimate its usability, and elaborate a processing strategy that will allow us to eliminate the flaws.

Let's look at the analytical tools available to us. They are few in number, but quite powerful:

- Monitoring (listening to) a recording
- Qualitative (visual) and quantitative (i.e., with various meters) analysis of the waveform and level of a recorded signal
- Qualitative and quantitative analysis of the instantaneous and classical spectrum of a recorded signal

Let's look at each of them in more detail.

4.1. Monitoring the Recording

First of all, listen closely to the recorded material many times. The goal of this listening is to decide whether the recording is suitable for further processing, and which fragments contain errors. If the same material was recorded repeatedly, you should choose the highest-quality takes. If there is no take entirely suitable for further processing, you may select several takes. You'll be able to assemble the required recording from fragments of different takes. If the takes were recorded with breaks, they might be stored in different files. We created the example file EX03_02.WAV without breaks, so the takes follow each other. In truth, the first version of the EX03_02.WAV file contained many more takes, but we cut the least successful (with the narrator's slips of the tongue and too loud external noises) to save the disk space and your time. In addition, we separated the remaining takes with rests, for convenience's sake.

It makes sense to listen to the sound while looking at the corresponding waveform (Fig. 4.1).

EX03_02.WAV contains five takes of the same phrase. After the first stage of analysis, we came to the following conclusions:

1. The first take (from 0:02 to 0:25) cannot be used in further work because outside sounds (voices in a neighboring room) are sometimes heard. It is reasonable to cut this fragment of the waveform to decrease the file size and file processing time.

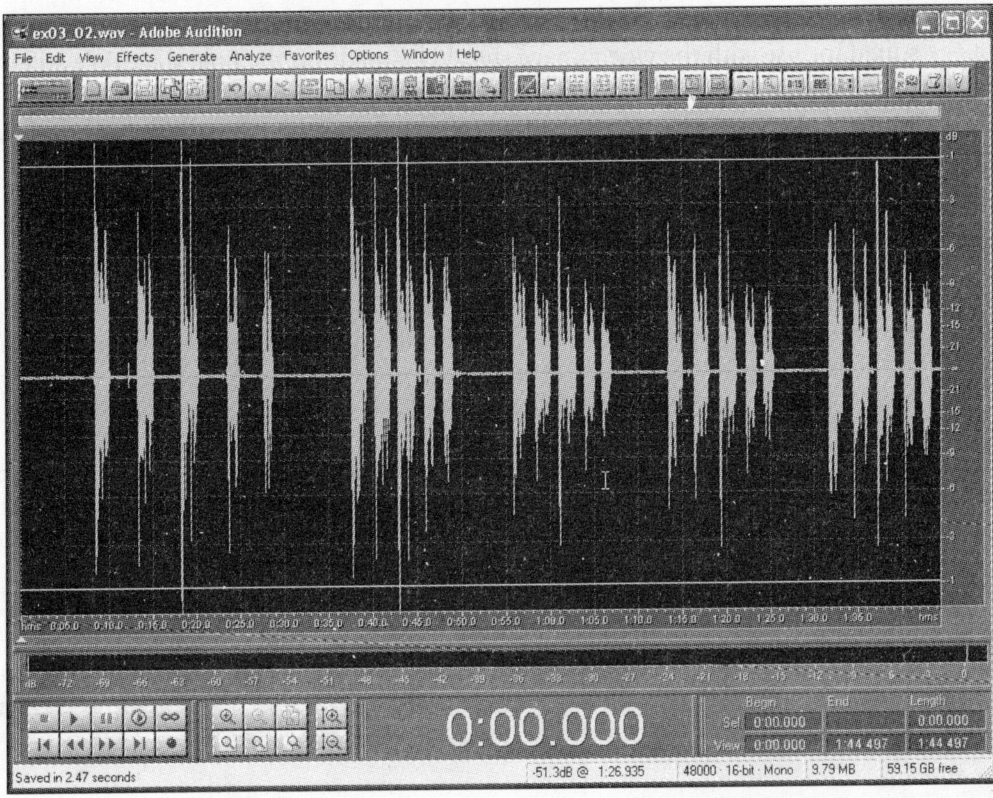

Fig. 4.1. Waveform corresponding to the EX03_02.WAV file

2. The second take (0:30–0:44) is recorded with microphone overload. The narrator sometimes spoke too loudly, which is why there are a few peaks that reach 0 dB, although most of the maximums of the waveform are about the level of –6 dB. In addition, ADC overflow took place because the recording was done without compression. It would be reasonable to cut this fragment too.
3. The third take (0:47–0:59) was recorded with a too low level. The narrator became tired by this take, and his voice grew weaker.
4. The fourth take (1:03–1:15) was recorded at a sufficiently high level and without overload. It doesn't contain obvious flaws, except noticeable sounds of the narrator's lips opening when he inhales. These sounds can be eliminated later. In addition, the narrator's voice became quiet by the end of the phrase. As a whole, the take can be used in work.
5. The fifth take (1:20–1:32) was recorded after a small break, during which the narrator took a rest and better understood his task. This take can be considered good

and used as the main one. The decision about which take (No. 4 or No. 5) is best suited for use with the video image should be made on the final stage. We still have to combine five audio fragments into one soundtrack. These are:

- Introductory part of the video clip, in which audio is synchronized with the picture
- Asynchronous audio for the video image of the book covers described by the narrator
- Central part of the clip, in which the narrator on the screen talks about the publishing house
- Next to the last part of the video clip, in which the video image of the best-sellers is accompanied by the off-screen voice
- Final part of the video clip, in which audio is again synchronized with video

Without analyzing the sound of the other parts of the video clip, it is impossible to decide, which of the two suitable takes is best. One criterion of the two fragments' compatibility is the degree of similarity of the narrator's intonations and the backgrounds of the recordings.

A similar visual analysis must be done for three takes of another asynchronous recording, contained in the file EX03_04.WAV.

When listening to a recording, watch the level meter. Using the meter, you can estimate the noise level in rests (in our case, from –55 dB to –48 dB) and the average and maximum signal level. You can also detect overload (see *Section 3.3*).

4.2. Obtaining Statistical Information on the Waveform Using the *Waveform Statistics* Dialog Box

Obtaining statistical information about a waveform is done with the **Waveform Statistics** dialog box, opened with the **Analyze > Statistics** command. The dialog box contains two tabs: **General,** with statistical information on the waveform parameters; and **Histogram,** with the histogram (value distribution) of the waveform samples.

The information here is useful when deciding whether it makes sense to try to eliminate certain distortions, and when you choose parameters to process the recorded signal dynamically.

4.2.1. *Obtaining Waveform Statistics on the* General *Tab*

The **General** tab (Fig. 4.2) contains statistical information about either the selection or the entire waveform.

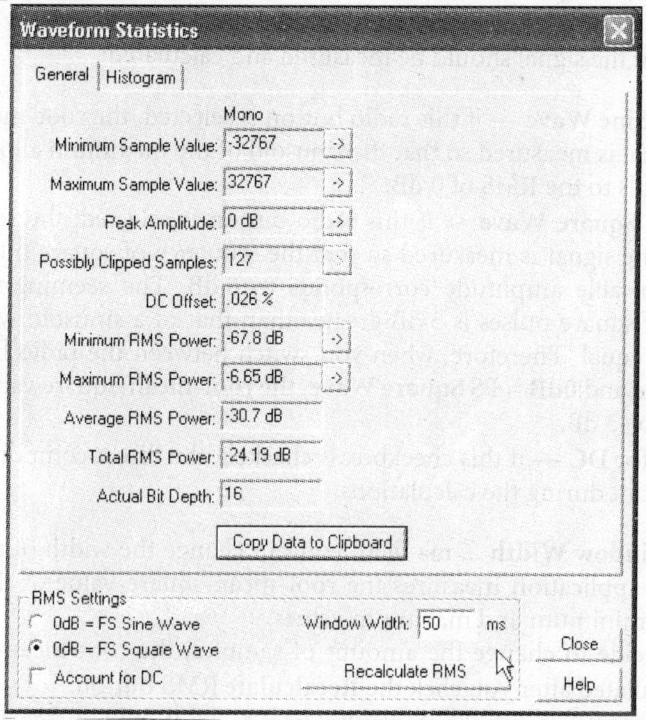

Fig. 4.2. Waveform Statistics dialog box, **General** tab

Two columns for the left and right stereo channels (or one column if the signal is mono) contain the following information:

- **Minimum/Maximum Sample Value**
- **Peak Amplitude**
- **Possibly Clipped Samples** — the number of samples that reach the analog-to-digital converter's maximum or minimum limit (i.e., the number of clipped samples)
- **DC Offset** — the average sample value (the level of the direct component offset in the selection)
- **Minimum/Maximum RMS Power** — the minimum or maximum root-mean-square value of the signal [1] (the width of the window for RMS computing is specified in the **Window Width** field at the bottom of the dialog box)
- **Average RMS Power** and **Total RMS Power** — variants of the signal's root-mean-square values
- **Actual Bit Depth** — the actual bit depth (resolution) of the audio data

The **RMS Settings** group contains options that determine how the root-mean-square value of the signal should be measured and calculated:

- **0dB = FS Sine Wave** — if this radio button is selected, the root-mean-square value of the signal is measured so that the sinusoid of the maximum allowable amplitude corresponds to the RMS of 0 dB.
- **0dB = FS Square Wave** — if this radio button is selected, the root-mean-square value of the signal is measured so that the sequence of square pulses of the maximum allowable amplitude corresponds to 0 dB. The seeming volume of a sequence of square pulses is 3 dB greater than that of a sinusoid when their amplitudes are equal. Therefore, when you switch between the radio buttons **0dB = FS Sine Wave** and **0dB = FS Square Wave**, the root-mean-square value of the signal is adjusted by 3 dB.
- **Account for DC** — if this checkbox is checked, the direct component will be taken into account during the calculations.

In the **Window Width ... ms** field, you can change the width of the time window, in which the application measures the root-mean-square value of the signal when it looks for the minimum and maximum values.

If you decide to change the amount of samples, the root-mean-square deviation will be recalculated after you click the **Recalculate RMS** button.

There are buttons with the -> symbol next to most of the fields. If you click one of these buttons, a marker in the waveform will be put at the sample corresponding to that parameter.

If you want to store the parameter values in a file to print them or insert the data into a Microsoft document, click the **Copy Data to Clipboard** button. The contents of the tab will be copied to the clipboard. Look at the statistics of the EX03_02.WAV file.

```
     Mono
Min Sample Value:      -32767
Max Sample Value:      32767
Peak Amplitude:        0 dB
Possibly Clipped:      127
DC Offset:             .026
Minimum RMS Power:     -67.81 dB
Maximum RMS Power:     -6.66 dB
Average RMS Power:     -30.71 dB
Total RMS Power:       -24.2 dB
Actual Bit Depth:      16 Bits

Using RMS Window of 50 ms
```

Notice the following parameters:

- `Possibly Clipped` = 127 — there are 127 clipped samples. They cause an unpleasant "choking" effect, and should be processed later to restore the shape of the signal in the clipped portions.
- `DC Offset` = .026 % — there is a small direct component in the waveform. During montage, this can cause clicks at the splitting points and junctions of fragments. The direct component also should be removed.

By selecting each of the five takes in turn and analyzing the selections, you can compare their main parameters (Table 4.1).

Table 4.1. Main statistical parameters of the takes

Parameter	Take No. 1	Take No. 2	Take No. 3	Take No. 4	Take No. 5
Possibly Clipped	45	82	0	0	0
Minimum RMS Power	–66.61	–56.91	–66.15	–66.48	–65.66
Maximum RMS Power	–7.58	–6.66	–11.24	–11.01	–9.93
Total RMS Power	–22.84	–20.35	–24.45	–24.56	–22.63

This comparison of the corresponding values of the parameters reveals that, judging by the number of possibly clipped samples, takes Nos. 3, 4, and 5 are the best. No. 4 seems to be the least noisy (an indirect indication of this is that its Minimum RMS Power value is the least). The "quietest" take is No. 4 (Total RMS Power parameter), and the "loudest" is No. 2. However, the latter is the most clipped take (see the `Possibly Clipped` parameter).

The value of the `Total RMS Power` parameter is small for all takes (from –24 dB to –20 dB). The voice will be very quiet compared with, say, music taken from a CD and mixed with the speech. This is why a dynamic range compression might be necessary during mixing.

4.2.2. Analyzing Sample Value Distribution on the Histogram Tab

The **Histogram** tab containing a *histogram* of the sample values in the waveform selection is shown in Fig. 4.3.

A histogram is a widely used (especially in probability analysis) form of representation of information about a random process.

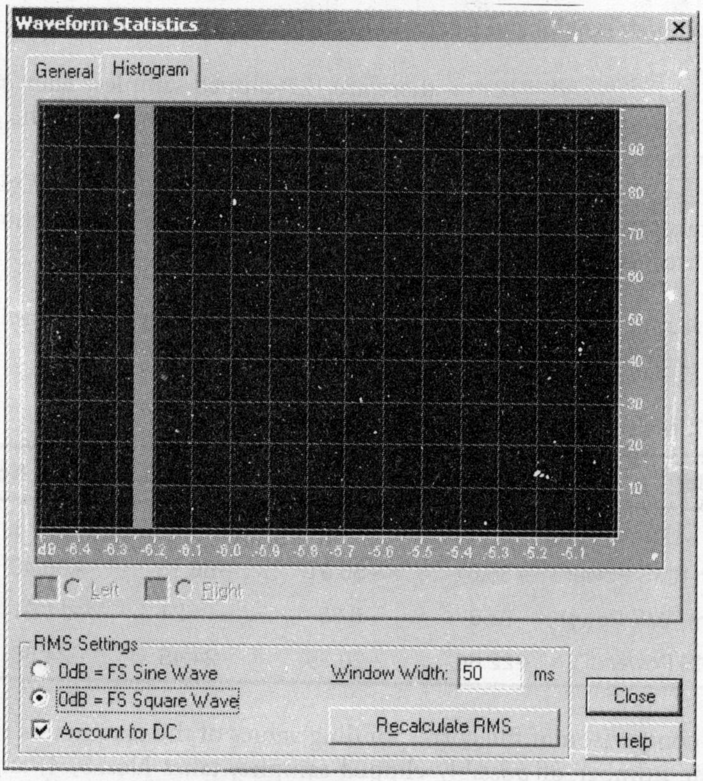

Fig. 4.3. Waveform Statistics dialog box, **Histogram** tab

In our case, a histogram displays how the number of samples whose root-mean-square values fall within a specified interval depends on a sample value measured in decibels. Too vague? Consider an example. Fig. 4.3 shows a histogram of a mono waveform containing a sinusoid signal generated with the **Generate > Tones** command. In this example, it is known that the generated signal amplitude was set to –3.2 dB. The histogram perfectly reflects this: All the samples are within the –3.25 dB to –3.20 dB range. There are no samples with other values in the analyzed signal. If you wish to change the amplitude of this signal (to boost the signal), you may set a gain of up to 3.2 dB without fear. No distortions will appear.

Signals whose properties aren't known in advance could be analyzed in the same fashion. The results of such an analysis would be useful when you make decisions concerning any amplitude conversions, such as boosting the signal or compressing its dynamic range. Consider another example. Fig. 4.4 shows the waveform of an actual vocal signal recorded in the EX03_02.WAV file (take No. 5). For your convenience, we copied this take to a separate file, EX04_01.WAV.

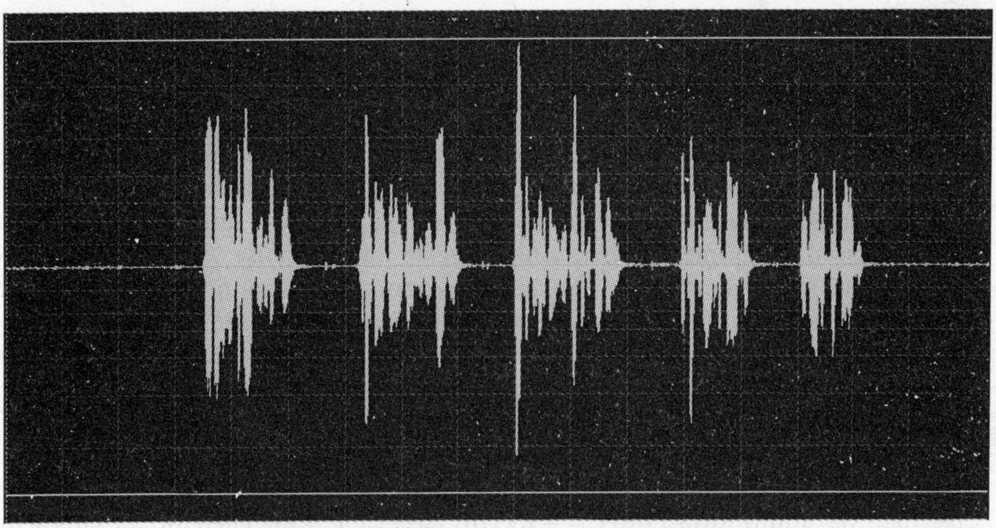

Fig. 4.4. Waveform of an actual speech signal

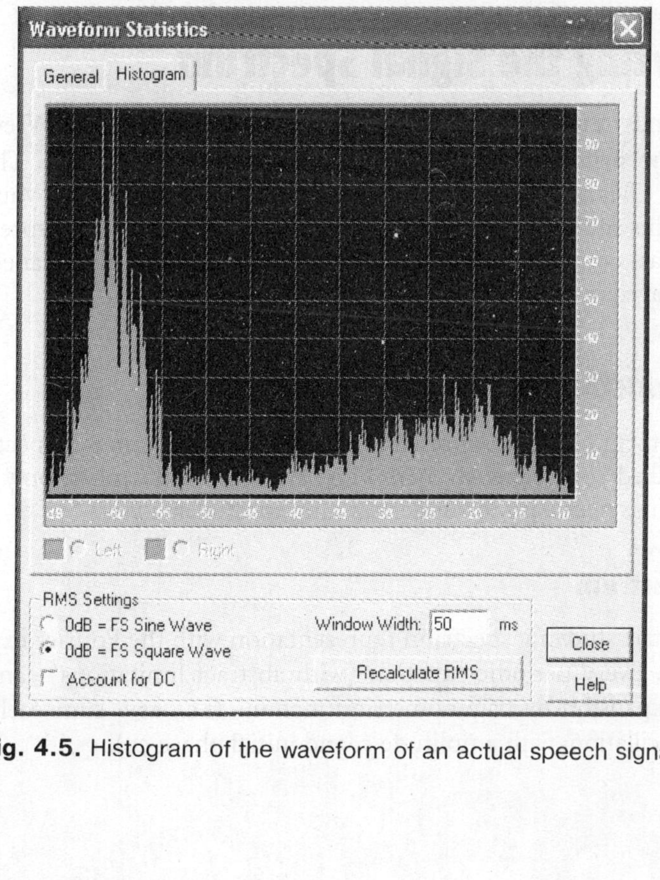

Fig. 4.5. Histogram of the waveform of an actual speech signal

Let's consider the histogram of this signal and decide how to process it best. It would be good to increase the average signal power as much as possible (thus increasing the apparent volume) and decrease the noise level. At the same time, it is desirable not to distort the signal.

First, it strikes the eye that the histogram isn't monotonous as the signal level decreases (we mean large values of the histogram components between –55 dB and –67 dB). It looks like the waveform was recorded either under unfavorable noise conditions or with equipment that has a high level of internal noise. Actually, this recording was made with good equipment, but in a room without sound insulation. We can conclude that the samples with values less than –55 dB are noise. Therefore, one stage of dynamic processing should involve noise reduction, and the initial threshold value could be about –55 dB. This should be adjusted during processing by estimating results aurally.

Second, the analysis of the histogram reveals that there are few samples with levels less than –10 dB, and there are almost no samples with levels less than –9 dB. Remember that Maximum RMS Power = –9.93 dB (see Table 4.1). Therefore, a satisfactory result can be obtained by limiting the signal to –9 dB and then amplifying it by 9 dB.

4.3. Analyzing the Signal Spectrum

The commands **View** > **Multitrack View**, **View** > **Waveform View**, and **View** > **Spectral View** switch between audio information display modes. The first mode is discussed in *Chapter 10*. The second mode is already familiar to you, as we've been working in this mode so far. In these two modes, the sound is represented as waveforms. The last command turns on a mode, in which the instantaneous signal spectrum is displayed in various brightness and colors.

4.3.1. Introduction to Spectral Analysis

The spectral form of signal representation and the instantaneous spectrum in particular are described comprehensively in [12]. Here, we will explain only the main terms and other things necessary for understanding spectral analysis.

Classic Spectrum

It is best to start studying spectrum representation with the Fourier expansion of a periodic signal. Every periodic function (with abstract limitations) can be represented as a series expansion by trigonometric functions (i.e., as a sum each item of which is a cosine oscillation, with amplitude c_k and initial phase φ_k).

The set of c_k coefficients is called the signal's *amplitude spectrum*, and the set of φ_k coefficients is called a *phase spectrum*.

The frequencies of all sinusoidal oscillations that make up the periodic function $s(t)$ are multiples of the main frequency $F = 1/T$. Individual components are called *harmonics*. The oscillation with frequency F is called the first harmonic ($k = 1$), the oscillation with frequency $2F$ is called the second harmonic ($k = 2$), and so on.

The Fourier series gives an expansion of a periodic function by trigonometric functions. This expansion also can be applied to a non-periodic function, considered the limiting case of the periodic function with the period increasing infinitely. If $T \to \infty$, then $F \to df$, and $2\pi k/T \to \omega$. (The ω parameter is the continually changing circular current frequency.) Then, the Fourier series becomes the Fourier integral. A non-periodic function can be represented only as the sum of an infinitely large number of oscillations, infinitely close to each other in frequency and with infinitely small amplitudes. The Fourier integral represents the non-periodic function as a sum of sinusoids and cosinusoids with a continuous sequence of frequencies. It is sometimes said that a non-periodic signal contains oscillations with all frequencies. It is pointless to talk about the amplitudes of individual spectral components, because these are infinitely small values.

Current Spectrum

The classic definition of the spectrum is based on the Fourier transform, when integration over time is within infinite limits, and the spectrum only depends on frequency. However, an infinite duration of any process is an abstraction that has nothing in common with reality.

If the function being analyzed is a reflection of a real-life physical process, the information about the spectrum is obtained only as the result of observations. Therefore, while analyzing the spectrum, we can perform calculations only from the starting moment of the observations until the current time t, rather than a moment in the infinite future.

The *current spectrum* is defined as the result of the Fourier transform, but with a variable upper limit of integration, for which the current time is taken. Therefore, the current spectrum is not only a function of frequency, but of time as well.

At the beginning of this section, we used the notion of a periodic function. The periodic function is just a useful mathematical abstraction; every natural process has its beginning and end.

An actual cyclic process is usually called "periodic" if it lasts long enough: The duration is measured in terms of the number of "periods," which must be much greater than one. The periodic nature of the process only appears over time, when its typical features become distinct. The current spectrum reflects the development of this process.

Thus, a periodic process is the limit that every actual repeated process can reach in time. Similarly, the spectrum (in its classic definition) of such a process is the limit that the current spectrum reaches as integration time extends to infinity. For example, when integrating over an infinite range, the spectrum of a sinusoid is the only line at the frequency equal to the frequency of the sinusoid.

How can we measure in practice the current spectrum of, say, a sinusoid? We could switch on the spectrum analyzer, then switch it off after a while. It turns out that we don't measure the spectrum of an infinite sinusoidal oscillation, but the spectrum of its "long" segment. Therefore, the spectrum of a rectangular pulse with sinusoidal filling is actually measured. This explains why, even for a sine oscillation, the spectral line widens as integration time is decreased, the sidelobes of the spectral function appear, and the zeroes of the spectral function move further apart. The spectrum of a rectangular pulse demonstrates this behavior as its length decreases [12].

Thus, the current spectrum shows the signal properties as they are actually generated and processed to a greater extent than a spectrum obtained over infinite time.

Instantaneous Spectrum

The instantaneous spectrum is simply a bridge between two methods of the process description: the frequency method and the time method. The spectrum calculated over infinite time and the current spectrum are too-coarse tools when the analyzed process is not stationary. To bring the frequency and time representations of the signal nearer to each other, the notion of an *instantaneous spectrum* was introduced. The instantaneous spectrum is the spectrum of a short segment of the process immediately preceding the current moment. This definition uses a sliding integration: The integration interval has a constant length, but it moves along the time axis. This interval is invariant relative to the current time. This definition of the spectrum is far removed from the one proposed by great mathematicians long ago. Nevertheless, the instantaneous spectrum is a soundman's or soundwoman's most effective tool for analyzing the properties of the sound that is being recorded or that was recorded earlier. Music created with a synthesizer is distinguished by the most noticeable instability of its timbre. Perhaps this is why the tools for analysis of the current and instantaneous spectrum have been long used in sound editors.

Weighted Spectrum

You are now acquainted with three approaches to spectrum calculation. However, there's more to mention. Here, we will carry on discussing spectral transformations and the influence of time on spectral analysis.

How can a single point on the spectrum curve be calculated? Formulas give a comprehensive answer to this question. However, we don't really want to use them, so we'll try to explain in plain English.

First, a frequency f_0 is selected. An actual or virtual oscillator forms a sinusoid with this frequency and with a certain amplitude. The signal being analyzed is normalized in amplitude. Starting at time t_0, the operations listed below are performed on this sinusoid, and the signal being analyzed, at the times $t_0, t_1, t_2, t_3, \ldots, t_i, \ldots, t_{N-1}$, in steps of Δt (the smaller Δt, the better):

1. A sample of the sinusoid is taken.
2. A sample of the signal being analyzed is taken.
3. These samples are multiplied.
4. The results of multiplication are added to the accrued total.

The process of spectrum measurement at frequency f_0 is terminated at a certain moment. The accrued total is divided by the number of the samples. The calculated value is memorized and possibly plotted as a point on the curve. Then, the accrued total is reset to zero, and the frequency is changed by Δf (i.e., a new frequency value f_1 is selected). This procedure is repeated until the frequency series $f_0, f_1, f_2, \ldots, f_{N-1}$ covers the entire specified range.

This procedure of calculating the spectral coefficient is nothing more than calculating the cross-correlation function of the signal being analyzed and the sinusoid with the specified frequency. In other words, while the spectral component is calculated, the degree of similarity between the signal being analyzed and the standard (basic) signal (a sinusoid, in this case) is discovered. We find out the proportion of the signal being analyzed that "contains" the sinusoid.

If the signal you are analyzing has already been recorded, and if you have a digital spectrum analyzer that can store the intermediate results of calculations for as long as necessary, it will be feasible to measure the current spectrum and the instantaneous spectrum using this procedure.

You might be wondering: Does the described mathematical algorithm correspond to the work of actual spectrum analyzers, and to analysis performed by the human ear and brain? Not quite.

The main problem is that both the instrument that analyzes the spectrum and human beings have finite memories, from which bygone events and the details of any process gradually disappear. This means that earlier samples of the signal being analyzed contribute less to the accrued sum of the products of the samples, which determines the value of the spectral coefficient.

The actual properties of the memory of the spectrum analyzers are taken into account by using *weight functions.* A weight function describes the contribution of the previous samples of the signal being analyzed to the calculated spectrum. The form of a *spectral window* illustrates the weight function.

The spectral analysis we spoke about earlier corresponds to the rectangular spectral window: The weight function is equal to one within the spectral window and to zero beyond it. When the current spectrum is analyzed, the beginning of the spectral window coincides with the beginning of the time interval, and its end coincides with the current moment. The current time moves forward, and the right side of the window moves, so the window width corresponds to the moment the analysis is terminated. If the instantaneous spectrum is calculated, the spectral window slides along the time axis without changing width.

However, the exponential weight function reflects the essence of the actual spectral analysis to a greater degree.

Rectangular and exponential spectral windows are most often used during spectrum calculation. The former corresponds to an ideal analyzer with an infinitely large memory; the latter successfully reflects the properties of the human brain and actual spectrum analyzers based on resonant filters. Other weight functions are also used, although less widely. It is difficult to give any particular recommendations about which function you should choose. Our only suggestion is that you stick to one weight function: Only then can you be sure that the analysis results differ because of the different signal properties, rather than due to different calculation methods. It is also reasonable to choose the same weight function when you work with the same signal and perform several tasks that use spectral transformations.

Fast Fourier Transform

Up to now, when discussing spectral representations, we have assumed that the signal is analog (i.e., is described by a continuous function). However, the computer can process only digital signals that are discrete in time and quantized by level. This is why the analog signal undergoes analog-to-digital conversion. Then, all necessary operations, particularly spectral analysis, are done on the digital signal, and a *discrete Fourier transform* (DFT) is done, rather than a common spectral transformation. The continuous time and frequency are replaced with corresponding discrete values, and addition is used instead of integration.

To calculate the discrete Fourier transform of a series of N elements, it is necessary to perform N^2 operations on complex numbers. If there are a few thousand processed arrays of digital samples of audio oscillations, it is difficult to use discrete spectral analysis algorithms (especially in real time). A way around this problem is the *Fast Fourier Transform* (FFT) algorithm, which significantly decreases the number of operations, because the input array processing is reduced to calculating the discrete Fourier transform for arrays with fewer numbers of elements.

Roughly, the amount of calculations using the Fast Fourier Transform algorithm is directly proportional to $N \times \log_2 N$, where N is the number of the signal samples. However, if you make a straightforward calculation of the spectrum without using fast transforms, the amount of calculations will be approximately directly proportional to $N \times N$. Without the Fast Fourier Transform, the performance of even the most advanced computer would be insufficient for filtration, spectral analysis, and synthesis of signals.

4.3.2. Analyzing Instantaneous Signal Spectrum in the Spectral View Mode

The **View > Spectral View** command turns on a mode, in which the instantaneous signal spectrum is displayed in various brightness and colors. Fig. 4.6 shows the distribution of the instantaneous signal spectrum recorded in the EX03_02.WAV file.

Fig. 4.6. Sound signal displayed as an instantaneous spectrum

What does the picture shown in the **Spectral View** mean? How can you use the information obtained by watching the instantaneous spectrum?

Time is plotted on the horizontal axis, and frequency on the vertical axis. The color and brightness of the display depend on the level of the spectral component in the analyzed waveform at a certain value. The brighter the display, the higher the level. As for color, the defaults are the following: Zero corresponds to black; as the level increases, red appears, and the maximum level is indicated in white. The color layout can be changed with the options of the **Spectral** page of the **Colors** tab in the **Settings** dialog box.

When looking at a spectral diagram, you can get a sense of how the main portion of the signal power is distributed by frequency over various points of the waveform. This information is useful when mixing down several tracks. It is desirable that the spectra of the track signals don't significantly overlap by frequency. This can be achieved with filtration. During processing signals with filters, spectral diagrams allow you to see the spectrum of the signal obtained as a result of processing and compare it with the spectrum of the original signal. Thus you can ascertain whether the processing is being done correctly.

It is extremely important that Adobe Audition's **Spectral View** allows you both watch the signal spectrum and edit the waveform. If you don't like a fragment, you can select it and work with it (or delete it completely).

Let's look at an example. Fig. 4.7 shows the instantaneous spectrum of a small waveform fragment from the EX03_02.WAV file. To make it easier to view all details, we selected this fragment and copied it to the EX04_02.WAV file.

This is the instantaneous spectrum of the signal that corresponds to the narrator's reading. The areas with a relatively wide spectrum correspond to words; those with a narrow spectrum are rests between them. You can see that between the phrases (where the mouse pointer is located), the instantaneous spectrum is wider than in the nearest neighborhood. An unnatural, suspicious peak is viewed there. A wide spectrum always corresponds to a quick drop of the signal or a short pulse. Most likely, there is a click there. Generally speaking, we could select the fragment that contains the peak in the middle, adjust the selection to zero crossings, and hit the <Delete> key. The click would be removed. When you have some experience, you'll do so in similar cases. However, for now we suggest you to look at the peak. For this purpose, select the **View** command in the **Waveform View** menu. You'll see a well-known image of a sound wave (Fig. 4.8). The waveform fragment we viewed in Fig. 4.7 is displayed, and the abnormal interval is selected.

Here is what we're looking for. It is a small, hardly noticeable sharp peak that corresponds to the 1.0 mark on the ruler. It is so small that it was difficult to find it even though we knew what we looked for and where. Imagine if you have to search for it by looking at the waveform! Most likely, you won't manage even if you do it slowly and thoroughly.

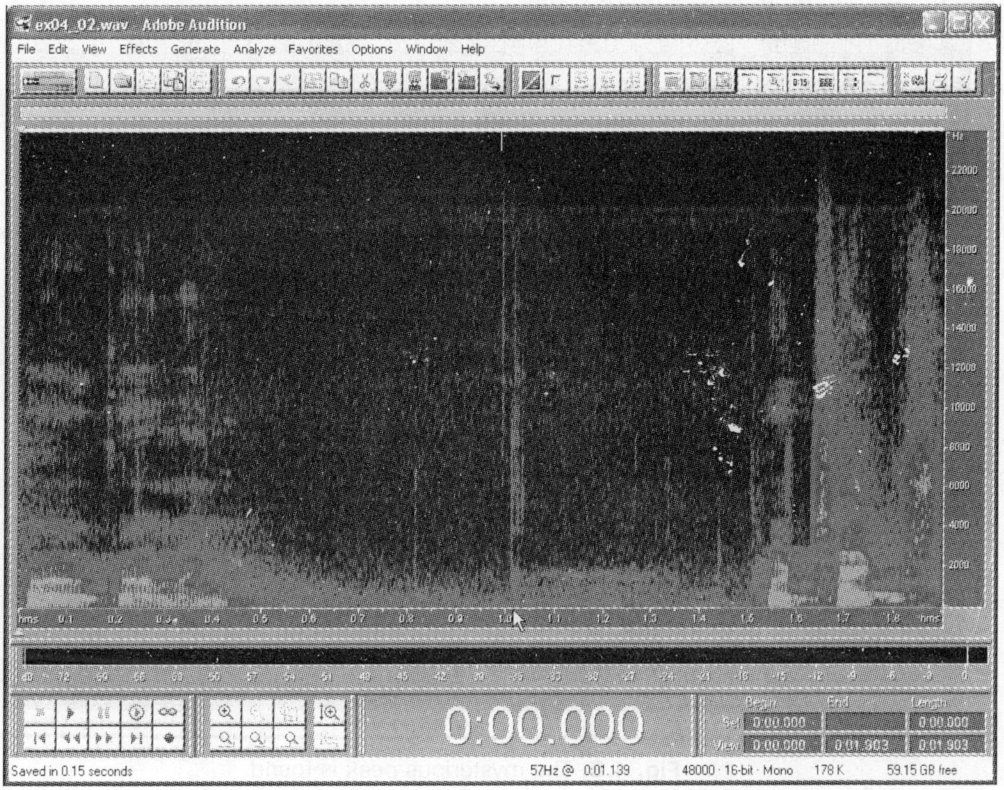

Fig. 4.7. Instantaneous spectrum containing an anomaly

Would anything bad happen if we didn't notice this anomaly? To answer this question, listen to the waveform fragment that includes this object. You'll hear a noticeable unpleasant "champing" sound: This is the sound of the narrator's lips moving apart after sticking to each other between words.

By analyzing the spectral representation, you can reveal any abnormally quick drops of the signal. Some of them have external causes, such as clicks, crackles, speech defects, etc. Sometimes, the drops appear during processing as a result of incorrect montage of a recording. For example, a user performs montage of fragments of two different signals, and at least one of them has a direct component or a very-low-frequency component. Or, a soundman or soundwoman splits a waveform into fragments but doesn't make sure that the split points coincide with zero crossings.

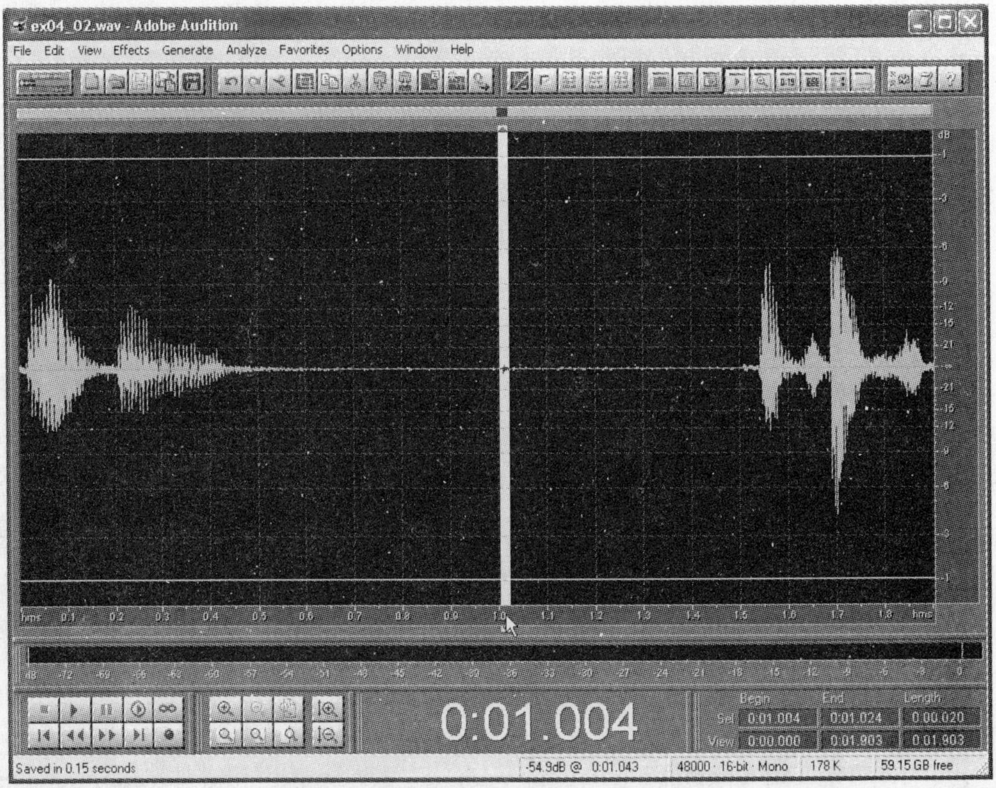

Fig. 4.8. The mysterious peak is found

4.3.3. Performing a Spectral Analysis with the Frequency Analysis Dialog Box

It would be strange if an editor such as Adobe Audition didn't allow the user to perform classical spectral analysis. There *is* such a tool in Adobe Audition, and it is accessed via the **Analyze** menu.

Select the **Analyze > Show Frequency Analysis** command to open the **Frequency Analysis** dialog box of the spectrum analyzer.

When you open the **Frequency Analysis** dialog box, the application performs a preliminary computation of a short waveform fragment beginning at the position of the marker. If a fragment of the waveform (or the entire waveform) is selected, the signal sample located at the middle of the selection is analyzed. This corresponds to a measurement of one value of the instantaneous spectrum.

Fig. 4.9. Spectrum analyzer dialog box

If you analyze the spectrum during the waveform playback, the picture will become "alive." The **Frequency Analysis** dialog box will display the sequence of the instantaneous spectrum values. A similar result can be obtained without starting playback. In the application main window, with the **Frequency Analysis** dialog box opened, grab one of the yellow triangles located above and below the working area and bound to the marker (with a yellow vertical dotted line) and move it left or right.

To perform spectral analysis of the waveform selection (or the entire waveform), click the **Scan** button. After a while, the spectrum computation will complete, and the picture will change. The result will correspond roughly to the classic spectrum, because the measurement is done over a large (though finite) interval.

The spectrum computation is done separately for the right and left channels. The spectrum curves of different channels are displayed in different colors.

If you find the dialog box with the spectrum diagram too small, you can resize it as always, i.e., with the mouse.

Now look at the diagram more closely. The frequency in hertz is plotted on the horizontal axis, and the levels of the signal components at certain frequencies are plotted on the vertical axis.

When the **Linear View** checkbox is checked, the horizontal axis is graduated linearly. In the linear view, it is more convenient to watch the spectrum in a whole, including its high-frequency portion. If you uncheck this checkbox, the horizontal axis will be graduated in the logarithmic scale. Remember that the logarithmic scale allows you to view the low-frequency portion of the spectrum in details. Compare Fig. 4.10, in which the frequency axis is graduated in the logarithmic scale, with Fig. 4.9, in which the spectrum of the same signal is shown in the linear view.

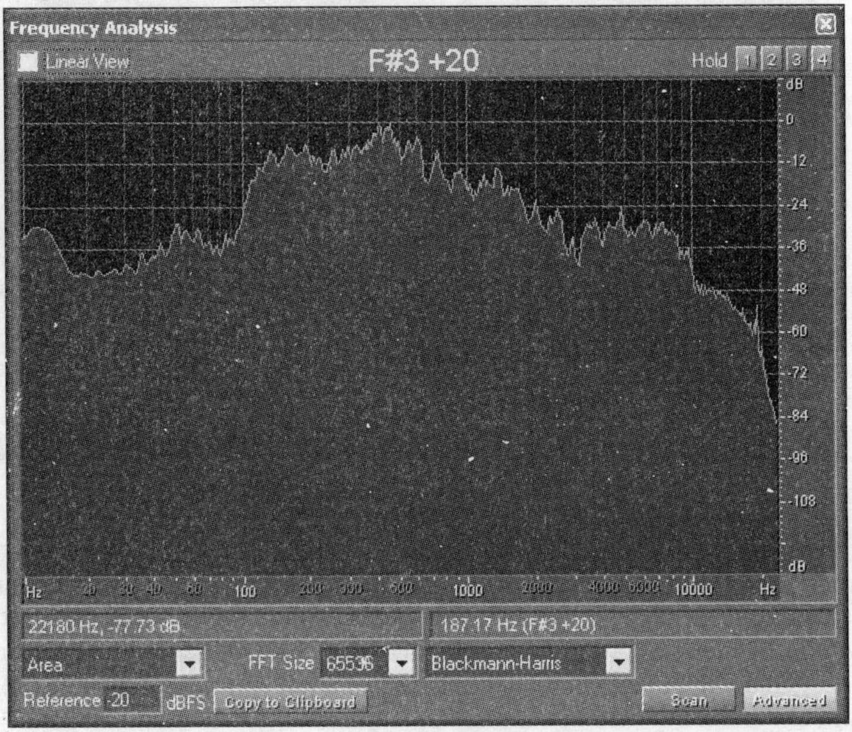

Fig. 4.10. Signal spectrum in the logarithmic scale on the frequency axis

Below the frequency axis and to the right, there is a field that displays the values of the spectral function for the left and right channels at the frequency, to which the mouse pointer is pointing (the frequency is also displayed in this field). This is true provided that the mouse pointer is within the coordinate field. When the mouse pointer moves, the parameter values change. If the mouse pointer is outside the coordinate field, the values of the three parameters don't change. They correspond to the frequency, at which the mouse pointer crossed the boundary of the coordinate field.

Notice that the numbers displayed in the **Cursor** field aren't the coordinates of the mouse pointer in the strict sense. In this field, you see the coordinate of the mouse pointer on the frequency axis and the corresponding spectrum value. This makes it simpler to measure the spectrum values. You don't have to aim at a particular point on the coordinate field. It would be enough for the necessary frequency value to appear in the **Cursor** field for the application automatically to display the spectrum value.

The field located to the right of the field we just described displays the frequencies of the spectral components of the signals from the left and right channels such that the maximum power is concentrated around these frequencies (these are the frequencies of the peaks on the diagram). This field also displays the notation of the pitch corresponding to the maximum of the spectral function (for the left and right channels separately). Standard notation is used (C, D, E, F, G, A, and B and accidentals). In Fig. 4.10, it is **F#**. The numbers in parentheses mean the following:

- Octave number (0 is the subcontra octave, 1 is the contra octave, 2 is the great octave, 3 is the small octave, etc.); in Fig. 4.10, it is **3**.
- Deviation from the precise pitch value of the desired tone in cents (a *cent* is a hundredth of a semitone) and the sign of the deviation; in Fig. 4.10, it is **+20**.

In Fig. 4.10, the measured frequency of the spectral function maximum is 187.17 Hz, which is slightly greater than the frequency of the note F#3 (at A4 = 440 Hz, this is 184.997 Hz). Therefore, the application correctly recognized the pitch (**F#3 +20**) that was 20 cents greater than the pitch of F#3.

The maximum frequencies of the spectral function can be different in the left and right channels. The pitch displayed at the top of the dialog box corresponds to the left channel signal.

The **Hold** group in the upper right corner of the dialog box consists of four colored buttons. If none of them is pressed, the spectral function envelopes of the signals from the left and right channels are displayed in different colors. If at least one button is pressed, the spectral function envelopes of the signals from the left and right channels are displayed in different hues of the same color. There are four colors: green, red, blue, and yellow. If several buttons are pressed, the rightmost gets the highest priority.

There is a drop-down list in the lower left corner of the dialog box that has five options for the style of the spectral function display.

- **Lines** — only the spectral function envelope is displayed.
- **Area (Left on top)** — both the spectral function envelope and its filling are displayed: The part of the coordinate plane lying under the envelope is filled with a color; the spectrum of the left channel signal is displayed on top of the right channel signal spectrum.

- **Area (Right on top)** — both the spectral function envelope and its filling are displayed: The spectrum of the right channel signal is displayed on top of the left channel signal spectrum.
- **Bars (Left on top)** — the filling of the spectral function is displayed as vertical bars. The spectrum of the left channel signal is displayed on top of the right channel signal spectrum.
- **Bars (Right on top)** — the filling of the spectral function is displayed as vertical bars. The spectrum of the right channel signal is displayed on top of the left channel signal spectrum.

If a mono signal is analyzed, you can select only out of three variants, as there are no layers.

By clicking the **Advanced** button, you can increase the number of the options available to you in the dialog box. The following advanced controls will appear:

- The **Reference ... dBFS** field
- The **FFT Size** drop-down list
- A drop-down list for choosing the weight function type
- The **Copy to Clipboard** button that makes it possible to copy frequency values and their corresponding spectral function values to the clipboard as text

You might need to move the diagram vertically to see the details of the spectral function in a particular interval. In the **Reference ... dBFS** field, you can specify the vertical offset of the spectrum diagram relative to zero. Don't forget to set this parameter to zero before you begin to measure the absolute values of the spectral function at particular frequencies. Otherwise, your measurements will include a constant error whose absolute value will be equal to the offset you entered.

The **FFT Size** drop-down list provides you with a few standard values of the sample size for FFT (the greater the value, the more precise the analysis, but the more time it takes). Another drop-down list, to the right of this, displays options for this transform, each of which has advantages and disadvantages.

The dialog box of the spectrum analyzer is modeless, i.e., is independent of the main window of the application. In other words, the **Frequency Analysis** dialog box can remain open while you're working in the main window (selecting a waveform fragment, moving the marker, generating sound oscillations, etc.). All changes to the waveform are immediately reflected by its spectrum. This is done intentionally, for the user's convenience. You can work with a waveform and watch the result of the spectrum analysis at once. In addition, if the FFT is small (e.g., 4,096 or less for an 800-MHz processor), it is possible to play sound and simultaneously watch the dynamics of its spectrum.

It should be mentioned that the **Frequency Analysis** dialog box is floating. You can dock it to the border of the main window if you wish.

Note that the frequency limit on the horizontal axis in the **Frequency Analysis** dialog box is set automatically: It depends on the sample rate of the waveform being analyzed.

If you look at the display closely, you'll notice that the maximum displayed frequency changes when you switch between the linear and algorithmic views.

Once you have some experience in working with the analyzer, and a professional intuition, you'll be able to look at the signal spectrum diagram and find, say, a small peak, in which the main power of noise in concentrated. After removing this peak from the signal spectrum with a filter, you'll make the signal-to-noise ratio much better.

Let's interpret the results of the spectral analysis of the audio signal from the file EX04_01.WAV (Figs. 4.9 and 4.10).

Remember that examination of the histogram led to the conclusion that those components of the recording with levels of less than –55 dB are noise. You can tell from Fig. 4.9 that the spectral function decreases to this level at a frequency of about 16 kHz. All spectral components above this threshold are caused by noise and can be suppressed with a filter later. In fact, even if you cut off high frequencies above 14 kHz, rather than 16 kHz, you wouldn't decrease the sound quality. As experience shows, a small (4 dB to 6 dB) increasing of the spectral function within the range from 14 kHz to 16 kHz is most likely caused by high-frequency wide-band noise, and it would be useful to get rid of it.

Now look at Fig. 4.10. You can see the low-frequency part of the spectrum. Notice the high level of low-frequency (less than 80 Hz) and very-low-frequency (less than 20 Hz) components. They aren't typical to speech. This is also noise, caused by cars passing by and ventilation appliances working in neighboring rooms. In a word, you should also use a filter to suppress signal spectrum components below 80 Hz.

Analyze the other signals contained in the files EX03_01.WAV, EX03_03.WAV, EX03_04.WAV, and EX03_05.WAV in a similar fashion.

As the analyzed signals are mono, the issue of mono compatibility control isn't urgent. However, you should know that Adobe Audition provides you with this ability. You can control a signal's mono compatibility with a built-in software stereo goniometer in the **Phase Analysis** window opened with the **Analyze** > **Show Phase Analysis** command. For details of how to use this analytical tool, see [3].

4.4. Summarizing the Results of the Analysis and Elaborating Work Plans

Well, what do we have? Several takes with the narrator's voice were recorded to accompany the video picture asynchronously. The most successful takes were selected, in which the narrator doesn't make mistakes, and the noise doesn't disturb the listeners, the DAC is rarely overloaded, and the natural reverberation level is relatively low.

Now we should do the following:

1. Cut unnecessary fragments out of the original file and process the junctions so that they are unnoticeable. If it is necessary to change the durations of rests, insert fragments with perfect silence (see *Chapter 5*).
2. Perform amplitude correction of the signal: gain, dampen, or normalize it (see *Chapter 5*).
3. Decrease the noise level (see *Chapter 5*).
4. Restore clips (see *Section 4.2.1* and *Chapter 5*).
5. Perform spectrum correction (see *Sections 4.3.2* and *4.3.3)* with frequency filters to suppress unwanted spectral components (see *Chapter 6*).
6. Perform the dynamic processing (see *Chapter 7*) to decrease the noise level and increase the average level (i.e., the volume) of the useful signal (see *Sections 4.2.1* and *4.2.2)*.
7. Process the recording with built-in effects (see *Chapter 8*) and plug-ins connected to Adobe Audition using DirectX (see *Chapter 9*).

All this should be done before the narrator's voice is inserted into your multitrack project (see *Chapter 10*) where it will be mixed with the music and then synchronized with the video (see *Chapter 11*).

It isn't unlikely that you will repeatedly return to certain stages of sound processing. This is why you should keep all files with intermediate results until you finish your project. The original and essential intermediate files must be kept "forever" (for the case your need to remix the project in another format or change its timing).

You should be aware that sound processing is a creative task. It cannot be described with an exact procedure that unambiguously prescribes the set and order of operations. Everything depends not only on the original material, but also the aesthetic criteria that guide you, your ability to appraise the results, your theoretical knowledge, and your skills in using the tools. In our case, we must take into account the limitations of the size of this book. This is why the plan we suggested should be considered as just one possible plan. In fact, each stage can have multiple branches, and the number of options for processing procedures is almost infinite; many of them will lead you to equally satisfactory results.

Getting Rid of Mistakes, Noise, and Distortions

Chapter 4 discussed the analysis of the EX03_02.WAV file that had been recorded from a microphone and stored in the EXAMPLES folder on the CD-ROM accompanying this book. As a result, we suggested plan for working with this file that included many operations available in Adobe Audition. Among other actions aimed at removing flaws from the recording, we suggested discarding bad takes, cutting out irrelevant sounds between words, and reducing noise.

In this chapter, we will look at editing operations related to changing the structure of a recorded audio track. In particular, we'll examine moving fragments from one time position to another, montage of fragments so their joins are unnoticeable to the ear, and placing waveforms one over another. In addition, we'll describe methods of converting amplitudes of audio oscillations, reducing noise levels, and clip restoration.

5.1. Deleting Unnecessary Material and Performing Montage

As you already know, when processing audio data recorded with a microphone, it is best to begin by deleting the worst takes and removing irrelevant sounds from the tests between words. Then you should take the best fragments from the remaining takes and montage them in the appropriate sequence.

To show you how to montage a recording, we'll use the EX03_02.WAV file located in the EXAMPLES folder on the disc that accompanies this book. So load it in the application first.

5.1.1. Moving the Selection Edges to Zero Crossings

The **Edit > Zero Crossings** submenu includes commands that can be used to move the beginning and end of a selected block to positions, at which the sound wave crosses the zero level. This level corresponds to the zero mark for the 16-bit format and to the value 127 for the 8-bit format. This function and the **Crossfade** function serve the same purpose: to prevent clicks at the beginning and end of an inserted fragment. The algorithm for searching for zero assumes that you can have two stereo channels whose waveforms differ. Below is a brief description of the submenu commands.

Using the **Adjust Selection Inward** command implies that the edges of the selection will be automatically moved to the nearest zero crossing inside the selection. Fig. 5.1 shows an example of an unsuccessful selection. You can see that the edges of the selection are at the points where the samples have nonzero values. If you cut this fragment and paste it to another waveform, clicks will be heard.

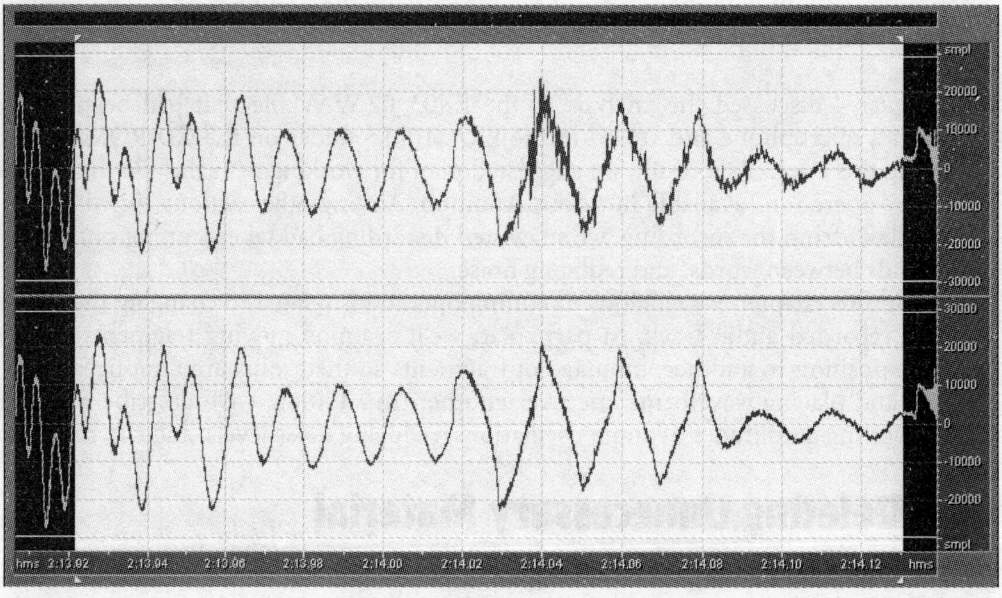

Fig. 5.1. Waveform selection

Fig. 5.2 shows the same waveform after executing the **Adjust Selection Inward** command. Compare the figures and make sure that the edges of the selected moved to the nearest zero crossings, thus approaching to each other.

Executing the **Adjust Selection Inward** command results in automatically moving the selection edges to the nearest zero crossings outside the selection.

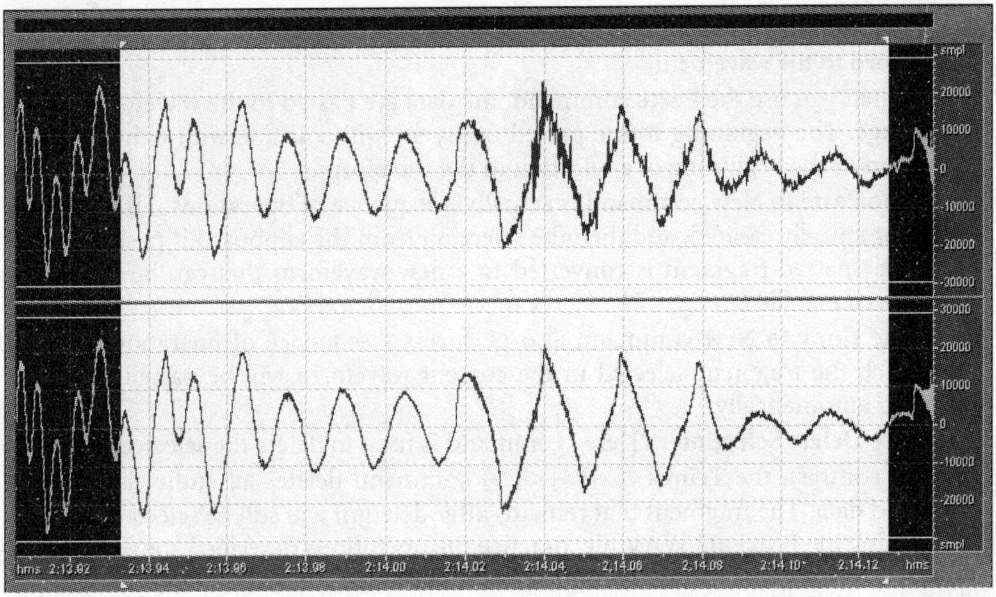

Fig. 5.2. Waveform selection with edges adjusted inward

The **Adjust Left Side to Left** command moves the left edge of the selection to the nearest zero crossings to the left.

The **Adjust Left Side to Right** command moves the left edge of the selection to the nearest zero crossings to the right.

The **Adjust Right Side to Left** command moves the right edge of the selection to the nearest zero crossings to the left.

The **Adjust Right Side to Right** command moves the right edge of the selection to the nearest zero crossings to the right.

Practice for a while by selecting fragments of the contents of the EX03_02.WAV file and moving the edges of the selections left and right.

5.1.2. Copying, Cutting, Deleting, and Pasting the Material

Commands that make it possible to copy, cut, and paste the material are available in the **Edit** menu.

To copy or cut a waveform fragment, you must first select it. The graphical and digital methods of making a selection are described in detail in *Section 2.3.*

When the commands **Copy** (<Ctrl>+<C>) and **Cut** (<Ctrl>+<X>) are executed, the data are put into the current clipboard.

The command **Paste** (<Ctrl>+<V>) and **Paste to New** paste data from the current clipboard to the waveform.

When you use the **Paste** command, the data are pasted to the waveform on the active page. The beginning of the pasted fragment will coincide with either the marker position or the beginning of a selection in the waveform.

The **Paste to New** command is actually a sequence of operations. First, a new page is automatically created, and then the selection from the clipboard is pasted to it. After that, the pasted fragment is converted to a new waveform that can be given a name and saved in a file.

The **Copy to New** command also performs a sequence of operations, as a result of which the fragment selected in the current waveform will be pasted to a new file created automatically.

The **Delete Selection** (<Del>) command is used to delete the selected audio block.

In contrast, the **Trim** (<Ctrl>+<T>) command deletes all audio data except the selected data. The fragment that remains after deletion will still be selected.

Using the EX03_02.WAV file, practice the operations described above.

5.1.3. Mixing Pasted Data with the Existing Waveform

The **Edit > Mix Paste** command deserves much attention. It is used to mix the audio data held on the clipboard with the waveform being edited. The **Mix Paste** command opens a dialog box shown in Fig. 5.3.

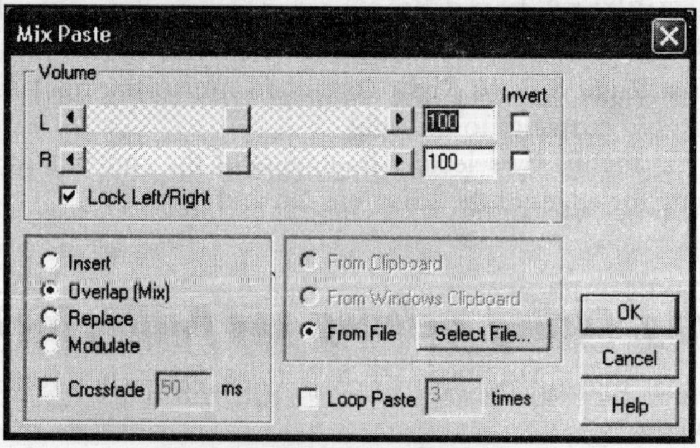

Fig. 5.3. Mix Paste dialog box

The **Volume** group contains the volume controls for the material pasted to the left (**L**) and right (**R**) channels. The volume is specified as a percentage (100% by default) with sliders or in digital fields. If you check the **Lock Left/Right** checkbox, the volume of both channels will change simultaneously. When the **Invert** checkbox is checked, the waveform is inverted before pasting. The word "invert" has many meanings; in this case, it means "multiply each sample by –1". The result will be to turn positive half-waves into negative, and negative ones into positive.

The lower left portion of the window contains radio buttons that allow you to select a paste method.

- **Insert** — the waveform being edited will be split, and its parts will be moved apart to make place for the contents of the clipboard.
- **Overlap (Mix)** — the material from the clipboard will be mixed with the waveform being edited.
- **Replace** — the material from the clipboard will replace the audio data that was in this part of the waveform before pasting.
- **Modulate** — paste with amplitude modulation. Each audio sample from the clipboard is multiplied by the corresponding sample of the waveform.

The **Crossfade** checkbox is used for switching on the crossfade mode, which is often very useful. Let's look at it more closely. When you select a block of audio data, the values of the samples at the edges of this block aren't necessarily equal to zero. This might cause unpleasant clicks when playing the material pasted from the clipboard. To eliminate these clicks, the crossfade mode is used.

If we look closely at the crossfade mode, we'll find that not only does Adobe Audition paste an audio block to a waveform, but it behaves "smartly," that is, controls the volume of the block. At the beginning of the block, its volume gradually increases from 0% to 100%, and not long before the block end, the volume gradually decreases. The time of changing the volume is specified in the field located to the right of the checkbox. It is so small (tens of milliseconds) that the listener doesn't notice. Such features are typical for not only this application, but also for professional studio equipment. Otherwise, audio recordings and TV and radio programs would contain numerous clicks caused by switching between hardware devices.

Enter the length of the time interval of changing the volume from 0% to 100% (or from 100% to 0%) into the **Crossfade** field.

The next group of radio buttons allows you to select the source of the pasted block:

- **From Clipboard N** — the internal clipboard. **N** here means the reference to the current clipboard. The application takes care that you are aware of which clipboard you're using.
- **From Windows Clipboard** — the system clipboard.
- **From File** — a file.

If you decide to paste data from a file (and select the appropriate radio button), you must select the file by clicking the **Select File** button (the file open window will open). Otherwise, pasting will be done from the clipboard, despite selecting **From File** radio button.

The **Loop Paste** ... checkbox makes it possible to paste the waveform contained in the clipboard repeatedly (the number of repetitions is specified in the field located to the right of the checkbox).

After you set all parameters, click the **OK** button or hit the <Enter> key.

You might have noticed that the **Mix Paste** command with its corresponding dialog box is a powerful tool for montage of recordings. If Adobe Audition was not a multitrack editor, this tool would be indispensable.

5.1.4. Undoing and Redoing Operations

Commands for undoing and redoing your actions are in the **Edit** menu. The first of them is **Undo**, which undoes the last operation. If you select it once more, one more editing step will be undone, and so on, until the possibility of undoing operations is exhausted. When it is impossible to undo an operation, the menu command **Undo** will be replaced with a gray item **Can't Undo**.

The **Redo** command recovers an operation that was previously undone.

The **Enable Undo** command makes it possible to turn the undo mode on and off (if the command is ticked in the menu).

To give the user the opportunity to use the **Undo** command, the results of each steps of work with the application are stored in special temporary files that can be large in size. If there is little free space on your hard disk, you can disable the undo mode, and the temporary files won't be created. In this case, you'll have to think over your every step, because you won't be able to undo wrong actions. We've already told you how you can set the maximum number of undo levels (see *Section 1.1.2*).

When you select the **Repeat Last Command** command (or hit the <F2> function key), the last command will be repeated.

You should be very careful! Adobe Audition will repeat the last command regardless of which waveform (whether current or another) you were editing. If the last command opened a dialog box with changeable options, its repetition will open this dialog box with the same settings as the last time.

You should note that not all commands can be repeated: The **Repeat Last Command** is available in the **Edit** menu only if the last command can be repeated.

5.1.5. Arranging the Structure of the Recorded File

The tools are ready, and you're familiar with the operations that allow you to montage the recording by moving, replacing, and deleting its individual fragments. It's time to move from words to deeds, that is, to arrange the structure of the EX03_02.WAV file from the EXAMPLES folder on the CD-ROM that accompanies this book.

When rearranging a waveform, bear in mind that this isn't the last stage of editing. You'll still have to perform noise reduction, filtration, and transformation of the dynamic range. It isn't unlikely that after one of these stages, you'll have to return to the montage and do it more finely and thoroughly. This is why you shouldn't try to "cure" all the "diseases" of the waveform at once. In particular, save a few of the longest fragments that contain no useful signal (recorded voice), but include only the noise typical to the room where the recording was made, or the background noise caused by electromagnetic interference induced in the signal circuits of the hardware.

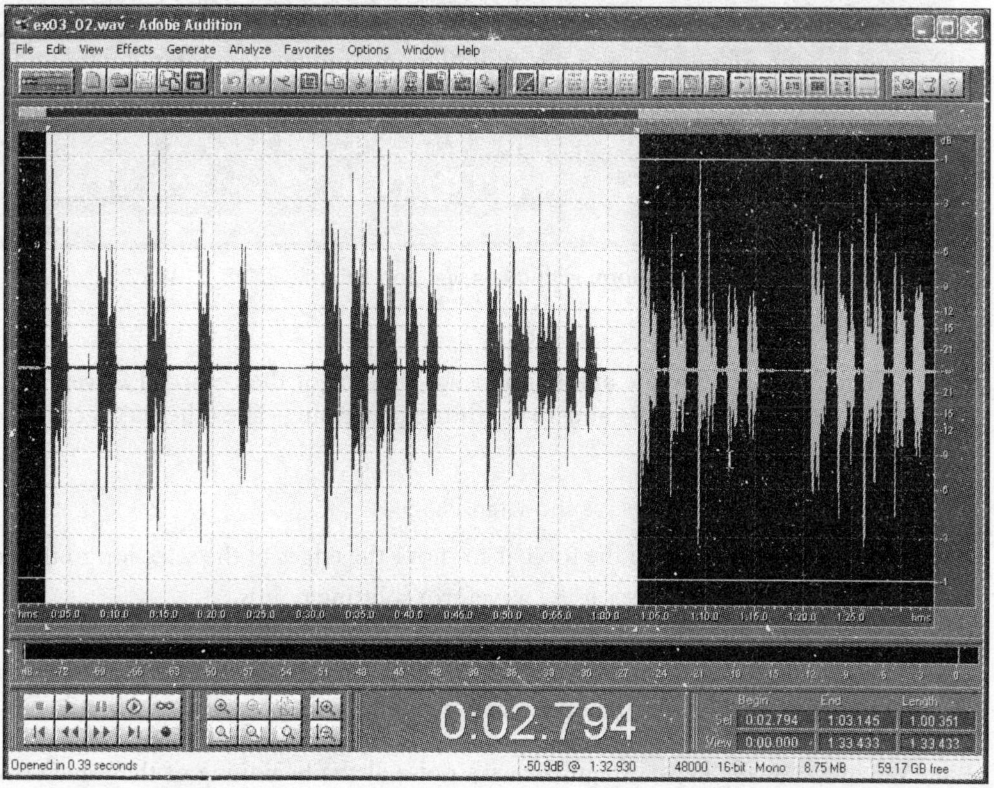

Fig. 5.4. Fragment to be deleted selected in the waveform (file EX03_02.WAV)

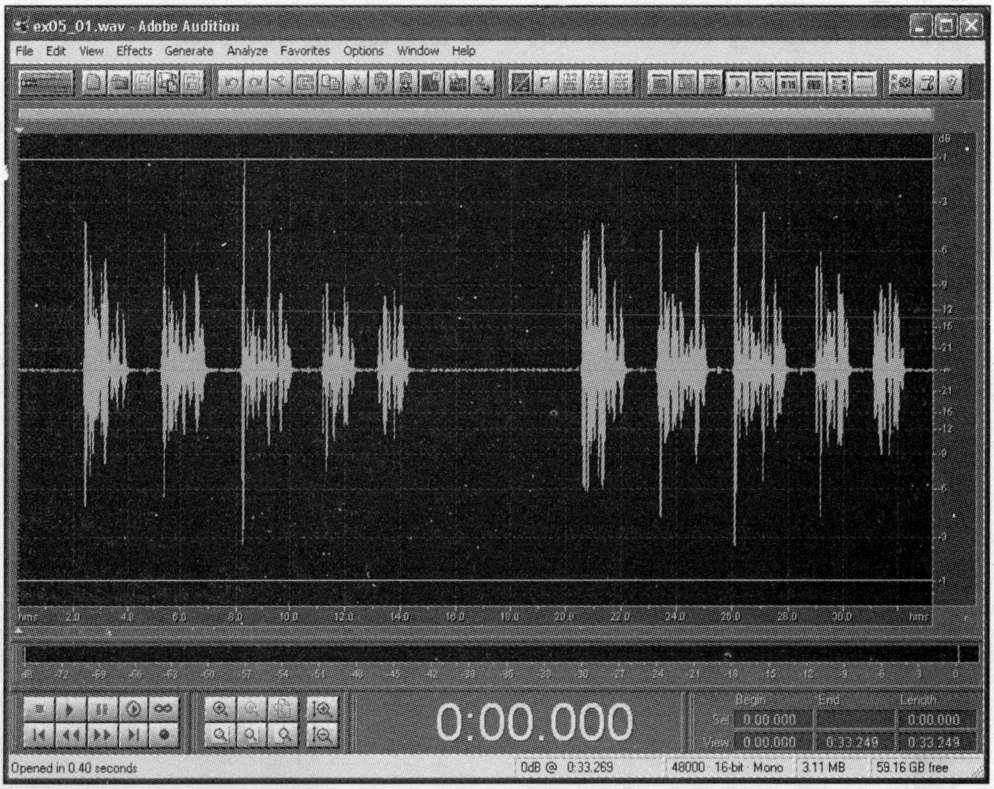

Fig. 5.5. Waveform with takes #4 and #5 (file EX05_01.WAV)

Remember that after the aural and visual analysis of the recorded waveform, we decided to leave only takes #4 and #5 for future processing. The other takes can be deleted. Proceed as follows:

1. Select the first three takes (as shown in Fig. 5.4).
2. Click the  button on the toolbar to move the edges of the selection to the zero crossings, to prevent clicks at the waveform splitting points.
3. Execute the **Edit > Cut** command or hit the <Delete> key.
4. The resulting waveform corresponds to takes #4 and #5 (Fig. 5.5). Save it in the EX05_01.WAV file with the **File > Save As** command.

We intentionally kept a fragment with noise at the beginning of the waveform as we will need it when performing noise reduction.

5.2. Processing Rests, Fragment Junctions, and Signal Amplitude

We deleted unwanted fragments from the EX03_02.WAV file that contains the narrator's voice recorded from a microphone, and saved the remaining material in the EX05_01.WAV file. This file doesn't contain fragments that are obviously bad. Nevertheless, its material still needs processing. During the current stage, we can do the following:

- Make the junctions between the fragments unnoticeable to the ear
- Edit the duration of rests between words and phrases
- Replace long rests containing noise with perfect silence
- Make the volumes of individual fragments approximately equal (especially if they originate from different takes).

You don't have to do all these operations in this order. If the result of analysis of the waveform shows that some of the operations aren't necessary, you may skip them.

5.2.1. Processing the Signal Level at Junctions

The signal level of a waveform selection (in particular, at the junctions of fragments) can be changed with the **Amplify** dialog box opened with the **Effects** > **Amplitude** > **Amplify** command. Although this dialog box is named **Amplify**, "amplification" should be treated here in a broad sense as "changing." Not only can you increase the signal amplitude, you also can decrease it. The **Amplify** dialog box has two tabs: **Constant Amplification** (Fig. 5.6) and **Fade** (Fig. 5.7).

Using the **Constant Amplification** and **Fade** tabs, you can select *constant* or *adjustable* change of the amplitude over the specified fragment.

With constant amplification, its amount is specified with the sliders **Amplification** (**L** and **R**) or digitally in the appropriate input fields. For example, if each of the fields displays 50, the amplitudes of the signals in the right and left channels will decrease by 50% over the entire selection.

With the **Lock Left/Right** checkbox, you can "bind" the controls for the right and left channels to each other. When the checkbox is checked, changing the position of one control will cause changing the position of the other.

With adjustable amplification on the **Fade** tab, you can specify how the gain must change from its initial value (**Initial Amplification**) to the final value (**Final Amplification**). For this purpose, sliders or input fields can be used. When you select the **Linear Fades** radio button, the gain changes linearly, and when you select the **Logarithmic Fades** button, it will change logarithmically.

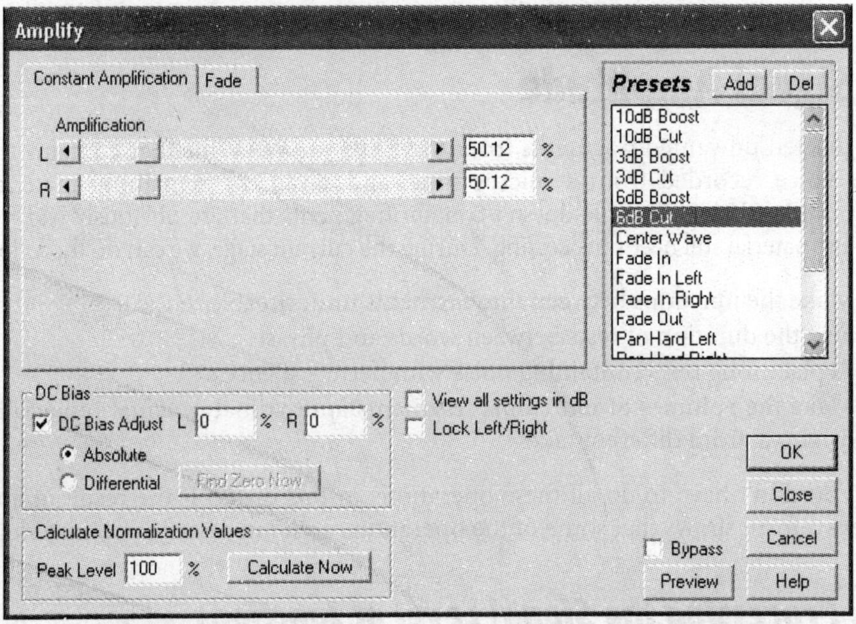

Fig. 5.6. Amplify dialog box; **Constant Amplification** tab

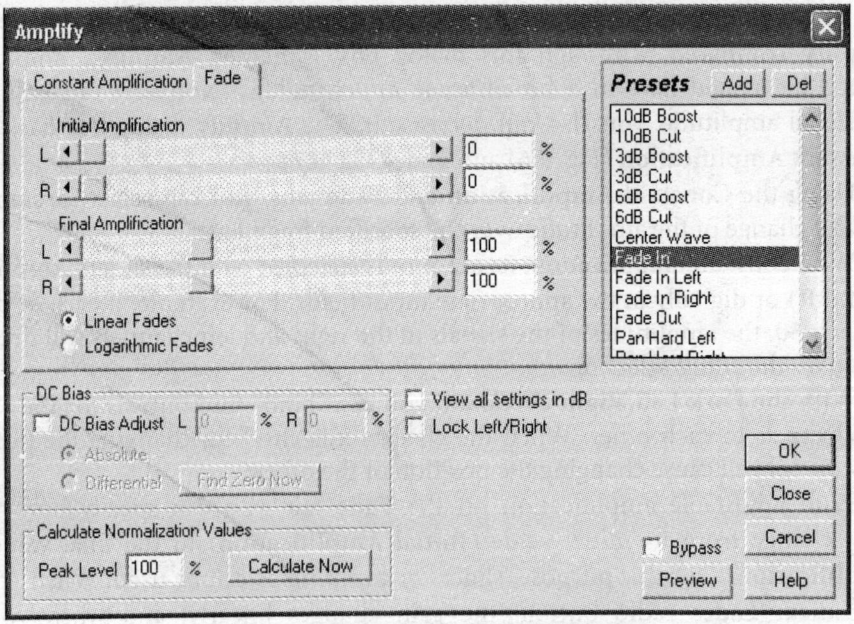

Fig. 5.7. Amplify dialog box; **Fade** tab

Depending on the state of the **View all settings in dB** checkbox, the values are specified as percentages or in decibels.

In the **DC Bias** group, you can adjust the bias of the audio signal relative to the specified level. Check the **DC Bias Adjust** checkbox and either specify the new value for the bias (select the **Absolute** radio button) or the increment as percentage (the **Differential** button). Adjusting the DC bias can be very useful. If the sound was recorded with a bias, or a bias appeared as a result of signal conversion in a sound editor (not Adobe Audition, which makes all conversions correctly), or the signal contains a large direct component or low-frequency components with large amplitudes, you should eliminate this sort of anomaly before you proceed with further processing. Centering the signal relative to the specified level will allow you the remove unwanted low-frequency components that usually cause clicks during montage of a recording.

The **Calculate Normalization Values** group contains controls for signal normalization. The **Peak Level** field displays the peak level of the signal. For example, 0 dB (or 100%) means that the audio signal must take the entire dynamic range.

By clicking the **Calculate Now** button, you tell the application to calculate the gain so that the signal will have the specified dynamic range after the **Amplify** operation is executed. Then the amplification controls will automatically take the appropriate positions.

In the **Presets** group, you can select standard presets for the controls in the **Amplify** dialog box.

Using the **Add** and **Del** buttons, you can add your own presets or delete the existing presets from the list. The **Add** button opens a dialog box in which you must enter a name for the new preset and click the **OK** button.

If you selected the mono format when creating or converting an audio file, the tabs look simpler, having fewer controls, input fields, and presets. Fig. 5.8 shows the **Constant Amplification** tab for a mono audio file, and Fig. 5.9 shows the **Fade** tab for the same file.

Out of all options of the **Amplify** window introduced in the preceding paragraphs, we'll use only one. It is designed for eliminating the direct component from the recorded signal. Remember that the original signal (EX03_02.WAV) contains a direct component. This was revealed by statistical data analysis: **DC Offset** = –.033% (see *Section 4.2.1*). Most likely, a portion of the original signal in the EX05_01.WAV file also contains a direct component. To check this, apply the **Analyze > Statistics** command to the selected waveform (EX05_01.WAV). Then look at the **General** tab of the **Waveform Statistics** dialog box. In this case, **DC Offset** = 0%. This means that there is no direct component in this signal. However, if there were a direct component in the signal being processed, it would be easy to remove it (to avoid clicks it might cause). This could be done as described below. Select the **Effects > Amplitude > Amplify** command to open the **Amplify** dialog box on the **Constant Amplification** tab (Fig. 5.6). We don't need to change the signal amplitude right now, so enter 100 into the field located to the right of the **Amplification** slider (100% corresponds to 0 dB).

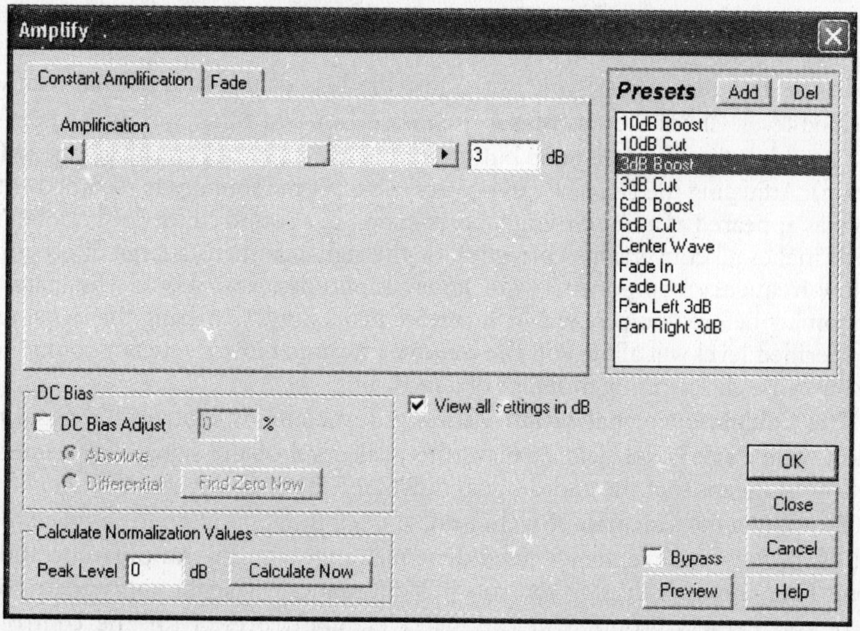

Fig. 5.8. **Constant Amplification** tab for a mono audio file

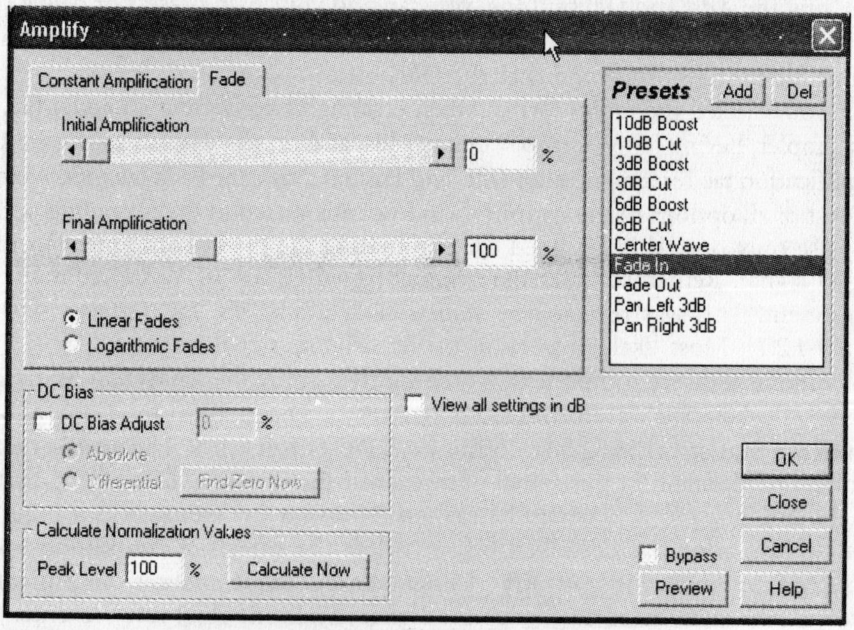

Fig. 5.9. **Fade** tab for a mono audio file

In the **DC Bias** field, check the **DC Bias Adjust** checkbox, select the **Absolute** radio button, and make sure that the field located to the right of the **DC Bias Adjust** checkbox displays zero (which is the default value). Click the **OK** button. The application will compute for a while, and then the waveform in the main window will shift up a little. If you now analyze the statistics with the **Analyze > Statistics** command, you'll see **DC Offset** = 0%. The offset is eliminated, and the direct component is removed.

5.2.2. Creating Perfect Silence in a Specified Fragment of the Waveform

If the recording contains long rests, the noise recorded along with the useful signal will be noticeable.

Adobe Audition gives you several methods for reducing noise in rests. One of them is replacing the sound in the rests with perfect silence. In practice, this means that the values of all the sound samples in a specified fragment are set to zero.

Perfect silence on a selected fragment of the waveform is created using the **Effects > Silence** command.

To better understand this function, compare Fig. 5.10 (an original signal) with Fig. 5.11 (the same signal after executing **Effects > Silence**).

The **Silence** command can be useful when the parts of the useful signal (words and phrases) are separated with long rests that contain nothing but noise (Fig. 5.10). It is indispensable when all fragments with the useful signal must remain in place and rests mustn't be deleted.

When it is allowed to move the fragments with the useful signal in time, you can simply cut the rests out of the recording or use a tool available in Adobe Audition for automating this procedure (the **Edit > Delete Silence** command [3, *Section 4.8*]).

Sometimes, it is necessary to "move apart" fragments to a certain distance by inserting rests with a specified duration between them. Of course, it makes sense to insert rests that don't contain noise. In such cases, it would be wise to use the **Generate > Silence** command that opens the **Generate Silence** dialog box with a field for entering the duration of a rest. After you click the **OK** button, the waveform will be split at the marker position, and an interval of a specified length with perfect silence will appear to the right of the splitting point. The left part of the original waveform will remain in place, and the beginning of its right part will move to the end of the newly created rest.

If rests are short and numerous, it becomes a tedious job to select each of them manually and replace noise with perfect silence. It would be wiser to use noise reduction. However, you should be aware that noise-reduction algorithms cannot achieve perfect silence, but can only decrease the noise level more or less successfully.

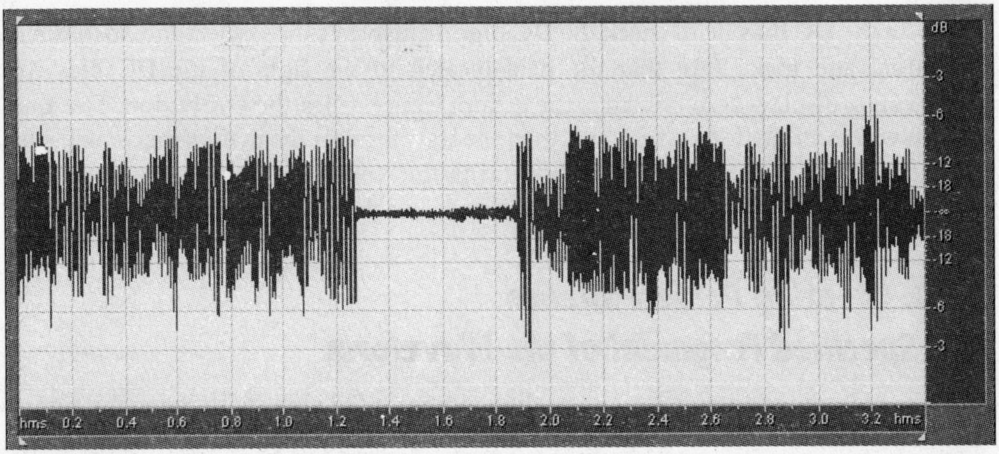

Fig. 5.10. Original signal

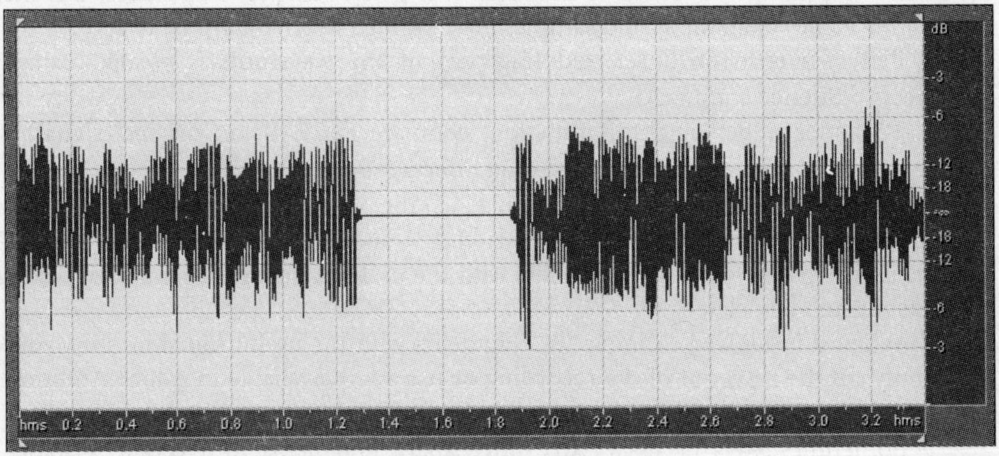

Fig. 5.11. Same signal processed with the **Silence** command

At the same time, some experts say that noise in rests should only be dampened, but should not be completely removed (for example, replaced with perfect silence). Abrupt jumps from ideally quiet fragments to fragments that contain noise along with a voice or music can be noticeable and irritate listeners.

We're not going to replace the rest between the takes in the EX05_01.WAV file with perfect silence. We're planning to apply one of the noise reduction tools available in Adobe Audition to this file. The algorithm computes the values of the spectrum components of the noise presented to it, and then subtracts them from the corresponding spectrum components of the "signal + noise" mix. If the waveform contains a fragment with perfect silence, it will be replaced with inverted noise. This means that if you decide to insert fragments with perfect silence into a waveform, you should do it *after* noise reduction rather than *before* it.

5.2.3. Waveform Normalization

Usually, normalization is applied when you don't want to use dynamic range processing but need to maximally increase the volume of the waveform and avoid overflow errors for all samples. Of course, it is possible to amplify the signal with the options of the **Amplify** dialog box, but this cannot guarantee that no overflow will take place. Normalization is equivalent to optimized amplification: The signal is amplified so that it gets maximum possible volume, but no distortions appear. Let's look at an example of this.

Select the **Effects** > **Amplitude** > **Normalize** command to open the small dialog box **Normalize** (Fig. 5.12).

Proceed with the waveform normalization proper.

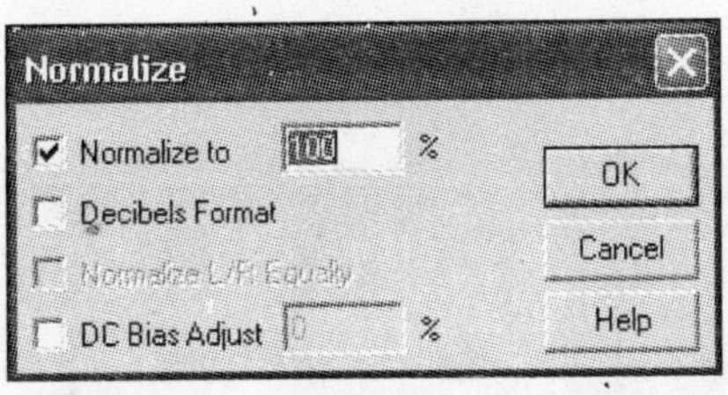

Fig. 5.12. Normalize dialog box

In the **Normalize to** input field, enter the level, to which the waveform should be normalized. The value should be specified in decibels or as percentages (depending on the state of the **Decibels Format** checkbox).

Click the **OK** button. The application will analyze the selection and detect a digital sound sample with the maximum absolute value (there can be several such samples, but it doesn't matter because the maximum values of the samples are equal).

The application automatically computes a factor such that when the maximum sample value is multiplied by this factor, the result is equal to the level you specified. Each of the samples in the waveform selection is multiplied through by this factor. As a result, the maximum sample takes the value you specified, and the value of the other samples will increase or decrease proportionally.

Fig. 5.13 shows an example of a waveform, in which the maximum sample is near the third second (this fragment is selected in the figure).

If you select the whole waveform, open the **Normalize** dialog box, enter 100 (or 0 dB) into the **Normalize to** field, and click the **OK** button. The result will be like that shown in Fig. 5.14.

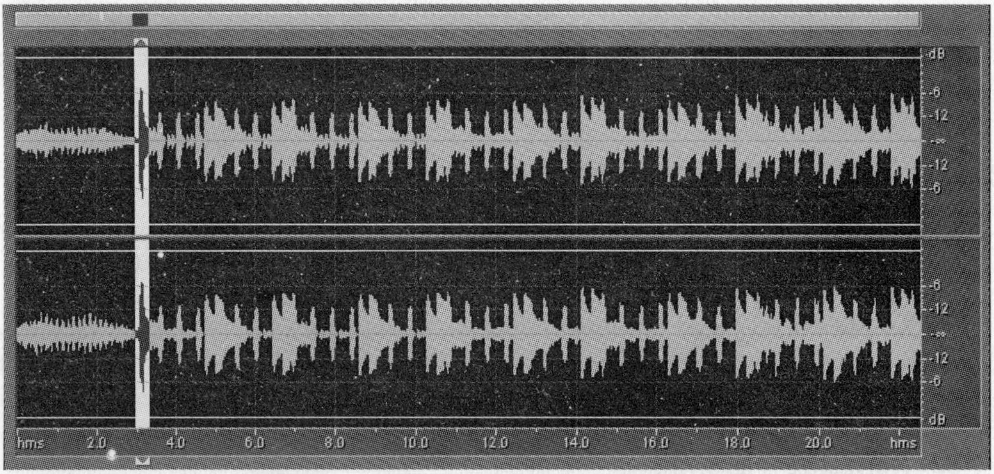

Fig. 5.13. Waveform before normalization

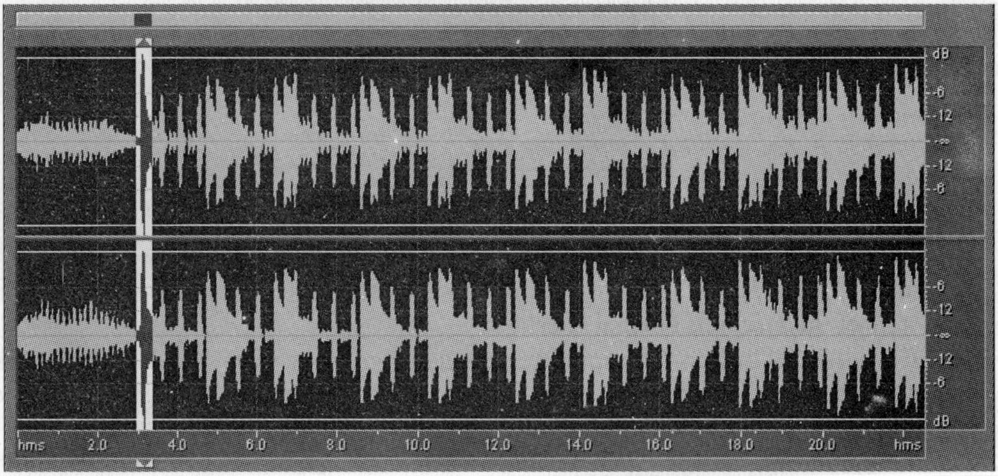

Fig. 5.14. Waveform after normalization

You can see from Fig. 5.14 that:

- The waveform diagram reaches the line that denotes the 100% level at the point of the maximum sample (in the figure, this fragment is selected).
- The values of the other samples increased.

There are two more checkboxes in the **Normalize** dialog box. If the **Normalize L/R Equally** checkbox is checked, normalization is done according to the following procedure:

1. Out of two stereo channels, the channel that contains the signal with the maximum amplitude is selected.
2. Based on this information, the signals of two channels are normalized simultaneously.

As a result, the signal of one channel will be hardly amplified to the maximum level. There's nothing bad in this; the signals in stereo channels don't need to be the same.

Sometimes, separate normalization of the stereo channels is required: For example, when the left and right channels contain completely different signals from different sound sources. In this case, it is useful to uncheck the **Normalize L/R Equally** checkbox.

The **DC Bias Adjust** checkbox controls signal centering about the zero level and the suppression of the low-frequency component.

Normalization isn't as harmless as it might seem. You shouldn't use it repeatedly on the same signal unless you have to. Any operation using numbers represented with a finite number of bits inevitably has errors. Such calculation errors are perceived by the ear as signal distortions. With repeated calculations, the errors accumulate, and the distortion becomes more noticeable.

Consider the waveform from the file EX05_01.WAV from the point of view of applicability of normalization. This waveform contains two takes of the material necessary for further work (Fig. 5.5).

It makes no sense to normalize this waveform, as it has samples that reach values close to maximum. A small level margin (about 1 dB) should be retained to avoid distortions that might appear in further signal processing.

Now, it's time to split the EX05_01.WAV file into two parts. Proceed as follows:

1. Cut the second take (selected in Fig. 5.5) with the **Edit > Cut** command.
2. Save the other take in a file under the name EX05_02.WAV with the **File > Save As** command.
3. Create a new project (**File > New**).
4. Paste the second take from the clipboard to the new project (**Edit > Paste**). The result is shown in Fig. 5.15 (we selected the fragment with noise at the beginning of the waveform).
5. Save it in a file under the name EX05_03.WAV with the **File > Save As** command.

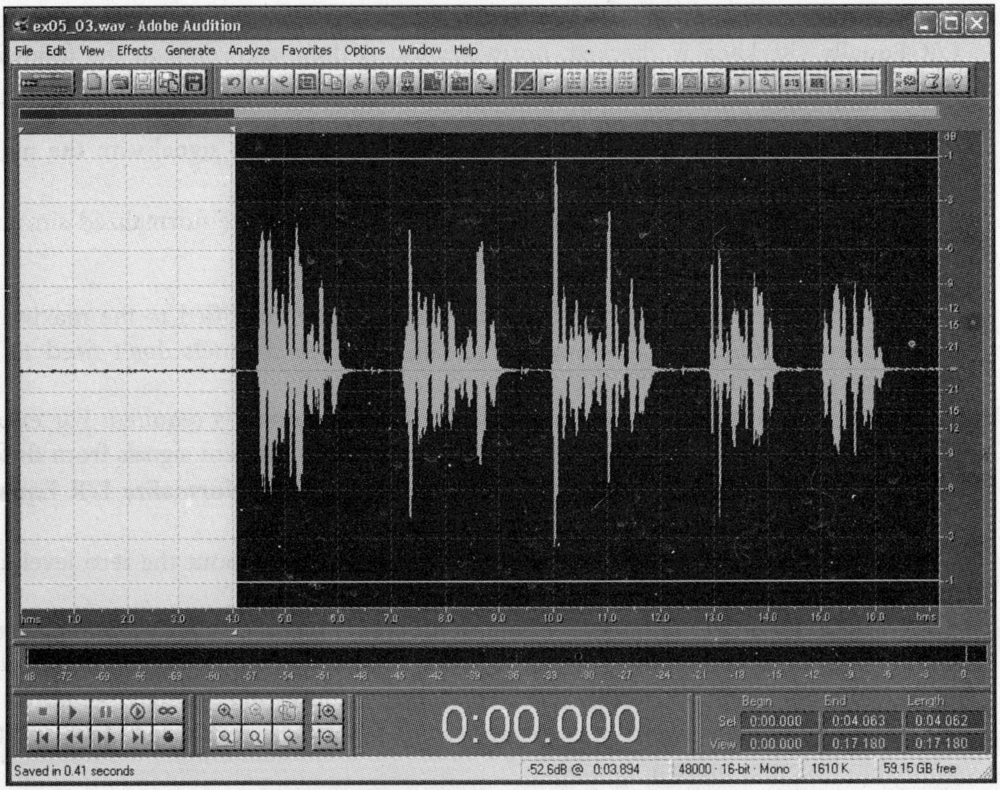

Fig. 5.15. Waveform (file EX05_03.WAV)

In our further work, if no problems appear, we'll use the take stored in the EX05_03.WAV file. The EX05_02.WAV file will be kept as a backup file.

5.2.4. Shaping the Amplitude Envelope

Sometimes, the tools for changing the signal amplitude discussed in the previous sections are insufficient. In some cases, you don't want to increase or decrease the whole signal, but you'd like to gain certain fragments, dampen other fragments, and leave the other ones untouched. This can be done with the **Create Envelope** dialog box opened with the **Effects** > **Amplitude** > **Envelope** command (Fig. 5.16). Using this dialog box, you'll be able to give the waveform amplitude envelope any shape you like.

You can see a coordinate plane. Time is plotted on the horizontal axis, and the signal level is plotted on the vertical axis. The length of the projection of the envelope on the time axis is equal to the length of the waveform selected in the working area of the main window.

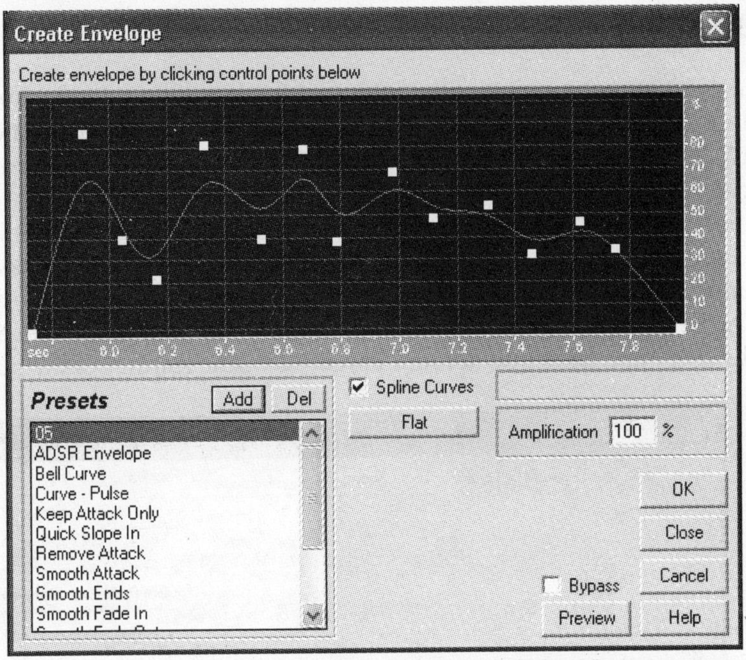

Fig. 5.16. Create Envelope dialog box

Here, you can draw an envelope that has any shape you like, for example, as shown in Fig. 5.16. The nodes are created by clicking the curve in the working area. By dragging them, you can shape the envelope as you like.

When might this be necessary? The shape of the envelope affects the spectral structure of the signal and, therefore, the timbre of the sound. For example, the pure note *A* is a sinusoidal oscillation with the frequency of 440 Hz. It sounds nasally and completely non-musically. However, if you replace the linear envelope of the waveform with a curve such as that shown in Fig. 5.16, the sound timbre will change dramatically. It will become musical, will "soar," and come "alive." For more details on how an envelope affects the timbre of the sound, see [1].

If you uncheck the **Spline Curves** checkbox, the smooth envelope curve will change to a broken line.

In the **Amplification** input field, you can enter the position of the highest point of the envelope.

If you click the **Flat** button, all the nodes will be deleted from the envelope, and it will turn into a line.

To save a successfully found envelope, click the **Add** button. In the dialog box that will open, enter a name for the preset and click the **OK** button.

5.3. Reducing the Noise Level

One of Adobe Audition's most remarkable functions is done with the **Noise Reduction** dialog box opened with **Effects** > **Noise Reduction** > **Noise Reduction** command (Fig. 5.17). When you learn how to use this simple but powerful tool, you might think that Adobe Audition can cope with any noise. You might even think that Adobe Audition can reduce any noise without detriment to the useful signal, no matter how much noise a recording contains. Of course, this isn't the case. There are distortions after noise reduction, but they are within reasonable limits, so a listener doesn't notice them. The developers of Adobe Audition managed to create an effective noise reduction technology that takes into account psycho-acoustic features of the human ear.

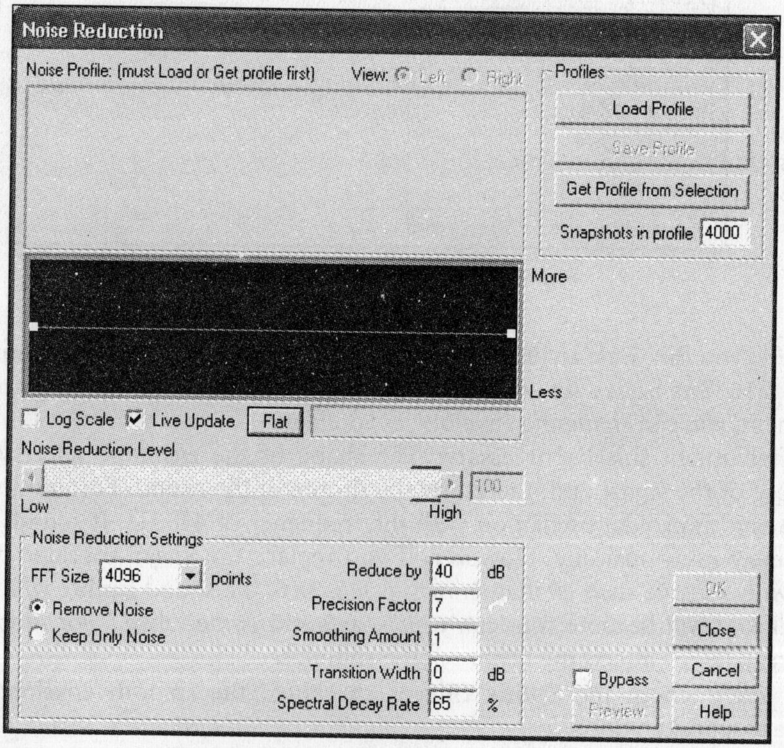

Fig. 5.17. Noise Reduction dialog box

To perform noise reduction, some information about the noise is required. The more statistical properties are available, the more effective is the noise reduction. Where can you get such information? The **Noise Reduction** function behaves like a police dog that wants a smell sample for a search. Adobe Audition "wants" a noise sample. Before you open the noise reduction dialog box, return to the application's main window and select a waveform fragment that doesn't contain useful information, but contains some noise typical for this waveform (microphone hissing, background noises, etc.). It is desirable that this fragment be as long as possible so that the application can obtain as much information about the noise as possible. The application will assume that the presented fragment contains only noise. Now open the **Noise Reduction** dialog box.

You should always leave a fragment with noise at the beginning of a waveform. Open the file EX05_03.WAV and select such a fragment (Fig. 5.15). Keep in mind that the longer the analyzed fragment, the more accurate the result of the analysis.

Click the **Get Profile from Selection** button. The application will collect information about the noise and display it in the coordinate field at the top of the dialog box (Fig. 5.18).

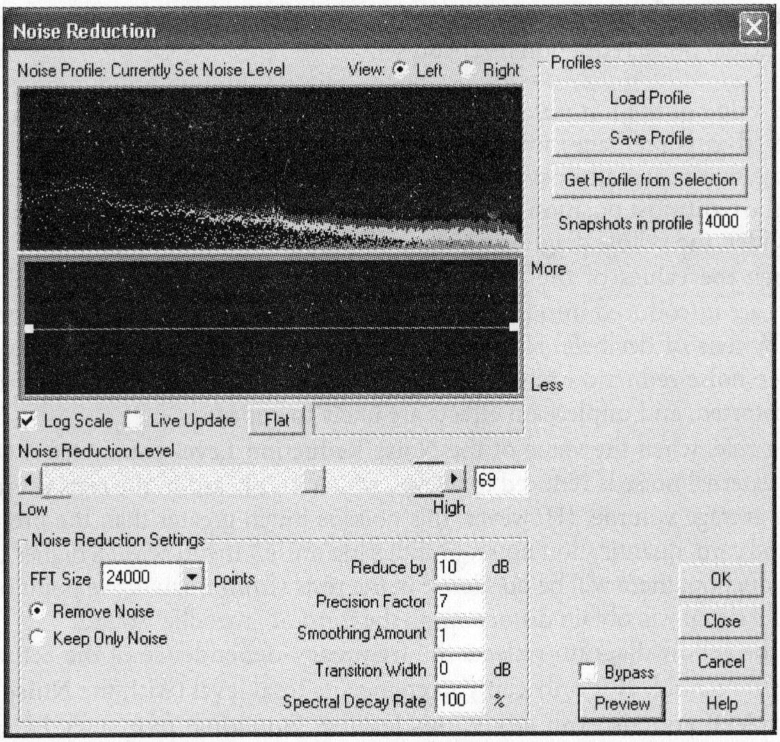

Fig. 5.18. Noise Reduction dialog box after getting information about noise

This is actually a frequency-response curve of the rejection filter that coincides with the spectrum of the analyzed waveform fragment. This isn't an ordinary frequency-response curve. You could say it is an "inside-out" curve. The higher its point on the coordinate plane, the greater the spectral component corresponding to this point will be reduced.

The frequency is plotted on the horizontal axis, and the values of the spectral components are plotted on the vertical axis. When processing is actualized, the noise reduction threshold will directly depend on the shape of the frequency-response curve. You can see as many as three diagrams on the coordinate field:

- The upper (red) one is a filter frequency-response curve that corresponds to the maximum noise reduction threshold.
- The lower (green) one is a filter frequency-response curve that corresponds to the minimum noise reduction threshold (the application creates these diagrams automatically after it gathers information about the waveform, and you can't change them).
- The middle (yellow) one is a filter frequency-response curve that corresponds to the actual noise reduction level you set.

The value of the last parameter is adjusted with the **Noise Reduction Level** slider or entered as percentages into the field located next to it. Play with this slider, and you'll see that at its leftmost position the yellow diagram merges with the green one, and at the rightmost position it merges with the red diagram. With the central position of the slider, the yellow diagram has its own shape.

When the values of the **Noise Reduction Level** parameter are small, almost no changes are introduced into the spectrum of the useful signal, and the noise can be reduced by tens of decibels. However, such a situation with noise isn't very common, and deep noise reduction might be required. In this case, the signal spectrum is likely to be distorted, and unpleasant effects are likely to appear.

As a rule, when the value of the **Noise Reduction Level** parameter is 60%, the recorded external noise is reduced to a level, which isn't heard in the rests during playback with an average volume. (However, this noise is much greater than the proper noise of the sound card, quantization noise, or dithering noise.) If you select a higher threshold of noise reduction, there will be no silence in the rests (from a subjective point of view), but the useful signal will obtain distortions in the form of "metallic" sound.

So the yellow diagram reflects the frequency-dependence of the actual noise reduction threshold. Not only can you change its total level (with the **Noise Reduction Level** slider), you also can adjust this level in individual frequency bands with the lower coordinate plane. To adjust the frequency dependence of the noise reduction threshold, use the diagram in this coordinate plane. As always, you can create nodes on the diagram by clicking it, and shape the curve by dragging the nodes. All your manipulations with the diagram will be instantly reflected on the yellow diagram in the upper coordinate plane. Thus, you have a tool for adjusting the curve automatically created by the application. This can be useful in complex cases when it is impossible to achieve good automatic noise reduction over the entire frequency band and retain high quality of the useful signal, and you have to look for a compromise.

The noise characteristics can be saved in a file with the **Save Profile** button. If you later want to reduce noise in an audio file recorded under the same noise conditions as the current one, it will suffice to click the **Load Profile** button and load the appropriate file with the noise characteristics. However, we don't recommend abusing this feature, because the noise characteristics of the room where you make recordings are constant only with good audio isolation. This isn't typical for home studios because it is impossible to achieve appropriate audio isolation at home. During one recording session, a car might be warmed up near your house; during another session, your neighbor might be trimming the lawn. These would be non-constant components of external noise. The advantage of the **Noise Reduction** function is that it can eliminate not only noise interference, but also regular background signals that are constant during processing the waveform or its fragments. In other words, if the car was rattling during a recording session, this sound can be removed almost completely. However, if you use this noise profile as a sample for processing an audio file recorded when the trimmer was working, it won't remove its sound from the audio file. Rather, the recording will be distorted because the application will try to remove the sound of the car engine that isn't present in the recording.

The number of snapshots for profile files can be specified in the **Snapshots in profile** field.

Everything we said above was just preparation for the noise reduction session. What should you do to get rid of noise?

If you select the entire waveform, including the fragments that contain only noise and fragments where noise is mixed with the useful signal, and use the **Noise Reduction** function, the application will perform optimized noise reduction.

You can make sure that the noise intensity has decreased. In Fig. 5.19, compare the fragments with and without noise located to the left and right of the edge of the selection. If automatic noise reduction is insufficient, use the **Noise Reduction Level** control or the corresponding input field.

Now you understand the purpose of the main controls of the **Noise Reduction** dialog box. It remains only to discuss a few useful options.

If you check the **Log Scale** checkbox, the logarithmic scale will be used on the frequency axis. You already know that this allows you to view the details of the low-frequency portion of the spectrum. When the checkbox is unchecked, the scale is linear, allowing you to analyze the high-frequency portion of the spectrum.

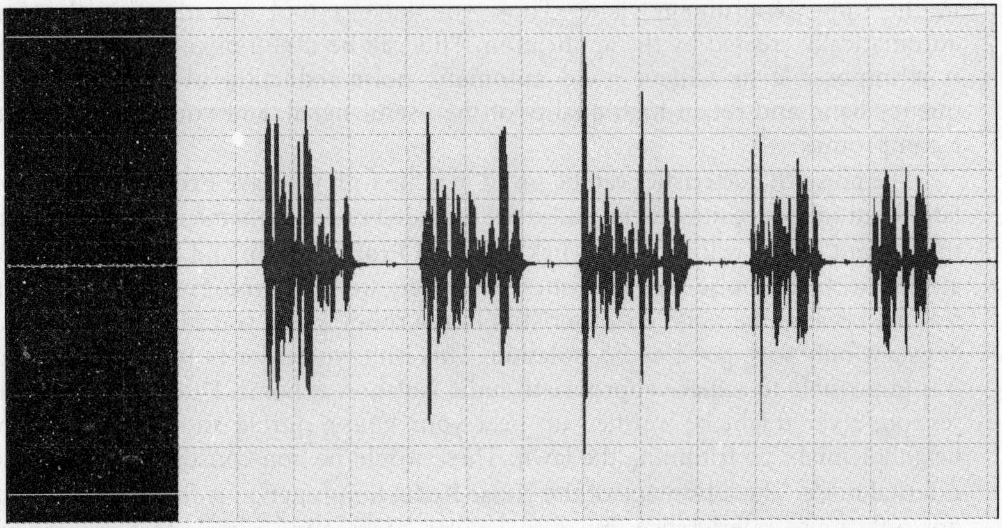

Fig. 5.19. Waveform (EX05_03.WAV) with noise reduced in the selection

When the **Live Update** checkbox is checked, the frequency-response curve is updated in real time. This means it will change continually as you move the nodes of the noise reduction diagram. Otherwise, the diagram in the upper coordinate plane will change only after you move a node in the lower coordinate plane and release the mouse button.

As always, a click on the **Flat** button resets the noise reduction diagram to its original form, a straight line.

To the right of the **Flat** button, there is a field where the coordinates of the mouse pointer are displayed (as a frequency and a level in percentage) when located within the lower coordinate field.

The **Noise Reduction Settings** group contains the settings of the noise reduction function itself. The **FFT Size** list contains the sizes of samples for the FFT operation used during the noise reduction. The greater the selected value, the better the sound processing, but the longer the processing time.

Taking into consideration the importance of noise reduction, we recommend you not to save time and select the maximum value of **FFT Size**.

If the **Remove Noise** radio button is selected, the noise will be deleted; if the **Keep Only Noise** radio button is selected, the noise will be kept, and the useful signal will be deleted. When can the latter be useful? You control the degree of noise reduction by setting the parameters of the noise reducer. You can get rid of noise almost completely, but this will significantly affect the useful signal. When you're listening to a processed recording, it is easy to make sure that there is no noise. However, it is much more difficult to find whether the useful signal is distorted. This is when the **Keep Only Noise** radio button can help you. Select it, process a waveform or its fragment (it is important that the waveform contains not only noise but the useful signal as well), and listen to the result. If you don't hear anything except noise, therefore, you chose the correct values of the noise reducer parameters. Undo the operation, select the **Remove Noise** radio button, and perform the final noise reduction without changing the settings.

If you failed to find the best combination of the parameters, you'll hear meaningful sounds through noise after you perform noise reduction with the **Keep Only Noise** radio button selected. This will indicate that some components of the useful signal were taken by the application for noise. Undo the operation, choose other parameter values (for example, move the **Noise Reduction Level** slider left) and try once more. After you achieve that the useful signal traces disappear, you can stop experimentation and proceed with noise reduction.

The **Precision Factor** field displays a factor that affects the precision of computation: The greater the factor, the better. However, when its value exceeds 10, no noticeable improvement in the sound quality can be heard, but the time taken for processing becomes much longer.

Rather than reduce noise instantly, the application can gradually transit from a waveform with noise to the waveform without noise. In the **Transition Width** field, enter a value of the parameter that affects the width of such transition. This will allow you to avoid noticeable changes in the noise level. By the way, it is unnatural when no noise is heard in rests, so some people don't like it.

The **Smoothing Amount** parameter is related to smoothening (averaging) the frequency-response curve. For noise with a large dispersion (such as white noise), you may leave the default value of 1 in this field. For noises with regular structures (such as background noise at 50 Hz), you should try to increase the value in the **Smoothing Amount** field. This can contribute to greater reduction of the regular noise at the cost of increasing the noise level a little. It would be difficult to give more detailed recommendations concerning preferable values of this parameter. If the results of noise reduction don't satisfy you, find the best value of the parameter using trial and error.

Thus, we reduced the noise in the EX05_03.WAV file. We don't need the waveform fragment with the noise sample any longer. We'll cut it and save the remaining portion of the waveform in a file under the name EX05_04.WAV.

5.4. Restoring Clips

The essence of *clipping* is that incorrect adjustment of the recorded signal level or its occasional increasing during recording causes an overflow of the analog-to-digital converter. Clipping reveals itself as an extremely unpleasant sound distortion. It is best not to use the material that contains clipping, and re-record it anew. But what should you do if this is impossible? Adobe Audition has an answer to this question.

Select the **Effects > Noise Reduction > Clip Restoration** command to open the **Clip Restoration** window (Fig. 5.20).

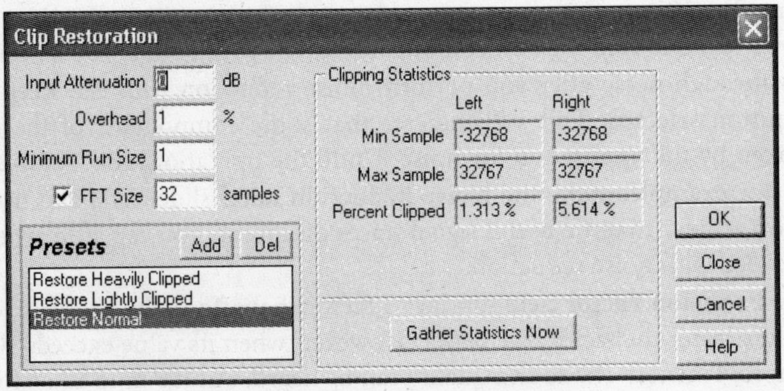

Fig. 5.20. Clip Restoration window

To understand the purpose of this window, consider an example. In Fig. 5.21, the left waveform was recorded with normal quality. The record level was such that none of the samples exceeded or even approached the maximum allowable value. In other words, this waveform doesn't have clipped samples. However, sometimes you can fail to find the correct recording level, and this leads to numerous clipped samples.

In the right waveform in Fig. 5.21, most of the samples are clipped. This waveform wasn't obtained by recording. Rather, we copied the left waveform and amplified its samples by 10 dB. We could record another audio file, but then it would be more difficult to appreciate a tool for clip restoration that we're going to introduce. Both the left and right waveforms display signals based on the same audio file, but distortions were intentionally introduced into the right waveform. If it were possible to compare their sound, you'd notice the difference: When playing the left waveform, you would hear a woman's pleasant voice; with the right waveform, you would hear gritting as if the coil in the speaker is damaged and touches the magnet.

You could try to decrease the level of the distorted signal, but this wouldn't help. The sound would become softer, but the distortions would remain.

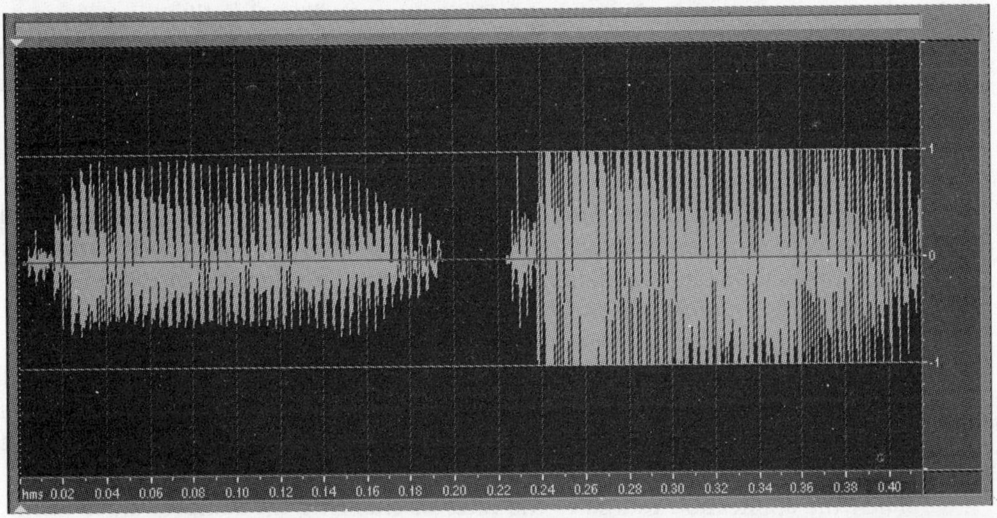

Fig. 5.21. Waveforms with normal quality (left) and with clipping (right)

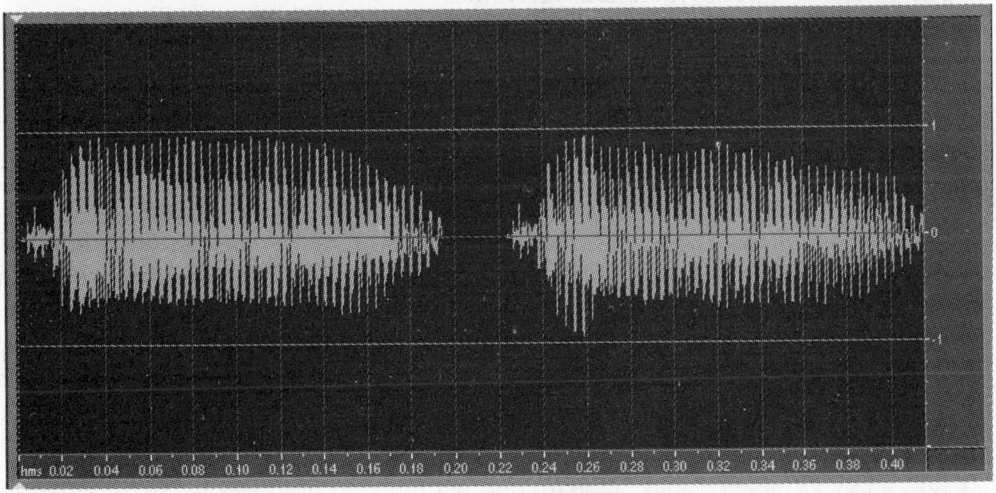

Fig. 5.22. Result of the **Clip Restoration** function

We should consider this audio file irrevocably damaged if there weren't the **Clip Restoration** dialog box in Adobe Audition. By selecting the clipped waveform and applying the clip restoration function to it, we obtained the waveform shown in Fig. 5.22 (right). The left waveform in the figure is the original waveform.

The major portion of the envelope of the clipped waveform is a straight line (Fig. 5.21), and the envelope of the processed waveform is a curve similar to the envelope of the original waveform. Of course, you'll notice difference if you compare the left and right waveforms in Fig. 5.22. Their sounds also differ. The timbre of the voice has changed, but the voice is pleasant, and the audio file can be heard without aversion and shudder.

It looks like a miracle! How could Adobe Audition know what shape the envelope had? No miracles, just science. This is interpolation based on statistical hypotheses.

Roughly speaking, Adobe Audition does the following. First, it divides the values of all waveform samples by a constant, such as 4. Thus, it provides itself with the ability to increase the values of individual samples later. The clipping threshold is also decreased with this division. If it was 100%, it becomes 25% after the division.

Then the application analyzes the series of samples whose values are equal to the clipping threshold. Suppose three such samples in succession were detected. Adobe Audition puts forward the following hypothesis: It is likely that the values of the first and last sample were indeed 25% during recording, and it is likely that without clipping the value of the middle sample would be greater than 25%.

Then the application estimates the rates of changing the sample values to the left and right of the clipped fragment and computes the value of the middle sample, using one of well-known interpolation algorithms.

This procedure is repeated for each detected series of clipped samples. Finally, the audio file is normalized.

Such an approach can undoubtedly restore clips. Nevertheless, it is obvious that the restored file won't be an exact copy of the file, which would be obtained with proper choice of recording mode.

There can be at least three sources of mistakes in the procedure:

- The hypothesis doesn't necessarily reflect the actual events. In our example, the middle sample might be equal to the clipping threshold, rather than exceeding it.
- The rate of changing the sample values isn't constant.
- If the series of clipped samples is long, the sample values that exceed the clipping threshold can change according to any law. The envelope can rise or decline monotonically, or it can oscillate.

Now let's look at the purpose of the options of the **Clip Restoration** dialog box (Fig. 5.20). We'll begin with the following fields:

- **Input Attenuation** — gains the signal before processing. This parameter affects the overall volume of the processed audio file. In essence, it bears information about the level to which the sample values of the audio file will be normalized. For reference purposes, the **Input Attenuation** value in the example shown in Fig. 5.21 was set to –10 dB.
- **Overhead** — is a value that determines a certain threshold: Samples that exceed it will be considered clipped. For example, if this parameter is 0%, only samples that

reach 100% will be considered clipped. When **Overhead** is 1%, samples that reach 99% will be considered clipped.

- **Minimum Run Size** — when the number of successive samples that reach the specified threshold is greater or equal to this value, the fragment is considered clipped.
- **FFT Size** — the sample size for FFT. As always, the greater its size, the more accurate the computations, but the longer the time.

The **Clipping Statistics** group displays the statistics for each of the stereo channels. These are the value of the minimum sample (**Min Sample**), the value of the maximum sample (**Max Sample**), and the percent of clipped samples (**Percent Clipped**). To obtain statistics, click the **Gather Statistics Now** button.

The **Presets** list consists of three lines:

- **Restore Heavily Clipped** — restores heavily clipped waveforms.
- **Restore Lightly Clipped** — restores lightly clipped waveforms.
- **Restore Normal** — processes waveforms whose clipping isn't noticeable to the eye. You can apply this processing to any audio file, just to be on the safe side. If it doesn't contain clipped samples, the processing will result in decrease of the normalization level by 1%.

We illustrated clip restoration with an example of a file that contained a lot of clipped samples. In actual practice, you should avoid using such material. However, we believe you won't make such a bad recording. The EX05_04.WAV file obtained from the fifth take of the recording (EX03_02.WAV) contains no clipped samples (see *Table 4.1*).

Chapter 6

Correcting the Spectrum

Chapter 4 introduced the spectrum analysis tools available in Adobe Audition. We looked at how to use them in practice to detect various anomalies that aren't always visible if the signal is displayed as a waveform but that are easily revealed in the spectrum. However, spectral representation would be of little use if there weren't tools for spectrum transformation. Of course, Adobe Audition provides such tools. There are many types of frequency filters, which allow you to transform the amplitude spectrum as you like. There are also a few processings, based on changing both the amplitude components of a signal and its phase spectrum, that make it possible to control the stereo field. These topics are covered in this chapter.

6.1. Understanding the Basics of Filtration

Filtration is comprehensively discussed in [1] and [3], so here we'll confine ourselves to a brief description of the essence of filtration and a classification of filters used in practice.

Filtration is a kind of processing of an electric audio signal with frequency selecting devices. Its goal is to change the spectrum (timbre) of the signal. The tasks of such processing can include the following:

- Amplitude-frequency correction (amplification or attenuation of individual frequency components)
- Complete suppression of the signal or the noise spectrum in a particular frequency band

For example, if the microphone, acoustic system, or another component of the audio channel has an uneven frequency-response curve, it can be smoothed with filters. If spectrum analysis reveals that a frequency range mainly contains noise and little signal, all oscillations in this range can be suppressed with filters.

Various devices are constructed to implement filtration: individual correcting and formant filters, devices for separating the sound into several channels according to frequency criteria (crossovers), two-band or multiband timbre controls (equalizers), presence filters, etc.

Filters implemented programmatically as components of music editors are based on spectral analysis. *Chapter 4* demonstrated how any signal can be represented as a set of harmonic expansion coefficients (sinusoid and cosine). Filtration is reduced to multiplying spectral coefficients by the appropriate values of the filter's transfer function. If the spectrum is represented in complex form, the signal is described by a set of amplitude and phase spectra, and the filters by frequency- and phase-response curves. A frequency-response curve is a frequency dependence of the filter's transfer ratio. A phase-response curve shows the frequency dependence of the phase shift of the output signal relative to the input signal. In this case, filtration is equivalent to multiplying the amplitude spectrum by the frequency response and algebraic addition of the phase spectrum to the phase response.

Due to the large number of multiplication operations, classical spectrum analysis takes a lot of processor time. It cannot be done at the actual processing rate with a large number of signal samples. To decrease the time of spectral analysis of discrete signals, special algorithms were developed that take into account the relationships between the various signal samples and exclude repeated operations. One such algorithm is the Fast Fourier Transform (FFT).

Depending on the position of the passband on the frequency axis, filters are divided into the following groups:

- Low-pass filters
- High-pass filters
- Band-pass filters
- Band-stop filters

The fragment of the frequency-response curve, in which the transfer ratio is not equal to zero corresponds to the passband of the filter. In contrast, the transfer ratio must be minimal (ideally, zero) within the stop (or suppression) band.

Strictly speaking, actual filters don't provide a zero value for the transfer function beyond the passband. The oscillations within the stop band still pass through the filter, but are significantly dampened.

Actual high-pass and low-pass filters are characterized by the following main parameters:

- The cutoff frequency
- The passband width
- The unevenness of the curve in the passband
- The steepness of the curve slope in the pass-to-stop transition area

For the band-pass filter, one more parameter is added: Q-factor, the ratio of the central filter frequency to its passband.

An example of a device that uses high-pass and low-pass filters is the timbre control (for high and low frequencies) available in almost every domestic amplifier, radio, or tape recorder. This device can also be considered the simplest equalizer. With it, you can adjust the sound of the system to your liking.

In addition to high-frequency and low-frequency timbre controls, many amplifiers and other systems have a center-frequency timbre control. This control actually adjusts a band-pass filter that is used to amplify or dampen the signal in a relatively narrow frequency band of the sound spectrum.

When working with Adobe Audition, you'll often use equalizers. *Equalizers* are devices that combine several filters and are designed to change the spectral properties (the timbre) of the processed signal. The first equalizer was used mainly as a device that compensates for the unevenness of certain segments of the audio signal amplification and transformation channel. When you have an equalizer, you can smooth out or "equalize" an initially uneven frequency-response curve. There are several types of equalizers that differ in purpose and construction, including:

- Graphic equalizers
- Parametric equalizers
- Presence filters
- Crossovers

A *graphic equalizer* is a set of band-pass filters with fixed central frequencies and variable gain that can be controlled with a slider. Sliders are commonly used as controls since their positions make up a sort of the frequency-response curve of the equalizer. This is why such equalizers are called graphic: The user "draws" the necessary frequency-response curve with the sliders.

Thus, a graphic equalizer is a set of band-pass filters that completely separate certain frequency bands. To enable the user to control the frequency-response curve within the whole area of audio frequencies, these filters are connected in parallel. The same signal is supplied to the inputs of all the filters, and the task of each filter is to amplify or dampen its "own" portion of the spectrum based on the position of the gain control (the slider).

The frequencies regulated using graphic equalizers are uniform, and are selected from several standard frequencies that cover the entire audio range and are separated by a certain interval. The interval can be an octave, half of an octave, or a third of it.

There can be up to several dozen adjustment bands.

The lowest-frequency filter of an equalizer doesn't have to be a filter. It can also be a low-pass filter. Similarly, the highest-frequency filter can be a high-pass filter.

Graphic equalizers are most often used for total signal processing, that is, for "finishing" the overall picture rather than filtering individual components. Using a graphic equalizer, you can approximately form the necessary frequency-response curve of the sound processing system or the acoustic system, i.e., increase amplification in some areas of the spectrum and decrease it in the others. However, a graphic equalizer (even a multiband one) is of little use for precise frequency correction, as the central frequencies of its filters are fixed and may not exactly coincide with the frequencies you want to emphasize, or may, conversely, suppress spectral components. In such cases, parametric equalizers come to your aid.

A *parametric equalizer* makes it possible to control not only the filter gain, but also the central frequency and quality (actually, the passband width). With some experience, you'll be able to set the values of these parameters precisely, to emphasize the sound of an individual instrument or remove unwanted noise (such as 60 Hz background noise or the self-excitement frequency of an acoustic system) with minimum influence on the other components of the audio image.

To create a frequency-response curve with a complex shape, multiband parametric equalizers are used. Each parameter of such an equalizer can be adjusted independently.

A *presence filter* makes it possible to create the impression that the instrument (or the singer) is in the same room as the listener. In fact, it is nothing more than an adjustable band-pass filter with a central frequency anywhere from 2 to 6 kHz. In a guitar control box, a presence filter makes it possible to make the guitar sound brighter and more noticeable among the sounds of the other instruments.

A *crossover* is a device that splits an input signal into several output signals, each of which contains only oscillations of a certain frequency range. A crossover is a set of band-pass and threshold filters (one for each output channel) with a shared input and individual outputs.

Although crossovers aren't equalizers in the strict sense, their working principles are the same.

It is well known that it is impossible to make a speaker that would reproduce all frequency ranges (high, middle, and low) equally well. If you narrow the range of the reproduced frequencies, making a speaker will become simpler, but several different speakers will be required to reproduce sound in all its range. In actual systems, the largest speaker reproduces low frequencies, and the smallest one reproduces high frequencies. Top-quality systems have a third speaker for middle frequencies.

For a speaker to operate normally, it is required that it receives only signals of the appropriate frequency range. To split a wide-band signal into several bands with different frequencies, crossovers are used.

After refreshing your knowledge of the terms related to audio signal filtration, you can proceed the main filters of Adobe Audition, available in the **Effects** > **Filters** submenu.

6.2. Introducing Adobe Audition's Main Filters

The filters available in Adobe Audition are listed in the **Filters** submenu (contained in the **Effects** menu):

- **Dynamic EQ** — equalizer with dynamic control of the adjustment frequency, gain, and bandwidth
- **FFT Filter** — filter based on the Fast Fourier Transform
- **Graphic Equalizer** — universal graphic equalizer
- **Notch Filter** — multiband notch filter
- **Parametric Equalizer** — seven-band parametric equalizer
- **Quick Filter** — eight-band graphic equalizer
- **Scientific Filters** — Bessel, Butterworth, and Chebyshev filters

So the **Filters** submenu contains commands related to filtration. Below we give brief descriptions of the filters opened with these commands.

6.2.1. FFT Filter — *a Filter Based on the Fast Fourier Transform*

The **Effects** > **Filters** > **FFT Filter...** command opens the **FFT Filter** dialog box (Fig. 6.1).

As its name implies, this dialog box implements a FFT filter based on the Fast Fourier Transform. Generally speaking, all the filters in the **Filters** submenu use FFT. Without FFT, even the most advanced computer would barely be able to cope with filtration, spectral analysis, and signal synthesis. Why is only this filter called an FFT filter? Most likely, because its dialog box (**FFT Filter**) has an interface similar to the interfaces of mathematical applications that implement the FFT. It even contains a special group **FFT and Windowing** that allows you to specify parameters significantly affecting the results of filtration.

The **FFT Size** drop-down list contains the sizes of samples for the FFT. The greater the size, the better the sound, but the longer the computation.

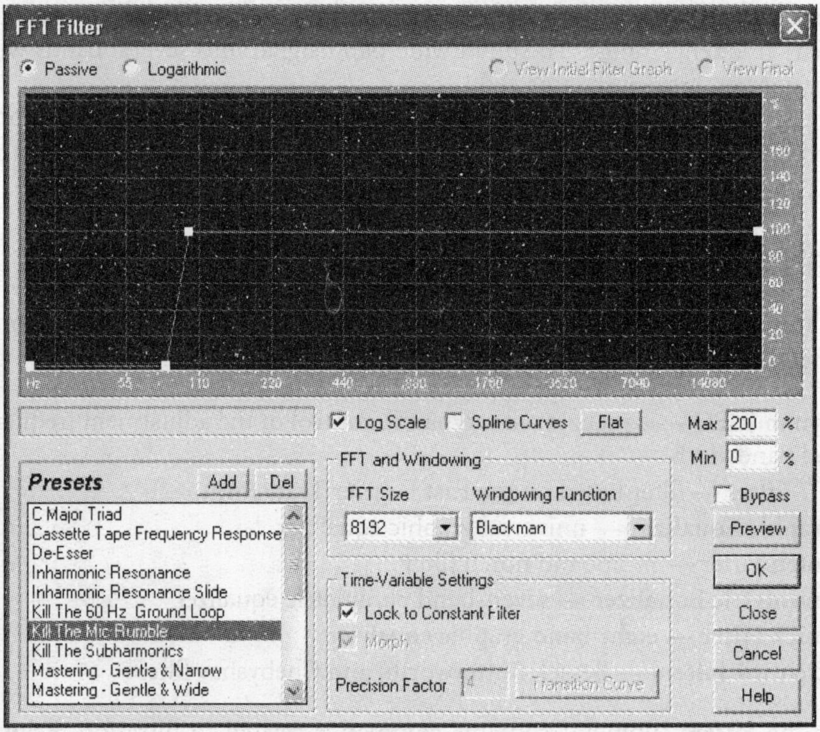

Fig. 6.1. FFT Filter dialog box

The **Windowing Function** drop-down list contains functions that determine the type of the time window and, therefore, the method of taking into consideration the history of the signal being analyzed.

The most eye-catching element of the **FFT Filter** dialog box is the coordinate field, which displays the filter's frequency-response curve. Frequencies are plotted on the horizontal axis, and the transfer ratio of the filter is plotted on the vertical axis.

In the **Passive** mode, the vertical axis is graduated in percentages. For example, 100% means that the signal is neither decreased nor increased by the filter. A value of 200% means that the amplitude of a particular spectral component is doubled, while the value of 50% indicates halving.

In the **Logarithmic** mode, the logarithmic scale is set on the vertical axis (the frequency-response curve is measured in dB).

If the **Log Scale** checkbox is checked, the logarithmic scale is set on the frequency axis. This makes it possible to view the details of the frequency-response curve in the low-frequency area. For example, in Fig. 6.1, the most informative portion of the frequency-response curve is in the frequency range from 55 to 110 Hz, and is well visible.

If the **Log Scale** checkbox is unchecked, the linear scale is set on the horizontal axis. This allows you to view the filter frequency-response curve in its natural form, with all proportions retained. However, you won't be able to see details in the low-frequency area. Neither mode is very suitable for precise graphical control over the shape of the frequency-response curve. For this purpose, the information field located under the frequency-response curve at the left side of the dialog box can be useful. This field displays the current coordinates of the mouse pointer. Therefore, a method for precise specification of a node point on the diagram (and, eventually, the shape of the entire frequency-response curve) does exist.

The **Spline Curves** checkbox makes it possible to turn on a spline approximation of the diagram. In this case, the filter frequency-response curve from Fig. 6.1 will look as shown in Fig. 6.2. You should be aware that not only the appearance of the diagram changes, but the actual frequency-response curve of the filter as well.

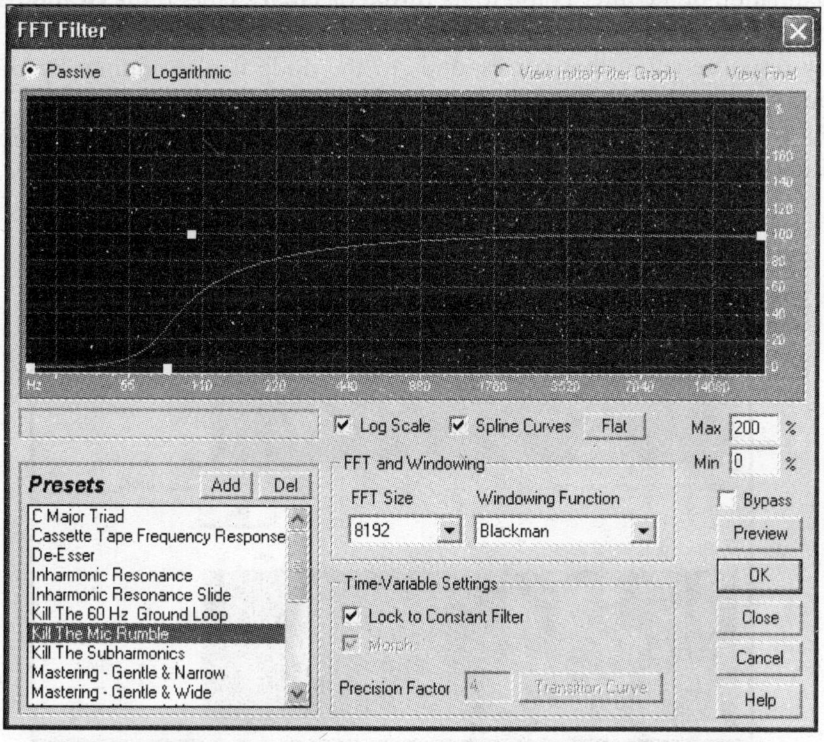

Fig. 6.2. Spline approximation of a filter frequency-response curve

When the **Lock to Constant Filter** checkbox is unchecked (in the **Time-Variable Settings** group), the frequency-response curve of the filter can change over the audio fragment according to your wishes. To achieve this, perform a few operations. Select the **View Initial Filter Graph** radio button and put node points on the curve with the mouse. This will be the initial filter graph. Then, select the **View Final** radio button and shape the final filter graph.

The controls of the **Time-Variable Settings** group turn on a mode, in which the initial shape of the filter frequency-response curve gradually transits to the final as the audio fragment is processed. This is achieved with the **Morph** checkbox. The **Precision Factor** field specifies how precisely the audio data is processed (how smooth the transition from the initial to final shape of the filter frequency-response curve is).

A click on the **Transition Curve** button opens a dialog box (Fig. 6.3), in which you can draw a curve to determine how the filter frequency-response curve should be transformed.

Here, the horizontal axis is a time axis, and the vertical axis shows the degree of approximation of the filter graph to its **Initial** or **Final** shape. If the **Graph response at point** checkbox is checked, the lower field of the dialog box will display the filter frequency-response curve that corresponds to the node you're adding. By clicking the **Flat** button, you can turn the curve into a line.

Fig. 6.3 shows the **Transition Curve** dialog box after clicking the left node of the transition curve. The lower field displays the initial frequency-response curve.

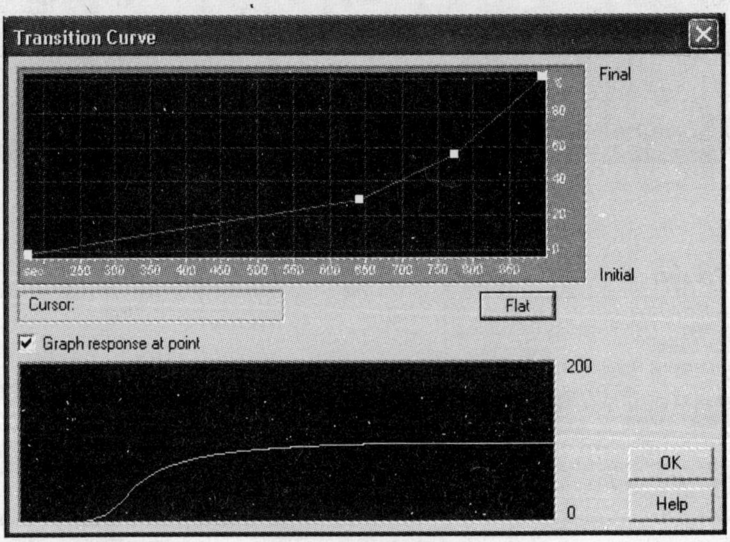

Fig. 6.3. Transition Curve dialog box

If you click the second node on the transition curve, the lower field will display the filter frequency-response curve at an intermediate moment of time. After a click on the right node on the transition curve, the final frequency-response curve of the filter will be displayed.

Now, return to the **FFT Filter** dialog box (Fig. 6.2). The **Presets** list contains quite a lot of presets. Here are just the most interesting ones:

- **C Major Triad** — a row of narrow-band filters adjusted to the frequencies of the *C major* chord of several adjacent octaves
- **De-Esser** — a filter that suppresses hissing sounds typical for some people's voices
- **Kit The 60 Hz Ground Loop** — a set of filters suppressing the background frequency (60 Hz) of the electric power supply and its higher harmonics
- **Kit The Mic Rumble** — a filter suppressing low-frequency noise received by the microphone
- **Only The Subwoofer** and **Only The Tweeter** — crossover filters that shape signals for the low-frequency and high-frequency speakers of the acoustic system

6.2.2. Quick Filter – *an Eight-Band Graphic Equalizer*

Quick Filter is indeed the quickest one available, but it is impossible to fine-tune its frequency-response curve. The quickest filter in Adobe Audition is just an eight-band graphic equalizer whose dialog box (Fig. 6.4) is opened with the **Effects** > **Filters** > **Quick Filter...** command.

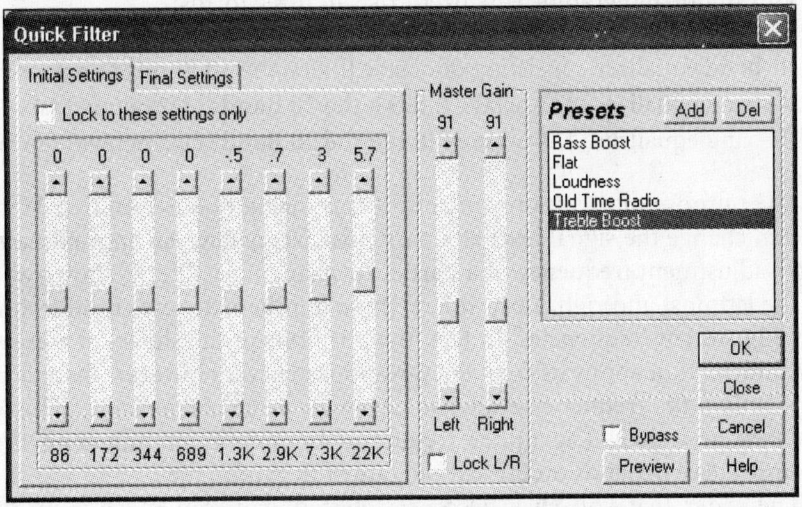

Fig. 6.4. Quick Filter dialog box

One advantage of this filter is the simplicity of its interface; it has no "excessive" controls. Like the other processings and effects in Adobe Audition, this filter is smart, i.e., when it moves on to work with an audio file that has a sample rate different from the previous one, all its elementary filters change their frequencies (and their uppermost and lowermost sliders change the cutoff frequencies).

The adjustment frequency is displayed below the corresponding control, and the gain/decay level is displayed above it.

Like with **FFT Filter**, you can implement a **Quick Filter** frequency-response curve that changes over time. To do this, specify the initial and final shape of the curve (the initial and final positions of the equalizer sliders). The **Lock to these settings only** checkbox must be unchecked. The initial frequency-response curve is specified on the **Initial Settings** tab, and the final one is specified on the **Final Settings** tab.

When the **Lock to these settings only** checkbox is checked, the frequency-response curve doesn't depend on time.

The sliders of the **Master Gain** set the level, to which the signals are gained after filtration. With the **Lock L/R** checkbox, you can bind the sliders of the left and right channels.

6.2.3. Graphic Equalizer — a Multiband Graphic Equalizer

The command **Effects > Filters > Graphic Equalizer...** opens a dialog box of the multiband **Graphic Equalizer**.

This multiband graphic equalizer exists in three forms:

- 10-band equalizer consisting of octave filters; the **10 Bands (1 octave)** tab
- 20-band equalizer (1/2-octave filters); the **20 Bands (1/2 octave)** tab
- 30-band equalizer (1/3-octave filters); the **20 Bands (1/3 octave)** tab (Fig. 6.5)

The purpose of the main controls of this dialog box is intuitive. With the sliders, you can change the signal level at a particular frequency. An approximate value of the center adjustment frequency of a particular elementary filter is shown above its slider. For the leftmost and rightmost sliders, these numbers denote cutoff frequencies rather than adjustment frequencies. In fact, the positions of the sliders of a graphic equalizer bear information about its frequency-response curve. However, there is a special field that displays the frequency-response curve for your convenience. This dialog box is very well arranged: The upper frequency boundary for adjusting the frequency-response curve depends on the sample rate of the audio file.

The slider that you click becomes selected. You can move it up or down with the mouse.

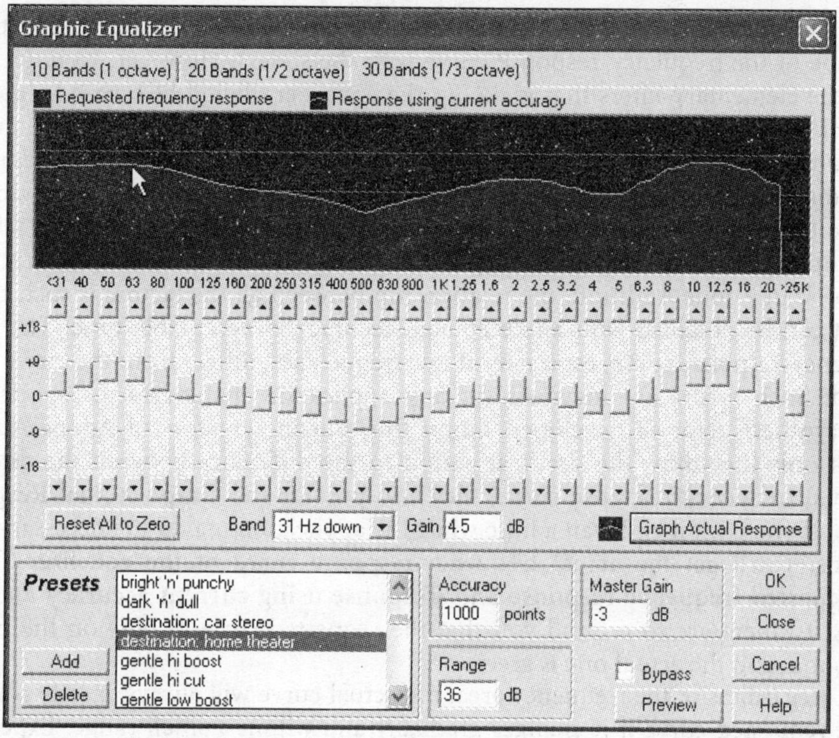

Fig. 6.5. 30 Bands (1/3 octave) tab of the **Graphic Equalizer** dialog box

In addition to the gain controls, there are following controls common for all bands:

- The **Reset All to Zero** button resets all the sliders to their zero positions.
- The **Band** drop-down list displays the exact value of the center frequency (or the cutoff frequency) of the selected filter.
- The **Gain** field allows you to enter a precise value of the signal gain for the center frequency (or the cutoff frequency) of the selected filter.
- The **Graph Actual Response** button allows you to obtain the actual frequency-response curve of the equalizer.
- The **Accuracy** input field displays the accuracy of processing (recommended values are from 500 to 5,000; the lower the low boundary frequency in the signal spectrum, the higher value should be specified).
- The **Range** input field allows you to specify the range, within which the slider should change the parameter (standard hardware equalizers usually have ranges from 30 dB to 48 dB).
- The **Master Gain** field allows you to enter the signal master gain.

Let's take a look at the **Graph Actual Response** button. You specify the desired shape of the frequency-response curve with the sliders. However, to implement each of the elementary filters that make up the equalizer, digital FFT-based algorithms are used. When modeling any process, a digital algorithm always gives an approximate result. The error depends on many factors, particularly on the number-representation format and the number of samples. When modeling an equalizer, the accuracy of the result additionally depends on the Q-factor of each filter, and on the selected law, according to which a particular parameter changes as the central adjustment frequency grows. In Adobe Audition, the relationship between all the factors is such that the result can be obtained with an acceptable accuracy in acceptable time. The actual frequency-response curve, especially at low frequencies, differs from the curve you specified. Such errors are inevitable in any application that performs spectral analysis or synthesis. Not all developers admit this, but the creators of Adobe Audition do. Not only they draw the user's attention to the difference between the desirable and actual frequency-response curve, they also provide the **Graph Actual Response** button. If you click it and wait a little while the application makes the necessary computations, you'll get the actual frequency-response curve of the equalizer. The words **Requested frequency response** and **Response using current accuracy** and the icons next to them are to remind you that the requested curve is blue on the black background, and the actual one is green.

Regardless of the frequency area, the actual curve will always exactly coincide with the requested curve if it changes gradually and within a small range. Experts recommend being very careful when using significant frequency adjustment.

The **Presets** list contains more than forty various presets, including:

- **Presence (Music)** — presence filter for selecting the musical accompaniment
- **Simple Bass Cut** — filter for decreasing the low-frequency level
- **Simple Bass Lift** — filter for increasing the low-frequency level
- **Simple Mid Boost** — filter for increasing the mid-frequency level
- **Vocal Presence (Boost)** and **Vocal Presence (Cut)** — presence filters for processing vocals (increasing or decreasing the signal level at frequencies typical for vocal parts)

6.2.4. Parametric Equalizer — a Seven-Band Parametric Equalizer

The command **Effects > Filters > Parametric Equalizer...** opens the **Parametric Equalizer** dialog box (Fig. 6.6). This is a seven-band parametric equalizer that makes it possible to specify practically any frequency-response curve with high accuracy.

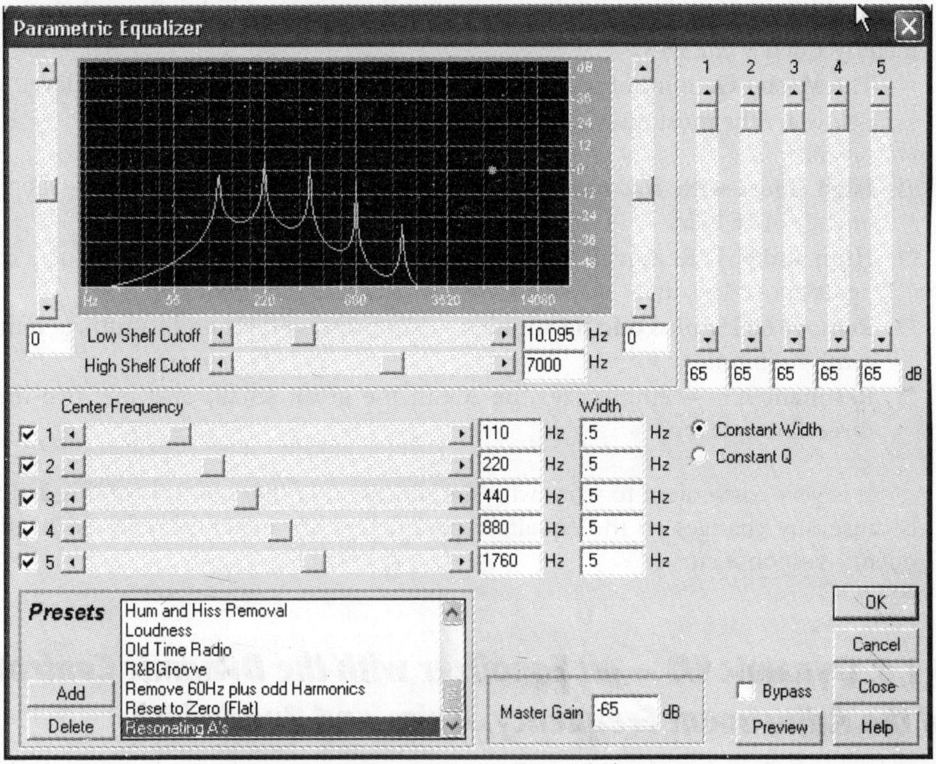

Fig. 6.6. Parametric Equalizer dialog box

The frequency-response curve is traditionally displayed in the upper part of the dialog box.

The sliders and input fields labeled **Low Shelf Cutoff** and **High Shelf Cutoff** are used to control the cutoff frequencies of the low-frequency and high-frequency shelf filters. The sliders located to the left and right of the coordinate field are used to adjust the signal gain/decay provided by these filters.

The **Center Frequency** group contains five checkboxes for filter selection and five sliders for center frequency adjustment. The exact values of the center frequencies are displayed in the fields to the right of the sliders. The **Width** column contains fields that allow you to enter new Q-factor values of the corresponding filters, thus changing their passband widths.

The level of the signal gain/decay provided by each of these filters is adjusted using the corresponding slider. These sliders are located in the upper right part of the dialog box.

If the **Constant Width** radio button is selected, the passband doesn't change when the filter frequency changes. If the **Constant Q** radio button is selected, its Q-factor becomes constant, i.e., the passband will become proportionally wider as the adjustment frequency changes.

The **Master Gain** input field is used for adjustment of the master gain level.

Below are the most interesting presets of the **Presets** list:

- **High Boost with 16k notch** — boosts high frequencies and suppresses the frequency of 16 kHz.
- **Hum and Hiss Removal** — suppresses components at 60 Hz and reduces components above 16 kHz.
- **Remove 60 Hz plus odd harmonics** — suppresses 60 Hz and its fifth, seventh, and ninth harmonics.
- **Resonant A's** — emphasizes the A's in the great, small, one-line, two-line, and three-line octaves.

It is very convenient to work with the sliders and other controls of this dialog box, because any changes to the equalizer parameters are instantly reflected by the frequency-response curve.

6.2.5. Dynamic EQ – *an Equalizer with the Dynamic Control of the Adjustment Frequency, Gain, and Bandwidth*

The **Effects > Filters > Dynamic EQ...** command opens the **Dynamic EQ** dialog box (Fig. 6.7), in which a one-band parametric equalizer with dynamic control of the adjustment frequency, gain, and frequency pass (or stop) bandwidth is implemented. The dialog box contains three tabs:

- **Frequency** — graphical control on the adjustment frequency of the filter (Fig. 6.7, *a*).
- **Gain** — graphical control on the gain in the pass (or stop) band (Fig. 6.7, *b*).
- **Q (bandwidth)** — graphical control over the Q-factor. With the center adjustment frequency fixed, the value of this parameter is inversely proportional to the pass (or stop) bandwidth of the filter (Fig. 6.7, *c*).

Using the **Dynamic EQ** filter is a matter of "drawing" time-dependence diagrams for parameters.

In the **Filter Type** group, you can select one of the filter types — **Low Pass, Band Pass**, or **High Pass** — and a transfer ratio of the filter in the stop band specified in decibels (in the **Stop Band_dB** field).

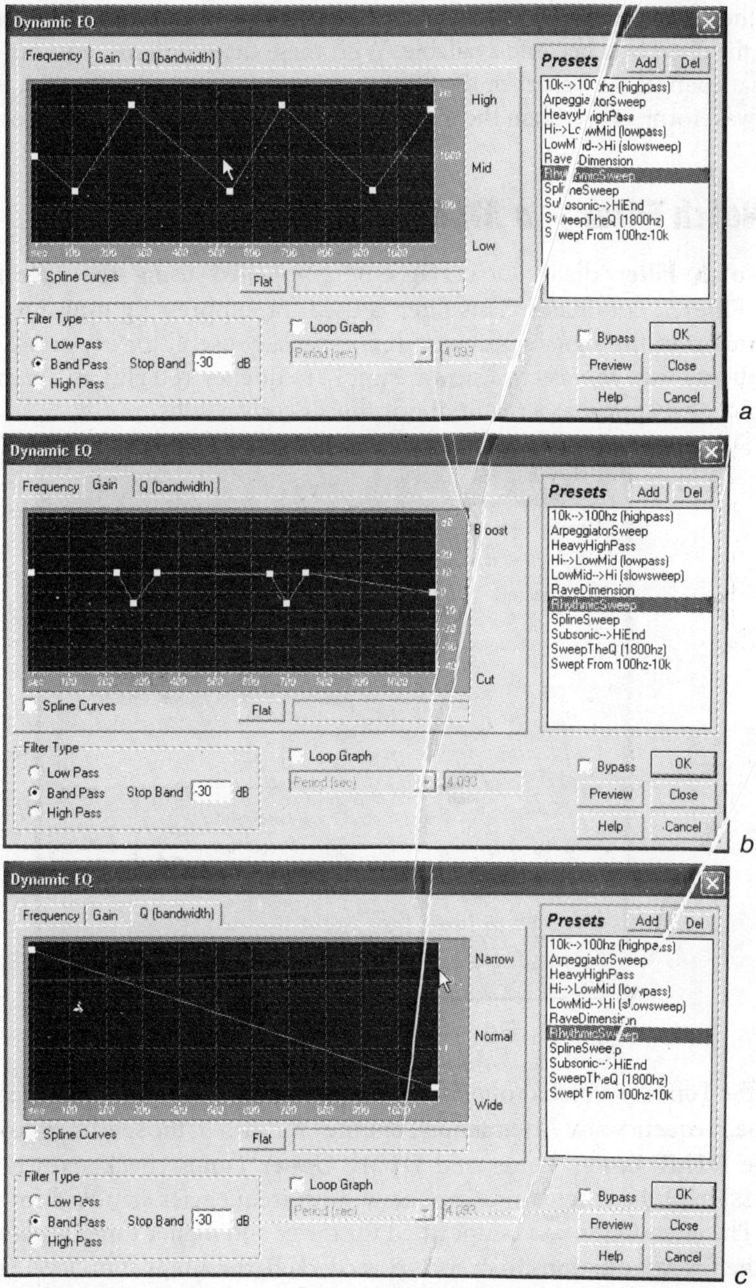

Fig. 6.7. Dynamic EQ dialog box, the **Frequency** (*a*), **Gain** (*b*), and **Q (bandwidth)** (*c*) tabs

If the **Loop Graph** checkbox is checked, the drop-down list and input field located under the checkbox become available. With these three options, you can loop the function that changes the values of the filter parameters so that this function is valid over the entire waveform, rather than the fragment, for which it was originally specified.

6.2.6. Notch Filter — *a Multiband Notch Filter*

The **Notch Filter** dialog box (Fig. 6.8) is opened using the **Effects** > **Filters** > **Notch Filter...** command. This filter is used for suppressing unwanted narrow-band components of the signal spectrum. It is especially useful for suppressing background components with the electric power supply frequency (60 Hz) and harmonics of this frequency that appear as a result of non-linear conversions.

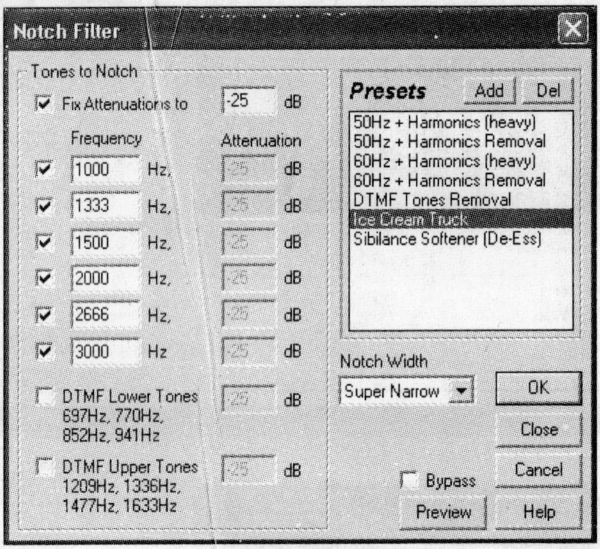

Fig. 6.8. Notch Filter dialog box

In the **Tones to Notch** group, you can select a frequency value and a degree of attenuation (the **Frequency** and **Attenuation** columns) for each of the spectrum components.

The **DTMF Lower Tones** and **DTMF Upper Tones** checkboxes turn on and off suppression of the spectrum components with frequencies standard for telephone dial tones. The attenuation can be specified for lower and higher tones separately.

If the **Fix Attenuations to** checkbox is checked, the attenuation level will be equal for all frequencies (it should be entered into the appropriate field). When this checkbox is unchecked, you can choose an individual attenuation level for each frequency.

In the **Notch Width** drop-down list, you can select the filter order [3], thus selecting the bandwidth: **Narrow, Very Narrow,** or **Super Narrow.** The recommend values of attenuation are the following:

- **Narrow** — no greater than 30 dB
- **Very Narrow** — no greater than 60 dB
- **Super Narrow** — no greater than 90 dB

The **Presets** list contains a number of interesting presets, including:

- **60 Hz + Harmonics (heavy)** and **60 Hz + Harmonics Removal** — two variants of filters suppressing background components that have the electric power supply frequency (60 Hz) and five harmonics of this frequency
- **DTMF Tones Removal** — a filter that suppresses the spectrum components with frequencies standard for telephone dial tones
- **Ice Cream Truck** — a filter that significantly (by 25 dB) increases the level of spectrum components with frequencies of 1,000 Hz, 1,333 Hz, 1,500 Hz, 2,000 Hz, 2,666 Hz, and 3,000 Hz

The dialog box we're talking about is called **Notch Filter**. The name implies that the filter must suppress certain frequencies and nothing more. However, the **Ice Cream Truck** preset conflicts with this logic, as it doesn't suppress the frequencies, but amplifies them. This led us to the idea that **Notch Filter** has hidden features not mentioned in the user's manual. After a few experiments with the filter, we discovered that the behavior of the filter (whether it attenuates or amplifies the frequency components of the signal) depends on the sign of the parameter entered in the **Attenuation** fields. For example, if you enter 25 dB, the application will interpret this command as: "Attenuate the frequency component by 25 dB". If you enter –25 dB, this will be treated as: "Attenuation by –25 dB", which is equivalent to: "Amplify by 25 dB".

6.2.7. Scientific Filters – *Bessel, Butterworth, and Chebyshev Filters*

The **Effects > Filters > Scientific Filters...** command opens the **Scientific Filters** dialog box, which contains a collection of "theoretical" filters of the following types:

- Bessel filter — the **Bessel** tab
- Butterworth filter — the **Butterworth** tab (Fig. 6.9)

- Chebyshev filter — the **Chebychev 1** and **Chebychev 2** tabs (unfortunately, the developers of Adobe Audition are unaware of the correct spelling of this great Russian mathematician's name)

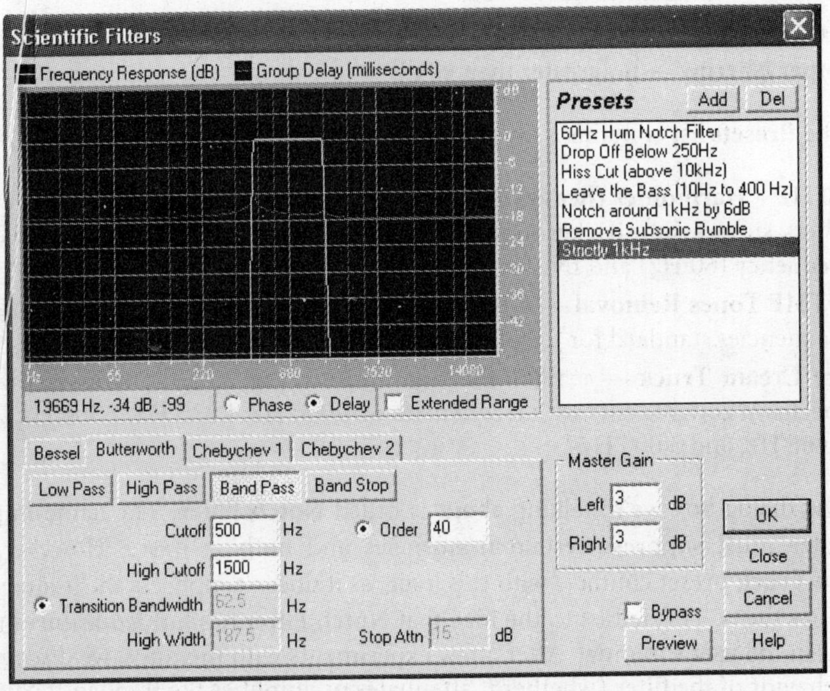

Fig. 6.9. Scientific Filters dialog box, **Butterworth** tab

The properties of these filters are comprehensively described in [3]. Now let's take a look at the interface of the **Scientific Filters** dialog box.

You can see two diagrams on the coordinate plane. One of them (yellow) is the frequency-response curve of the filter, and the other (red) is either the phase-response curve (if the **Phase** radio button is selected) or the frequency-dependence curve of the signal delay in the filter (if the **Delay** radio button is selected).

Below the coordinate plane, there is a field that displays the coordinates of the mouse pointer: the frequency, the frequency-response value, and the phase-response value. The **Extended Range** checkbox is used to switch between two ranges of the frequency-response display. When the checkbox is unchecked, the range of the displayed frequency-response values is from –54 to 12 dB. Otherwise, it is from –120 to 12 dB.

The buttons **Low Pass, High Pass, Band Pass,** and **Band Stop** allow you to select a class for each of the four filters (**Bessel, Butterworth, Chebychev 1**, or **Chebychev 2**):

- **Low Pass**
- **High Pass**
- **Band Pass**
- **Band Stop**

The set of filter parameters is determined by the class and type of the filter. For the **Low Pass** and **High Pass** filters, you can specify only the **Cutoff** frequency. However, for the filters **Band Pass** and **Band Stop**, this parameter means a low cutoff frequency. For the band filters, the high cutoff frequency is specified in the **High Cutoff** field.

For all filter classes except **Bessel**, you should specify four more parameters:

- **Order** — the order of the filter.
- **Transition Bandwidth** — for example, for a band-pass filter, this means a transition between the stop band and the pass band); when this parameter is selected, the filter order is set automatically (and vice versa).
- **High Width** — the high transition bandwidth (for example, for a band-pass filter, this means a transition between the pass band and the stop band); this parameter can be specified only for band filters.
- **Stop Attn** — attenuation of the spectral components in the stop band.

For the **Chebychev 1** and **Chebychev 2** filters, you can specify the maximum ripple of the frequency-response curve in the pass and stop bands: **Pass Ripple** and **Actual Ripple**.

The master gain is specified in the **Master Gain** group (for the left and right channel separately).

The **Preset** list contains seven very interesting presets.

- **60Hz Hum Notch Filter** — a Bessel filter of the second order that is used to suppress the background noise component with frequency 60 Hz. Unlike the similar filters discussed earlier, this one practically doesn't affect the neighboring frequency components.
- **Drop Off Below 250 Hz** — a Butterworth filter of the sixth order that suppresses spectral components with frequencies below 250 Hz.
- **Hiss Cut (above 10 kHz)** — a Chebyshev filter of the sixth order that suppresses spectral components with frequencies above 10 kHz.
- **Leave the Bass (10Hz to 400 Hz)** — a Chebyshev filter of the second order that suppresses all frequencies except those typical for the bass (from 10 to 400 Hz).

- **Notch around 1kHz by 6dB** — a Chebyshev filter of the seventh order that notches components in the nearest neighborhood of the frequency 1 kHz.
- **Remove Subsonic Rumble** — a Butterworth filter of the 18th order that suppresses subsonic spectral components (below 27 Hz).
- **Strictly 1 kHz** — a Butterworth filter of the 40th order whose passband is exactly 1 kHz.

When a filter becomes more complex (its order increases), it becomes possible to implement an almost ideal rectangular frequency-response curve. There will be no distortions of the signal amplitude in the passband of such a filter. However, the phases of the spectral components in the passband of this filter are actually unpredictable. This affects even the timbre of a mono file, to say nothing of a stereo file.

6.2.8. Going on with Our Project

On previous stages of our project, we obtained the file EX05_04.WAV with a reduced noise level. Now, we have to perform frequency filtration to improve the spectrum of the signal stored in the file. Our choice of the filter parameters should be based on the spectral analysis of the signal.

Remember that in *Section 4.3.3* we examined the results of the spectral analysis of the signal stored in the file EX03_02.WAV. Then, we drew the conclusion that all spectral components above 16 kHz are caused by wide-band high-frequency noise and should be attenuated using a filter. The level of low-frequency components with frequencies below 80 Hz (not typical for speech) is also high. This is noise from cars and ventilation appliances that passes through the windows and walls into the room where the recording was made. The results of the spectral analysis of the signal, stored in the EX03_02.WAV file, are likely to come in useful for processing the signal stored in the EX05_04.WAV file, because the EX05_04.WAV file is a part of the EX03_02.WAV file. However, nothing prevents us from making an analysis of the EX05_04.WAV (Fig. 6.10, *a*).

As we supposed, there are no significant differences between the spectrum of the fragment and that of the entire signal. Therefore, we can stick to our plan of filtration. Of the numerous filters available in Adobe Audition, choose **FFT Filter**. Draw a frequency-response curve to attenuate components below 80 Hz and above 14 kHz (Fig. 6.10, *b*).

Use this filter and perform a spectral analysis of the processed signal. The result is shown in Fig. 6.10, *c*. The unwanted spectral components are suppressed. We stored the obtained signal in the EX06_01.WAV file. If you listen to it, you'll find that, compared with EX05_04.WAV, the sound became clearer, and noise was reduced.

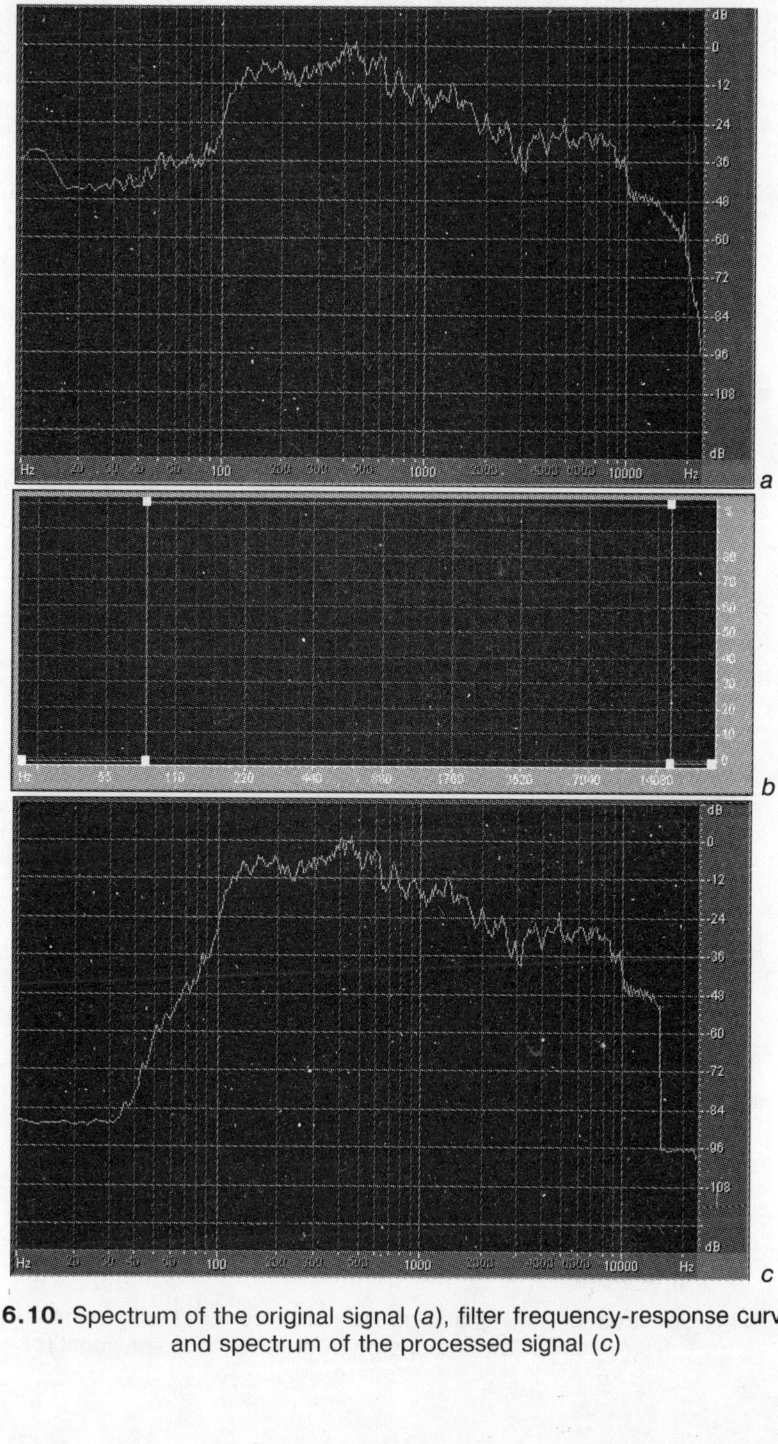

Fig. 6.10. Spectrum of the original signal (*a*), filter frequency-response curve (*b*), and spectrum of the processed signal (*c*)

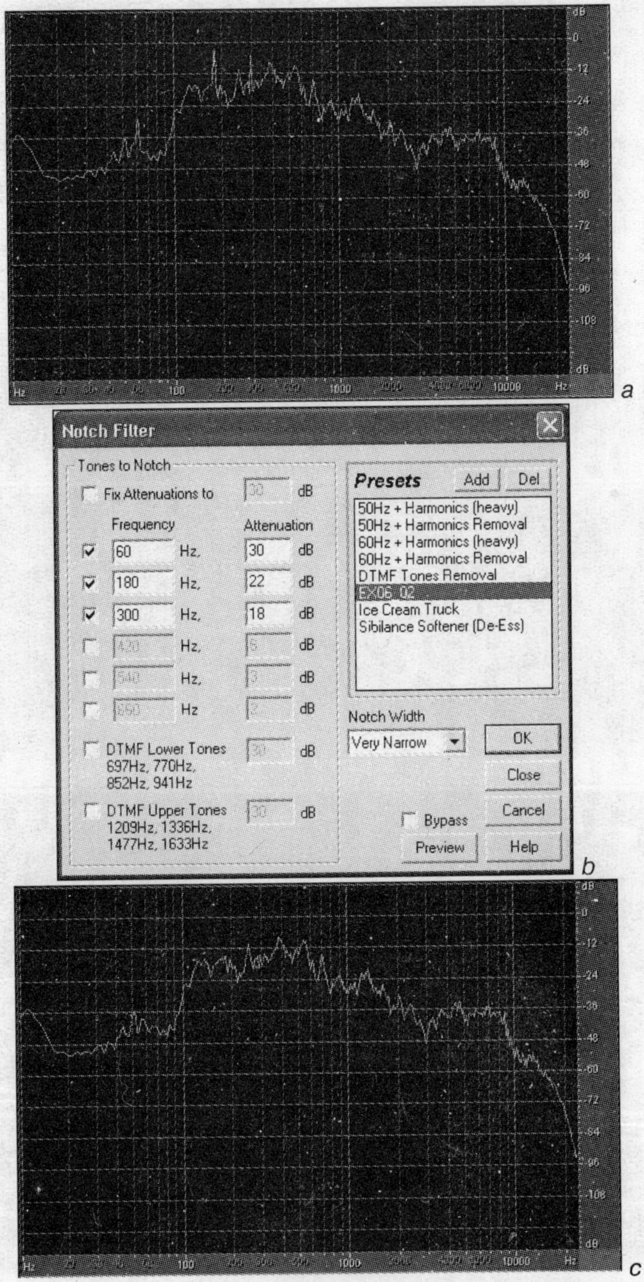

Fig. 6.11. Spectrum of the signal with alternating current background component (*a*), filter settings (*b*), and spectrum of the processed signal (*c*)

volume. The sound seems to become "denser." No wonder: Compression allows you to obtain the growth of the average power of the undistorted signal. In essence, compression is automatic control of amplification. When the signal level becomes too high, the gain is reduced; and when the signal level decreases to the normal value, the initial amplification is returned.

The result of compression depends on a good choice of the values of several main parameters, the most important of which are:

- Threshold
- Compression ratio
- Makeup gain
- Attack time
- Release time

Let's look at these parameters in more detail.

The *threshold* determines the level that, when exceeded by the signal, makes the compressor control the amplification (sometimes, it is said that the compressor is active). While the signal level is below the threshold, the compressor doesn't affect the signal (it is passive or off). The threshold value determines whether the processing will affect just individual peaks, or the signal will be compressed continually.

The *compression ratio* determines the degree of the dynamic range compression of a signal whose level is above the threshold. Numerically, it is equal to the ratio of the signal level at the output of the active compressor to the signal level at its input. For example, a compression ratio of 2:1 means that change in the input signal level by 2 dB causes change in the output signal level by only 1 dB. This ratio is often used, but sometimes you'll have to set greater values. If the compression ratio is set to, say, 20:1 or more, this is actually the limitation mode. This means that if a signal exceeding the set level is supplied to the input, the signal at the output will practically not be amplified. A compression ratio of ∞:1 would correspond to absolute limitation. In practice, however, this result is achieved with ratios greater than 20:1.

The attack time determines how quickly the compressor responds to signals with levels above the threshold. With greater values of the **Attack Time** parameter, the compressor is unlikely to respond to abrupt changes in the input signal level. Peaks will be present at the compressor output. If the value of the **Attack Time** parameter is small, it will be possible almost to exclude signal peaks when its level increases abruptly. However, such a sound may be insufficiently emphasized.

The release time is the time, during which the compressor exits the active state after the signal level falls below the threshold. If the release time is too large, the compressor remains in the active state for longer, and affects the dynamic range even when it is undesirable. This results in a sound pulsation effect noticeable to the ear, because compression doesn't smooth the signal. With a shorter release time, greater smoothing occurs. However, if the output signal level permanently oscillates around the threshold value, the "choking" effect can materialize. Your search for the best release time will be based on looking for a compromise. For instrumental music, it is usually recommended that a release time of about 500 msec be chosen as a starting point for finer adjustments. This corresponds to an interval between two bars for a tempo of 120 quarters per minute.

A *makeup gain* can be necessary to compensate for signal decay that can take place with certain types of dynamic processing. For example, if you limit the signal at the level of –5 dB, its dynamic range will become narrower, and the sound will become quieter. In such a situation, gaining the signal by 5 dB can be useful.

The perception of music depends on the dynamic range, because the dynamics allow a musician to convey the emotional contents. If you completely smooth the dynamics and make an even, average level, you'll obtain music that will be uninteresting to listen to.

An inexperienced singer usually makes significant variations in volume. As the result, some words are lost under the accompaniment, while others are very loud. This is why compression is always used during vocal recording.

If a singer encounters problems with hissing sounds, changing the type of the microphone or its location may improve the situation. If this doesn't work, the compressor can be used in the *de-esser* mode during mixing. In this mode, whistling and hissing consonants are removed from the vocal part.

If you use an external equalizer and filtration to suppress all low frequencies at the control channel input, the compressor will respond to only high-frequency sounds. In this case, the signal controlling the compressor will be made up of only those components of the original signal that whistle and hiss. This is the operating principle of a de-esser. The frequency components that must be influenced are chosen by ear. The equalizer inserted into the channel that controls the compressor must amplify frequencies within a range from 4 to 10 kHz. However, you'll have to find an exact requency-response curve. To do this, first listen to the audio signal without compression by passing the signal through an equalizer and adjusting its filters until the whistling sound is heard best. Parametric equalizers are suitable for this purpose.

Adobe Audition's virtual dynamic processing device has a filter that allows you to implement a de-esser. A few de-essers are included in the presets that come with the application.

If you select an equalizer frequency of about 50 Hz, it will help you to eliminate unpleasant sounds caused by plosive consonants from vocal recording. (The worst of the plosive consonants is "p.") However, it would be better to diminish these sounds at the recording stage with a microphone with acoustic filters or a cross-hatched screen, rather than try to correct things during mixing.

7.2. *Dynamic Range Processing* Virtual Dynamic Processing Device

Adobe Audition provides two virtual dynamic processing devices:

- ❒ **Dynamic Range Processing**
- ❒ **Hard Limiting**

In this book, we consider only **Dynamic Range Processing,** because you'll need this tool for work with the project. You can read about **Hard Limiting** in [3].

The **Dynamic Range Processing** dialog box (Fig. 7.1) is opened with the **Effects > Amplitude > Dynamics Processing** command. The dialog box is an exterior, visible component of universal virtual dynamic processing. Depending on the parameter values selected, it can be a gate, a compressor, an expander, a limiter, or a de-esser. The type of processing and the values of the parameters can be specified either graphically or digitally.

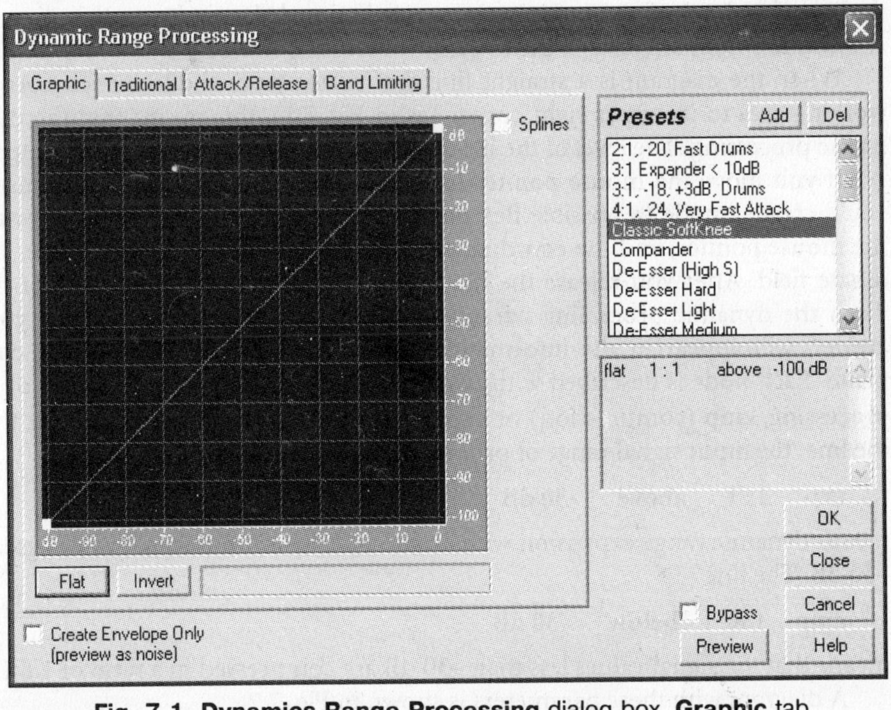

Fig. 7.1. Dynamics Range Processing dialog box, **Graphic** tab

There are four tabs in the **Dynamics Range Processing** dialog box:

- **Graphic** — used for graphically changing the type and parameters of the dynamic processing
- **Traditional** — used for the same purpose as the **Graphic** tab, but the parameters are controlled in a traditional fashion (digitally)
- **Attack/Release** — used for selecting parameters that affect switching the dynamic processing on and off
- **Band Limiting** — allows you to select the frequency range that should be processed

7.2.1. The Graphic *Tab*

Let's look at the **Graphic** tab of the **Dynamics Range Processing** dialog box, shown in Fig. 7.1.

A large part of this tab is taken by a coordinate field.

The value (in decibels) of the input signal level is plotted on the horizontal axis, and the value of the output signal level (also in decibels) is plotted on the vertical axis. Thus, the diagram shows how the level of the output (processed) signal corresponds to the specified level of the input (unprocessed) signal. Deep down, this diagram is an amplitude-response curve of the dynamic processing device.

When the diagram is a straight line that passes from the lower left corner of the working area to its upper right corner (as in Fig. 7.1), this means that there is no dynamic processing. The level of the input signal is equal to the level of the output signal.

If you move the mouse pointer to the diagram and click the left mouse button, you'll create a node (a possible flex point). Keeping the mouse button pressed, move the mouse pointer, and the coordinates of the node will be displayed under the coordinate field. After you release the mouse button, you'll fix the position of the node. Then the dynamic processing parameters corresponding to the diagram you've just created will appear in the information field located to the right of the coordinate plane. Each node is described with two lines. Each line begins with a type of dynamic processing, **cmp** (compression) or **exp** (expansion), followed by a ratio. At the end of the line, the input signal range of processing is displayed. For example,

exp 2:1 above -30 dB

means dynamic range expansion with a ratio of 2:1 for input signal values greater than –30 dB. The line

cmp 1.8:1 below -30 dB

means that the signal values less than –30 dB are compressed in a ratio of 1.8:1.

A diagram with these parameters is shown in Fig. 7.2.

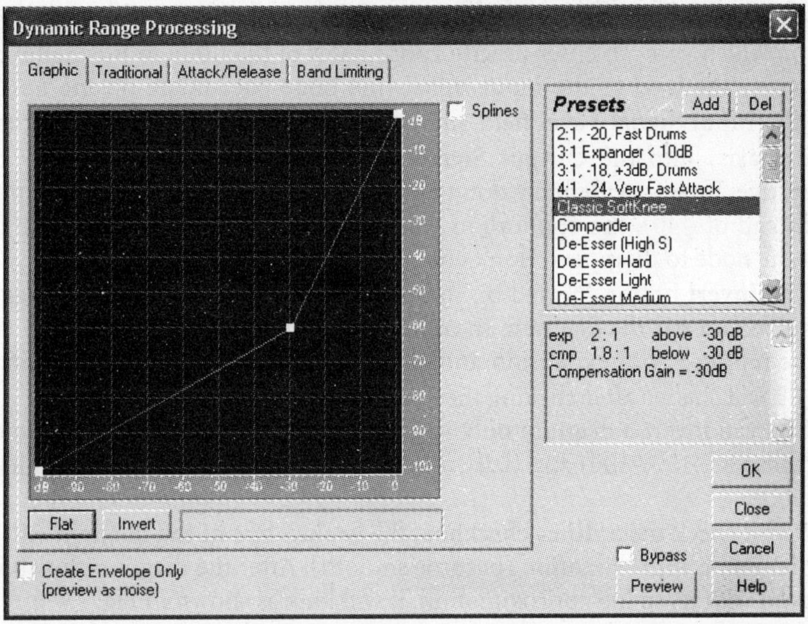

Fig. 7.2. Sample diagram

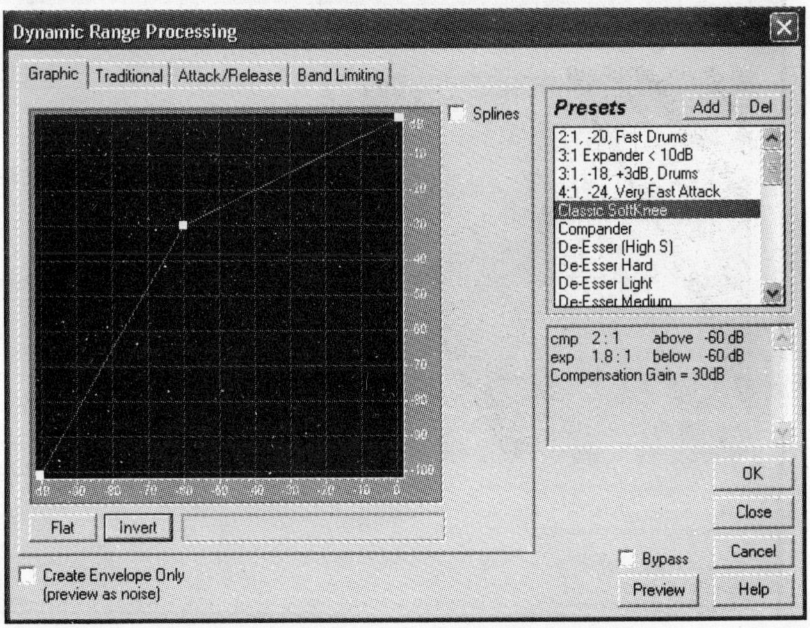

Fig. 7.3. Result of clicking the **Invert** button

A double left click (or a single right click) on a node opens the **Edit Point** dialog box, in which you can enter precise coordinates of the node in the digital form. To do this, enter the level of the input signal (the node coordinate on the horizontal axis) into the **Input Signal Level** field and enter the output level (the node control on the vertical axis) into the **Output Signal Level** field. The valid range for these values is negative. If you accidentally don't enter the "-" (minus) sign (for example, you enter 40 instead of –40), the application will substitute the invalid value with zero. If you want the node to disappear, don't enter anything into these fields.

The **Invert** button located on the **Graphic** tab of the **Dynamic Range Processing** dialog box inverts the diagram. In other words, on the resulting diagram compression will be replaced with expansion and vice versa. Fig. 7.3 shows how the diagram from Fig. 7.2 will change after clicking the **Invert** button.

You can invert a diagram only when it passes between two corner points with the coordinates (–100,–100) and (0,0), and each node is located higher than its nearest left neighbor.

If you check the **Splines** checkbox, the broken line of the diagram will be replaced with its spline approximation (become smooth). After the diagram shown in Fig. 7.3 is replaced with its spline approximation, it will look as shown in Fig. 7.4.

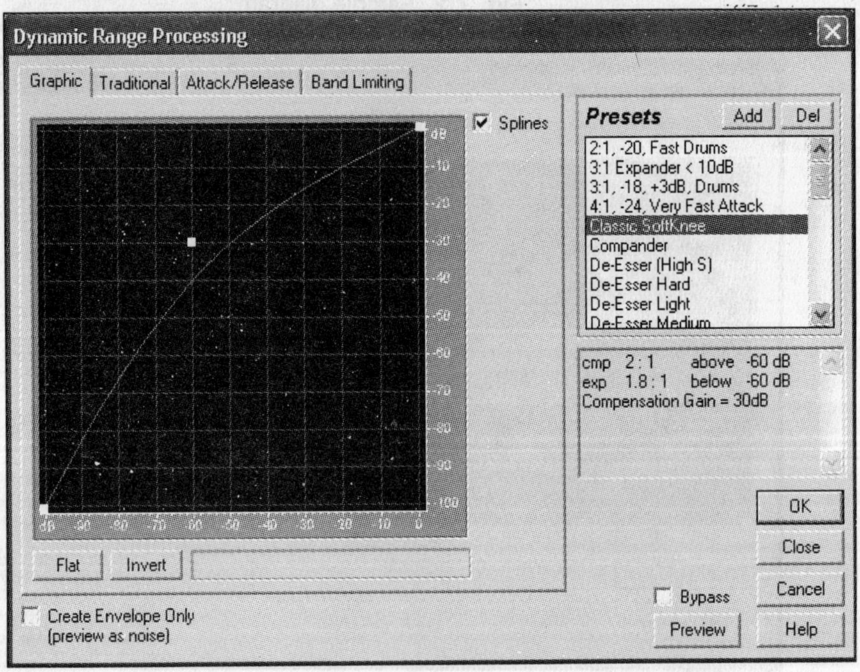

Fig. 7.4. Diagram with the **Splines** checkbox checked

You should be aware that not only the diagram shape changes, but also the actual input-value dependence of the output value.

The **Flat** button returns the diagram to its default shape (makes it a straight line; all nodes are removed).

If you check the **Create Envelope Only** checkbox and click the **OK** button, you'll create the waveform's amplitude envelope. When working on our project, we don't need the envelope, and so will not discuss it here. If you are interested in it, refer to [3].

7.2.2. *The* Traditional *Tab*

The **Traditional** tab of the **Dynamics Range Processing** dialog box contains the same information as the **Graphic** tab. However, here the information is in the digital form, rather than graphical.

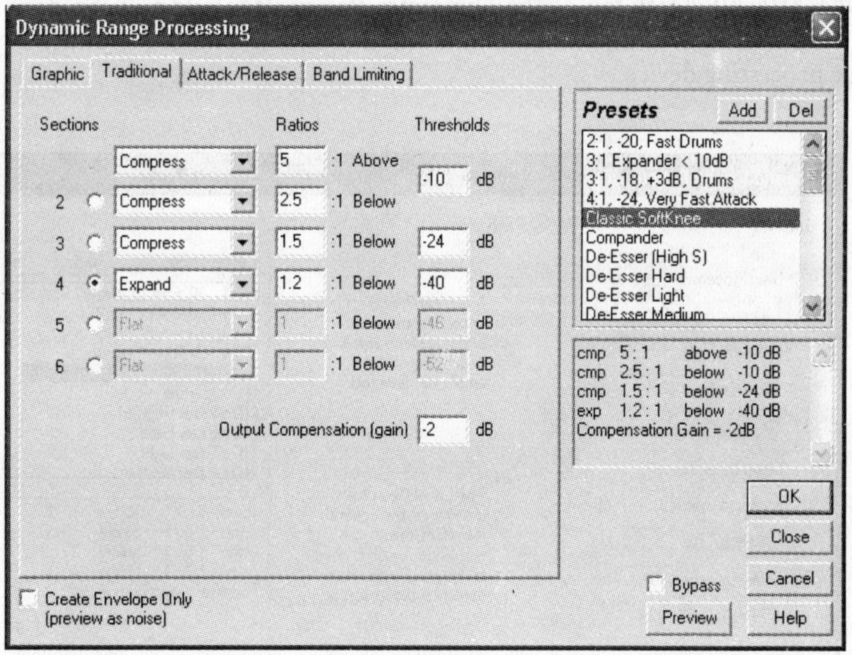

Fig. 7.5. Dynamics Range Processing dialog box, **Traditional** tab

The radio buttons numbered from 2 to 6 correspond to the nodes on the diagram. However, there can be more than six nodes.

There is a drop-down list to the right of each radio button. Each list displays the type of the dynamic range processing on the diagram portion located higher than the corresponding node. The contents of these lists can be edited by selecting one of three kinds of dynamic range processing: **Expand**, **Compress**, and **Flat** (in the latter case, nothing changes).

The fields of the **Ratios** column display the values of the dynamic range transformation ratios. They can be changed both by editing the input fields and by changing the angles of the lines that make up the diagram.

In the fields of the **Thresholds** column, you can edit the values of the threshold (the levels to which the diagram nodes correspond).

The **Output Compensation (gain)** field allows you to change the output gain to compensate for changes in the signal level during processing it with the effect.

7.2.3. The Attack/Release *Tab*

On the **Attack/Release** tab of the **Dynamics Range Processing** dialog box, you can edit the parameters of the amplification and detection channels [3] of the virtual dynamic processing device.

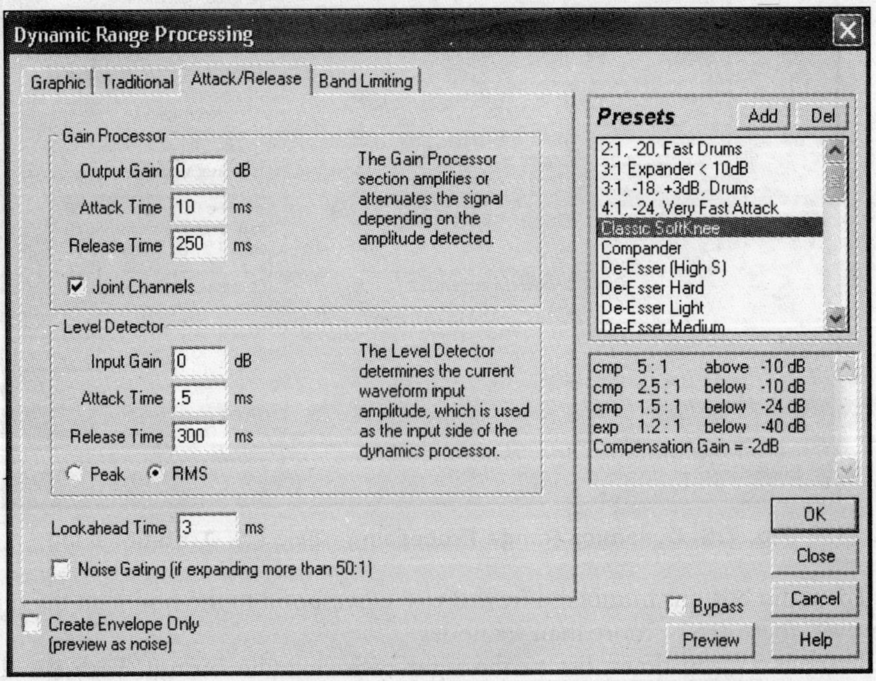

Fig. 7.6. Dynamics Range Processing dialog box, **Attack/Release** tab

The **Gain Processor** group contains the **Joint Channels** checkbox and the following input fields:

- **Output Gain**
- **Attack Time (Out)**
- **Release Time**

The **Level Detector** group contains the following input fields:

- **Input Gain**
- **Attack Time**
- **Release Time**

Using the **Peak** and **RMS** radio buttons, you can select the type of the amplitude detector, either peak or root-mean-square [3].

In the **Lookahead Time** field, enter the time interval, by which the dynamic processing device must look ahead for the appearance of an abrupt signal drop.

7.2.4. The Band Limiting *Tab*

On the **Band Limiting** tab of the **Dynamics Range Processing** dialog box, you can specify the limiting frequencies for the processing range (**Low Cutoff** and **High Cutoff**).

The options of this tab make it possible to process individual spectrum components of the signal, rather than the whole signal. For example, with the parameter values shown in Fig. 7.7, dynamic processing will be done only within the frequency range typical to whistling sounds in speech. This is how a virtual de-esser is implemented.

In the list of presets of the **Dynamics Range Processing** dialog box, you can find implementations of all useful dynamic processing methods. Below is a brief description of them:

- **De-Esser (High S)** — suppresses whistling sounds; compresses signals with levels greater than –30 dB (with the 3:1 ratio) in the frequency range between 5.5 kHz and 14 kHz).
- **De-Esser Light** — suppresses whistling sounds; compresses signals with levels greater than –24 dB (with the 1.5:1 ratio) in the frequency range between 4 kHz and 12 kHz).
- **Gate That Compressor! (-50 Thr)** — is a complex dynamic processing that combines a gate, expander, and compressor; it cuts off noises, amplifiers quiet sounds, and muffles loud ones. It can be useful for improving the quality of recordings on magnetic tapes.

- **Noise Gate @ 10dB** — compresses signals with a level less than –19.6 dB (with the 18.7:1 ratio); expands the dynamic range of signals with levels from –19.6 dB to –10 dB (in a ratio of 8.93:1).

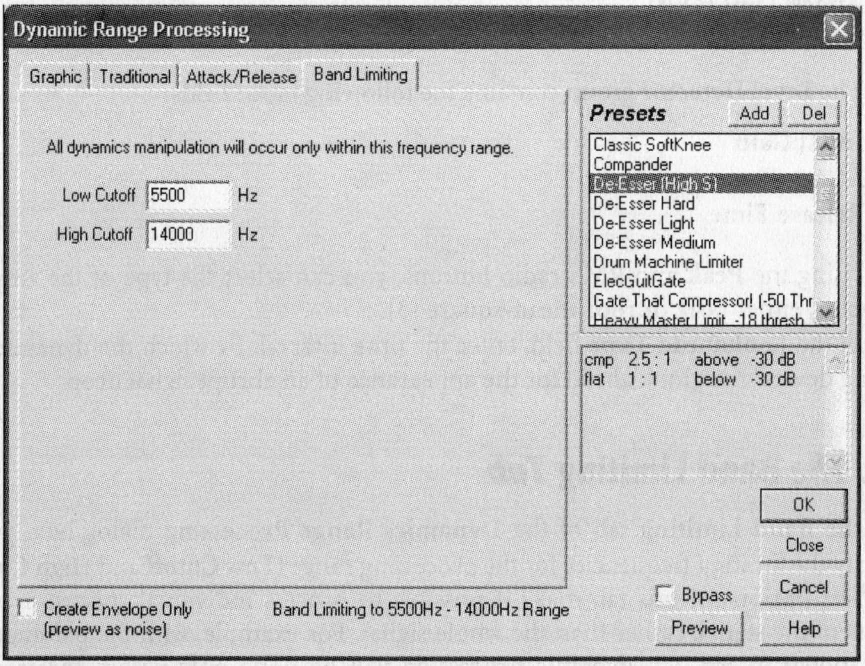

Fig. 7.7. Dynamics Range Processing dialog box; **Band Limiting** tab

Here, we don't need to worry about the time parameters of the virtual gain processor and level detector, to make it easier for you to understand the presets. You can find the time parameters on the **Attack/Release** tab.

7.3. Going on with Our Project

During the previous stages of our project, we obtained the EX06_01.WAV file, in which the noise is reduced and unwanted components of the signal spectrum are attenuated with filtration. At this stage, it doesn't matter that irrelevant sounds can be heard in the recording when the narrator inhales. The file will be split into separate phrases later, and the unwanted sounds can be deleted then. On the other hand, dynamic signal processing is next up. We'll have to select tentative values of the parameters and then adjust them by controlling the results aurally. The irrelevant sounds we mentioned earlier can significantly hamper this, because the dynamic range processing device will take them into account. Therefore, it is reasonable to eliminate these sounds before the dynamic processing. In fact, we did this and saved the results in the EX07_01.WAV file.

Earlier, examining the statistical properties of the signal (the original take stored in the file EX04_01.WAV) led us to conclude that the average level of the signal was low, and the speech would be quieter than a musical background taken, say, from a CD (see *Section 4.2*). This is why the signal should be compressed and then amplified. We also said that one of the stages of dynamic processing could be a threshold noise reduction (with the initial threshold about –55 dB). As follows from an examination of the histogram (see *Section 4.2.2*), a good result can be obtained by limiting the signal to –9 dB and then amplifying it by 9 dB. However, the dynamic and noise properties of the signal saved in the EX07_01.WAV file differ from those of the original signal because of the previous processings. This is why it would be reasonable to perform a statistical analysis of the contents of the EX07_01.WAV file. Load this file and select the **Analyze > Statistics** command to open the **Waveform Statistics** dialog box.

The data on the **General** tab indicates that the signal still has a low average level (the value of the **Total RMS Power** parameter is about –22 dB), and average level of the signal peaks also remained almost the same (**Maximum RMS Power** = –9.92 dB). An examination of the histogram allows us to conclude that the noise reduction has increased the dynamic range (samples with levels about –78 dB have appeared). At this stage, it would be reasonable to use the following types of dynamic processing:

- Dynamic range compression with the threshold of –20 dB and in a ratio of 1.5:1
- Threshold noise reduction (with a tentative threshold between –55 dB and –50 dB)

When we implemented this plan, we found that the threshold noise reduction caused a "choking" effect: The noise level was still high, and useful fragments of speech were cut off at the threshold of –50 dB. Nevertheless, this direction of the processing had been chosen correctly. We had to experiment a little while controlling the changes in the sound of the fragment. We managed to decrease the noise while simultaneously increasing the subjective volume by combining compression of the signal components with high levels and the expansion at lower levels. We obtained the desired result after we used the **Splines** option and shaped a smooth curve for the complex dynamic processing shown in Fig. 7.8.

The obtained signal was saved in the EX07_02.WAV file. Since no compensation for decreasing the signal level was done during the dynamic processing, we additionally normalized the signal to the –1 dB level and saved the result in the NSINC1.WAV file.

In summary, the NSINC1.WAV file was obtained from the file EX03_02.WAV. The following operations were performed: Based on a comprehensive analysis, we selected the best take; it was saved in a separate file; the signal saved in this file was subjected to noise reduction, filtration, and dynamic processing; and a few short fragments with unwanted sounds between phrases were cut from the signal. We also performed similar operations on the EX03_04.WAV file and saved the result in the file NSINC2.WAV.

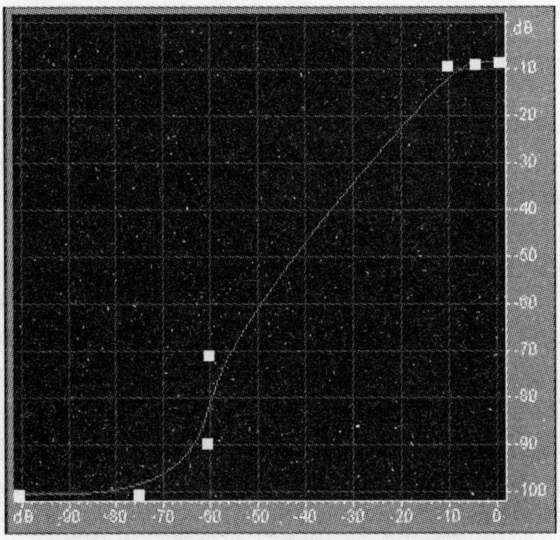

Fig. 7.8. Smooth processing characteristic

As for the other original files, EX03_01.WAV, EX03_03.WAV, and EX03_05.WAV, we performed the same operations, but without cutting the unwanted sounds between phrases. The point is that this material must be used in the project synchronously with the recorded video, so we mustn't change time intervals between phrases and words. "Extra" sounds should be replaced with silence by selecting the fragments that contain them one-by-one and by using the **Effects > Silence** command. The results of processing the files EX03_01.WAV, EX03_03.WAV, and EX03_05.WAV were saved in the files SINC1.WAV, SINC2.WAV, and SINC3.WAV, respectively. The listed files are also stored in the EXAMPLES\CH_07 folder.

Chapter 8

Built-In Effects

Adobe Audition possesses a powerful toolkit for creating effects. The number of effects that can be obtained with this editor is tremendous. This chapter will look at effects based on signal delay. The **Effects > Delay Effects** menu includes commands that open the dialog boxes of corresponding effects: **Chorus, Delay, Dynamic Delay, Echo, Echo Chamber, Flanger, Full Reverb, Multitap Delay, QuickVerb, Reverb**, and **Sweeping Phaser**. A comprehensive description of all these effects is given in [3]. For reasons of space, here we have to omit descriptions of effects that are unlikely to be used for human voice processing, because they might make speech unintelligible. These are **Chorus, Flanger**, and **Sweeping Phaser**.

Note that it is too early to process our project files with these effects. This should be done when the work with the track containing the narrator's voice is completed, and the fragments of the recording (both synchronous with the video and asynchronous) are put in the correct order. You could process these fragments individually, but in this case, you would have to remember the parameters of the effects. If the parameters differ, the acoustic environment around the sound will be different in different fragments.

Nevertheless, we'll give you an idea of how our file would sound if we applied some of the available effects to it in turn.

8.1. Introducing *Delay* and *Echo* Effects

The need for the delay effect emerged with the beginning of stereo usage. The very nature of a human ear implies that in most cases, the brain receives two audio signals at different times. If the sound source is in front of the listener, i.e., on a line perpendicular to the line connecting his or her ears, the direct sound from the source will reach both ears at the same time. In the other cases, the distances from the sound source to the ears are different, so one of the ears perceives the sound first.

Delay is first of all used when a recording of a voice or acoustic musical instrument using only one microphone is "inserted" into a stereo composition. This effect is the basis of techniques for creating stereo recordings. However, delay can be also used for one-time repeating of certain sounds. What delay must be selected? The answer to this is determined by a number of factors. First, you should take into account aesthetic criteria, the artistic goal, and common sense. The delay time for the main signal and a copy of it to be distinguished is less for short and abrupt sounds than for longer sounds. The delay can be greater for compositions performed at a slow tempo than for those performed quickly.

If there is a certain volumetric ratio of direct and delayed signals, the psychoacoustic effect of changing the apparent position of the sound source on the stereo panorama may occur. Indeed, a piano "saltation" is a very difficult thing to justify from both the aesthetic point of view and from the point of view of reality, when the real piano sound is to be performed. Like any effect, delay should be applied within reasonable limits.

This effect is implemented with devices that can make a delay of an acoustic or electric signal. Most often, this is a digital delay line. Of course, before using the digital delay line, the signal must be first converted into digital form. After the copy of the signal passes the delay line, digital-to-analog conversion is done. The original signal and the delayed copy of it can be either separately directed to the different stereo channels or mixed together in various proportions. The total signal can be directed either to one of the stereo channels or to both.

In sound editors, delay is implemented programmatically (mathematically) by changing the relative numeration of the samples of the original signal and the copy of it.

Virtual delays, like their hardware prototypes, always have controls for the depth and the modulation frequency of the delayed signal, as well as a control of the feedback factor. The signal is sent from the output back to the delay line. The decay time is set using the feedback control. To turn a one-time repetition into a real echo, you should increase the feedback factor. As a rule, both actual and virtual devices have a control, using which you can find the delay time corresponding to the tempo of your composition.

8.1.1. A Simple Delay Effect

Use the **Effects > Delay Effects > Delay** command to open the **Delay** effect dialog box (Fig. 8.1).

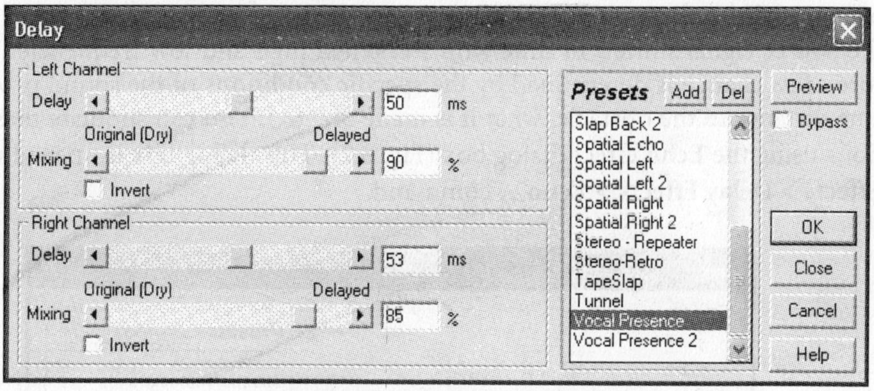

Fig. 8.1. Delay effect dialog box

The **Left Channel** and **Right Channel** groups contain the delay setting controls for each stereo channel.

You can specify the delay time in milliseconds with the **Delay** control, or directly in the field to the right of it.

Similar interface elements enable you to specify the level of the delayed signal mixed to the source signal as a percentage. These are marked **Mixing**. The state of the **Invert** checkbox determines whether the phase of the mixed signal is to be inverted.

Traditionally in Adobe Audition, there is a list of presets (**Presets**) in this effect's dialog box. By clicking the **Add** button, you can open a dialog box, in which you can specify the name of a new preset. To delete a selected preset from the list, click the **Del** button.

8.1.2. The Echo Effect

The next effect, which is more complex, is **Echo**. The main difference between this effect and a simple delay is that the delayed copies of the signal are subject to additional processing: Their spectrum is changed. Sound processed with the **Echo** effect is more natural than sound processed with the **Delay** effect. In nature, an echo is produced as a result of sound waves repeatedly bouncing off obstacles (e.g., off houses, walls, mountains, etc.). Various spectral components of sound are reflected from the obstacles in various ways. The lower the frequency (the longer the wavelength), the easier it is for the wave to overcome a obstacle by going around it. On the other hand, it is very difficult for a high-frequency wave to overcome even a simple obstacle. Such a wave does not go through the obstacle, but is reflected off it and partially absorbed, turning into heat energy. However, you should not ignore the fact that high-frequency sound waves attenuate faster than those with a low frequency do when propagated in the air. In conclusion, we can surmise that an echo contains the source signal shifted in time with weakened high and low frequencies. The nature of its change is determined by the specific conditions of the sound propagation (the distance to the obstacle, what it is made of, etc.). You can simulate these conditions using the **Echo** effect dialog box (Fig. 8.2). This dialog box is opened using the **Effects > Delay Effects > Echo...** command.

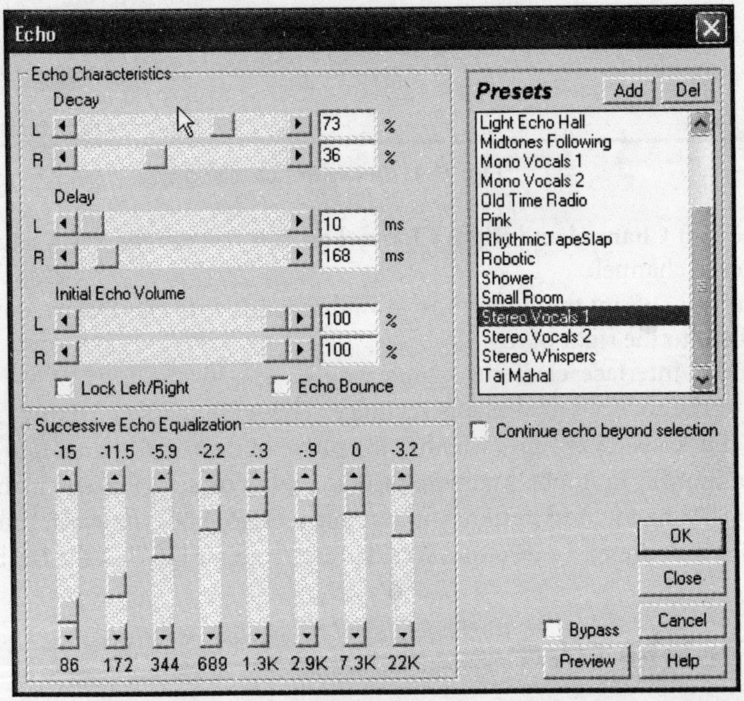

Fig. 8.2. Echo effect dialog box

The **Decay** control is used to specify the level of the delayed signal (as a percentage relative to the source signal), the echo level and, consequently, the time of its existence. The **Delay** control is used to specify the time (in milliseconds), for which the signal will be delayed. The **Initial Echo Volume** control is used to specify the level, with which the echo will be mixed to the source signal.

The **Successive Echo Equalization** group is an equalizer you can use to change the spectrum of the delayed signal.

Check the **Continue echo beyond selection** checkbox if you want to retain a gradual attenuation of the echo outside of the selected fragment of the waveform.

If the **Lock Left/Right** checkbox is checked, the corresponding controls of the left and right channels are combined.

If the **Echo Bounce** checkbox is checked, the echo will be emphasized.

The **Presets** group contains a list of presets for various types of echoes.

The file EX08_01.WAV contains an example of the signal obtained after the file NSINC1.WAV was processed with the **Echo** effect (the **Stereo Whispers** preset).

8.1.3. The Dynamic Delay Effect with Dynamically Controlled Parameters

The **Effects > Delay Effects > Dynamic Delay** command opens the **Dynamic Delay** effect dialog box (Fig. 8.3).

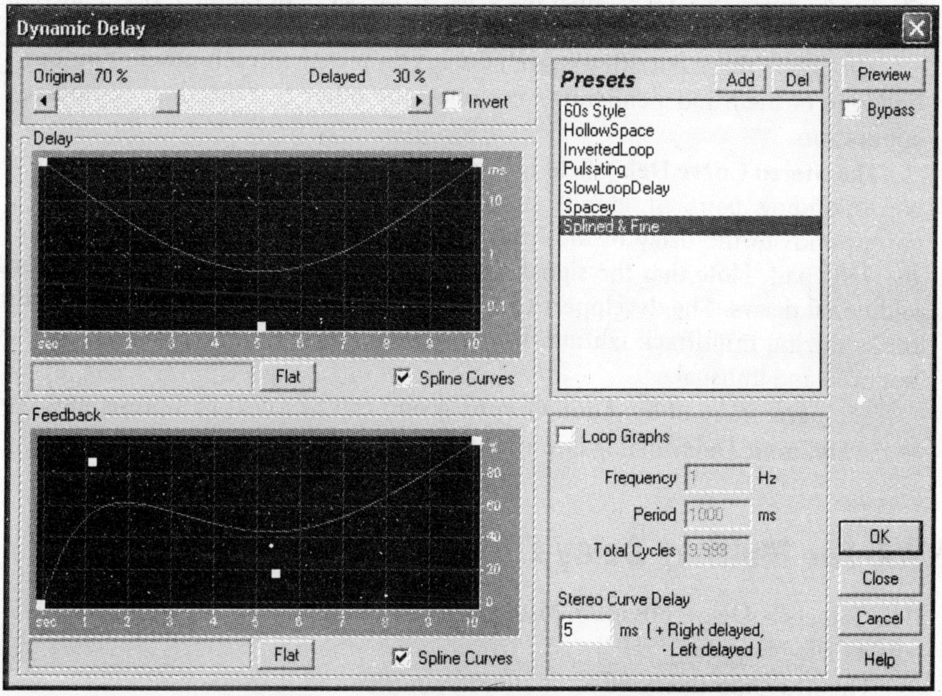

Fig. 8.3. Dynamic Delay effect dialog box

The **Dynamic Delay** dialog box implements a delay, but the controls available make it possible to dynamically (using the curves) change the values of the two most important parameters of the effect: the actual delay (the **Delay** coordinate plane) and the feedback ratio (the **Feedback** coordinate plane).

There is no need to describe the purpose of the **Original — Delayed** slider, the **Spline Curves** and **Invert** checkboxes, or the list of presets: You encountered these controls many times in the dialog boxes of other effects, as well as when changing the shapes of graphs.

It is worthwhile, however, to look at the peculiarities of the effect's operation with different states of the **Loop Graphs** checkbox. If it is unchecked, the graphs illustrate the change of the delay and feedback ratio over the entire selected fragment of the waveform. If the **Loop Graphs** checkbox is checked, the graphs relate to a single loop. Here, you work with a fragment whose time parameters are specified in the fields of the **Loop Graphs** group:

- **Frequency** — frequency of the cycle repetition
- **Period** — period of the cycle repetition
- **Total Cycles** — total number of cycles in the selected fragment of the waveform

The above three parameters are closely connected to each other. You can specify only one of them independently (any one); the other two are then computed by the application.

The **Stereo Curve Delay** field is used to specify the value of the time shift between corresponding pairs of graphs in the right and left channels. A positive value corresponds to the delay of the "right" pair of graphs, and a negative one to that of the "left" pair. Note that the signals of the right or left channels do not undergo any additional delays. The developers recommend that you apply this method to different tracks during multitrack editing. If you do, the effect will turn out to be very pronounced and unusual.

The parameters of the **Loop Graphs** group can be saved in a preset and displayed in the **Dynamic Delay** dialog box after the preset is loaded.

8.1.4. The Multitap Delay *Effect*

The **Effects > Delay Effects > Multitap Delay** command opens the **Multitap Delay** effect dialog box (Fig. 8.4).

The **Multitap Delay** effect is the combination of a delay, echo, filter, and reverberation (see *Section 8.2*).

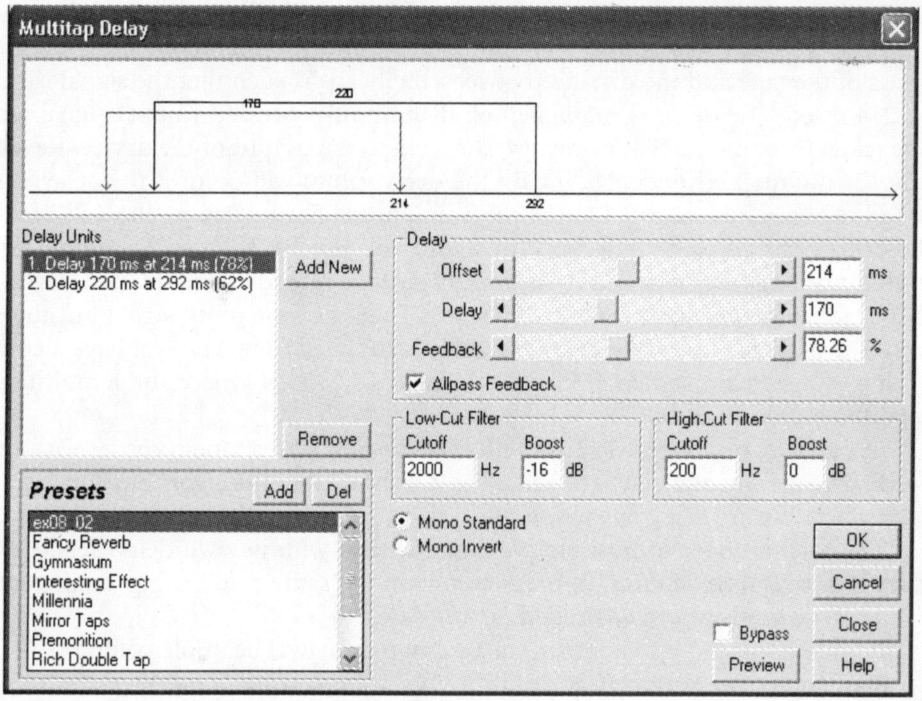

Fig. 8.4. Multitap Delay effect dialog box

The diagram in the upper part of the **Multitap Delay** dialog box shows the algorithm of sound processing with the effect. The algorithm is made up of cycles. Each cycle on the graph corresponds to a line with arrow. The figures shown at the beginning of the line mean the shift of the echo relative to the source sound. The figures above the line indicate the signal delay in the feedback loop.

The algorithm of the effect shown in Fig. 8.4 consists of two cycles. For example, in the first of them, a single delay is done by delaying the signal by 214 msec, and the reverberation occurs due to the delayed signal being fed into the feedback loop with a delay time of 170 msec.

This is rather vague, isn't it? This is not particularly surprising, since the effect itself is very complex. An analogy with a classical tape-recorder reverber is helpful in understanding it. The principle of creating an echo signal in tape-recorder reverbers is as follows. The original signal is recorded on the tape using the magnetic recording head. When this point of the magnetic tape reaches the playback head after a certain time interval, the signal is read. This signal, with decreased amplitude, is sent for recording via the feedback loop. This creates an effect of repeated sound reflection with a gradual decay. The sound quality is determined by the parameters of the tape recorder.

If there are two magnetic heads in the reverber, one for recording and the other for playback, you can implement very simple delay and reverberation. Let's say that the speed of the tape and the distance between the heads is such that the signal is delayed by 214 msec. The delay is implemented if the non-processed (input) signal and the one taken from the playback head are supplied to the output of the device. Reverberation (or multitap echo, depending on the delay value) will occur if the delayed signal (of a lower level) is returned to the recording head. The multitap echo will occur, but the delay between each "reflection" of sound will also be 214 msec. Suppose that one more recording head is added to the imaginary tape recorder, and the tape passes from this head to the playback head in 170 msec. Then, not the input signal but the signal from the playback head (the delayed signal) is supplied to it. You will have a complete analog of the circuit shown in Fig. 8.4: a single delay of 214 msec and a multitap echo repeated every 170 msec.

In other words, one cycle of the effect corresponds to a tape recorder with two recording heads and one playback head. Fig. 8.4 shows that the algorithm consists of two cycles; here, we are using five heads (including one recording head).

The total number of possible cycles is 10, each with its own delay, feedback, and filtration parameter settings. In order to obtain the same result using a tape recorder, 29 magnetic heads would be needed.

If one cycle is put into another, the multitap delay will be implemented.

Select a variant of the effect circuit from the **Presets** list. The **Delay Units** list will then contain the parameters of each delay cycle displayed. Using the controls of the **Delay** group or the corresponding fields, you can adjust the following parameters of each cycle:

- **Offset** — offset relative to the source sound
- **Delay** — delay in the feedback loop
- **Feedback** — ratio of the feedback

Changing the positions of the first two controls is displayed in the cycle graphs. Note that all controls, fields, and options control the current cycle parameters: the one currently selected in the **Delay Units** list.

You can add another line to this list by clicking the **Add New** button. If there was at least one cycle, the newly created one will have the same parameters. If no cycles existed before clicking the **Add New** button, click any element of the **Delay** group so that the cycle graph appears.

In order to delete a cycle, select it in the **Delay Units** list and click the **Remove** button.

Check the **Allpass Feedback** checkbox to prevent a direct component from appearing in the processed signal.

The **Low-Cut Filter** and **High-Cut Filter** groups contain fields that you can use to enter the cutoff frequency (**Cutoff**) and amplification (**Boost**) of the filter that cuts off the lower frequencies (**Low-Cut Filter**), and the one that cuts off the higher frequencies (**High-Cut Filter**), respectively. If, however, you enter values greater than zero in the **Boost** fields, the corresponding frequencies will not be cut off but amplified. We do not recommend that you do this, since a phenomenon similar to self-excitement in an acoustic system may occur: The level of each subsequent delayed signal will be higher than that of the previous one. Sometimes, to obtain an effect of a continuous or even increasing echo with a specific timbre, you might want to enter positive values in the **Boost** fields. However, to simulate the self-excitement of the acoustic system, you can simply enter a **Feedback** parameter value greater than 100%.

Use **Left Only**, **Right Only**, **Discrete Stereo**, and the other radio buttons to select the source channels to be processed: left, right, both, or combinations thereof for various signal processing algorithms (such as addition, subtraction, or inversion).

It is useless to try to describe in words the processing algorithms provided in the **Presets** list.

The file EX08_02.WAV contains an example of the signal obtained after the file NSINC1.WAV was processed with the **Multitap Delay** effect with the parameter values that are shown in Fig. 8.4.

8.2. Introducing the *Reverb* Effect

Reverberation is one of the most interesting and popular audio effects. Essentially, the original audio signal is mixed with copies of itself delayed for various time intervals. In this sense, reverberation resembles delay. The difference is that the number of delayed copies of the signal can be much greater for reverberation than for delay. Theoretically, the number of copies can be infinite. In addition, the greater the delay time of a copy during reverberation, the less the amplitude (volume) of the copy. The effect depends on the time intervals between the copies of the signals and the rate of decreasing their volumes. If the intervals between the copies are small, the reverberation effect proper is achieved. An impression of a large resonant room appears. The sounds of musical instruments become saturated, "three-dimensional," and have a rich timbre. The singers' voices become more melodic, and flaws become less noticeable.

If the intervals between copies are large (more than 100 msec), it would be more correct to speak not of reverberation but an echo effect. The intervals between the sounds become distinguishable. The sounds stop merging and seem to be reflected from remote obstacles.

For example, the primary audio signal emitted by the acoustic system is a sharp pulse. The acoustic system is on the stage of an auditorium. The direct sound reaches listeners' ears first. This signal reaches the listeners by the shortest route, so it has more energy than the other signals. The direct signal carries only the information on the position of the source to the right or left of the listener.

The earlier (primary) reflections reach the listener with some delay. This component of the sound field undergoes one or two reflections from the surfaces (the walls, floor, and ceiling). When interacting with these surfaces, the sound wave is not only reflected, but it also loses some of its energy, which heats these surfaces. Therefore, the strength of the primary reflections is less than that of the direct signal (but not by much). The primary reflections are heard as quite audible echo signals. The time lags between them are quite large, since the difference in the distances that the signals travel to reach the listener is also large. For example, the wave may be reflected from the side or rear wall. It is quite possible that some of the waves related to the primary reflections will undergo not one but several such reflections. The early reflections contain information not only on the performer's location, but also on the size of the auditorium. It is early reflections that contribute the most to the impression of the size of the acoustics of the auditorium. The early reflections are considered copies of the primary signal that lag behind the direct signal by no more than 60 msec.

The secondary and following (late) reflections are sound waves reflected repeatedly from each surface. As the number of reflections grows, their strength is considerably reduced. In addition, the sound spectrum is changed. Because of the difference in the reflecting surfaces and the materials that they are made of, the different spectral components of the signal are reflected differently: Some of them are absorbed more intensively, and so are attenuated more quickly.

As the number of secondary reflections grows, they are dispersed and become more numerous. Gradually, they stop being perceived as separate sounds and merge into one gradually attenuated echo. This is reverberation.

Theoretically, attenuation lasts indefinitely. To make it possible to compare different reverberation processes (and mainly the reverberation properties of auditoria) in practice, the concept of reverberation time was introduced. The *reverberation time* is the time over which the level of the reverberating signal decreases by 60 dB.

The main device for implementing reverberation is a device that creates the echo signal. The history of such devices is rather interesting.

Along with the echo chambers, steel plates, or rather large pieces of sheet metal, were used to imitate reverberation. Oscillations were introduced into and taken from them using devices similar in their construction and operation to electromagnetic headphones. The reverberation was flat (not 3D), and the signal had a typical metallic tinge.

In the mid 1960s, spring reverbers were used to obtain the reverberation effect. Using an electromagnetic transducer connected to one end of the spring, mechanical oscillations were excited that reached the other end of the spring, which was connected to a sensor, after a delay. The effect of the sound repetition was caused by the repeated reflections of mechanic oscillations from the ends of the spring. The sound quality in a spring reverber was very low. The spring reacted to any vibrations in the air and floor, there was unavoidable feedback between the acoustic system and the spring, and the sound had a pronounced "metallic" tint. The time of the reverberation could not be controlled.

These imperfect devices were replaced by tape recorder reverbers.

With the development of digital technology and appearance of integrated circuits containing hundreds and thousands of digital delay elements within one chip, high-quality digital reverbers were developed. In such devices, the signal can be delayed for any time necessary both for reverberation and for echo. The feedback loop sends parts of the signal from the output back to the delay line, and a repeated echo occurs. The feedback ratio should be less than one; otherwise, the level of each new echo will be increased and not attenuated, and an effect similar to self-excitation in an acoustic system may occur.

Such reverbers are widely used by musicians and sound producers.

8.2.1. The Simple Reverbers QuickVerb *and* Reverb

The **Effects > Delay Effects > QuickVerb** command opens the **QuickVerb** effect dialog box (Fig. 8.5).

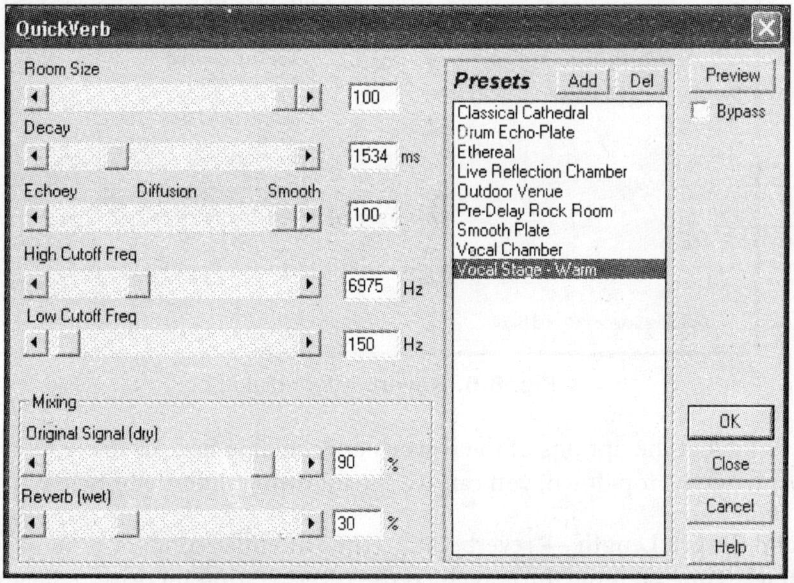

Fig. 8.5. QuickVerb effect dialog box

The effect seems to be well named: You can indeed specify the processing parameters quickly using it, as there are only a few of them:

- **Room Size** — size (length) of the simulated room.
- **Decay** — decay time of the reverberating signal.
- **Diffusion** — character of the reverberation: **Echoey** is a reflected sound that is very similar to an echo, and **Smooth** is a fuzzy sound that is reflected from many objects.
- **High Cutoff Freq** — high cutoff frequency of the range processed by the reverber.
- **Low Cutoff Freq** — low cutoff frequency of the range processed by the reverber.
- **Mixing** — controls for the ratio between the amplitudes of the source (**Original Signal (dry)**) and processed (**Reverb (wet)**) signals.

The next effect is also reverberation. Setting its parameters is done using the options of the **Reverb** effect dialog box shown in Fig. 8.6. This dialog box is opened with the **Effects > Delay Effects > Reverb** command.

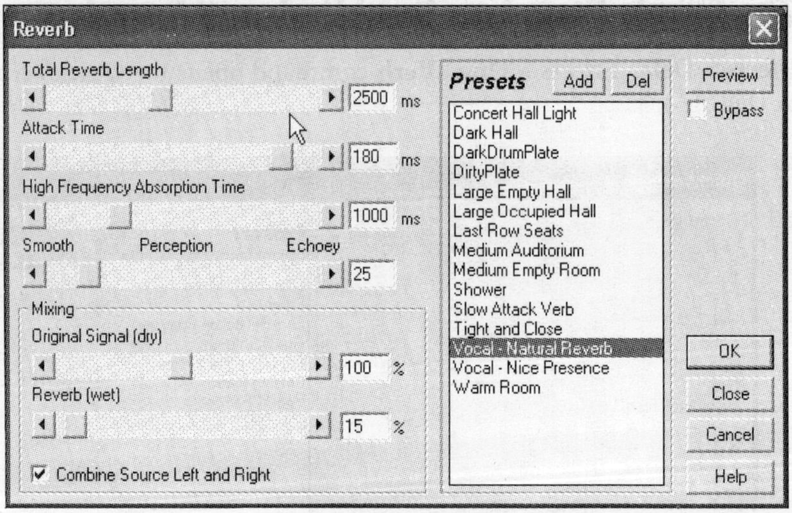

Fig. 8.6. **Reverb** effect dialog box

Let's look at the options of the **Reverb** effect dialog box. In the left part of the dialog box, from the top down, you can see the following sliders and fields:

- **Total Reverb Length** — reverberation time in milliseconds.
- **Attack Time** — time, during which the reverberation increases (the appearance of sound reflected from objects at different distances).

- **High Frequency Absorption Time** — decay time of the high-frequency components of the spectrum because of their absorption by the propagation media and the reflecting obstacles.
- **Perception** — nature of the reverberation: **Smooth** indicates a fuzzy sound reflected from many objects; **Echoey** is a reflected sound that resembles echo.

The **Mixing** group is used to specify the mixing parameters of the source (**Original Signal (dry)**) and processed (**Reverb (wet)**) signals.

The checked **Combine Source Left and Right** checkbox enables you to combine the signals of the stereo channels into one signal and then calculate the reverberation and the further mixing of the processed original (stereo) signals. The calculation is twice as fast as for each individual signal, but the original stereo image of the sound is destroyed.

The **Presets** list provides the traditional set of reverb variants: simulation of the acoustics of various rooms, popular algorithms of the reverberation simulation, etc.

8.2.2. *A Universal Reverber* Full Reverb

The universal reverberation **Full Reverb** is used in Adobe Audition to simulate an acoustic space in detail. The effect has several unique features:

- Realistic simulation of early reflections
- Ability to change the size and acoustic properties of the simulated room
- Simulation of a reflecting surface of any material
- Ability to change the absorption properties of the space within the room
- Correction of the reverberation signal frequency spectrum using a three-band parametric equalizer

The **Effects > Delay Effects > Full Reverb** command opens the **Full Reverb** effect dialog box, which contains three tabs: **General Reverb** (Fig. 8.7), **Early Reflections** (Fig. 8.8), and **Coloration** (Fig. 8.9).

Let's look first at the controls of the effect dialog box that are common to all tabs.

The **Mixing** group contains controls for the following parameters:

- **Original Signal (dry)** — level of the non-processed signal
- **Early Reflections** — level of the early reflections
- **Reverb (wet)** — level of the processed signal

The checked **Include Direct** checkbox enables a phase shift of the sound oscillations in the right and left channels, with the purpose of matching the directions of the primary reflections with the location of the sound sources on the stereo panorama.

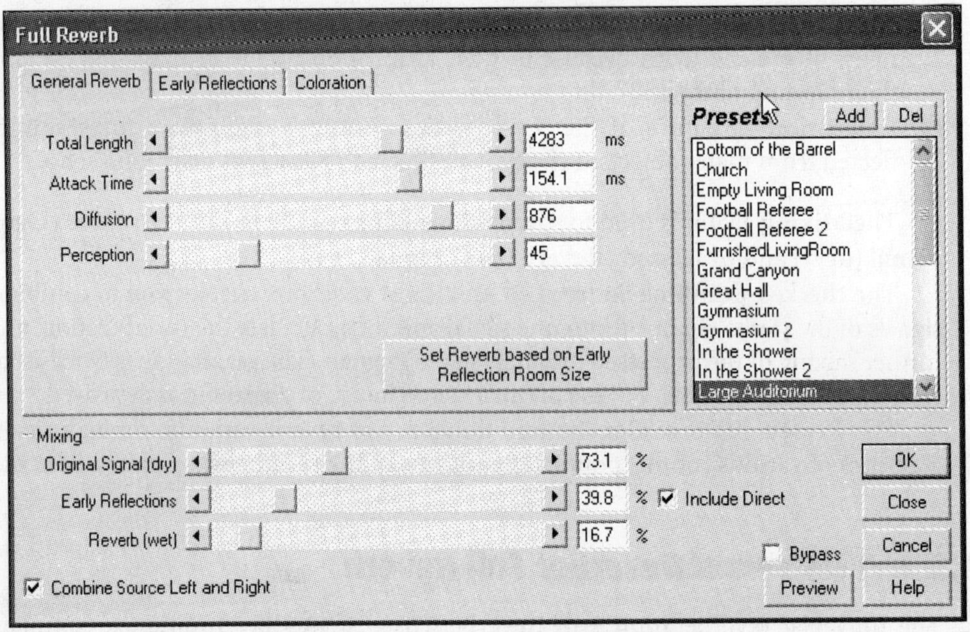

Fig. 8.7. General Reverb tab of the **Full Reverb** effect dialog box

The checked **Combine Source Left and Right** checkbox combines the left and right channels of the sound source before processing with the effect, with the purpose of reducing the calculation time. The stereo image of the sound source is destroyed.

If the **Bypass** checkbox is checked, the signal bypasses the effect.

In addition to the static part, the dialog box of the effect contains three tabs: **General Reverb**, **Early Reflections**, and **Coloration**. Let's examine these tabs.

The **General Reverb** tab (Fig. 8.7) contains the controls for the general reverberation parameters:

- **Total Length** — total reverberation time
- **Attack Time** — time to achieve the effect's maximum level
- **Diffusion** — absorption properties of the sound propagation media
- **Perception** — shows how the reverberation is perceived: from the fuzzy sound typical to reflection from many closely positioned obstacles to a clear multiple echo
- **Set Reverb based on Early Reflection Room Size** — automatic matching of the general reverberation parameters to those of the early reflections, room, and propagation media

The **Early Reflections** tab is shown in Fig. 8.8.

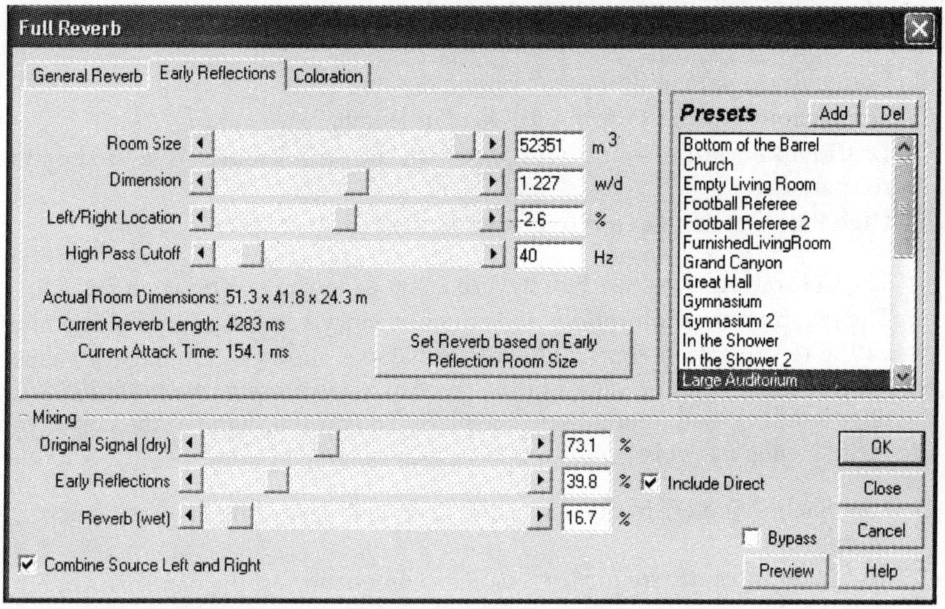

Fig. 8.8. Early Reflections tab of the **Full Reverb** effect dialog box

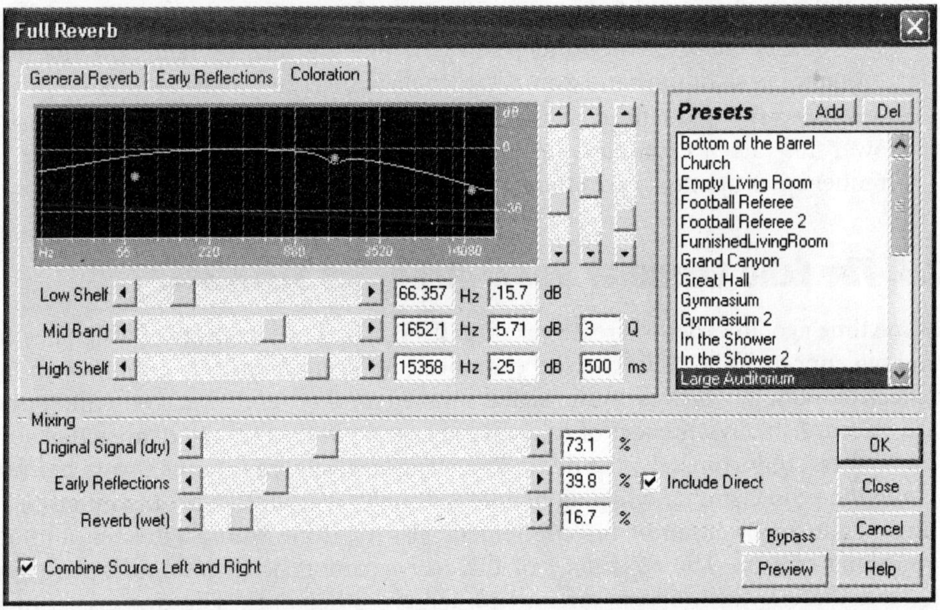

Fig. 8.9. Coloration tab of the **Full Reverb** effect dialog box

The parameters specified on the **Early Reflections** tab are as follows:

- **Room Size** — size of the room in cubic meters
- **Dimension** — room's width relative to its length
- **Left/Right Location** — the point, at which the sound source is located on the stereo panorama
- **High Pass Cutoff** — cutoff frequency of the high-pass filter

The **Coloration** tab of the **Full Reverb** effect dialog box is shown in Fig. 8.9.

The graph on the **Coloration** tab is the frequency-response curve of the filter that passes the reverberation signal. The horizontal axis shows the frequency values, and the vertical one shows the values of the frequency-response curve in decibels. In fact, the filter is a three-band parametric equalizer. To edit the shape of the curve, you can use the following controls:

- **Low Shelf** — cutoff frequency of the filter that passes the low-frequency spectral components.
- **Mid Band** — center frequency (resonance frequency) of the band-pass filter.
- **High Shelf** — cutoff frequency of the filter that passes the high-frequency spectral components.
- The three vertical controls to the right of the graph control the level of the signal amplification/attenuation by each of the three filters of the parametric equalizer.
- **Q** — quality factor of the band-pass filter. The greater this value, the sharper the resonance peak of the band-pass filter (the narrower its passband).
- **ms** — reverberation time of the high-frequency components of the signal (the lower this value as compared to the total reverberation time, the quicker the high-frequency components are attenuated in the processed signal).

8.2.3. The Echo Chamber *Room-Acoustics Simulator*

Some time ago, in order to create various effects based on the delay of a signal, studios and big concert halls included echo chambers. An *echo chamber* is a room with highly reflective walls, in which an audio signal source (speaker) and a receiver (microphone) are placed. Actually, this sort of echo chamber is a reduced model of an actual auditorium where, unfortunately, the desired acoustic atmosphere can not always be created. Using the echo chamber, you can handle (although with difficulty) the intensities and time of the propagation of re-reflected signals by setting sound-reflecting or sound-absorbing screens. The advantage of the echo chamber is that sound attenuation is natural there (which is very difficult to achieve otherwise). The drawbacks of such chambers are their relatively small sizes. Therefore, because of their own resonance, the signal spectrum is distorted in the mid-band frequencies. Another problem is reliable acoustic insulation of the echo chamber. The main drawback, though, is that the echo chamber cannot be a widely used tool for obtaining delay effects, since it is too cumbersome and expensive.

So what is left for musicians who would like to use an echo chamber but have no such opportunity? The answer is in Adobe Audition. It has a built-in echo chamber (of course, not a room itself, but a mathematical simulator). What is this for? The echo chamber differs from all the other devices by using real 3D reverberation. In the other devices, this is not actually reverberation, but a pitiful, two-dimensional (sometimes one-dimensional) copy. The echo chamber simulator allows you to simulate the acoustic of any room. It is even better than an actual echo chamber, since it allows you to quickly change the size of the simulated room and the reflective properties of the walls, floor, and ceiling. Moreover, this is not one but two echo chambers, with separately set coordinates of the sound sources and receivers.

Notice that a similar effect is implemented as a plug-in for Cakewalk Pro Audio and SONAR [2].

The **Echo Chamber** dialog box opened using the **Effects** > **Delay Effects** > **Echo Chamber** command is shown in Fig. 8.10.

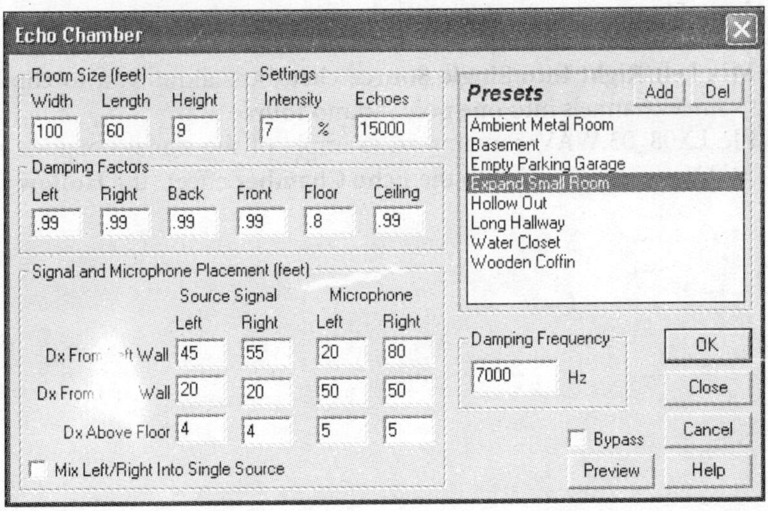

Fig. 8.10. Echo Chamber dialog box used for modeling sound propagation in a 3D room

Let's consider the options of the **Echo Chamber** dialog box.

The **Room Size (feet)** group is used to specify the room size (in feet): **Width**, **Length**, and **Height**.

The **Settings** group is used to specify the intensity (**Intensity**) and number of simulated reflections (**Echoes**).

The **Damping Factors** group is used to specify the damping factors for the materials that the walls, floor, and ceiling are made of:

- **Left** — left wall
- **Right** — right wall
- **Back** — back wall
- **Front** — front wall
- **Floor** — floor
- **Ceiling** — ceiling

The **Damping Frequency** field is used to specify the upper frequency of the processed spectrum of the signal. Frequencies exceeding this frequency are dampened.

The **Signal and Microphone Placement (feet)** group is used to specify the positions of the source signal (the **Source Signal** columns), as well as of the microphone or listener (the **Microphone** columns) in the virtual chamber. There are actually two sources: the signals from the left and right source channels. There are also two microphones (the listener's ears), and you can use three coordinates to specify the position of each of them:

- **Dx From Left Wall** — distance from the left wall
- **Dx From Back Wall** — distance from the back wall
- **Dx Above Floor** — height above the floor

The **Mix Left/Right Into Single Source** checkbox allows you to combine the left and right source channels into one point sound source.

The file EX08_03.WAV contains an example of the signal obtained after the file NSINC1.WAV was processed with the **Echo Chamber** effect (the **Hollow Out** preset).

Chapter 9

Using DirectX Plug-Ins

In Adobe Audition, you can use effects (plug-ins) connected to the application using DirectX. This significantly extends Adobe Audition's already numerous sound processing options, provided that DirectX plug-ins are installed in your system.

9.1. Using DirectX Plug-Ins in Adobe Audition

After installing Adobe Audition, execute the **Effects > Enable DirectX Effects** command, and the **DirectX** submenu will appear in the **Effects** menu. After initializing the DirectX plug-ins, the **Enable DirectX Effects** item will disappear from the menu.

If any plug-ins were installed after the installation of Adobe Audition, it is likely that you will not see them in the **DirectX** submenu. Apply the **Effects > Refresh Effects List** command so that Adobe Audition can find and recognize all DirectX plug-ins.

The **DirectX** submenu displays the names of all the effects that the application recognized as DirectX effects compatible with Adobe Audition. In practice, however, this means that some of the effects listed in the **DirectX** submenu may have nothing in common with sound processing. For example, you might find plug-ins used for image compression and digitization.

In order not to return to the external plug-ins issue, we'll move on to another item of the **Effects** menu (**Unsupported**), which in certain cases can also be missing from the application. **Unsupported** is a submenu that appears in the **Effects** menu only when there are plug-ins in the system that Adobe Audition has discovered, but has found to be unsuitable for joint use. The **Unsupported** submenu is an original means of "illusion destruction" — a sort of a herald communicating the bitter truth to the user. When you installed the plug-ins, you planned to use them together with Adobe Audition. You cherished these hopes, and if they failed to work at a crucial point, you would be in a difficult situation. Fortunately, the **Unsupported** submenu warns you in due time.

So, the **Effects > DirectX** command opens the **DirectX** submenu. The rest depends on which DirectX plug-ins are installed on your computer and the way they are designed.

Before you start working with a plug-in in the **Waveform View** dialog box, select the material to be processed (the whole waveform or its fragment). Then find the required effect in the submenu system and open the corresponding dialog box with a mouse click.

Unlike earlier versions of Cool Edit, Adobe Audition supports real-time mode for DirectX plug-ins. However, you can connect a real-time effect only to a track of the multitrack editor (*Chapter 10*).

Using DirectX effects in the **Waveform View** dialog box is possible only by recalculating the audio data for the selected fragments of the current waveform. To try the effect parameters, you can use the pre-audition button (**Preview** or **Purchase**) available in the effect dialog box. After you make sure aurally that the parameters of the effect were correctly specified to obtain the desired result, click the **OK** button in the effect dialog box. The data in the selected fragment of the waveform will be recalculated.

In the next section, we describe one of plug-ins of the Waves Platinum Native Bundle 4 package.

9.2. Using RVox: a Gate, Compressor, and Limiter

RVox is a gate, vocal compressor, and limiter combined in one plug-in (Fig. 9.1). Controlling it is very easy because:

- Automatic control of the input signal level is provided.
- Dynamic parameters (attack and release time) are unavailable for editing.

The plug-in is contained in the Renaissance Collection kit of the Waves Platinum Native Bundle 4 package.

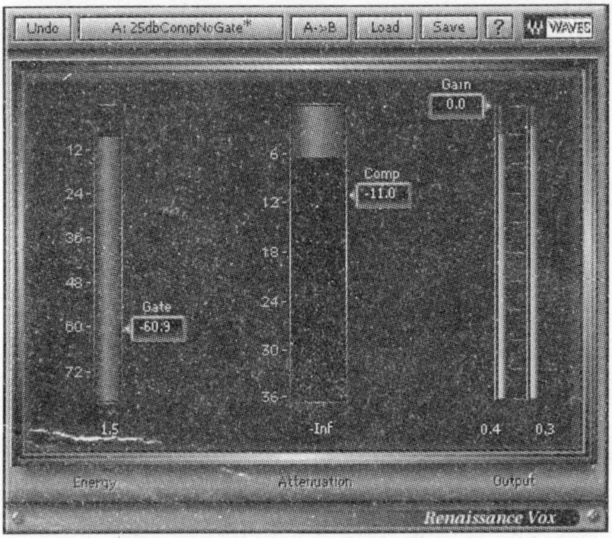

Fig. 9.1. RVox plug-in dialog box

There are different opinions concerning the processing done inside the plug-in. Some people think it is a sort of gating and compression. However, the user manual does not talk about gating, but about "descending expansion," which was intended for mild noise reduction in the overlapping area. Apparently, by this area the developers mean an interval within the low-level area between the gate's attack and release thresholds.

The **Gate** slider controls a generalized parameter related to the thresholds. In fact, the area, which includes a smooth bend of the response curve, is moved along the level axis with this slider.

In the compressor, also just one parameter, **Comp**., is available for adjustment. Taking into account that the plug-in has automatic adjustment of the makeup gain, we can conclude that **Comp.** replaces two parameters of a typical compressor: threshold and compression ratio. In essence, **Comp.** determines the absolute value of compression, rather than its relative value. This is why this parameter is measured in dB. To avoid internal clipping, an additional processing, i.e., limiting, is used.

The third control (**Gain**) adjusts the output signal level.

Discussing this plug-in was a deliberate choice. It turns out that using it for dynamic processing of a signal recorded in the EX07_01.WAV file gives good results. With **Gate** = 25 and **Comp** = 9, not only the subjective loudness increased, but the noise level decreased significantly. The processed signal is saved in the file EX09_01.WAV. You can make sure that it is quite competitive with the signal saved in the NSINC1.WAV file, which was obtained using Adobe Audition's own tools.

Chapter 10

Mixing a Multitrack Project to Stereo

In many sound editors, mixing an audio composition from individual files is done using one pair of stereo tracks. In Adobe Audition, this procedure can be done in the **Edit Waveform View** mode using only standard operations such as cutting, pasting, copying, and mixing. In essence, montage doesn't differ much from traditional gluing together fragments of magnetic tape. Of course, electronic montage is much more convenient than working with a pair of scissors, a brush, glue, and a press. However, the procedure of assembling fragments requires a lot of time to fit them together and achieve a balance in the resulting mixes. Adobe Audition provides you with a fundamentally new tool for montage. This is the multitrack environment, which can be called "an editor in the editor." In addition, the multitrack mode is the main one in Adobe Audition; the application enters it immediately after start.

10.1. Inserting Audio Data into a Multitrack Environment

So the main job — montage of individual waveforms of a finished audio composition to a project — is done in the multitrack editor.

To insert a current waveform into a multitrack project, use the **Edit > Insert in Multitrack** command. However, the waveform being edited is often present in your multitrack project. For example, suppose you make a recording in the multitrack editor, switch to the waveform editing mode, and perform all necessary processing there. In this case, you don't need the **Edit > Insert in Multitrack** command: Just switch to the multitrack mode to continue working on the project.

Jumping ahead slightly: The multitrack editor window contains many tracks, one under another. It also contains its marker. If you select the **Insert in Multitrack** command of the **Edit** menu while working in **Edit Waveform View**, the waveform on the active page will be inserted into a multitrack editor track, and the beginning of the inserted waveform will be at the position of the marker.

When you use the **Edit > Insert in Multitrack** command for the first time, the waveform will be inserted in the first available track. The next insertion will be made in the next track, and so on. You can change this order: For example, you can insert several waveforms in the same track or skip some of the tracks.

The **Edit > Insert Play List Multitrack** command allows you to insert waveforms from the files listed in the **Play List** into the multitrack environment. This command is one of the tools that help you automate processing of a large number of files. Rather than manually insert files in the multitrack environment one by one, you can make a list of them and use the **Insert Play List Multitrack** command. A description of working with the **Play List** is given in [3, *Section 5.4*].

To learn how to work in the multitrack environment, insert one of the example files on the CD-ROM, such as EX09_01.WAV.

10.2. Working in the Application Main Window: the *Multitrack View* Mode

To switch to the multitrack environment (**Multitrack View**) from the waveform editing mode, either select the **Multitrack View** in the **View** menu, click the 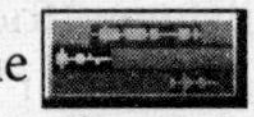 button, or press the <F12> key. The application main window will look like that shown in Fig. 10.1.

In this window, you can see many elements that are already familiar to you. These are the transport controls, the tools for zooming in and out, the time indicator, the input fields for the beginning, end, and length of a selection, the signal meter, and the status bar. As always, the main menu is at the top of the window.

However, this is the only resemblance to the window we saw when working in the **Edit Waveform View** mode. The difference is that there are only seven rather than ten main menu commands in the multitrack environment, and, most important, the main window contains many pairs of stereo tracks rather than just one pair. If you zoom out vertically as far as possible and use the scroll box on the scrollbar, you'll be able to count the tracks, of which there are 128.

Fig. 10.1. Application main window in the **Multitrack View** mode

10.2.1. The Basics of Working in the Adobe Audition Multitrack Environment

Waveforms in the multitrack environment are displayed as colored blocks. Each of them contains a waveform, the name of the file that contains the waveform, and some other elements. These blocks are like the bricks that can be used to build a composition in the multitrack environment.

The blocks can be moved in time and between the tracks. You also can split them or mix them down to one stereo or mono track. However, it is impossible to edit an individual waveform in the multitrack environment. To edit it, click the desired block, and the application will enter the mode of editing the selected waveform. After you cut unnecessary portions out of the waveform, suppress noise, perform dynamic processing and filtration, apply effects, do normalization, etc., just switch to the multitrack view.

We should also mention that the edges of a block do not necessarily coincide with the edges of the waveform. A block can contain a selected fragment of a waveform. In addition, the same waveform can be used in different blocks. Different variants are possible. For example, one block can contain one fragment of the waveform, another block can contain another fragment, and yet another block can contain the entire waveform. Naturally, if you modify a waveform shared by several blocks, the changes will affect all these blocks.

It is possible to control the volume and panorama of a waveform on each track and apply real-time effects to the tracks. However, adjusting the volume and panorama and applying effects are done here by recomputing the values of the digital audio samples during playback, and no changes are made to the waveforms.

You can place existing waveforms on the tracks, and you can also record them while in the multitrack environment. In addition, it is possible to perform multichannel recording in the multitrack environment by simultaneously recording signals from several sound sources to different tracks.

You can include MIDI files and video files in the AVI format into a multitrack project. It is impossible to edit them in Adobe Audition, but you'll be able to synchronize your multichannel project with MIDI music or video images.

The possibility of working with video is very important. Although multitrack video editors (such as Adobe Premier) allow the user to edit audio, they have much fewer options than Adobe Audition.

In practice, work with video in Adobe Audition is done as follows. Import an AVI file that generally contains video and audio streams. You can include only the video clip in your multitrack project. Put the video on one track, and its sound track from the AVI file will be automatically put on another track. You can open this block in the waveform editing mode, clean it of noise, perform dynamic processing, etc., and then return to the multitrack mode and put music at appropriate places in the film by putting the corresponding waveforms on unused tracks. You can record sound for the film anew by muting or erasing the original sound track and recording with one or more microphones in a studio. When playing a multitrack project, video will be played in an individual window. This gives you the ability to score the film for sound.

For more details on working with audio for video, see *Chapter 11*.

When the work is completed, use a special command to mix the audio and video to a new AVI file. The video will remain unchanged, and the sound will be new (or edited).

Thus, the simplest way to use Adobe Audition as a multitrack editor is as follows:

1. Create a new session (with the **File > New Session** command) or open an existing one (with the **File > Open Session** command).
2. Starting from the required time mark, perform recording or insert ready waveform blocks into the appropriate tracks.
3. Process the newly recorded waveforms after switching to the waveform editing mode (with clicks on the corresponding blocks).
4. Back in the multitrack editor, split, move, delete, or combine blocks as you wish.
5. Perform mixing. Adjust the volume and panorama of the tracks, apply real-time effects to them, and create automation envelopes that will allow you to control desired parameters.
6. Use the **File > Save Mixdown As** or **Edit > Mix Down to File > All Waves** command to save the obtained composition as one stereo audio file. If the project contains video, change the last step to the following. Select the **File > Save Mixdown to Video As** command and save the results of your work in an AVI file.

What is a session? In essence, a *session* is an SES file, a multitrack project of your composition that contains the following data:

- The paths to the files with the waveforms located on the tracks (i.e., included in this session)
- Information on assigning the waveforms to particular tracks
- The playback start time for each waveform
- The attributes of the tracks and buses and the parameters of the effects connected to the tracks and buses
- Automation

A session file takes little space because it doesn't contain any digital audio samples. You might say (if we forget about files and disks for a while) that from a user's point of view, a session is a set of waveform images on the tracks of the multitrack editor.

At the same time, the waveforms exist independently of the session. You can edit, save, close, and delete them. In addition, you can create several sessions that use the same audio files.

If an audio file is used in the current session and you try to close it (with the **Edit > Close** command of the waveform editor), a warning message telling you that the corresponding block will disappear from the multitrack project will appear. If you delete or move an audio file with an operating system tool and then try to open a session that uses it, a standard dialog box asking you to specify the path to this file (or another file that could be used instead) will appear. If you click the **Cancel** button, the corresponding block will never appear in the multitrack project.

Keep in mind that all the waveforms used in a session must have the *same* sample rate.

When creating a new session with the **File > New Session** command, a dialog box opens in which you must choose a sample rate for the entire project. If you try to insert a file with a sample rate other than the sample rate of the project, the application will suggest you to create a copy of this file, and then it will convert the waveform taking into account the new sample rate and add this converted copy of the original file to the multitrack session. Before the conversion, you'll be able to change the file format (stereo or mono) and the audio signal resolution.

10.2.2. Recording Sound. Connecting Effects to Tracks and Buses. Locking Tracks

Adobe Audition allows you to import MIDI and AVI files. Information contained in these files will be put on MIDI and video tracks, respectively. In other words, there are three types of tracks: audio, MIDI, and video.

A video track has only one attribute: the track name. A MIDI track has the following attributes: **V** (volume), **S** (Solo), **M** (Mute), and a tracks-to-MIDI-ports map that is opened by clicking the **Map** button.

Let's look at audio track attributes in greater detail.

There is an attribute field at the beginning of each track. The set of its elements depends on both the track type and the sizes of the attribute fields. The latter, in turn, depend on the vertical zoom level and the position of the right edge of the track attribute fields. In addition, there are three buttons above the track attribute fields that allow you to change the order of the displayed attributes:

- **Vol** — the volume and panorama attributes will be displayed first.
- **EQ** — the equalizer parameters will be displayed first (each audio track has a three-band parametric equalizer).
- **Bus** — parameters related to the output of the track signal to a specified bus will be displayed first (these are discussed later).

The field with the audio track attributes is shown in Fig. 10.2. Its upper part contains the track name. The default names of tracks are **Track 1**, **Track 2**, etc. To change the name, just click it and enter another name via the keyboard.

Fig. 10.2. Audio track attributes

The **R**, **S**, and **M** buttons turn on and off the record, solo, and mute modes, respectively.

- **R** — when the record mode is on, the recording of the signal from the specified input to this track will start as soon as you click the **Record** button on the transport panel.
- **S** — when the solo mode is on, only this track will be heard (or all tracks whose **S** buttons are pressed).
- **M** — when the mute mode is on, this track will be muted, and you won't hear it in the total mix.

After you click the **Out 1** button, you'll be able to select output ports for the track in the **Playback Devices** dialog box (Fig. 10.3).

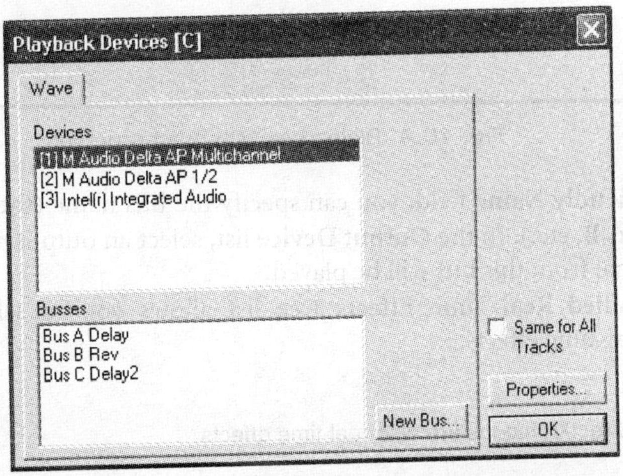

Fig. 10.3. Playback Devices dialog box

In the **Devices** list, you can select an output port, through which the audio information from this track will be played. If you select an item in this list and click the **Properties** button, the **Device Ordering Preference** dialog box described in *Section 1.3* will open. Among other things, this dialog box allows you to select devices that will be available in the **Devices** list of the **Playback Devices** window.

Notice the **Busses** list (which is empty by default). This is a list of the available buses. Buses are used to group tracks together. You can create a bus and specify it as an output port for several tracks. By connecting real-time effects to this bus, you can process the signals from the track group with these effects.

To create a new bus, click the **New Bus** button. A dialog box with the properties of the newly created bus will open (Fig. 10.4).

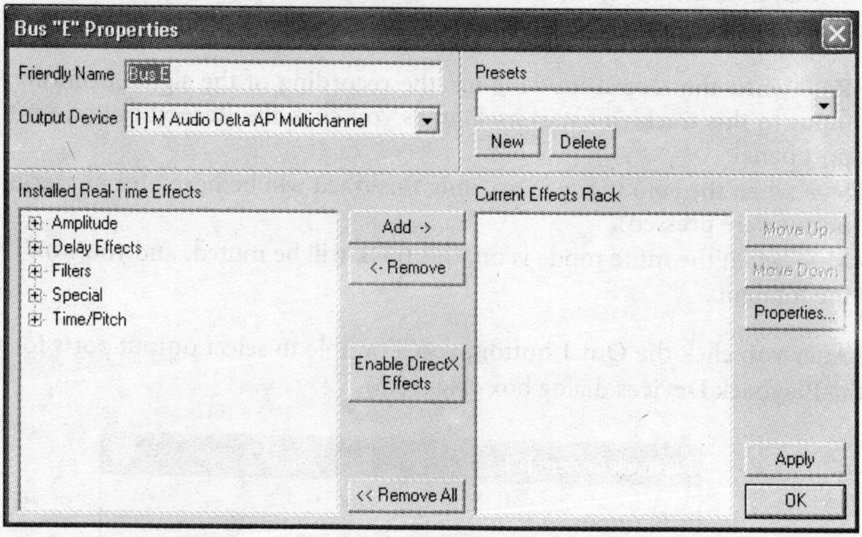

Fig. 10.4. Dialog box with bus properties

In the **Friendly Name** field, you can specify the bus name (the default bus names are **Bus A**, **Bus B**, etc.). In the **Output Device** list, select an output port, through which the audio signal from this bus will be played.

The **Installed Real-Time Effects** tree list allows you to select one of Adobe Audition's real-time effects.

All DirectX plug-ins are also real-time effects.

By clicking the **Add->** button, you can move the selected effect to the **Current Effects Rack** list. This is how effects are connected to a bus (Fig. 10.5). In the same way, you can connect more effects to the bus.

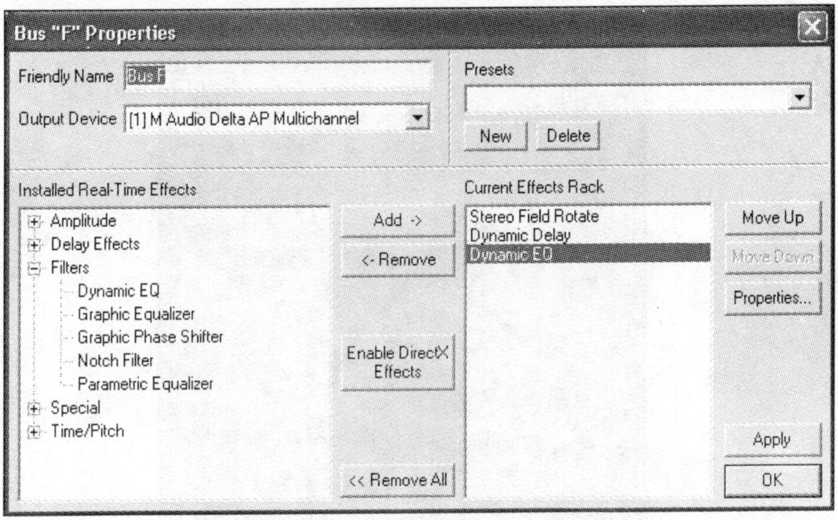

Fig. 10.5. Connecting effects to a bus

The order of connection of the effects to the bus can be significant. If you select an effect in the **Current Effects Rack** list, the buttons **Move Up** and/or **Move Down** will become available. They make it possible to move the selected effect up or down the list.

If you click the **Properties** button, a dialog box with the effect properties will open (Fig. 10.6).

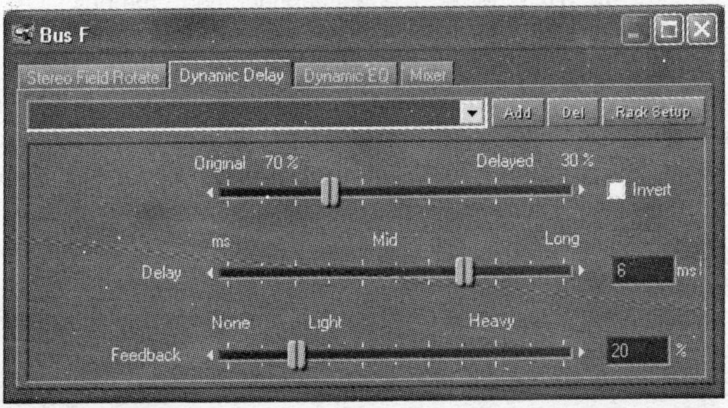

Fig. 10.6. Dialog box with properties of effects connected to the bus

This dialog box has several tabs that correspond to the connected effects. The last tab is called **Mixer** (Fig. 10.7). With this mixer, you can route the signal between the effects connected to the bus.

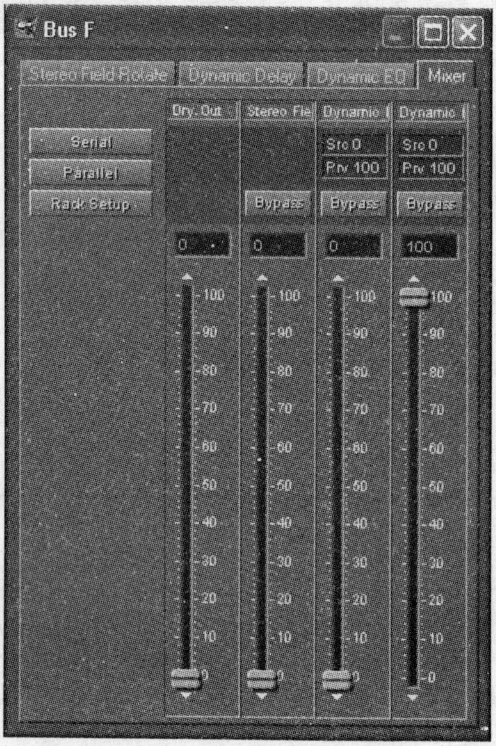

Fig. 10.7. Mixer of effects connected to the bus

The first strip of the mixer is always called **Dry Out**. It contains a fader that controls the level of the unprocessed signal at the bus output. Next are effect strips. Each of them also has a fader that is used to control the level of the signal sent from the effect output to the output audio port. The **Bypass** button is used to bypass the corresponding effect. The **Prv** field shows the level (as percentage) of the signal received from the output of the previous effect. The position of the fader doesn't affect the level of the sent signal.

To change the parameter value displayed in a digital field (such as **Prv**), click this field, hold the mouse button, and move the mouse left or right.

The **Src** field displays the level of the original unprocessed signal supplied to the effect's input.

The buttons **Serial** and **Parallel** actually set the factory settings of the mixer:

- **Serial** — sets serial processing the signal with the effects. The mixer settings are such that the input of the subsequent effect is connected to the output of the previous effect, and the signal from the last effect is sent to the output audio port.
- **Parallel** — sets parallel processing the signal with the effects. The original unprocessed signal is sent to the output of each effect, and the signals from the outputs of the effects are sent to the output audio port.

The **Rack Setup** button opens a dialog box with the properties of this bus (Figs. 10.4 and 10.5).

Now let's return to the **Playback Devices** dialog box (Fig. 10.3). If you check the **Same for All Tracks** checkbox, the output audio ports selected in this dialog box will be set for all tracks after you click the **OK** button. There are identical checkboxes in other dialog boxes, and, will not mention them further.

Consider the other audio track attributes. The input audio port is a port, from which recording will be done. The corresponding button is located in the track attribute field. Its default name is **Rec 1**. A click on this button opens the **Record Devices** dialog box shown in Fig. 10.8. In this dialog box, you can select an input audio port (**Wave**), recording mode (**Left Cannel**, **Right Channel**, or **Stereo**), and digital signal resolution (**16-bit/32-bit**).

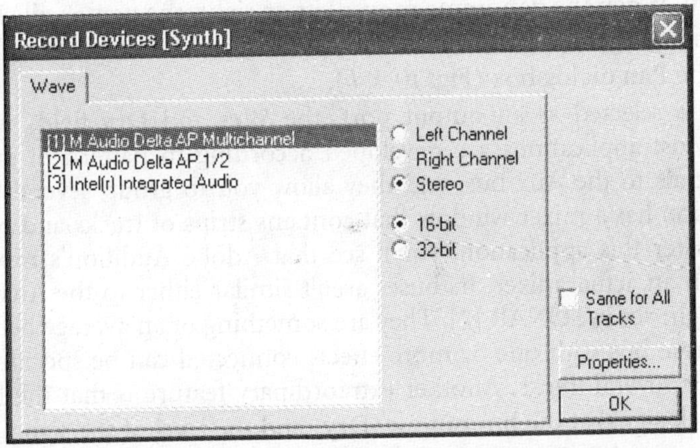

Fig. 10.8. Record Devices dialog box

If you click the **Properties** button, the **Device Ordering Preference** dialog box described in *Section 1.3* will open. After you close the **Record Devices** dialog box by clicking the **OK** button, the name of the **Rec 1** button of the corresponding track might change to **Rec N**, where *N* is the number of the input audio port specified for the track.

Now you know enough to try to record on the track. Prepare one or more tracks for recording: Specify input audio ports by clicking the **Rec 1** buttons, click the **R** buttons, and set the marker to the position, at which recording is to start. Start recording by clicking the **Record** button on the transport panel. If everything is all right, recording will start. You can stop it by clicking the **Stop** button on the transport panel or hitting the spacebar on the computer keyboard.

We already encountered the marker when working in the waveform editing mode. It is a vertical line of yellow dots that specifies the position, at which the recording or playback will start or the waveform will be inserted.

Recording might fail to start if the device selected as a signal source doesn't support the sample rate used in the session, for example, if the input audio port of a voice modem supports sampling at 8 kHz, and you selected a rate of 48 kHz when creating the session.

The next audio track attributes we're going to look at are volume and panorama. The volume display field is denoted by the letter **V** followed by the signal level value in dB. You already know one method of changing the value in a digital field: "Drag and drop." There is another method for this. Right-click the field. The **Vol** dialog box shown in Fig. 10.9, *a* will open. Adjusting the track volume with this dialog box is more convenient.

The panorama digital field is usually located above the volume field, and its default name is **Pan 0**. When the panorama moves left or right, the name will change to **L** or **R** and deviation from the center will be indicated as a percentage. A right click on this field opens the **Pan** dialog box (Fig. 10.9, *b*).

If a bus is selected as an output port, the **Wet** and **Dry** fields will be available (Fig. 10.2). Most applications are developed according to pattern of an actual mixer. They have sends to the Aux bus, and they allow you to group several tracks together. Adobe Audition has a mixer window that contains strips of tracks and buses. However, after you master this application, you'll see that Adobe Audition's mixer has little in common with an actual mixer. Its buses aren't similar either to the Aux buses or main buses you might see in SONAR [2]. They are something of an average between SONAR's buses. The same bus with one or more effects connected can be specified as an output audio port for several tracks. Another extraordinary feature is that the level of the unprocessed track signal at the bus output (**Dry**) and the level of the signal processed with the effects connected to the bus (**Wet**) can be adjusted independently for each track.

A parametric equalizer necessarily connected to each of the tracks can be considered a sort of a real-time effect. The fields **L**, **M**, and **H** allow you to adjust the signal gain or decay provided by three filters. Double-click any of these fields. The **Track Equalizers** dialog box (Fig. 10.10) will open.

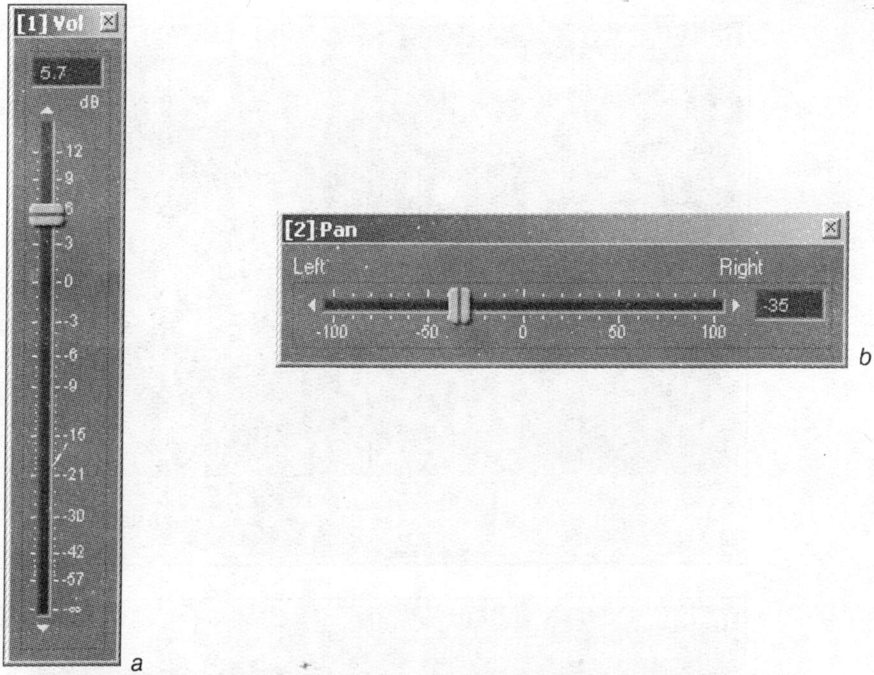

Fig. 10.9. Dialog boxes for volume (*a*) and panorama (*b*) adjustment

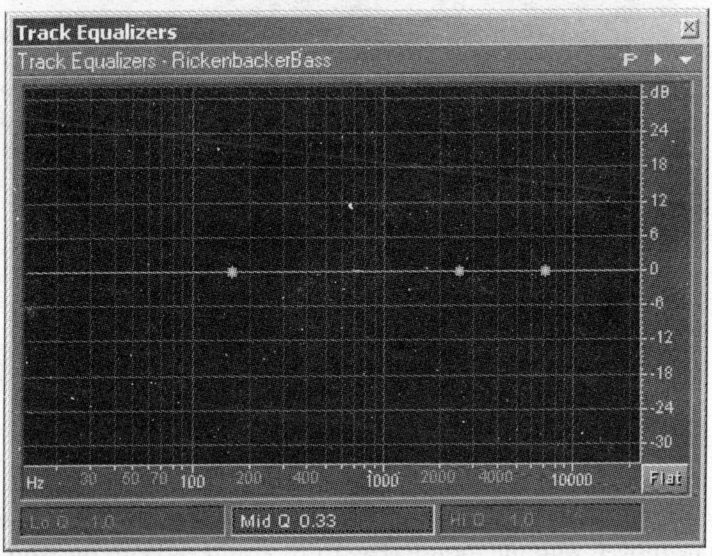

Fig. 10.10, *a*. Dialog box for shaping the frequency-response curve of the track equalizer

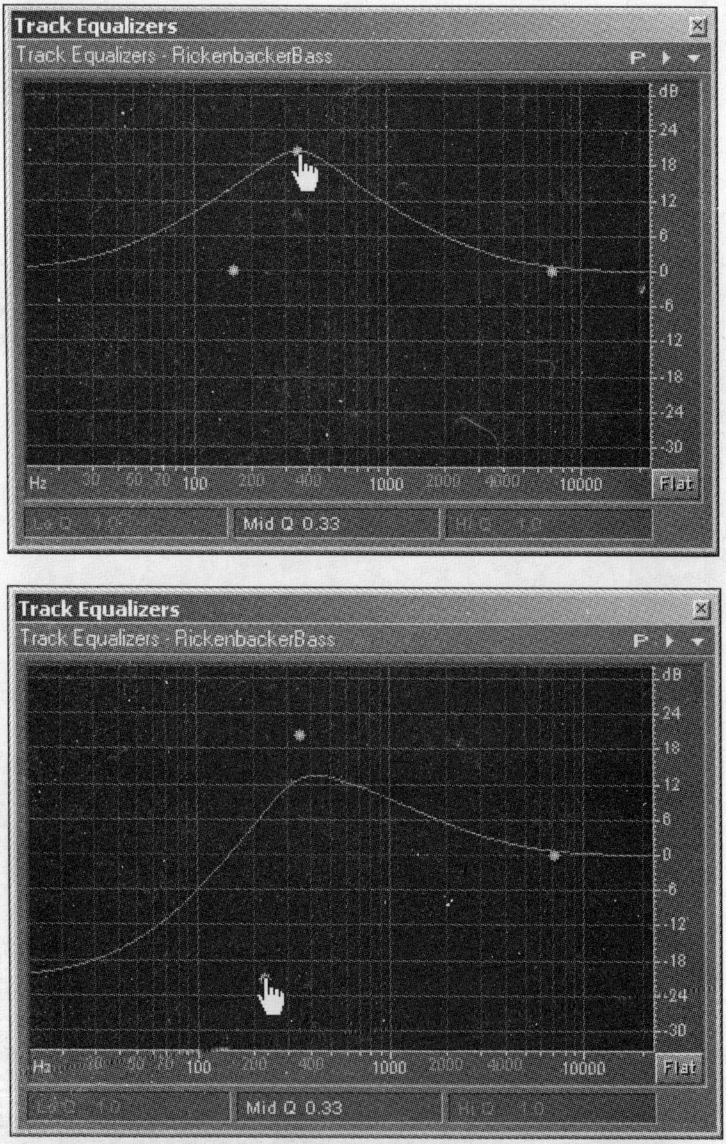

b

c

Fig. 10.10, *b–c*. Dialog box for shaping the frequency-response curve of the track equalizer

Three white dots (Fig. 10.10, *a*) correspond to the center frequencies of the filters. They can be moved with the mouse (Fig. 10.10, *b* and *c*). With the **Mid Q** field, you can adjust the quality of the middle filter. The qualities of the other filters (**Lo Q** and **Hi Q**)

cannot be changed by default. By clicking the **Flat** button, you can reset the equalizer settings, after which its frequency-response curve becomes linear. With the ▶ button, you can switch to another mode of controlling the filter (Fig. 10.11).

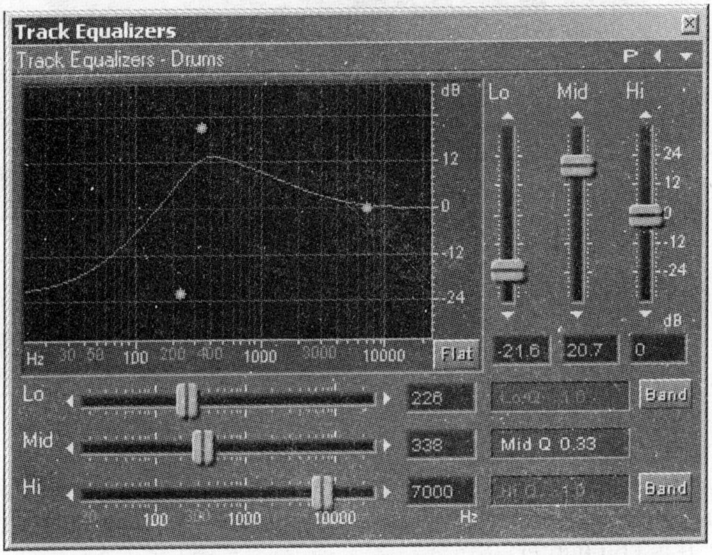

Fig. 10.11. Another way of controlling the track equalizer

In this mode, you can control the center frequencies of the filters and the signal gain or decay with both white dots and sliders. You can adjust the parameters very precisely by clicking the triangles at the end of the slider controls.

The **Band** buttons switch the filter types; the low-pass and high-pass filters (**Lo** and **Hi**) turn into band-pass filters (same as **Mid**). After that, their quality parameters — **Lo Q** and **Hi Q** — become editable.

The **P** button located in the upper part of the window opens the **EQ Presets** dialog box, which allows you to save the current equalizer settings as a preset.

Why is the window being discussed called **Track Equalizers** (plural) and not **Track Equalizer** (singular)? Don't close the window and click any track. You'll see that the track name appears at the top of the window, and the frequency-response curve becomes different from the curve of the track, for which the window was opened. This is because the **Track Equalizers** window shows the equalizer settings of the current track. Now, click the ▼ button and try to select different tracks as current. It will turn out that the **Track Equalizers** window has several tabs with equalizers, each of which corresponds to a particular track (Fig. 10.12).

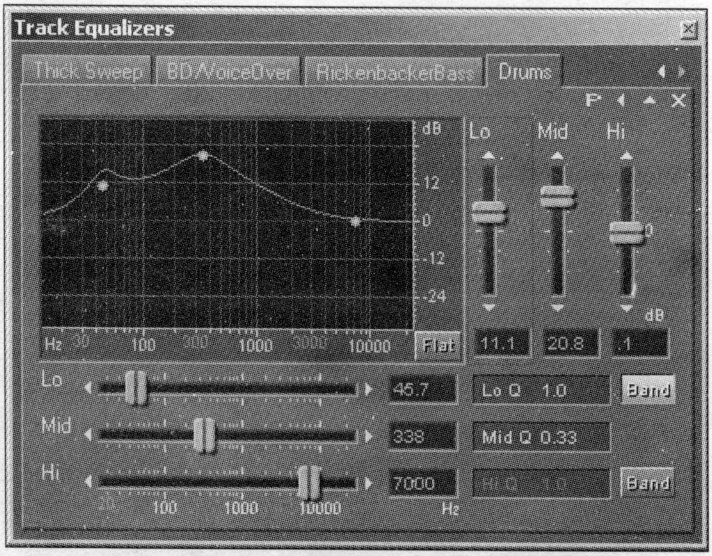

Fig. 10.12. Several equalizers in one window

You might have noticed that Adobe Audition uses the notion of a *current track*. The current track is selected by clicking. The current track differs from the other tracks by color: It is a bit lighter.

Among the track attributes, you'll notice the **Eq /A** (or **Eq /B**) button that has a direct relationship to the track equalizer. The equalizer settings you made are stored in one of two registers. You can switch between the registers with this button. One register stores one set of settings, the other register stores the other settings. You can switch between the settings during playback, thus selecting the best variant (the button name will change between **Eq /A** and **Eq /B**). A double click on this button is a useful technique. As a result, the settings from the current register will be copied to the second register.

So far, we have only considered a situation, in which effects are connected to a bus. Of course, you can connect effects directly to a track. If no effect is connected to a track (which is the default case), a click on the **FX** button opens the **Effects Rack** dialog box (Fig. 10.13).

We already came across a similar window when connecting effects to a bus. However, that window had another name.

Connect the desired effects by selecting them in the tree list **Installed Real-Time Effects** and clicking the **Add->** button to add them to the **Current Effects Rack** list. You can enter a name for the set of effects connected to the track into the **Friendly Name** field. However, the default name isn't bad: **FX** and the track number. Now, click the **Properties** button to access the parameters of the effects. There is another method for connecting effects to a track that involves using an organizer (see *Section 10.2.7*). Just select the desired effect in the **Effects** tree list and drag it to the desired track. In any case, the window shown in Fig. 10.14 will open.

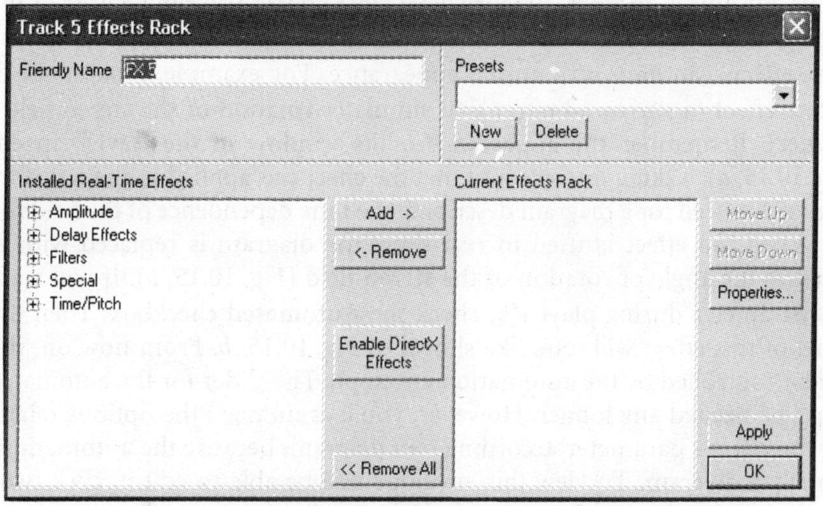

Fig. 10.13. Dialog box for connecting real-time effects to a track

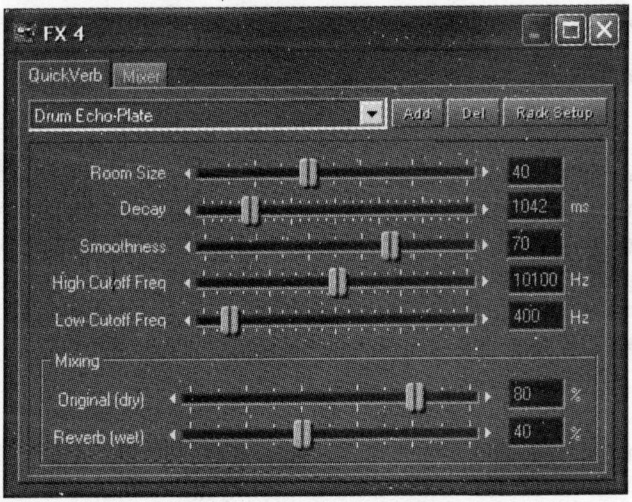

Fig. 10.14. Effect properties

This window contains several tabs that are used to switch between the sets of parameters of different effects. The last tab is called **Mixer**. As its name implies, this tab contains the effect mixer. We gave its detailed description when talking about effects connected to a bus.

All effects built into Adobe Audition can be divided into real-time ones and those that can be used only when destructively editing a waveform. There are also multitrack effects, but this is another category. Real-time effects also can be used in the waveform editing mode. However, in the multitrack mode, the windows with the properties of these effects can have an unusual appearance. For example, look at the **Stereo Field Rotate** effect (a surround effect that simulates rotation of the stereo field around the listener). Remember the appearance of its window in the waveform editing mode (Fig. 10.15, *a*). Taking into account that the effect was applied to the waveform selection, there was a need for a diagram describing the time dependence of the field rotation.

When the effect is used in real time, the diagram is replaced with a slider that specifies the angle of rotation of the stereo field (Fig. 10.15, *b*). If you want to control this parameter during playback, check the **Automated** checkbox. Then the parameter panel of this effect will look like shown in Fig. 10.15, *b*. From now on, the parameter will be controlled by the automation envelope. The slider for the automated parameter won't be needed any longer. However, you'll again need the options related to changing the effect's parameter according to a diagram, because the automation envelope is actually a diagram. To view this envelope and be able to edit it, click two buttons located on the toolbar of the main window:

Edit Envelopes — turns on the mode of editing automation envelopes.

Show FX Parameter Envelopes — turns on the mode of displaying automation envelopes of real-time effects.

A horizontal line with nodes looking like little white rectangles will appear on the track, to which the effect in question is connected. By adding new nodes and moving the available ones, you can shape the curve that shows how the parameter being automated changes with time. This curve is an automation envelope. Working with envelopes will be described comprehensively later.

Real-time effects do not all have automated parameters.

Only real-time effects can be used in the multitrack mode, so we'll call them simply "effects" for brevity's sake.

Another track attribute closely related to effects is the **Lock** button. It can make your work much easier. We already mentioned it, and now we'll look at it more closely.

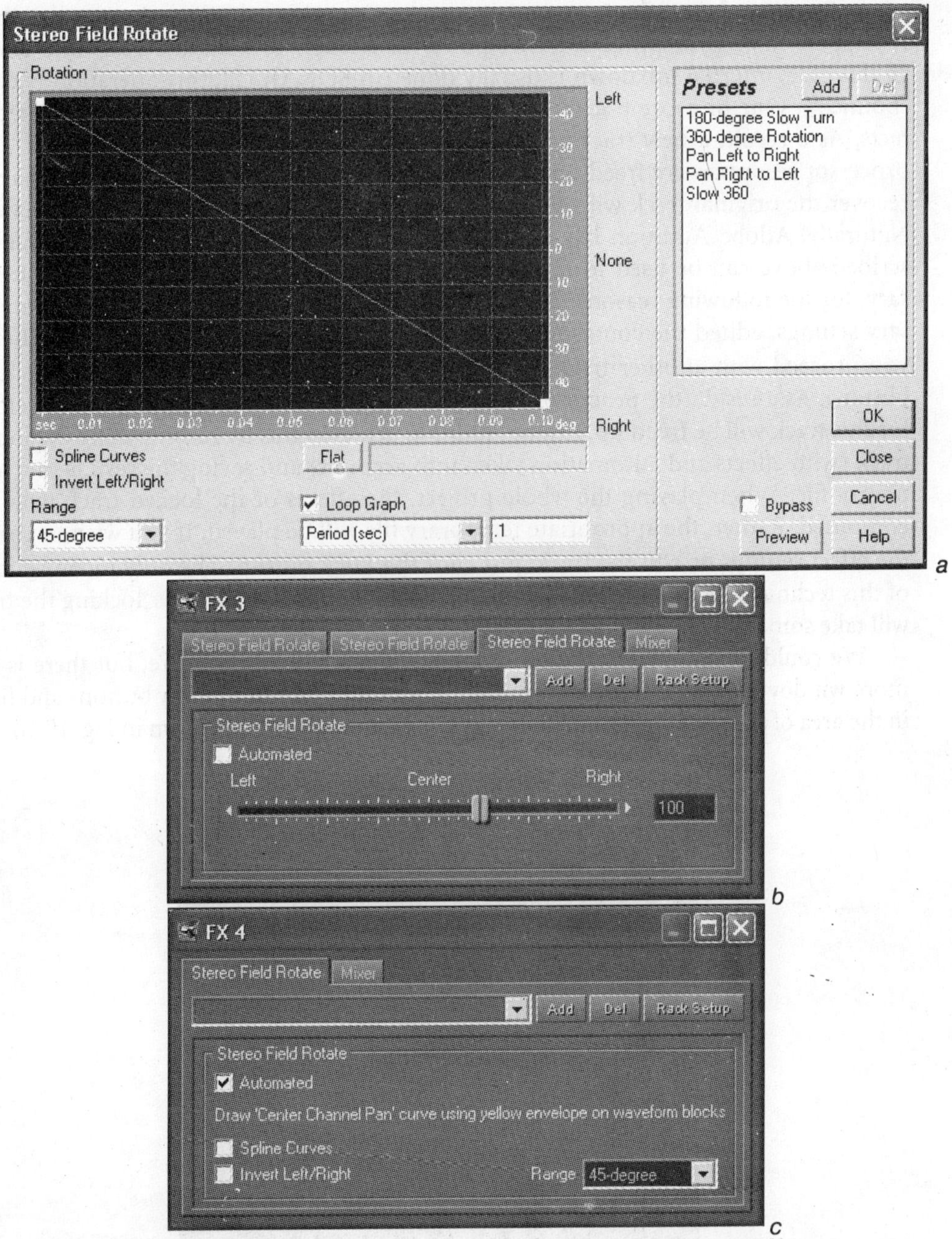

Fig. 10.15. Parameters of the same effect when used in the waveform view (*a*), as a real-time effect (*b*), and as an automated real-time effect (*c*)

Suppose you're mixing a composition using a multitrack musical or audio editor. It happens that your processor isn't powerful enough to compute real-time effects. In this case, internal mixdown is usually done (in SONAR [2], this operation is called "bounce"). One or more tracks are recomputed taking into account the connected effects. As a result, a new track appears. The original track is muted (or deleted), and processor resources are freed up. If you decide to change effect settings, you'll have to recover the original track with the real-time effects connected, and make the changes. Naturally, Adobe Audition has a set of mixdown commands, and the technique described above can be used to free up processor resources. However, this isn't necessary, for the following reasons. Suppose you connected effects to a track, made necessary settings, edited the contents of the track, and used automation envelopes. Before you proceed with another track, you can lock the current one (by clicking the **Lock** button). As a result, the processor resources taken for computing the real-time effects for this track will be freed up. Adobe Audition achieves this by recomputing the locked track (with effects and automation taken into account) and saving the results in a temporary file. When playing the whole project, the effects of the locked track won't be computed. Rather, the appropriate temporary file will be played. If you wish to change the effect settings or edit the track, just click the **Lock** button. The only inconvenience of this technique is that the recomputation of the temporary file after locking the track will take some time.

We could finish the description of the audio track attributes here, but there is one more window that we cannot ignore. Right-click on a place free of any buttons and fields in the area of the audio track attributes. You'll see the dialog box shown in Fig. 10.16.

Fig. 10.16. Track properties

This dialog box displays all the attributes described above, but in a form convenient for editing. In addition, it can contain attributes of several tracks at once. Don't close this dialog box, and click several tracks. You'll see new tabs with these tracks' names appearing in the dialog box.

10.2.3. Inserting Existing Waveforms in a Project. Working with Blocks

We discussed how to add waveforms to a project by recording them. However, there is nothing to prevent you from adding previously recorded waveforms or waveforms stored in a sample library.

There are several ways of doing this:

- In the multitrack editor, insert a waveform that doesn't belong to the session and is opened on the current page in the **Edit Waveform View** mode (use the **Edit > Insert in Multitrack** command of the waveform editor).
- In the multitrack editor, insert any waveform currently loaded in Adobe Audition (with the command **Insert > Waveform_Name**; here and hereafter, we mean multitrack editor commands).
- Insert a waveform from any audio file, i.e., load the file in Adobe Audition and put it at the desired place in the track (with the **Insert > Wave from file** command).
- Use the **Insert > Video from file** command to insert a video file in the multitrack editor; the video will be put on one track (a video track), and the sound track from the file will be put on another track (an ordinary audio track).
- Use the **File > Open Waveform** command to load a waveform in Adobe Audition, then use the **Insert > Waveform_Name** command to put the waveform on one of the tracks.
- Load one or more waveforms in the **Session** while in the **Multitrack View**.
- Mute a waveform in Adobe Audition and use the organizer to drag the waveform from the organizer to the desired track (*Section 10.2.7*).

How can you specify the position, at which the waveform should be put? We already covered the current track, which is specified by clicking either a track or the field with its attributes. The current track is highlighted with a color: It is brighter (lighter). In Fig. 10.17, the current track is the third track (from top).

Like the waveform editor, the multitrack editor displays a marker that indicates the position where recording or playback will start. This marker also determines the position in the track where the waveform will be inserted.

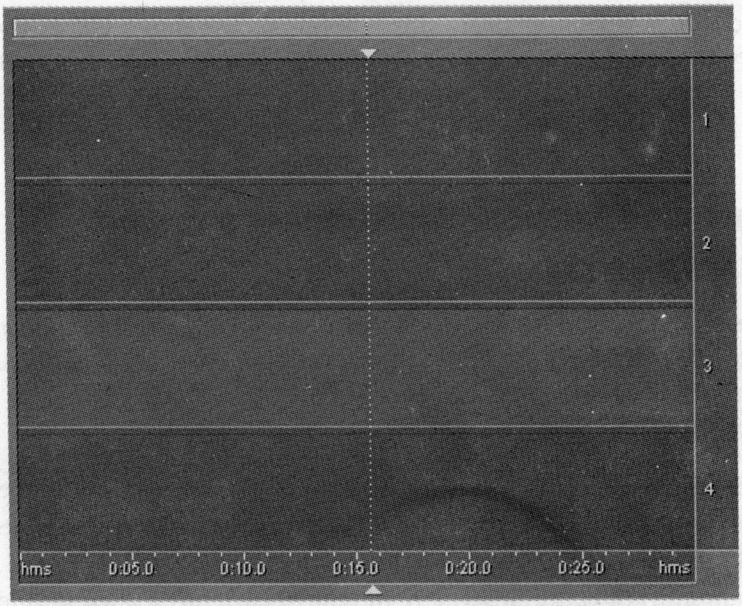

Fig. 10.17. Waveform insertion position

After a waveform appears in the multitrack environment, it is more correct to call it a *block*. There is a couple of reasons for this:

❐ The waveform is contained in a graphic object that can be moved.
❐ Blocks can contain not only a sequence of audio samples (a waveform), but also automation envelopes and a number of attributes discussed later.

It is very easy to move a block. Grab it by clicking the right mouse button and drag it to the desired position in the desired track.

Sometimes, it is necessary to perform operations simultaneously on several blocks that must be previously selected. A group of blocks is selected by clicking them while keeping the <Ctrl> key pressed. There is another method as well: While keeping the <Ctrl> key and the left mouse button pressed, draw a rectangle over the desired blocks with the mouse pointer.

To move several blocks, grab any of the previously selected blocks with the right mouse button, and drag it and the other blocks to a new position.

Not only adjacent blocks can be grouped together. To select several random blocks, click each of them while keeping the <Ctrl> key pressed.

Sometimes, it is necessary to select not individual blocks, but a fragment of a multitrack project covering several blocks or fragments of blocks. What for? For example, you might want to perform a mixdown of this multitrack project to one waveform.

Position the mouse pointer on any of the horizontal lines separating the tracks at the point where the selection should begin. Click and hold the left mouse button and move the mouse pointer to the end point of the selection. After you release the mouse button, you'll see a gray vertical band. You've just selected a project fragment that includes fragments of all existing tracks. Bear in mind that the blocks aren't selected. It is a fragment of the composition that is selected.

You can select one or more blocks within the selection. As a result, parts of blocks can be selected if the edges of the selection cross these blocks. To do this, press the <Ctrl> key and click the block whose fragment you want to select on the area where the gray vertical band crosses the block. The block will be highlighted, and its fragment will be selected.

If you need to select fragments of several overlapping blocks, stick to the same procedure. The only difference is that in the closing stage you should keep on holding the <Ctrl> key pressed and click the fragments of all blocks you need.

What are you going to do if you need to create a copy of a block? Maybe try to copy it to the clipboard? Nothing will come of it: There is no such command. You can perform copying using one of the following methods:

- Insert the same waveform in the project again.
- Keeping the <Ctrl> key and the *right* mouse button pressed, drag the desired block to the place where the copy should be put (the block will remain in place, and the copy of it will appear at the specified position).

The first method can't be called a "pure" copying. The next insertion of a waveform will make a new block appear, and all its attributes will have the default values. The second method is true copying because both waveforms and their attributes are copied.

Splitting blocks can be done as follows:

1. Click the split point (the block will be selected, and the marker will be put at that point).
2. Click the  **Split Blocks** button on the toolbar or select the **Edit** > **Split** main menu command or the **Split** command of the pop-up menu (the pop-up menu is opened by right-clicking).

To delete blocks, select one or more blocks, a fragment of a block, or fragments of several blocks, and hit the <Delete> key.

If you want not only to delete a block from the session, but also unload it from Adobe Audition, select it and hit the <Shift>+<Backspace> shortcut.

Sometimes, it can be useful to combine a few blocks in a group, after which the blocks can be moved or deleted as a complete entity and you don't have to select each individual block, i.e., the blocks of one group would behave as if they were one block. To group blocks:

1. Select the desired blocks.
2. Click the **Group/Ungroup blocks** button on the toolbar or select the **Edit > Group Blocks** command or the **Group Blocks** command of the pop-up menu.

You can lock one or more blocks. This operation has nothing in common with locking tracks, and its only result is that it will be impossible to move blocks. Locking blocks is easy:

1. Select the desired blocks.
2. Click the **Time Lock Block(s)** button on the toolbar or select the **Edit > Lock In Time** command or the **Lock In Time** command of the pop-up menu.

A "lock" icon will appear in the lower left corner of the locked block. Unlocking is done in the same fashion as locking. Click the button or use the same commands as described above.

10.2.4. Working with Loops and Grooves. Editing the Project Parameters

There are two loops, ANALOGUE_JUMPER_C_140BPM.WAV and BREAK_LOOP_A_132BPM.WAV, in the EXAMPLES\CH_10\LOOPS folder on the CD-ROM that accompanies this book. These files contain all necessary settings, so the application will consider them as loops after you load them in a multitrack project. Loops differ from all other blocks by having the icon in the lower left corner of the block.

Fig. 10.18, *a* shows two loop blocks. The tempo of one loop is 140 beats per minute, and the tempo of the other is 132 beats per minute. However, if you start playback of the project, there won't be any discrepancy between the loops. They will be played in the tempo specified for the entire project.

In addition to the WAV files, the mentioned folder contains a project file LOOPS.SES. This project already contains two loops with different original tempos. You may experiment with them.

Another way, in which loop blocks differ from other blocks, is that they can be stretched. Fig. 10.18, *b* shows the upper loop block stretched so that it crosses the right boundary. The block is cyclically filled with the periods of the loop.

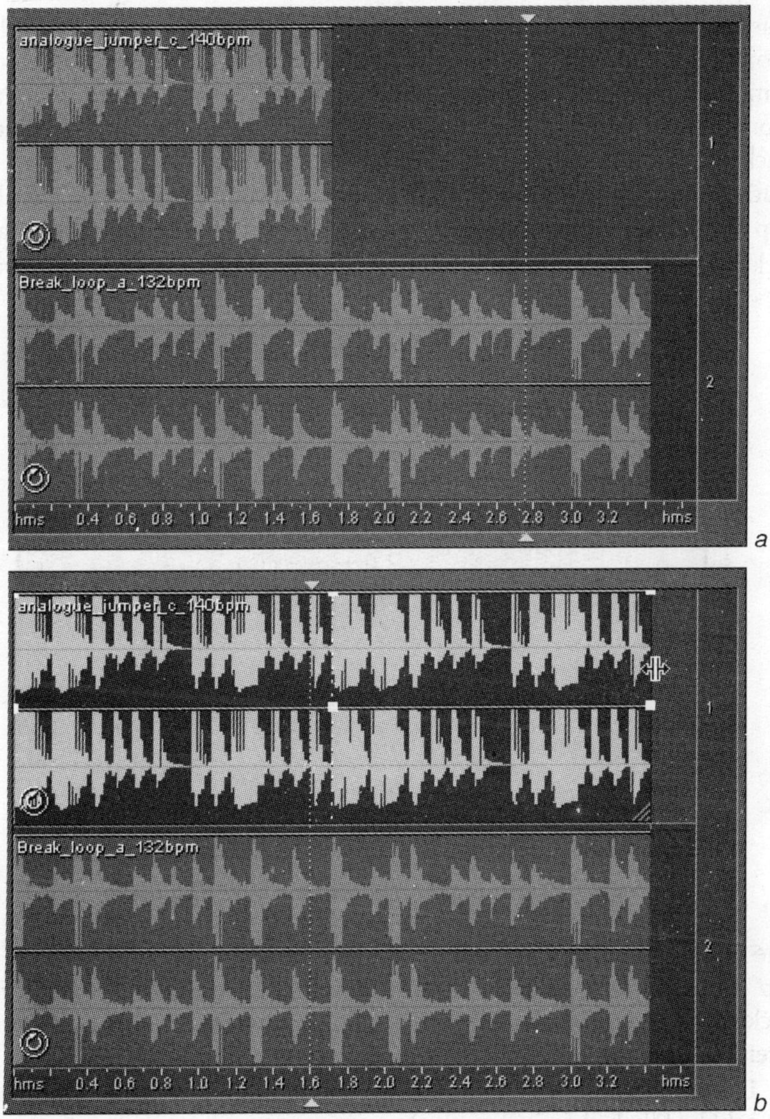

Fig. 10.18. Loop blocks

The loops given as examples are downloaded from **www.looperman.com**, which has a lot of free loops. If you wish to prepare a loop for use in a multitrack project, you'll find all necessary information in [3].

Adjusting the loop tempo is done "on the fly," during its playback within a multitrack project. For the sake of interest, double-click a loop block, thus switching to the waveform editing mode. You'll notice that when the loop is played, its tempo doesn't differ from the tempo it initially has. Despite the change in the loop block length in the multitrack project, its length in the waveform editor doesn't change.

Return to the multitrack mode if necessary and right-click any of the blocks. Select the **Loop Properties** command in the pop-up menu. This command is available for any block type. The **Wave Block Looping** dialog box shown in Fig. 10.19 will open.

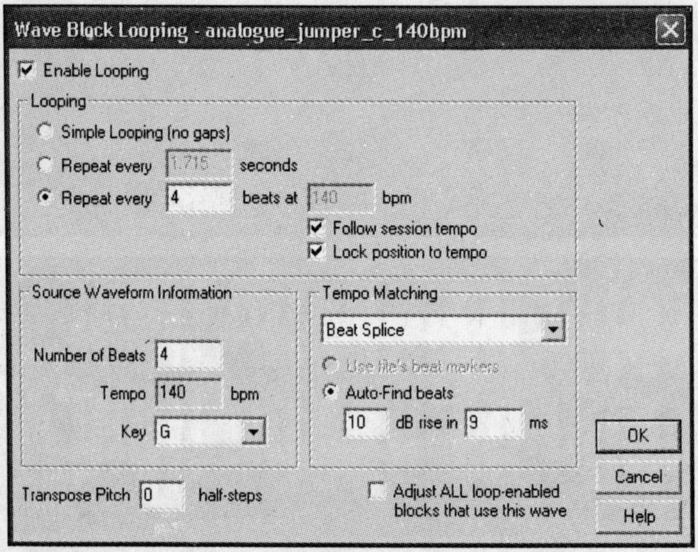

Fig. 10.19. Dialog box with the loop properties

If the **Enable Looping** checkbox is checked, the application "knows" that this block is a loop. In principle, you can loop any waveform if it makes sense. If you uncheck this checkbox, the loop block will turn into an ordinary block that cannot be stretched, and its tempo won't be adjusted to the tempo of the project.

The **Looping** group contains looping parameters that determine how the loop block should be filled when its length changes:

- **Simple Looping (no gaps)** — no tempo adjustment.
- **Repeat every x seconds** — the waveform of the loop is repeated every **x** seconds.
- **Repeat every x beats at y bpm** — every **x** beats are repeated at tempo **y**.

By default, the last of these modes is selected, and the **Follow session tempo** checkbox is checked. If you uncheck this checkbox, the parameter we denoted as **y** will become available, and you'll be able to specify a loop tempo other than the project tempo.

If the **Lock position to tempo** checkbox is checked, the loop block length won't change when the loop tempo changes. For example, if the tempo increases, the loop block will contain more periods than before but the length of the block will remain the same. If you uncheck the **Lock position to tempo** checkbox, the number of periods in the loop block won't change with changing the tempo. Therefore, the length of the loop will change.

The **Source Waveform Information** group includes some of the parameters of the original waveform of the loop that are described in [3, *Section 5.10*] (the same section covers the **Tempo Matching** group, which includes loop tempo correcting algorithms and their parameters).

The lower part of the **Wave Block Looping** dialog box (Fig. 10.19) contains the following options:

- **Transpose Pitch ... half-steps**
- **Adjust ALL loop-enabled blocks that use this wave**

Remember that the term "waveform" isn't a synonym for "block". The same waveform can be used in several different blocks and with different looping parameters.

We've mentioned project tempo several times. Find the **Session Info** panel in the main window (Fig. 10.20). It can be opened with the **View > Show Session Properties** command or the <Alt>+<3> shortcut.

Fig. 10.20. Session Info panel

In the **Session Info** panel, you can specify a multitrack project's tempo (the **Tempo** field), number of beats per bar (**beats/bar**), and tonality and time (the **Key** fields).

The presence of these parameters in a sound editor seems unnatural. It is easy to change the key and tempo when music is represented as MIDI commands, but this isn't the case when it comes to music "assembled" of WAV files. Nevertheless, you already know that loops can adjust themselves to the project tempo that is specified in this panel. As for grooves, they can additionally adjust to the project tonality also specified in this panel. Let's define the difference between the notions "loop" and "groove" more precisely. From the application's point of view, a groove is actually a loop consisting of melodic sounds. The application cannot differentiate by itself which sounds (percussion or melodic) are present in a waveform. When editing loop properties (see Fig. 10.19), you tell the application whether it must consider the waveform a rhythmic loop whose tonality doesn't matter (the **Key** parameter is set to **Non-voiced**) or a groove with a specified tonality (the value of the **Key** parameter is other than **Non-voiced**).

Changing the tonality of the entire project will affect only the tonality of grooves, the blocks for which the value of the **Key** parameter is other than **Non-voiced**.

There are two buttons on the **Session Info** panel (Fig. 10.20):

- **Metronome** — turns on the metronome
- **Advanced** — opens the **Advanced Session Properties** dialog box with an extended set of project parameters, including those that influence the metronome's operation

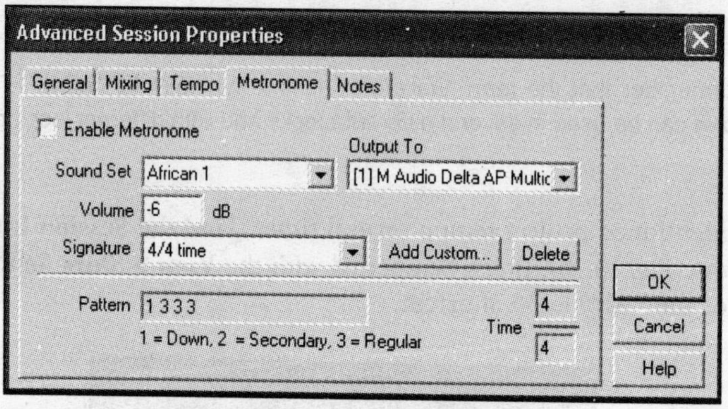

Fig. 10.21. Advanced Session Properties dialog box, **Metronome** tab

The **Advanced Session Properties** dialog box contains several tabs. It would be logical to begin with the **Metronome** tab, which defines the metronome settings (Fig. 10.21).

- The **Enable Metronome** checkbox duplicates the metronome button on the **Session Info** panel.
- The **Sound Set** drop-down list contains a set of sounds used in the metronome.
- **Output To** displays an audio port, through which the metronome sound is output.
- **Volume** displays the volume.

- **Signature** displays the time.
- **Pattern** is a field that displays the metronome pattern, a series of digits that correspond to beats. The first digit corresponds to the first beat, the second to the second, etc. The digits 1 to 3 denote different sounds, and zero denotes the absence of sound. You can define the name of a custom metronome pattern that will be available in the **Signature** list and create an appropriate pattern. To do this, click the **Add Custom** button. The dialog box shown in Fig. 10.22 will appear.

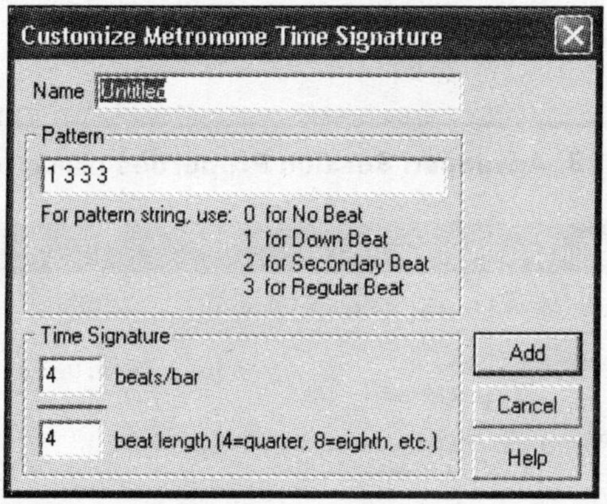

Fig. 10.22. Dialog box for a metronome template

In the **Name** field, enter a metronome pattern name that will be available in the **Signature** list. In the **Pattern** field, enter the pattern proper with digits from 0 to 3 separated by spaces. In the **beats/bar** field of the **Time Signature** group, enter the number of beats in a bar, and in the **beat length (4=quarter, 8=eighth, etc.)** field, enter the beat length.

Let's now go back to the **Advanced Session Properties** dialog box and open **General** tab (Fig. 10.23).

SMPTE Start Time Offset determines a delay between receiving a project play command and the beginning of the actual playback. The delay might be needed when Adobe Audition is used with devices synchronized via the SMPTE protocol. By clicking the **Format** button, you can change the format, in which the delay value is displayed. For example, **Samples** is the number of sound samples, **Decimal (hh:mm:ss.ddd)** is the *hours:minutes:seconds:fractions-of-a-second* format, etc.

The **Key for Voiced Loops** list displays the project tonality (this is equivalent to the **Key** list on the **Session Info** panel).

The **Mixing** tab of the **Advanced Session Properties** dialog box is shown in Fig. 10.24.

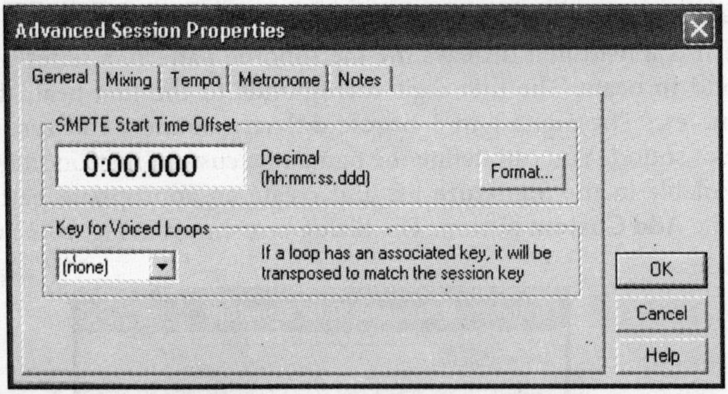

Fig. 10.23. Advanced Session Properties dialog box, **General** tab

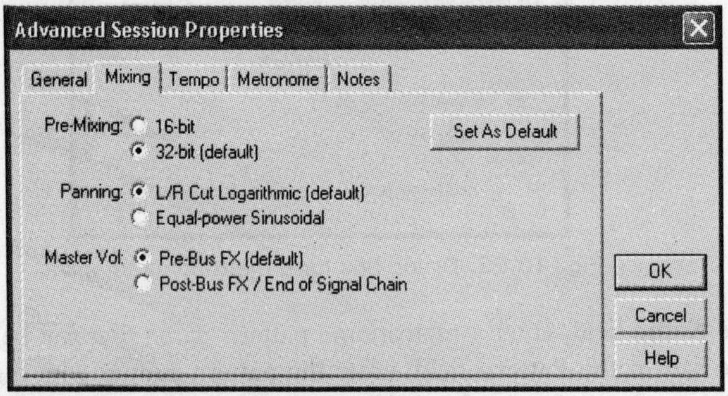

Fig. 10.24. Advanced Session Properties dialog box, **Mixing** tab

In the **Panning** group, you can select the panning method:

- **L/R Cut Logarithmic (default)** — panning is achieved by decreasing the signal level in the opposite stereo channel logarithmically.
- **Equal-power Sinusoidal** — when panning, the signal level in one channel is decreased, and in the other channel, it is increased; as a result, the total power of the signal is retained.

In the **Pre-Mixing** group, you can select the resolution of the digital signal obtained during background mixing to 16 bits or 32 bits (by default). If you click the **Set As Default** button, the settings done on this tab will be default when creating a new project.

So what is background mixing? Computation related to sound processing requires a lot of processor time. Although Windows is a multitask operating system, there is usually a lot of processor time. Since computers are personal, most events they process are generated by the user. This means that your computer is practically idle between the commands you give. Of course, it runs various system processes, but these take much less time than, say, computing a reverberation effect. What is the clock rate of your computer? Suppose 2 GHz. Therefore, the processor has billions of idle ticks between your commands. Adobe Audition doesn't waste this time, thanks to background mixing. The application continually monitors all changes in the parameters of tracks, blocks, effects, etc. and mixes your project. If you change any block settings, the application recomputes the mix that contains this block. When you start the playback of your project, Adobe Audition will be ready to play it because all necessary computations (or at least some of them) will be completed and saved in temporary files by that moment. If necessary, background mixing continues during the playback.

You can introduce changes in your project during the playback. They will be processed by the application, and you'll hear them. The progress of background mixing is indicated by the indicator , located below the track attribute fields. During the process, the application accesses the hard disk intensively.

Of course, background mixing is done only when necessary. If the application has completed computing the mix of the whole project, and you don't give any new commands, it won't perform background mixing. The entire progress indicator will be light green.

The **Tempo** tab of the **Advanced Session Properties** dialog box is shown in Fig. 10.25.

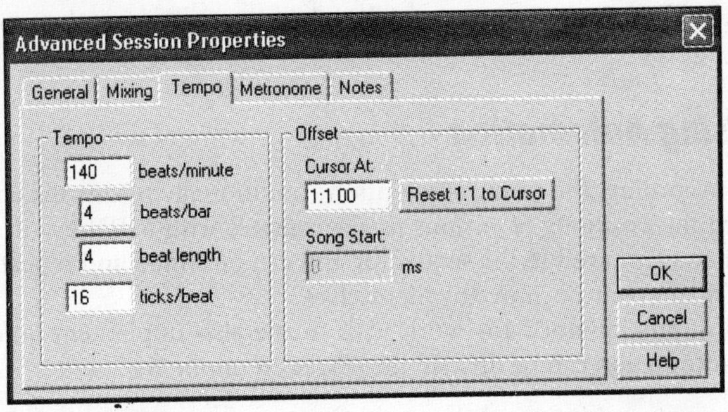

Fig. 10.25. Advanced Session Properties dialog box, **Tempo** tab

The **Tempo** group contains editable parameters related to the project tempo (they partly duplicate the fields of the **Session Info** panel):

- **beats/minute** — tempo
- **beats/bar, beat length** — time signature
- **ticks/beat** — the number of ticks in a beat

Beats are divided into ticks that can be considered time marks used by the application when performing various synchronization tasks.

The **Cursor At** field in the **Offset** group specifies the offset of the ruler. If you click the **Reset 1:1 to Cursor** button, the marker position will correspond to the zero on the ruler.

The **Notes** tab of the **Advanced Session Properties** dialog box is shown in Fig. 10.26.

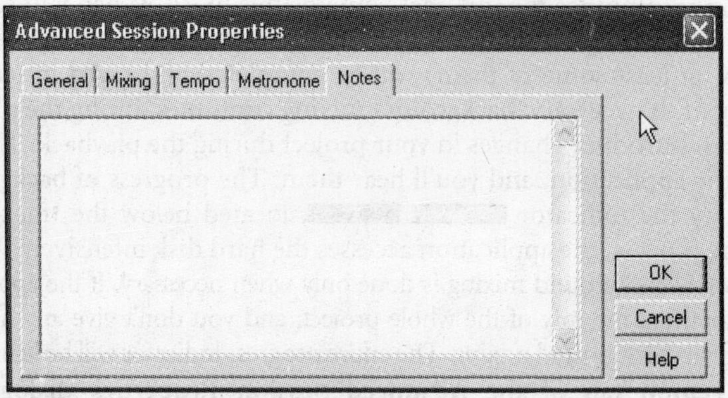

Fig. 10.26. Advanced Session Properties dialog box, **Notes** tab

Here, you can enter your notes and comments concerning the project and nothing more.

10.2.5. Using Automation

In sound recording, the term "automation" traditionally means the ability to write the changes to the positions of various mixer controls with MIDI events. All of a soundman's actions are saved in the sequencer and can be edited and repeated. During playback, the mixer controls move by themselves.

Applications intended for work with music also implement automation. In this context, automation can be divided into three components:

- The user writes the movements of virtual controls (MIDI controllers) in the form of automation envelopes.
- The automation envelopes are created "from scratch" and edited graphically.
- The application changes the automated parameters when it plays a multitrack project.

Adobe Audition implements the second and the third components of automation. The application doesn't allow you to write the changes you're making to the settings of tracks, effects, etc., when playing a project. Naturally, the application responds to these changes, but they are not saved as diagrams of time-dependence of any parameters. However, you can create and graphically edit automation envelopes that will control various parameters during project playback. In fact, automation envelopes are time-dependence diagrams of parameters. For example, the higher the volume envelope, the louder the sound in the corresponding block portion. Conversely, using envelopes, you can, for example, muffle background music when a narrator is speaking (we assume that his or her voice is recorded in a block placed in parallel with the block containing the background music on another track).

A panorama envelope should be treated as follows. The higher the curve, the further to the left the sound source; the lower the curve, the further to the right the sound source. The center of the panorama corresponds to the horizontal central line in the block.

Automation envelopes of effect parameters can be treated as follows. The higher the curve, the greater the value of the automated parameter; the lower the curve, the lesser the parameter value.

Below are the buttons on the toolbar and the corresponding commands of the main menu relating to automation curves:

 (the **View > Show Volume Envelopes** command) — shows or hides volume envelopes

 (the **View > Show Pan Envelopes** command) — shows or hides panorama envelopes

 (the **View > Show Wet/Dry Mix Envelopes** command) — shows or hides envelopes of the **Wet/Dry** parameter (which reflects the ratio of the level of the signal processed by an effect to the original signal level)

 (the **View > Show FX Parameter Envelopes** command) — shows or hides automation envelopes of effect parameters

 (the **View > Show Tempo Envelopes** command) — shows or hides tempo envelopes in MIDI files added to the project (these envelopes are stored directly in the MIDI files and are unavailable for editing)

 (the **View > Enable Envelope Editing** command) — turns on and off the mode of automation envelope editing.

First press the  and  buttons and release the other ones. A broken line will be visible over each block. This is an automation envelope. In essence, it is a time-dependence diagram of the signal level. Only the envelope of the selected block is available for editing. If you click a block (thus selecting it), the envelope nodes (knee points) will appear. You can create a new node. Move the mouse pointer to the envelope (the pointer will look like this:) and click. A new node will appear. When the mouse pointer is over a node, a hint will appear that displays the value of the automated parameter at this point (Fig. 10.27).

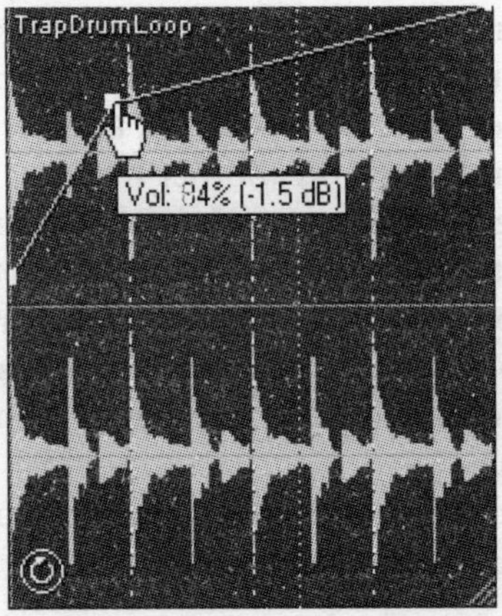

Fig. 10.27. Volume envelope and the value of the automated parameter

You can create as many nodes as you wish to shape the envelope by moving the nodes with the mouse.

It is often useful to approximate envelopes with splines. Then the envelope will look like a curve running smoothly over the nodes, rather than a broken line. This option is enabled in the following manner. Right-click a block (you can first select several blocks), and the pop-up menu of the block will appear. Select the **Envelopes** command and then select one of three types of envelopes:

- **Volume**
- **Pan**
- **FX Mix**

Then select the **Use Splines** command for the selected envelope (Fig. 10.29).

The appearance of an envelope without approximation and with a spline approximation is shown in Fig. 10.28, *a* and *b*.

If approximation is disabled, the envelope is built using first-order interpolation, i.e., the nodes are connected with lines.

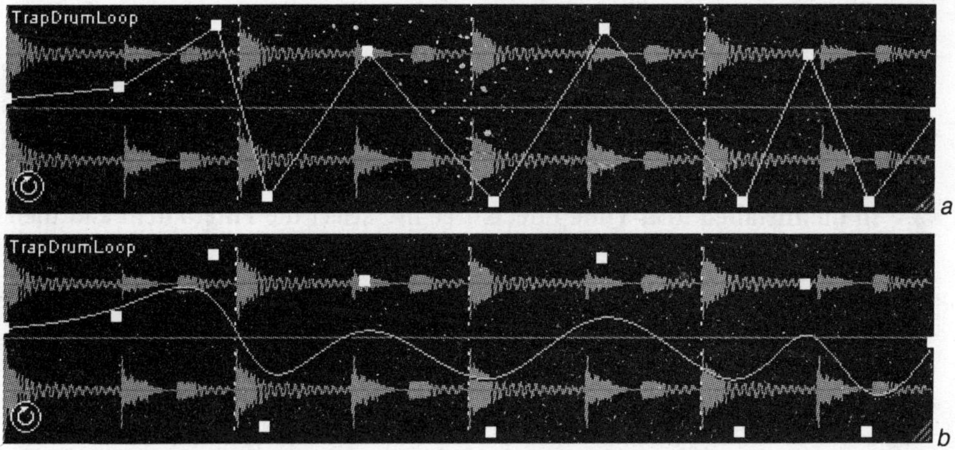

Fig. 10.28. Envelopes: (*a*) common; (*b*) spline-approximated

The **Use Splines** command is in the same submenu as the **Clear Selected Points** command (Fig. 10.29), which can be useful when you need to delete a few nodes.

Fig. 10.29. Part of the block pop-up menu

Before you use this command, select a fragment of the multitrack project that contains the envelope nodes you want to delete. Then right-click the block containing these nodes to open the pop-up menu.

There is a simpler way of deleting an envelope node. Grab the node with the mouse and drag it away from the block.

Try to automate an effect in practice, for example, a filter with dynamic control of the parameters (the filter that implements the "wah-wah" effect). Let one track contain a block that should be processed with this effect. This is the track we will experiment with. Here are the stages of this process:

1. Connecting the effect to the appropriate track
2. Selecting the parameters to automate
3. Creating envelopes

Now let's look at the procedures involved in these stages.

Connecting the Effect to the Appropriate Track

1. Click the **FX** button in the track attribute field. If no effect is connected to the track, the **Effects Rack** window will open. If effects are already connected to the track, the window with their parameters will open. In this window, click the **Rack Setup** button, and the **Effects Rack** window will open.
2. In the **Installed Real-Time Effects** tree list, select the **Filters** item and then select the Dynamic EQ item.
3. Click the **Add->** button and then the **OK** button. The effect will be connected to the track.

Selecting the Parameters to Automate

Click the **FX** button in the track attribute field. Since at least one effect is connected to the track, the effect parameter window will open.

If more than one effect is connected to the track, go to the **Dynamic EQ** tab (Fig. 10.30). In the bottom part of this tab, select the filter type with one of the following radio buttons: **Low Pass**, **Band Pass**, or **High Pass**.

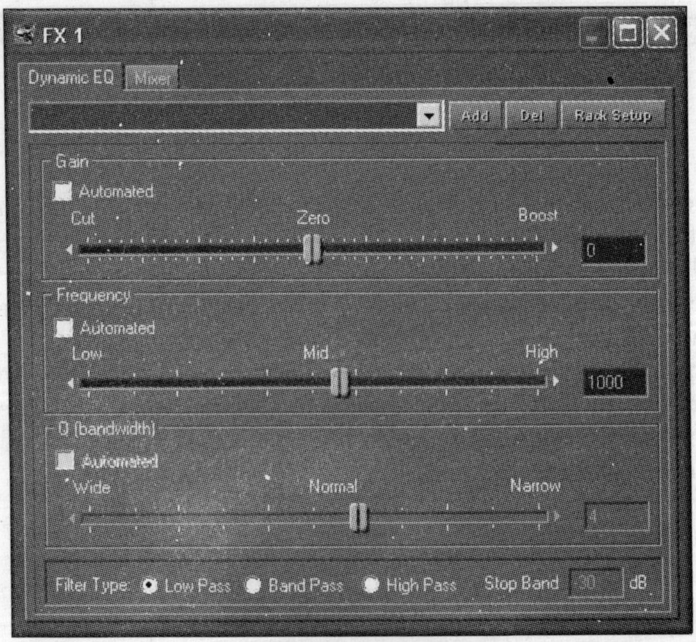

Fig. 10.30. Parameters of the **Dynamic EQ** effect

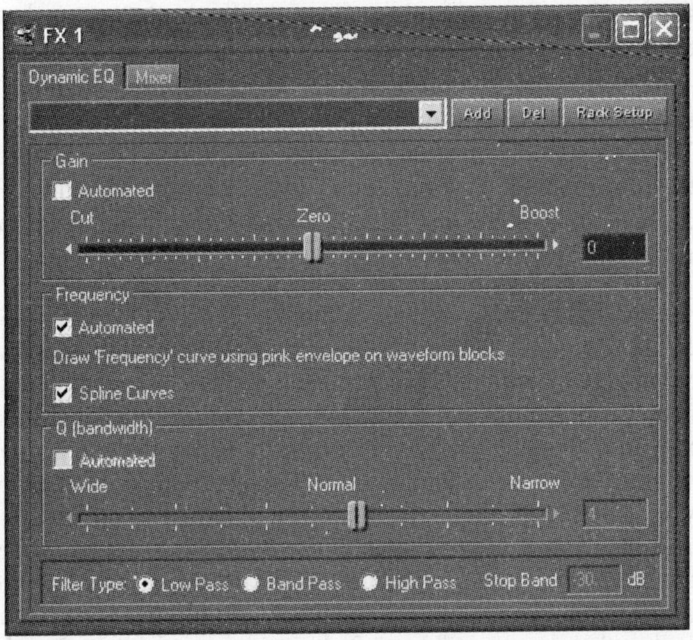

Fig. 10.31. Frequency parameter of the **Dynamic EQ** effect is selected for automation

Three parameters of this effect are available for automation. These are the output gain (**Gain**), the cutoff frequency (**Frequency**), and the quality (**Q**). The last parameter is available only for the band-pass filter. Check the **Automated** checkboxes for those parameters that should be automated (we chose only one: **Frequency**). The window will look like that shown in Fig. 10.31.

If necessary, check the **Spline Curves** checkboxes to enables spline approximation of the envelopes of the parameters being automated.

Close the effect parameter window or move it aside so that it doesn't get in the way.

Creating Envelopes

1. Use the **View > Enable Envelope Editing** command or the button located on the main window toolbar to enable the envelope editing mode. Use the button or the **View > Show FX Parameter Envelopes** command to access the automation envelopes of the effect parameters. Click the block whose envelopes you're going to edit.
2. By default, envelopes look like horizontal lines. As there can be more than one envelope, first find the envelope you want to edit. To do this, move the mouse pointer to each envelope in turn and watch the status bar of the main window.

It will display the name and value of the parameter that controls the envelope, to which the mouse pointer is moved. We chose the **Frequency** envelope.

3. Create nodes by clicking the envelope. Move them so that the envelope takes the shape you want. If any nodes appear by mistake, drag them away from the block. You can select a fragment of the project being edited, start loop playback, and listen to the results of your actions as you edit the envelope. To start the loop playback, select the **Options > Loop Mode** command and start the playback with an appropriate transport control.

We saved the results of our actions in the file FX-AUTOMATION.SES in the folder EXAMPLES\CH_10\FX-AUTOMATION on the CD-ROM that accompanies this book.

To complete this section, let's quickly recap on the important points.

Information concerning the shapes of automation envelopes relates to a *block*, rather than a track. In other words, the shapes of envelopes are properties of a block. At the same time, a list of available automation envelopes is a property of a *track*. You can try an experiment. Move the block, for which we've created an envelope, along one track, and then move it to another track. You'll find that envelopes typical to one track (such as envelopes of the parameters of certain effects connected to the track) disappear on another track. If you return the block to the original track, the envelopes will appear again, but their shapes will be default, i.e., horizontal lines. To give the envelopes their previous shapes, you'll have to use the **Edit > Undo** command at least once.

10.2.6. Introducing Pop-up Menus of Tracks and Blocks

Pop-up menus of tracks and blocks contain most commands of the application's main menu related to editing a multitrack project. It is more convenient to select these commands in the pop-up menus accessed by right-clicking on an object being edited.

The Track Pop-up Menu

The track pop-up menu is opened by right-clicking on a track portion that is free from blocks. Commands selected in this menu will be applied to the track that was clicked. Some of the commands were discussed earlier, some other commands open windows that were also discussed (in Adobe Audition, it is generally possible to open a window in several ways).

Consider the rest of the commands.

- **Insert** — opens a submenu, in which you can select a source of data added to a multitrack project. The **Insert** submenu includes the following commands:
  - **Empty Wave** — creates a block that doesn't contain a waveform. The size of the block is defined by the width of the previously selected project fragment. If no selection was made, the command is unavailable.

- **Empty Wave (Mono)** — is similar to the previous command, but the created block is in the mono format.
- **Wave from File** — inserts a WAV file in the project.
- **MIDI from File** — inserts a MIDI file in the project.
- **Video from File** — inserts the video image from an AVI file in the project.
- **Audio from Video File** — inserts the sound track from an AVI file in the project.
- **File/Cue List** — opens the **Insert Into Multitrack** window with a list of waveforms and cues loaded in Adobe Audition [3, *Section 5.3*].

In addition, the Insert menu allows you to select a waveform out of those loaded in Adobe Audition.

- **Mix Down to Track (Bounce)** — opens a submenu with commands related to the internal mixdown (mixing several blocks to one):
  - **All Waves** — mixes down all blocks.
  - **Selected Waves** — mixes down only the selected blocks.
  - **All Waves (Mono)** and **Selected Waves (Mono)** — commands similar to the previous ones, but the result is saved in the mono format.

The following commands of the track pop-up menu switch the states of the track attributes:

- **Mute Track** — mutes the track.
- **Solo Track** — makes the track solo.
- **Solo Current Track Only** — makes the track solo and resets the **S** (solo) attributes of the other tracks.
- **Arm Track for Record** — prepares the track for recording.

The following commands of the track pop-up menu open dialog boxes in which various track parameters are available for editing:

- **Track Volume** — opens a dialog box with a volume control.
- **Track Pan** — opens a dialog box with a panorama control.
- **Effects Settings** — opens a dialog box with effect parameters if at least one effect is connected to the track; otherwise, opens the **Effects Rack** dialog box.
- **Rack Settings** — opens the **Effects Rack** dialog box, in which effects can be connected or disconnected.
- **Playback Device** — opens the **Playback Devices** dialog box, in which you can select an output audio port for this track.

- **Recording Device** — opens the **Recording Devices** dialog box, in which you can select an input audio port, from which recording will be done; in addition, you can select a format (stereo or mono, and resolution).
- **Track Equalizer** — opens the dialog box of the track equalizer.
- **Track Properties** -— opens a dialog box with the track properties.

It only remains to discuss two commands of the track pop-up menu:

- **Select All Blocks in Track** is self-explanatory.
- **Insert/Delete Time** opens a dialog box with the same name (Fig. 10.32) that allows you to insert a rest into a multitrack project (move apart the blocks on all tracks) or delete the selection. Before using this command, it makes sense to select a fragment in the project and free up the selection from blocks by moving them to the right or deleting. After the command is executed, the blocks that were partly contained in the selection will be cut by an edge of the selection.

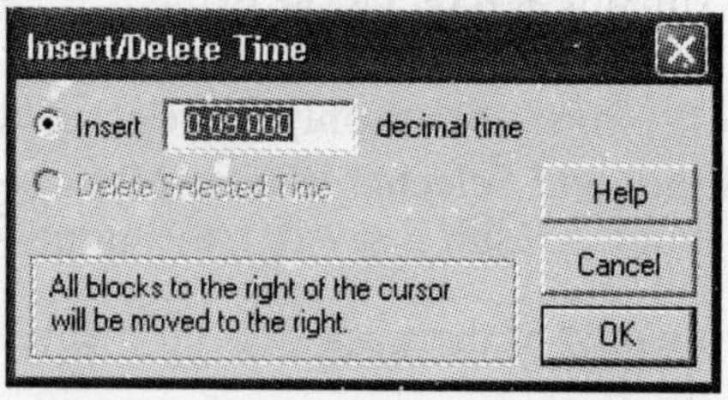

Fig. 10.32. Insert/Delete Time dialog box

There are two radio buttons in the **Insert/Delete Time** dialog box:

- **Insert** inserts a rest whose length is specified in the format selected in the **View > Display Time Format** submenu.
- **Delete Selected Time** deletes the selection.

The Block Pop-up Menu (If Only One Block Is Selected)

The block pop-up menu is opened by right-clicking on a block. Commands selected in this menu will be applied to the block that was clicked. Below are the commands of the block pop-up menu:

- **Edit Waveform** — opens the waveform of the block in the editing mode.
- **Loop Properties** — opens the **Wave Block Looping** dialog box (see *Section 10.2.4*). If looping is enabled for this block, a tick is displayed next to the **Loop Properties** command.
- **Allow Multiple Takes** — turns the **Multiple Takes** mode on and off. If you have several attempts at recording on approximately the same area on a track, the older

material will be overrecorded by the new one. In the **Multiple Takes** mode, all takes are retained. You can select a desired take in the **Take History** submenu. In fact, the **Multiple Takes** mode allows you to put different blocks on the same place on a track. By selecting the **Delete This Take** command of the **Take History** submenu, you can delete the current take.

- **Adjust Wave Block Volume** — opens a dialog box with a volume control. Volume adjustment will be applied to the block, and not to the entire track.
- **Adjust Wave Block Pan** — opens a dialog box with a panorama control. Panorama adjustment will be applied to the block.
- **Wave Block Properties** — opens a dialog box that makes it possible to set the main block properties (Fig. 10.33):
    - **Volume** — the vertical slider control
    - **Pan** — the horizontal slider control
    - **Filename / Path** — a field for assigning the block a new name other than the name of the file that contains the waveform
    - **Time Offset** — a field with the offset of the block relative to the beginning of the track
    - **Block Color** — a slider control for the block color
    - **Mute** — a checkbox that mutes the block
    - **Lock in Time** — a checkbox that prohibits the block from moving to another time position
    - **Lock for Play Only** — a checkbox that prohibits recording over the block

Fig. 10.33. Wave Block Properties dialog box

- **Mix Down to File** — performs mixing the block down and saves the mix in a file. You might think this command makes no sense for one block because its waveform already exists as a file. However, executing this command results in computation of a new waveform taking into consideration track parameters (volume, panorama, etc.) and the effects applied to the track that contains this block.
- **Mix Down to File (Mono)** — is similar to the previous command, but mixing down is done in the mono format.
- **Block Color** — opens a dialog box with the same name for selecting the block color (Fig. 10.34).

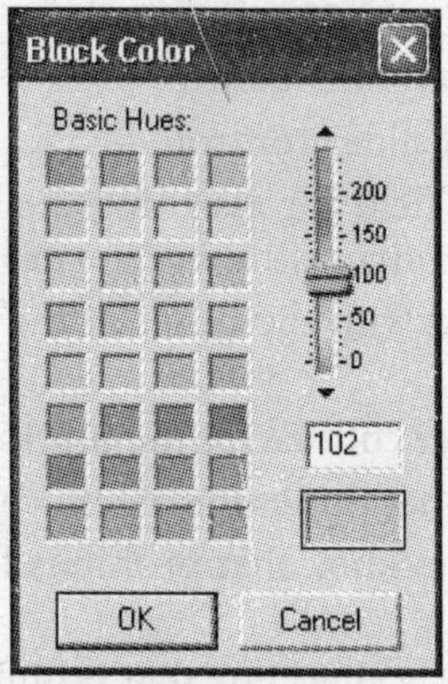

Fig. 10.34. Block Color dialog box

Using this dialog box, you can change the block color. It is interesting that you cannot select an unsuitable block color, for example, such that graphic elements will melt into the background.

- **Punch In** — performs the following operations:
  - Splits the original block along the edges of the selection; as a result, two or three independent blocks appear
  - Turns on the **Lock for Play Only** mode for the blocks located outside the selection
  - Turns on the **Allow Multiple Takes** mode for the blocks located inside the selection

As a result of these actions automatically performed by the application, you can record as many takes as you like to the selection. You don't risk erasing the material outside the selection, and you'll be able to choose the best take later.

- **Crossfade** — opens a submenu whose commands automatically build a volume envelope within the selection in the block. The volume will fade in or out, depending on which part of the block is selected (whether it is closer to the beginning or end). The following types of fade in/out are possible:

- **Linear**
- **Sinusoidal**
- **Logarithmic In** (concave)
- **Logarithmic Out** (convex)

Logarithmic laws of changing the volume over time are most natural.

- **Loop Duplicate** — opens a dialog box with the same name that allows you to create several consecutive copies of the block (Fig. 10.35).

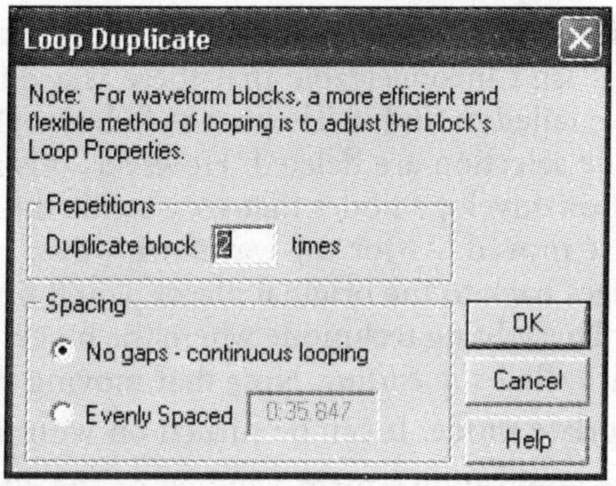

Fig. 10.35. Loop Duplicate dialog box

In the **Duplicate block ... times** field, specify the number of the copies of the block. If the **No gaps - continuous looping** radio button is selected, the copies of the block will follow each other without gaps. If the **Evenly Spaced** radio button is selected, you can specify the interval between the copies of the block.

- **Convert to Unique Copy** — creates a copy of the waveform of the block that substitutes the original waveform. The new waveform is saved in a new file. When applied to a loop or groove, this command gives interesting results. Suppose the waveform of a loop actually contains one measure of a rhythmic part. If you stretch the loop block so that it takes several measures, the contents of its waveform won't change. The waveform will contain one measure as before. If you then use the **Convert to Unique Copy** command, a new waveform will appear that will have as many measures as the original block. As for the block, it won't lose the properties of a loop.

The following three commands of the block pop-up menu relate to the block properties already familiar to you:

- **Mute Block** — self-explanatory.
- **Lock in Time** — locks the block from being moved.

- **Lock for Play Only** — locks the block from recording.
- **Split** — splits the block at the marker position or by the edges of the selection. You already came across this command in *Section 10.2.3*.
- **Merge/Rejoin Split** — connects the block with adjacent blocks. If the blocks have different origins (contain different waveforms), this operation is called merging. The waveforms are merged with overlapping and a crossfade 30 milliseconds long. If the blocks were obtained as a result of splitting (with the **Split** command), the operation is called rejoining. In this case, they must follow in the same sequence as after execution of the **Split** command.
- **Adjust Boundaries** and **Trim** — perform the same action, although they have different names. It isn't inconceivable that there is a difference between the two commands, but we failed to find it. They act as follows. The fragments of the block that are outside the selection are deleted. However, this isn't a complete deletion. Only the automation envelope nodes that are outside the selection are deleted, and the block edges are moved. As for the waveforms, they remain untouched. If you drag the block edges back to the original places, you'll find that nothing happened to the waveform. This editing technique where the block edges aren't bound to the waveform edges is called *slip editing*. Note that moving the block edges is possible only in an appropriate mode. It can be turned on with the  button located on the toolbar of the application's main window or the **View > Enable Block Edge Dragging** command.
- **Cut** — has nothing in common with the command of the same name that cuts a selection onto the clipboard. This command splits the block at the edges of the selection and deletes the selected portion.
- **Full** — moves apart the block edges so that they coincide with the edges of the waveform.
- **Remove Block** — removes the block, but doesn't close the corresponding waveform file.
- **Destroy Block (remove & close)** — removes the block and closes the corresponding waveform file.
- **Envelopes** — opens a submenu with commands that are already familiar to you (see *Section 10.2.5*).

The Block Pop-up Menu (If a Block Group Is Selected)

The block pop-up menu is opened by right-clicking on any of the selected blocks provided that at least two blocks are selected. Commands selected in this menu will be applied to all selected blocks. The pop-up menu of *blocks* contains much fewer commands than the pop-up menu of a *block* does. (Many commands of the former menu have names identical to the names of the commands in the latter menu and perform the same actions, but with the selected block group rather than with one block.) We'll describe only a few specific commands of the block group menu:

- **Group Blocks** — groups and ungroups the selected blocks.
- **Group Color** — opens a dialog box with the same name that allows you to change the color of the block group.
- **Align Left** — aligns the selected blocks along the left edge of the block that was right-clicked to open the pop-up menu.
- **Align Right** — is similar to the previous command, but the alignment is done along the right edge of the block.
- **Crossfade** — opens a submenu containing the commands for automatically building a volume envelope. You already encountered these commands, but then they worked with one block. If you apply them to several blocks, the envelopes will be built so that the volumes of some overlapping blocks will fade out, and those of the other overlapping blocks will fade in. The term "crossfade" means an overlapping effect, in which one sound gradually transits to another.

10.2.7. Using the Organizer

The **View > Show Organizer Window** command opens the **Organizer** panel that is used for making work with files and effects more convenient.

The panel looks like an organizer that you can refer to to recall details concerning editing waveforms. The most important thing is that the **Organizer** panel allows you to execute many operations without accessing the main menu.

The panel contains three tabs:

- **Files** — contains options for working with files
- **Effects** — opens an effect window
- **Favorites** — executes your favorite operations

The *Files* Tab. Options for Work with Files

The **Files** tab of the **Organizer** panel is shown in Fig. 10.36.

The main portion of the **Files** tab is occupied by a scrollable list of opened files. At the top of the tab, there are the buttons . By clicking them, you can perform a few "popular" file operations:

 **Open File** — opens a file.

 **Close Files** — closes the files selected in the list on the **Files** tab.

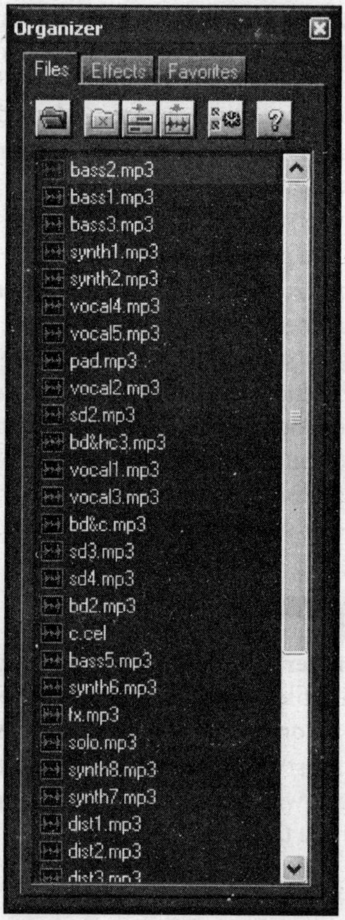

Fig. 10.36. Files tab of the **Organizer** panel

Insert Into Multitrack — inserts the selected files into the multitrack editor. When inserting, the application might ask you to let it convert the file format.

Edit File — makes the page with the file selected in the list current. (If a page is current it means it is displayed and available for editing.) This button is inactive when the file displayed in the current page is selected in the list. You also can switch between pages by double-clicking the necessary files in the list.

Advanced Options — turns on advanced options. After these options are turned on, the **Files** tab looks as shown in Fig. 10.37.

The rightmost button doesn't need explanations. It opens the online help.

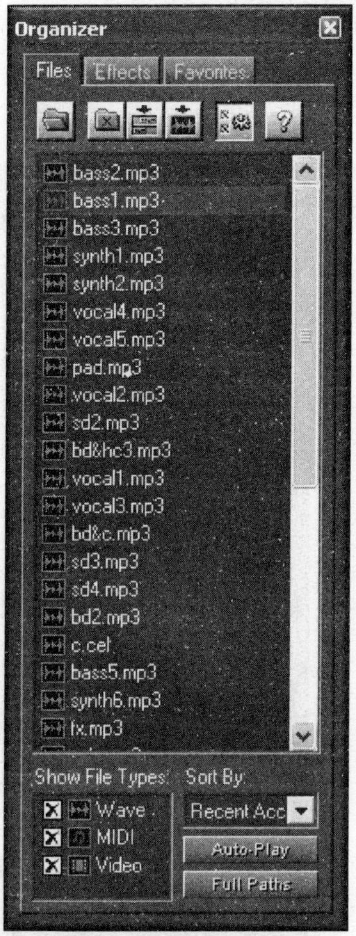

Fig. 10.37. Files tab of the **Organizer** panel; advanced options turned on

The lower left part of the tab contains the file type filter for the files displayed in the list. It is assumed that you may work with audio, MIDI, and video files. The list will show the names of the files of the types, for which the checkboxes in the **Show File Types** group are checked.

The drop-down list **Sort By** allows you to select how the files will be ordered (sorted) in the list.

If the **Auto-Play** button is pressed, the next file you select in the list will be played automatically.

If the **Full Paths** button is pressed, the full paths to the files will be shown in the list in addition to the file names and extensions.

The *Effects* Tab. Opening an Effect Window

The **Effects** tab of the **Organizer** panel lists effects available in Adobe Audition (Fig. 10.38).

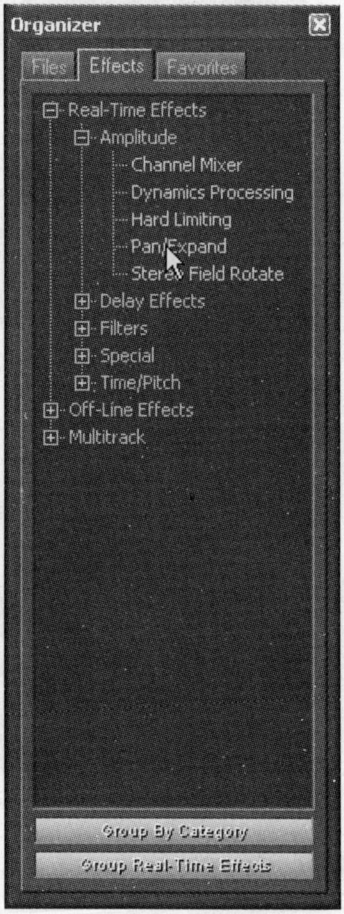

Fig. 10.38. Effects tab of the **Organizer** panel

To open the window of an effect, click its name in the list. The list is organized depending on the states (pressed or released) of the buttons **Group By Category** and **Group Real-Time Effects.**

If none of the buttons is pressed, the available effects are listed in alphabetic order.

If the **Group By Category** button is pressed, the effects are grouped by their functionality.

If the **Group Real-Time Effects** button is pressed, the effects are displayed as a tree with three branches. At the lowest level of the hierarchy, you see a list of effects. The effects whose names are highlighted can be used in real time.

In Adobe Audition, all effects are divided into three categories:

- **Real-Time Effects** — can be used both in the waveform editing mode and the multitrack mode
- **Off-Line Effects** — can be used only in the waveform editing mode
- **Multitrack**

By these categories, the effects can be grouped in the tree list of the organizer. In fact, all Adobe Audition effects are plug-ins, and the organizer displays their list. In principle, multitrack effects can be *connected* to a track by dragging them from the organizer to the track. However, you shouldn't do so because effects of this category can be *applied* only to selected blocks within a selection in a multitrack project. You can call them from the organizer by double-clicking the necessary effect's name. It is recommended that you use multitrack effects only through the **Effects** menu.

Multitrack effects can be applied to one or two selected blocks (depending on a particular effect). However, you must first select an area in the multitrack project that includes these blocks.

If an effect is to be applied only to two blocks, they must overlap!

The result of using multitrack effects is the creation of a new block. The application has three multitrack effects: **Envelope Follower**, **Frequency Band Splitter**, and **Vocoder**. They are comprehensively described in [3].

The *Favorites* Tab. Executing Your Favorite Operations

The **Favorites** tab of the **Organizer** panel is used to execute your favorite operations (Fig. 10.39).

By *favorite operations*, we mean the editing functions, effects, processing scripts, and external applications that you use most often. You can collect the favorites in one list and in one menu. For details on how the **Favorites** menu is used, see [3, *Chapter 9*].

Here we'll just mention that the **Favorites** menu and the **Favorites** tab of the **Organizer** panel completely duplicate each other. The dialog box used for editing the list of favorites can be opened both from the **Favorites** menu and the **Favorites** tab of the **Organizer** panel. To do this, click the **Edit Favorites** button on the **Favorites** tab of the **Organizer** panel, or select the **Edit Favorites** command in the **Favorites** menu.

Fig. 10.39. Favorites tab of the **Organizer** panel

In the multitrack mode, the **Organizer** panel looks the same as in the waveform editing mode; there are no new options or tabs. However, the capabilities of this panel are best revealed in the multitrack mode. You should think of the organizer as a palette of effects and files that can be used as building blocks for your composition.

The **Files** tab (Fig. 10.37) displays all files loaded in Adobe Audition. Grab a necessary file and drag it to the necessary place in your multitrack project.

The **Effects** tab (Fig. 10.38) displays the effects tree. However, only the effects related to the **Real-Time Effects** category are available in this list. If you need to connect an effect to a track, grab the effect and drag it to the track. After that, the window with the parameters of the effects connected to this track will open on the tab that corresponds to the newly connected effect.

That about wraps it up on the peculiarities of using the organizer in the multitrack mode.

10.2.8. Working with the Mixer

The availability of a mixer window in applications designed for work with music and sound has become a tradition. There is a mixer in Adobe Audition too. You can open its panel with the **View > Show Mixers Window** command or the <Alt>+<2> shortcut.

There is a master section with the total volume fader at the left side of the mixer.

The appearance of the rest part of the panel depends on which tab is selected, **Track Mixer** (Fig. 10.40) or **Bus Mixer** (Fig. 10.41).

Fig. 10.40. Mixers panel, the **Track Mixer** tab

Fig. 10.41. Mixers panel, the **Bus Mixer** tab

On the **Track Mixers** tab, each strip corresponds to one of the tracks. To the right of the track mixer, there is a column of buttons that determine the set of track attributes displayed by the mixer. We clicked all the buttons, so Fig. 10.40 shows the complete appearance of the mixer. The fields and track attribute buttons on the mixer correspond to the track attribute fields in the main window. Perhaps the only difference is that the mixer includes the volume fader (the main window uses digital fields to control the volume of the tracks).

As the name of the **Bus Mixer** (Fig. 10.41) implies, each of its strips corresponds to a bus. The only exception is the last strip that always has only one active button, **New**, for creation of a new bus.

The **Out** button opens a window with the properties of the corresponding bus. The main purpose of this window is to connect effects to the bus and specify the output audio port, to which the signal from the bus will be sent. The **Config** button opens a window with the properties of the effects connected to the bus. The last tab in this window corresponds to the effect mixer. All these windows were described in detail in *Section 10.2.2.*

In addition to the buttons mentioned above, each of the bus mixer strips has a volume fader, a pan control, and the **M** (Mute) and **S** (Solo) buttons.

The last thing to mention is that the mixer panel is floating. You can drag it to any place in the main window. It is also resizable.

10.3. Further Work with the Project

Previous chapters looked at how to process sound recorded from a microphone in the **Edit Waveform View**. This mode is sufficient for recording and processing sound that doesn't need to be strictly synchronized with a picture. It is in this mode that we created the file with a narrator's voice. According to our scenario, the video clip should include a recorded narrator's voice reading a text and accompanying a video presentation of various musical and audio equipment. In fact, we prepared two files for this purpose, EX07_01.WAV and EX09_01.WAV. Based on the same original material, these files differ in methods of processing the dynamic range (see *Sections 7.3* and *9.3*).

In *Chapter 8*, we introduced Adobe Audition's built-in effects, but postponed using them until we have the sound synchronized with video. In addition, we're planning to add a musical background to the narrator's voice. Not only would this liven up the project, but also make it possible to veil some shortcomings of the narrator's voice, which we failed to get rid of regardless of all our efforts.

The listed tasks should be fulfilled in the **Multitrack View**. However, to process the sound synchronized with the video, we'll have to repeatedly enter the waveform editing mode (and return).

The techniques of using Adobe Audition as a multitrack editor that supports multichannel recording can be generally described as follows:

1. Perform one-channel recording (using aliasing) or multichannel recording in the multitrack mode.
2. Edit the recorded waveforms and waveforms obtained from external sources (such as a sample library, digital audio CD tracks, or the sound track of a digital video) in the **Edit Waveform View** mode.
3. Return to the multitrack mode and perform montage and mixing of the composition based on the edited waveforms with real-time effects and automation applied.

If the goal of our project were creation of a musical audio composition, we would complete the description of this process in this chapter. However, to create a video clip, you need to know how sound is exported from a video file to Adobe Audition, and how it is imported from Adobe Audition to a video file. This is why we're going to continue working on the project after we discuss peculiarities of working with digital video.

Chapter 11

Creating a Soundtrack for a Movie

You may have noticed that Adobe Audition is a powerful universal sound editor that, in skilful hands, can work wonders with sound. You can record sound from various sources, process it with any conceivable effect, and mix complex compositions containing many voices sounding simultaneously. In addition, in the multitrack mode, the application supports work with a video track (though only one) in addition to audio tracks. This makes Adobe Audition a tool for editing the sound for a digital video. Adobe Audition isn't a video editor. It doesn't allow you to process a video image with effects and montage a movie. For this purpose, you would have to use special applications (such as Adobe After Effects and Adobe Premiere Pro), which are beyond the scope of this book. Our task is quite simple: We'd like to show you how to arrange joint use of audio and video editors so that you can process a soundtrack and synchronize it with a video image in Adobe Audition.

11.1. Exporting a Movie from Adobe Premiere Pro

Adobe Premiere Pro, Adobe After Effects, and Adobe Audition can be used in various combinations. For example, you can prepare video clips containing special effects in Adobe After Effects, create audio clips in Adobe Audition, and then import all these in Adobe Premiere Pro for final mixing. We assume that Adobe Premiere Pro is the main tool for video montage, and Adobe Audition is used for soundtrack montage. Therefore, we're going to stick to the following procedure when creating our project.

1. All video montage is done in Adobe Premiere Pro. At this stage, soundtracks for the clips are left unprocessed.
2. An Adobe Premiere Pro project is exported to Adobe Audition as an AVI file (the quality of the video recording doesn't matter in this case).
3. The soundtrack for the video image from Adobe Premiere Pro is created in Adobe Audition practically from scratch: Audio clips of the narrator's voice are processed, various sounds and music are added, and effects are applied. The soundtrack imported into Adobe Audition from the AVI file is used only for auxiliary purposes (to synchronize blocks with video).
4. The soundtrack created in Adobe Audition is mixed down to one WAV file of a mono, stereo, or 5.1. format.
5. The obtained WAV file is imported into the original Adobe Premiere Pro project. The original unprocessed audio clips are removed or muted, i.e., the WAV file created in Adobe Audition replaces the original soundtrack of the Adobe Premiere Pro project.
6. The full-screen video with the top-quality soundtrack is output from Adobe Premiere Pro to a tape or DVD.

Suppose a movie is shot, captured to a video file with a computer, and its montage is done in Adobe Premiere Pro. As early as the stage of creating an Adobe Premiere Pro project, you should take care that the format of the project's digital sound corresponds to the format of the digital sound of the captured video files. Therefore, the Adobe Audition project should also have the same format. The most important thing is that the sample rates in the Adobe Premiere Pro and Adobe Audition projects must be the same. Later, this will allow you to avoid excessive conversion of audio data and retain high soundtrack quality. A sample rate of 48 kHz is used in our project.

In Adobe Premiere Pro, select the work area, i.e., the project fragment that must be exported. Use the **File > Export > Movie** main menu command or the <Ctrl>+<M> shortcut to export the movie. A standard file-saving dialog box named **Export Movie** will open. Before you click the **OK** button and export the movie to a file with a specific name, you should make a few settings. Click the **Settings** button in the **Export Movie** dialog box. The **Export Movie Settings** dialog box will open. The **General** section of the dialog box (Fig. 11.1) contains general properties of the file being exported. Here are the most important of them:

- **File Type**. Select **Microsoft AVI.**
- **Range**. Select **Work Area Bar.**
- Check the **Export Video** and **Export Audio** checkboxes.

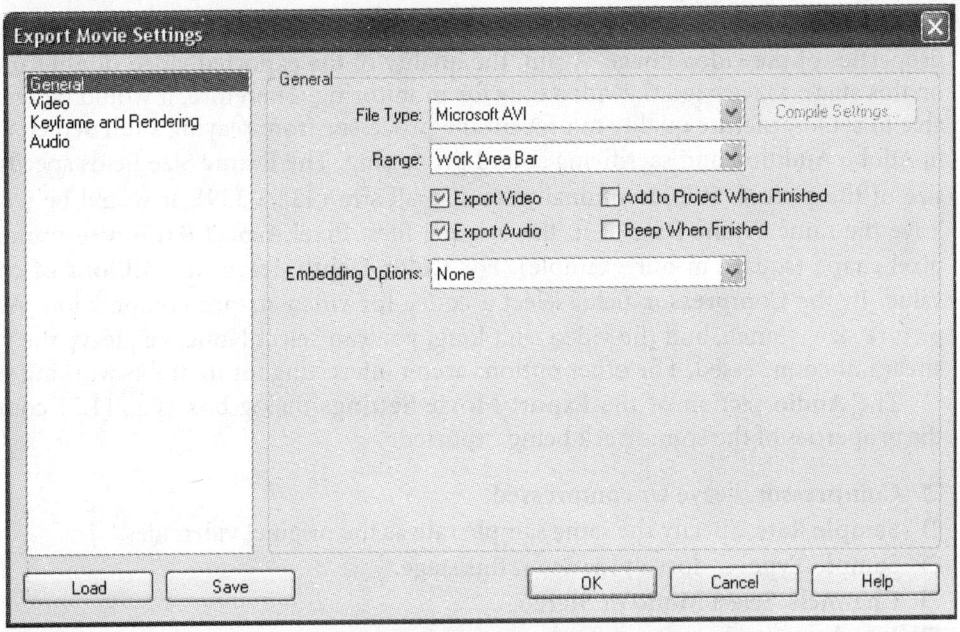

Fig. 11.1. General settings of the exported file

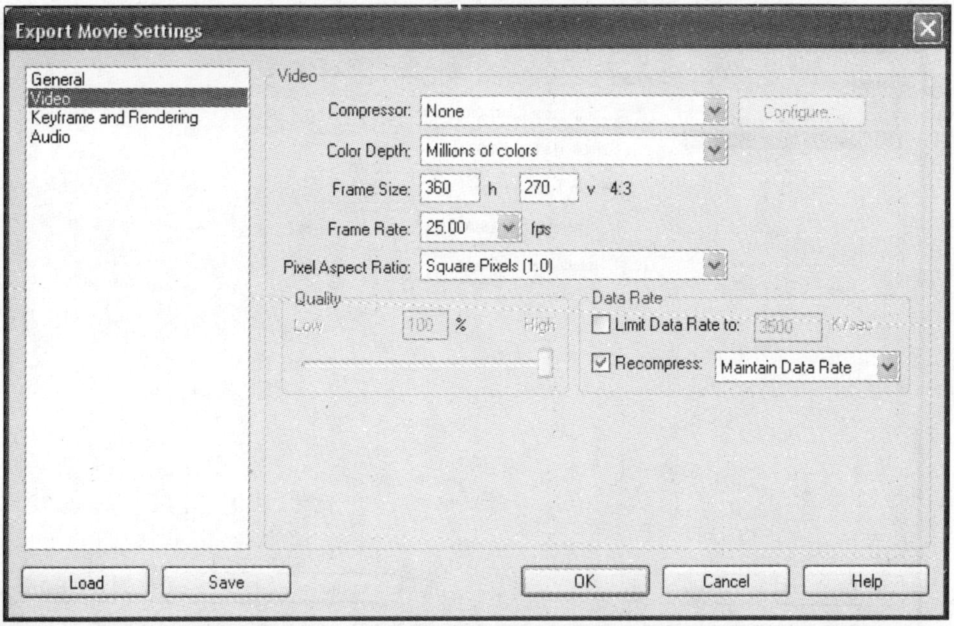

Fig. 11.2. Properties of the exported video

The **Video** section of the **Export Movie Settings** dialog box (Fig. 11.2) contains the properties of the video image. Again, the quality of the exported video doesn't matter on this stage, as we need the video only for monitoring. Therefore, it would be reasonable to set low picture quality to prevent the processor from playing a full-screen video in Adobe Audition and sacrificing sound processing. The **Frame Size** fields specify the size of the picture. We intentionally set a small size (452 × 339). It would be wise to leave the same **Frame Rate** as in the original files. **Pixel Aspect Ratio** determines the pixel shape (square in our example). For **Color Depth**, leave the **Millions of colors** value. In the **Compressor** field, select a codec for video stream compression. As the picture size is small, and the video isn't long, you can select **None**, i.e., leave the video stream uncompressed. The other options aren't interesting for us at this working stage.

The **Audio** section of the **Export Movie Settings** dialog box (Fig. 11.3) contains the properties of the soundtrack being exported:

- **Compressor**. Leave **Uncompressed.**
- **Sample Rate**. Specify the same sample rate as the original video files.
- **Sample Type** — doesn't matter at this stage.
- **Channels**. Select **Mono** or **Stereo.**
- **Interleave** — doesn't matter.

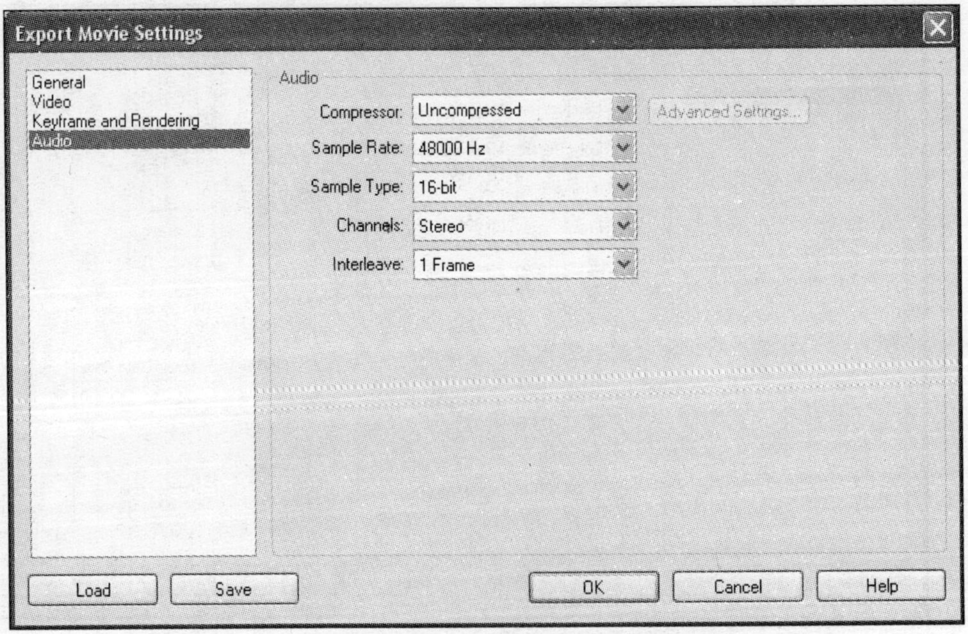

Fig. 11.3. Properties of the exported audio

Click the **OK** button to close the **Export Movie Settings** dialog box, and click the **OK** button in the **Export Movie** dialog box to export the video file. Exit Adobe Premiere Pro.

The file we obtained as a result of the export is available on the CD-ROM that accompanies this book, in the EXAMPLES\CH_11 folder (the file PREMIERE.AVI). The EXAMPLES\CH_11 folder also contains the other example files related to this chapter.

To view the AVI files, install the Standard DivX Codec(FREE) available at **http://www.divx.com/divx/**.

11.2. Importing the Movie into Adobe Audition

If we mixed a mono or stereo soundtrack of the movie in Adobe Premiere Pro, we could do at least its mastering in Adobe Audition. (Mastering is the final processing of a recording before publishing that includes dynamic processing, equalization, eliminating flaws, etc.) For this purpose, we could enter the **Edit Waveform View** and select the **File > Extract Audio from Video** command to extract audio data from the AVI file. With this command, we could, for example, get the soundtrack of a movie and process it with Adobe Audition's tools. The command opens the **Choose a video file** dialog box. Except for its name, this dialog box doesn't differ from the other file-open dialog boxes.

However, our task is to mix down a soundtrack in Adobe Audition, so this command is of little use in this case. We'll choose another way. Switch to the **Multitrack View** mode and create a new session with the **File > New Session** command. In the new project, select the same sample rate as in the Adobe Premiere Pro project (48 kHz). Use the **File > Save Session** command to save the session in the folder that contains the Adobe Premiere Pro project. It is convenient to put all files related to one project in one folder. Now import the movie from the AVI file. For this purpose, use the **Insert > Video from file** command. A standard file-open dialog box will open. In this dialog box, select the AVI file you exported from Adobe Premiere Pro (PREMIERE.AVI). If import of the AVI file completes successfully, two independent tracks will appear in your multitrack Adobe Audition project (Fig. 11.4): a video track and an audio track extracted from the AVI file. These tracks are independent because their blocks are not related to each other. In addition, the **Video** window will open that will display the video picture corresponding to the current position of the play cursor. This window can be shown/hidden with the **View > Show Video Window** main menu command. If you have two displays connected to your computer, it would make sense to move the **Video** window to the other display (to keep it from covering the multitrack project window).

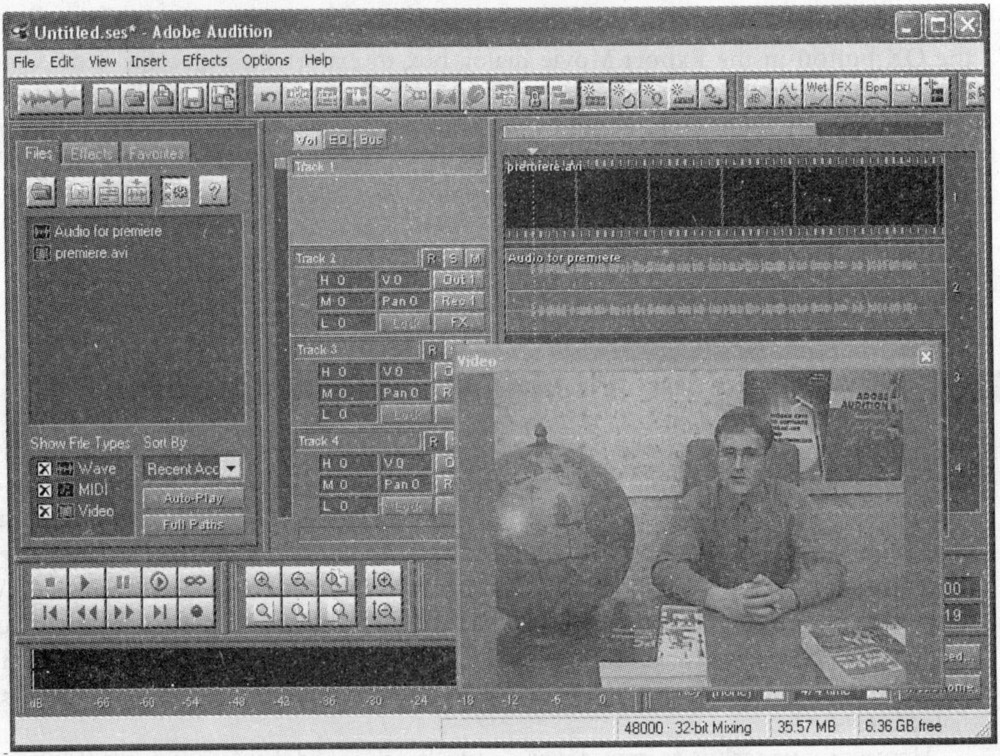

Fig. 11.4. Movie imported into Adobe Audition

11.3. Synchronizing Audio with Video

From now, we'll use the **Insert > Wave from File** command to add necessary files to our multitrack project. These can be various sounds (from sample libraries), music, loops, and a narrator's (or actors') speech. In general, a non-professional video camera, even with an external microphone, doesn't provide as high sound quality as semi-professional audio equipment (including a computer with an advanced sound card). Therefore, simultaneous audio recording with a computer or a studio tape recorder might be required during shooting a movie. The obtained files should be first processed in the **Edit Waveform View** mode and then inserted into the multitrack project. In our case, these are the files SINC1.WAV, NSINC1.WAV, SINC2.WAV, NSINC2.WAV, and SINC3.WAV that are located in the EXAMPLES\CH_11\SPEECH folder.

What should be done to synchronize top-quality sound blocks with the video image? The answer is simple. The blocks must be synchronized with the imported soundtrack, rather than with the video. However, you should first make sure that the starting points of the video blocks coincide in time with the starting points of the soundtrack blocks (Fig. 11.5). If they don't, it is very easy to make them coincide:

- You can move them to the beginning of the multitrack.
- You can move one block so that its beginning is on the same vertical line as the beginning of the other block.

Fig. 11.5. Starting points of the video blocks coincide in time with the starting points of the soundtrack blocks

If the  **Snap to Blocks** button is pressed on the toolbar, Adobe Audition will take care of synchronizing blocks with a precision of one sample (any moved block will "stick" to the vertical edges of other blocks). Blocks are moved with the right mouse button pressed.

Let's proceed with the next stage: synchronizing the blocks and the soundtrack imported from the original AVI file to Adobe Audition. Fig. 11.6 shows fragments of two tracks when the waveform display is greatly zoomed in. The upper track contains a block that corresponds to a low-quality soundtrack recorded with the microphone of a non-professional video camera. The lower track contains a block obtained by recording the same sounds with top-quality equipment. Place the marker at the front edge of the upper waveform. Move the lower block horizontally with the right mouse button pressed until the front edge of the lower waveform reaches the marker. As a result, the waveforms are synchronized with each other and the video image. The precision of synchronization is a few sound samples.

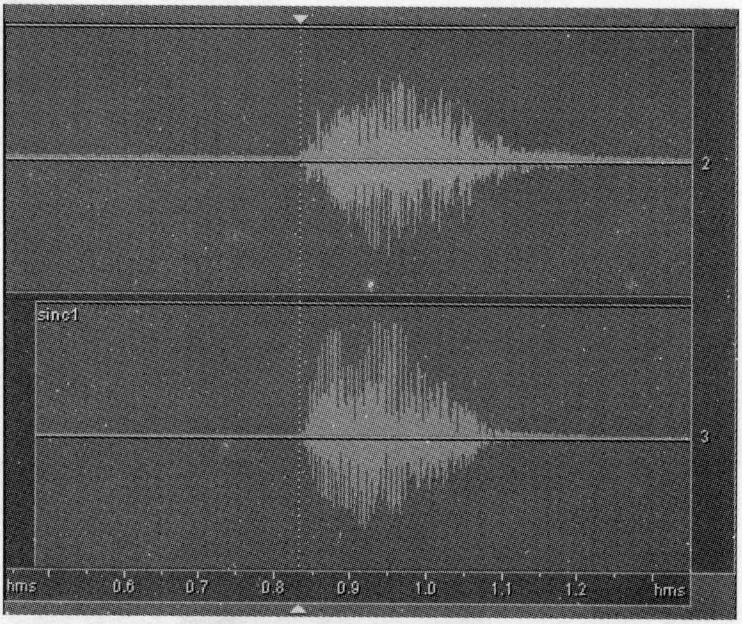

Fig. 11.6. Synchronizing two blocks by the front edges of the waveforms

This example is somewhat far-fetched. When blocks are long, synchronization only by one front edge might be insufficient. Since the blocks were recorded on different equipment, and the clocks of different devices aren't synchronized, the waveform offset will be accumulated. In other words, if you align waveform edges at some point, they will appear desynchronized at another point. What should you do in such a case? There are two ways out:

- Use the **Split** command of the pop-up menu to split the lower block into a few shorter blocks and synchronize each of them with the video.
- Record video using a professional video camera with an external microphone and a high-quality preamplifier.

The second method should be preferred.

After you use these techniques to synchronize the blocks of SINC1.WAV, SINC2.WAV, and SINC3.WAV with the video (the ALIST.SES project file), you can remove or mute the original soundtrack imported with the AVI file.

WAV files with background music for our project are located in the folder EXAMPLES\CH_11\MUSIC.

11.4. Making a Soundtrack

In this section, we'll describe a few simple tricks used for mixing down a multitrack project in Adobe Audition.

Fig. 11.7 illustrates a crossfade: a gradual transition of the sound of one block into the sound of another block. This can be done using amplitude envelopes: Within the same time interval, the envelope of the upper block falls, and the envelope of the lower block rises.

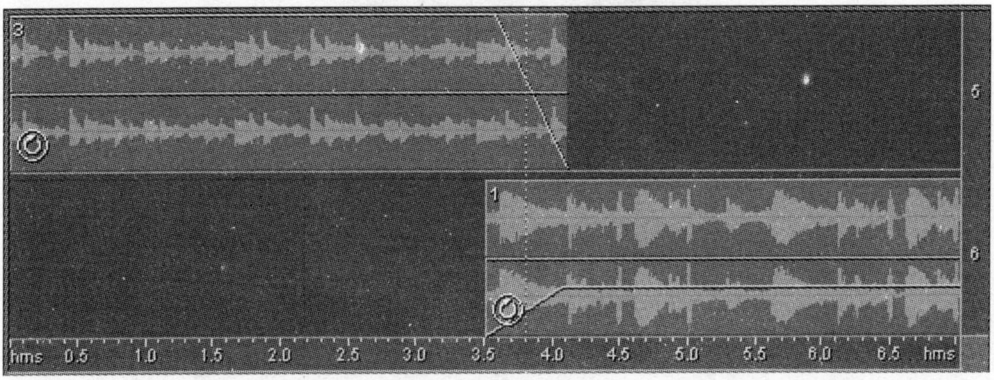

Fig. 11.7. Gradual transition of one block into another (crossfade)

To obtain "dense" sound of speech on appropriate tracks, you can use dynamic processing as a serial effect. For this purpose, click the **FX** button in the track field in the **Effects Rack** dialog box (see *Section 10.2.2*), connect the **Dynamics Processing** effect (see *Section 7.2*), and create a response curve similar to that shown in Fig. 11.8.

For tracks whose signals are processed with serial effects, it is reasonable to use the **Lock** attribute (see *Section 10.2.2*) to diminish the load on the processor.

In the project described in this book, all audio files with speech have already undergone dynamic processing. Therefore, we won't apply it to the project tracks.

Effects like reverberation should be used as serial effects. Click the **Out1** button in the track field. The **Playback Devices** dialog box will open (see *Section 10.2.2*). Click the **New Bus** button to create a bus (and name it, for example, **reverb**). Select the newly created bus and click the **Properties** button. In the bus properties dialog box, connect the **Reverb** effect to this bus (see *Section 8.2*). Select the effect and click the **Properties** button to open its dialog box. In this dialog box, select the **Mixer** tab and set the **Dry Out** control to zero, and the **Reverb** control to 100 (as a result, there will be only the processed signal at the output of the effect).

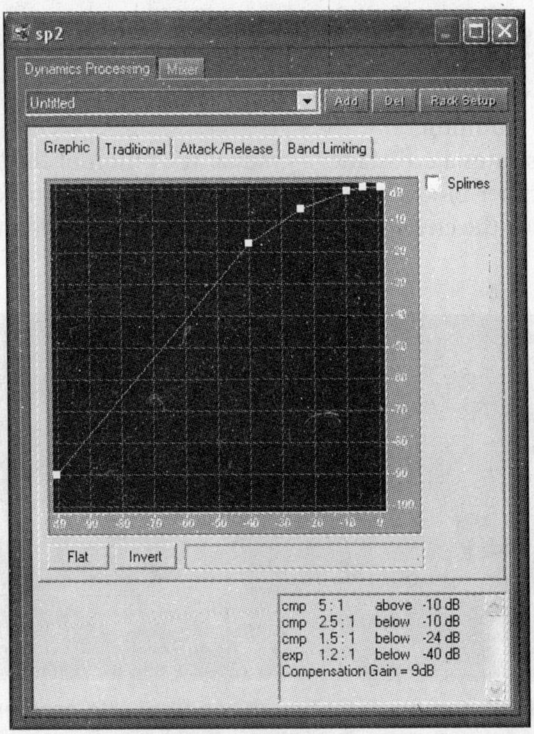

Fig. 11.8. Response curve of the voice signal compressor

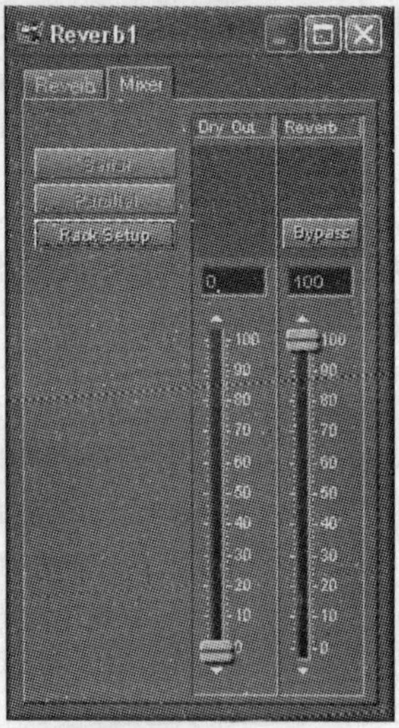

Fig. 11.9. Mixer tab of the effect's dialog box

Now you can use the **Wet** and **Dry** attributes to control the volume of the signal that was or wasn't processed with the reverb effect. If you wish to control the depth of the effect, its parameters, or panorama in the speaker, you can use automation envelopes (see *Section 10.2.5*).

The result of mixing down our project was saved in the ALIST.SES file.

11.5. Viewing the Results and Moving the Mixed-down Soundtrack to the Adobe Premiere Pro Project

Mixing down a multitrack project requires a lot of computer resources. This is why the video may play jerkily. To view the result of your work comfortably, you can use the **File > Save Mixdown to Video As** command. All audio tracks will be mixed down to one stereo pair and saved in an AVI file along with the video. The soundtrack can be compressed with the MP3 algorithm to decrease the size of the AVI file. The resulting AVI file can be viewed with Windows tools (our file is named PREMIERE_STEREO.AVI). If you notice that some sounds are ahead of the events (are heard earlier than they should be) or fall behind them, you'll have to return to the Adobe Audition project and correct the problem.

When you are satisfied, you should save the created soundtrack as a WAV file. To do this, select the project fragment taken by video and use the **File > Save Mixdown As** command.

In the Adobe Premiere Pro project, use the **File > Import** command to import the file with the soundtrack prepared in Adobe Audition. Audio tracks in the Adobe Premiere Pro project can be muted. After that, you can output the full-screen movie with the high-quality soundtrack to a tape or DVD.

Up to now, we have been talking about a stereo soundtrack. The next chapter covers obtaining a soundtrack in the 5.1 format.

Mixing a Project to the Surround Panorama

Since audio recording first appeared, both listeners and designers have been eager to make the recorded and played sound as close to the original as possible. The developers of audio equipment do their best to approach to the ideal. They struggle against noise, minimize distortion, and expand the frequency and dynamic ranges of the elements of the audio signal recording/transmitting/playing channel. In addition, they try to make the sound field created by acoustic systems give the listener information about the directions of the sound sources and the acoustic properties of the room in which the recording took place.

12.1. Historical Notes: From Stereo to Surround

In the first stage of development, audio recording and broadcasting were mono. The sound heard from a loudspeaker was changed out of recognition compared with the "live" sound in a concert hall: The balance between different musical instruments was distorted, the timbre was distorted, and, most important, the spatial properties were lost. This was a very serious disadvantage. The human ear is capable of finding the directions to the sound sources which helps us orientate ourselves in the environment. If all sounds are heard from the same point, it seems unnatural.

The first experiments on obtaining surround sound were carried out as long ago as the 1930s. Comparative tests of multichannel and mono systems produced astonishing results. It was found that even when two separate channels were played, the subjective quality of the sound significantly improved. The most astonishing thing was that experts preferred stereo sound even when they were offered mono recordings with objectively higher quality. The decisive advantage was the possibility of spatial localization of the imaginary sound sources (Fig. 12.1).

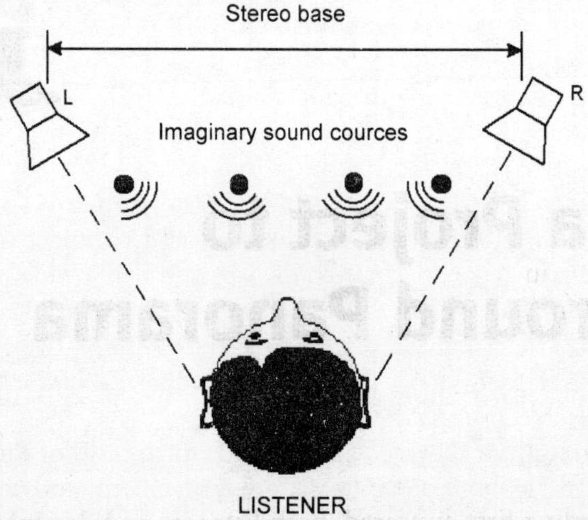

Fig. 12.1. Distribution of imaginary sound sources in a stereo panorama

During the first stage, developers decided to confine themselves to only two channels. Of course, this was mainly because of the limitations of devices of the time: Vinyl records actually allowed only two full-value channels. Stereo sound provides a certain transparency: The parts of individual instruments become more distinguishable against the background of the orchestra. Besides, a stereo system can convey a sort of a sound impression of the room where the recording was made. Stereo records and stereo record players, stereo tape recorders, and stereo broadcasting appeared with time. However, stereo sound has a significant disadvantage: It lacks the natural nature of an actual sound field, and stereo panorama is limited to the angle between the directions to the speakers, and thus is a plane.

One of the first attempts to overcome the demerits inherent to stereo systems was quadraphony (to play back quadraphonic recordings, four acoustic systems are used). The first home quadro systems appeared in early 1970s and everybody hoped they had a brilliant future. However, they failed, for several reasons. The imperfection and high price of four-channel recorders/players played a certain role. However, the main reason was that new sound quality didn't appear with change from stereo to quadro at the time. The quadraphony of 1970s didn't provide surround panorama: The listener felt the usual stereo panorama in front of him or her and another stereo panorama behind him or her. The human ear perceives audio signals from different directions differently: The signals coming from front are noticed better than those coming from behind. Quadraphony ignored this; a quadraphonic system was symmetrical about the axis between the frontal and rear areas of the surround panorama. As a result, the imaginary sound sources weren't localized clearly in the frontal area of the surround panorama. All the imaginary sound sources were positioned in one plane, between the front and rear speakers, so there still wasn't any three-dimensional sound. In addition, in those days there weren't computers and effects processes that could provide a soundman or soundwoman with convenient controls for moving the sound sources within the surround panorama, and quadraphonic equipment was too expensive. So, quadraphony stepped back, and stereophony won and started to develop toward making devices smaller, increasing their technical properties and operating quality, and changing to new media: compact cassettes and compact discs. Audio recording companies and manufacturers of audio devices still had a wide field of operations and a large sales market. They have repeatedly offered users complete replacement of their audio collections. The musical material collected on vinyl records during the preceding decades was updated first for mono tape recorders, then for stereo cassette recorders, and now is offered to music fans on laser discs.

However, stereophony seemed to surrender at the end of the 20th century. Digital audio recording technologies and capacious, convenient, and cheap media eliminated the problem of storing long multichannel recordings. In addition, an urgent demand arose for sound conveying acoustic properties of the ambience. The virtual graphic worlds of computer games are becoming increasingly complicated and close to the reality and, therefore, require appropriate sound. Cinema, which sustained a crisis during its contest with television, has been revived in the form of home movie theaters and movie theaters with a new format, whose main difference from their predecessors is not in terms of the image but a fundamentally new sound (however, image quality has also improved due to DVD and advanced projection technologies).

The new epoch in audio recording began as a result of research conducted by the engineers at Dolby Laboratories (**http://dolby.com**). This was a basically new approach to multichannel audio transmission. It differed from traditional methods in that to store audio signals of two additional channels, the developers used matrix coding, i.e., mixed the additional channels to the main two channels. The way of positioning the acoustic systems also changed. In addition to acoustic systems located in the corners of the room as of the quadraphonic tradition, a central channel was added between the right and left front channels to maintain the wide stereo base for spectators sitting to one side, and the surround channel was positioned behind the spectators. Thus a new system of the movie-theater sound, Dolby® Stereo, appeared. The Dolby® Stereo format was first used in "Star Wars" in 1975.

The Dolby® Pro Logic® system became a playback system of completely new quality that was compatible with the old audio recording standard. It used a decoder that implemented a spatial focusing of audio images, and a technology used to decrease the mutual interference between channels. Dolby® Pro Logic® also made it possible to delay the sound signal in the rear channel. Thus it became possible to adjust the properties of the "standard movie theater," for which multichannel sound was mixed during movie production to the geometric and acoustic properties of the actual room.

Then the epoch of digital coding and digital recording of multichannel surround audio began, and Dolby® Digital appeared. Digital audio coding uses the AC-3 algorithm (Dolby's third generation audio coding algorithm). AC-3 is an algorithm for multichannel sound compression (the number of independent channels being from one to six) with a certain loss. It uses advances in psychoacoustics, taking into account the peculiar features of the human ear to decide what portion of the audio signal information can be discarded unnoticeably to the ear. Three-dimensional acoustic images, clearer details, natural movements of sound sources from the frontal area to the rear, and stereo sound in the rear area have all contributed to the success of the system.

The next step in the evolution of the surround audio systems was the Dolby® Digital EX system, which can be considered a superstructure based on Dolby® Digital. Like Dolby® Digital, the Dolby® Digital EX system can encode up to six independent channels (the 5.1 format), but the information of one or two additional surround channels is mixed to the left and right rear channels using matrix encoding. Because of this, it was possible to maintain back compatibility with Dolby® Digital equipment, and at the same time, the introduction of the additional surround channels (6.1 or 7.1) made it possible to obtain even more precise localization of sound sources in space using Dolby® Digital EX equipment.

At present, it is possible to talk about the increasing popularity of a new consumer format, DVD audio. Audio data in this medium can be stored using different encoding algorithms, including Dolby® Digital. However, thanks to the large capacity of a DVD medium (4.7 GB on a one-layer-disk), it is no longer necessary to compress audio information. DVD audio allows you to store multichannel recordings in formats up to 24 bits/96 kHz without any compression and, therefore, without any loss.

12.1.1. Introducing the 5.1 Format

Currently, the main consumer format of surround recordings is 5.1.

The designation 5.1 shows the number of channels and carries no information concerning a particular method of multichannel audio encoding. The format uses five channels (front left, central, front right, rear left, and rear right) with the full frequency range and one low-frequency channel (with a range from 3 Hz to 120 Hz) connected to the subwoofer, an acoustic system capable of producing low-frequency sounds (Fig. 12.2).

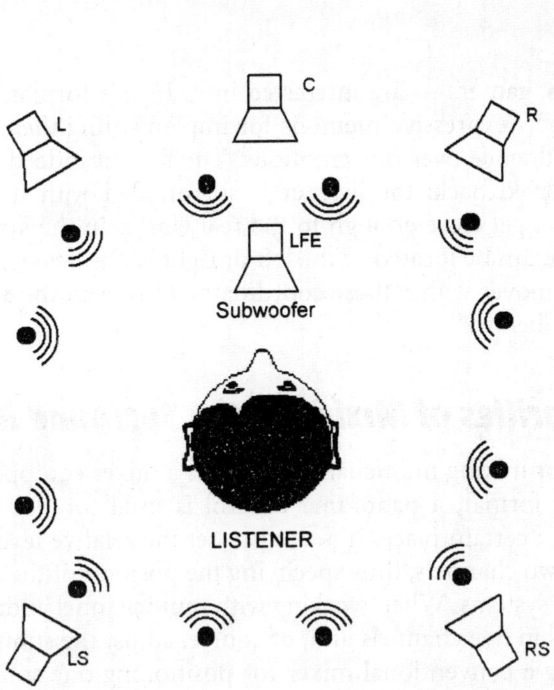

Fig. 12.2. Positioning the sound sources in the 5.1 system

In the 5.1 system, the surround panorama is shaped. Since our ears actually cannot determine the direction of a very low frequency sound source, the location of the subwoofer doesn't matter. The subwoofer is also used in conventional stereo systems. The low-frequency spectral component of the total signal from the stereo channels is supplied to the subwoofer channel. As a result, the playback of bass frequencies is ensured. However, in the 5.1 system, the sixth channel plays a special role. It should be considered as an independent low-frequency effect channel, rather than a low-frequency component of a multiband acoustic system.

Experts agree that the 5.1 format is the most promising, since it is supported by the major manufacturers. It is important that appropriate media (DVD) are available.

Even though a uniform standard hasn't been adopted yet, and a number of encoding systems for the 5.1 format exist concurrently, the fiasco of "primitive" quadraphony is unlikely to be repeated, even if more than one different encoding system survives. The basic difference of the 5.1 format from the quadraphony of 30 years ago is that now the signal has a digital form, so the creation of a universal decoder capable of working with sound encoded with different systems won't encounter any difficulties and won't make devices much more expensive.

The manufacturers of audio and video devices, computers, computer accessories, and software are all concerned about the success of the 5.1 format. Consumers —

viewers, listeners, gamers — are interested in it. In this format, sound producers and musicians find new expressive methods for implementing their creative ideas and increasing their influence over our emotions. The format indeed imparts a new quality to the sound played back: the listener is surrounded with it. However, the virtual world still doesn't get close enough to the real world. In the synthesized audio space, the sound source can be located to the left or right of the listener, in front of or behind him or her, and moves within these coordinates. However, the actual sound space also has "above" and "below."

12.1.2. Peculiarities of Mixing to the Surround Panorama

The main tool for mixing multichannel audio is a mixer equipped with panning tools. With the stereo format, a panorama control is used for positioning the imaginary sound source at a certain place. It is used to set the relative levels of the audio signals sent to each of two channels, thus specifying the position of the sound source between the two acoustic systems. When working with multichannel audio, you have to control a similar process in five channels and, of course, adjust the subwoofer channel. This is why, when using a conventional mixer for positioning one sound source, it is necessary to manipulate using multiple controls. Notice that the positions of the faders controlling the signal level and the positions of the panorama controls in each channel are difficult to correlate with the position of the imaginary sound source on the surround panorama. It is even more difficult to make the sound source move along a specified trajectory. This is only possible in mixers with automation. A joystick would be very convenient as a surround panorama control in a mixer designed for work with multichannel audio.

In addition, a mixer capable of working with surround audio must have multiple outputs (as many as the number of channels). For example, in the 5.1 system, the mixer must have at least six outputs. The equipment of a stereo audio studio is fairly expensive, and the price of a 5.1 studio is frightening!

Multichannel recorders are also expensive. They must have six or more channels, and it is desirable that they have a bit depth no less than 24 bits.

Mixers and digital tape recorders are multichannel in grain. This is why certain models designed for work with stereo sound can be more or less conveniently used in a 5.1 studio. As for equalizers, dynamic processing devices, and, particularly, effects, things are a little more complicated. Of course, you could provide six channels by connecting together three two-channel devices. However, any meaningful adjustment of the parameters would be impossible in this case.

Digital tape recorders and hardware mixers can be well replaced by software multitrack studios and their built-in virtual mixers, which allow the user to control the panorama with an ordinary mouse.

Not every owner of a home stereo studio can afford a monitoring acoustic stereo system. However, when mixing to stereo, a suitable way around is to have inexpensive monitoring headphones. However, stereo headphones won't be sufficient in the 5.1 format. You cannot manage without five wide-band acoustic systems (and a subwoofer).

When working with stereo audio, the main requirements of monitors are the smoothness of their frequency-response curves, low distortion levels, and the complete identity of the two acoustic systems. Similar requirements could be made of five wide-band monitors of the 5.1 format. At first glance, they would seem to have to be completely identical. However, in this case you would be mixing to the surround panorama under conditions other than those under which many listeners of your composition will be listening. The fact is that most owners of home movie theaters have rear acoustic systems that are weaker than the front ones. In addition, the rear acoustic systems can be constructed differently from the front speakers. In turn, the central acoustic system often differs from the extreme front ones. It might turn out that the listener's impression won't correspond to your intentions.

As for the low-frequency channel of the 5.1 system, the subwoofer mustn't be used when mixing a musical composition if no special effect, such as an explosion or a gunshot, is present in the composition according to the artistic intention.

Original musical compositions mixed to the surround panorama haven't yet become widely popular. Multichannel sound exists mainly as a supplement to video. Obviously, approaches to panning the sound track of movie and panning a musical composition should differ. When accompanying a video, the main sound source should be put in front of the viewers, because they are watching the action on the screen. The rear channels should be used to impart spatial features to the sound and to implement special effects. Of course, when working with surround music, one can use the approaches approved in the movie production. For example, you can put the main sound source in front of the listener and use the rear channels for creating the acoustics of the ambience and moving secondary sound sources. Nevertheless, when it comes to a musical composition created independently of any video, the creator is free to use new expressive tools inherent to the surround panorama. For example, you can "put" the listener among the musicians and move the entire field or individual sound sources around the listener or away from him or her.

However, you shouldn't abuse the special effects of panning. For example, it is hardly reasonable to create a virtual piano whose keyboard, judging by the sound, encircles the listener. Drum sounds and, especially, sudden loud sounds heard from the rear channels will make the listeners turn around by reflex or even to jump from fright. As a result, your song could go flop: Who will like it?

When working on stereo recordings, we have to intentionally restrict the usage of the stereo panorama features as applied to certain musical instruments. These restrictions will be caused not only by artistic, but by technical reasons. For example, it would be pointless to move the bass from the center of the stereo panorama. First, the stereo effect in the low-frequency band is very weak. Second, if you pan the bass left or right, one of the speakers will appear to be underloaded. Similar problems are also typical for 5.1 systems, although low-frequency sounds there are emitted by the subwoofer. One of these problems is related to the usage of the central channel. In movies, it is used to bind the dominant sounds to the picture so that the spectators sitting far from the center perceive these sounds as coming from the screen. In music, sounds that are sent equally to the left and right stereo channels (the main vocal, bass, and certain drums) should be distributed over the central and front channels. This will allow you to avoid overloading the central channel. In addition, sounds are more distinct when some of them are directed to the central channel and others are sent to the left and right front channels.

When mixing to the surround panorama, additional signs appear that allow the listener to select individual parts by ear. These are the direction to the sound source within 360° and, to some extent, the distance to it (the panorama depth). This is why it isn't necessary to use frequency filtration to emphasize certain signals against the background of others, to change the volumes of the instruments during the song, or to compress individual audio signals.

12.2. Positioning Sound Sources on the Surround Panorama with *Multichannel Encoder*

Load the multitrack project to Adobe Audition. Select the **View > Multichannel Encoder** main menu command available in the **Multitrack View** mode to open the **Multichannel Encoder** dialog box (Fig. 12.3).

The **Multichannel Encoder** dialog box contains controls that allow you to:

- Select the track to be processed
- Specify an algorithm for conversion of the format of the audio data recorded to this track
- Measure and adjust the levels of individual components of the sound field
- Put the imaginary sound source at any position in the surround panorama
- Create a graph of the movement of the imaginary sound source in space
- Mix a multitrack stereo project down to a surround file

The **Track List** field contains a list of tracks available in the loaded multitrack project. The waveform corresponding to this track will be displayed on the **Waveform Display** (Fig. 12.4). This display also shows panning envelopes that specify the trajectory of the imaginary sound source movement in the "left/right" coordinates (this envelope is yellow) and the "front/rear" coordinates (the green envelope).

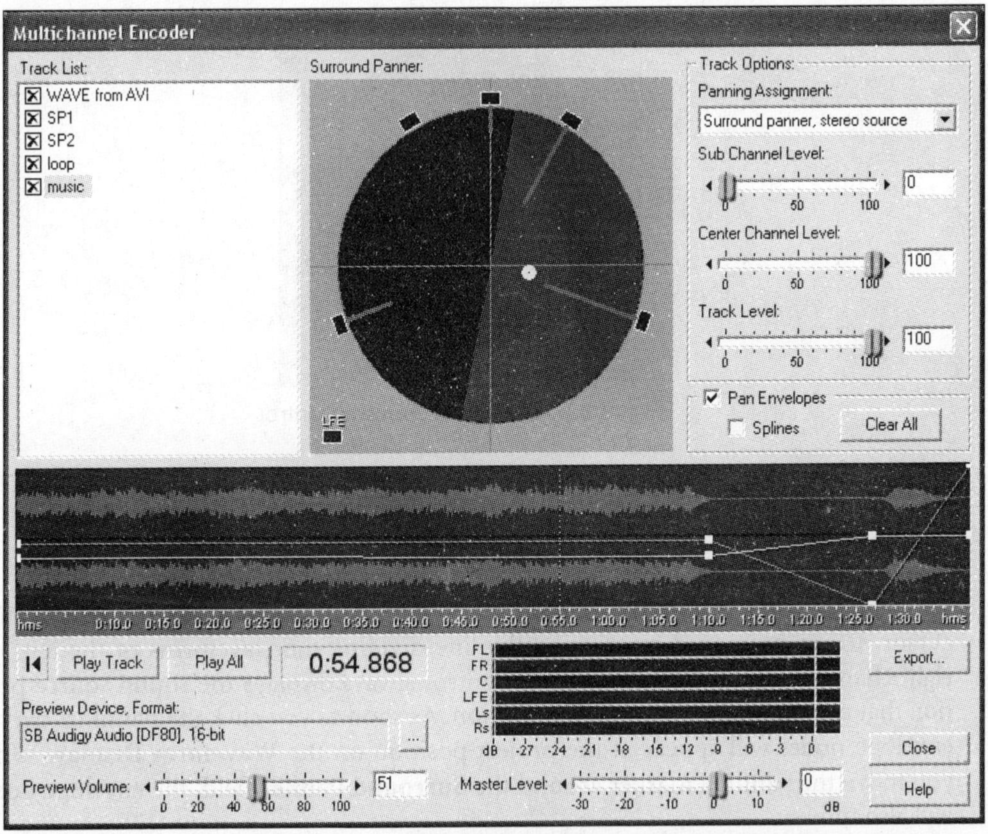

Fig. 12.3. **Multichannel Encoder** dialog box

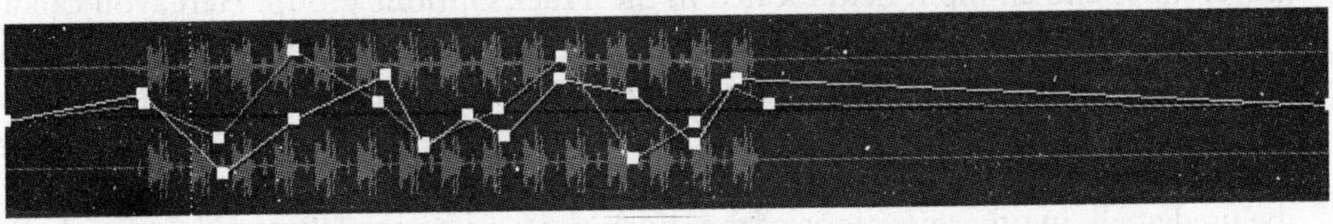

Fig. 12.4. Waveform and panning envelopes on the **Waveform Display**

The envelope is shaped by creating and moving the nodes of the graph. To create a node, click the envelope. To move it, drag it with the mouse.

You might feel that the positions of the nodes of the graph don't give an idea of how the imaginary sound source is positioned on the surround panorama. To make sound source positioning clearer, the **Surround Panner** control combined with indicators is provided (Fig. 12.5).

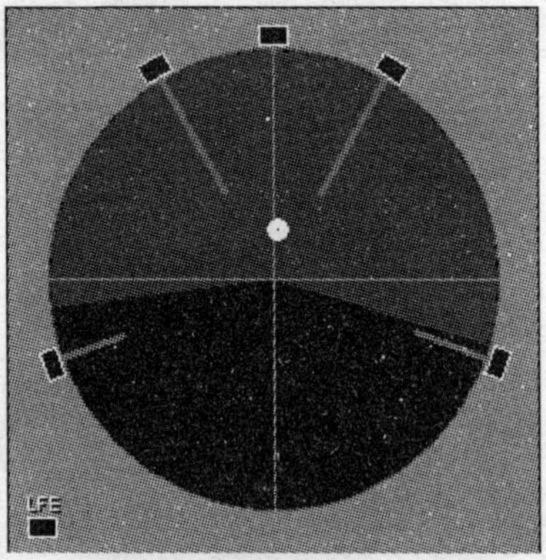

Fig. 12.5. Surround Panner control

The length of each line coming from the front, rear, or central "speaker" indicates the corresponding signal level. The blue sector is the stereo field area of the source. The position of the sound source on the surround panorama is indicated with the *panning marker* (a light circle). The marker can be moved with the mouse.

The yellow vertical dotted line on the **Waveform Display** is the project position cursor. It can be moved by clicking the line dividing the waveforms of the left and right channels. The **Surround Panner** control always displays the sound source position that corresponds to the project position. As soon as you click the panning marker, envelope nodes will appear at the project position on the **Waveform Display**. When you move the panning marker around the **Surround Panner** field, the envelope nodes will also move.

To adjust the signal level in the low-frequency effect channel, use the **Sub Channel Level** slider and an input field located in the **Track Options** group. Here, you can also find sliders for the signal level adjustment in the center channel (**Center Channel Level**) and for the entire track (**Track Level**). The **Center Channel Level** slider determines the contribution of the center channel to creating the position of the imaginary sound source. If you move this slider to its leftmost position, the center channel won't be used at all. In other positions of the slider, the load on the left and right front channels will be partly shifted to the center channel.

If you uncheck the **Pan Envelopes** checkbox, the envelopes will become unavailable for viewing and editing. When the **Splines** checkbox is checked, the broken-line envelopes will be approximated with splines. By clicking the **Clear All** button, you delete all nodes you've created, and the envelopes turn into straight lines.

The **Panning Assignment** drop-down list located at the top of the **Track Options** group contains several options for audio data conversion. Here, you can select the type of the source material and the format to which it will be converted. For example, if you select the **Surround panner, stereo source** item, the signal from the source track will be converted to the 5.1. format while retaining the stereo properties of the sound source (for example, if the source was distributed over the stereo panorama, this property will be kept after the source is put on the surround panorama). If you select the **Surround panner, summed to mono** item, the sound source will be converted to mono, regardless of its original properties, and become a dot on the surround panorama. Here are the other conversion options:

- **LFE only** — The signal is directed only to the low-frequency effect channel.
- **FL + FR, stereo** — The signal is directed to the left and right front channels while retaining the stereo properties of the sound source.
- **Ls + Rs, stereo** — The signal is directed to the left and right rear channels while retaining the stereo properties of the sound source.
- **Center + LFE, stereo** — The signal is directed to the center channel and to the low-frequency effects channel while retaining the stereo properties of the sound source.
- **Center only, mono** — The signal is converted to mono and sent to the center channel.
- **FL only, mono** — The signal is converted to mono and sent to the front left channel.
- **FR only, mono** — The signal is converted to mono and sent to the front right channel.
- **Ls only, mono** — The signal is converted to mono and sent to the left rear channel.
- **Rs only, mono** — The signal is converted to mono and sent to the right rear channel.

After you select a particular conversion option, the corresponding changes will be reflected on the **Surround Panner** control.

By clicking the box denoting an acoustic system (including **LFE**), you can direct the signal of the selected track to the desired channel. The appropriate mode will be automatically selected in the **Panning Assignment** list.

Therefore, on the first stage of mixing a composition to the surround panorama, each of the imaginary sound sources can be panned individually.

By playing only one track (the **Play Track** button) or the whole mix (the **Play All** button), you can estimate the results by ear.

To listen to a mix in the 5.1 format, you'll need a sound card supporting this format and an appropriate acoustic system.

The **Preview Device, Format** field displays the name of the device (the sound card) used to listen to the results of surround panning and the data-output format to it.

To the right of the **Preview Device, Format** field, there is a button that opens the **Multichannel Preview Options** dialog box (Fig. 12.6).

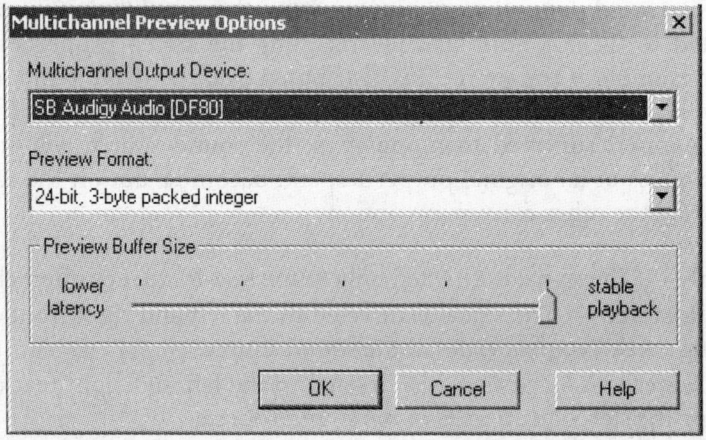

Fig. 12.6. Multichannel Preview Options dialog box

In this dialog box, you can change the device (**Multichannel Output Device**) and the format of the output audio data (**Preview Format**). Using the **Preview Buffer Size** slider, you can specify the size of the buffer used in this process. A home computer usually has two devices that can output sound: a sound card and a voice modem. The latter is completely unsuitable for musical purposes. Of course, the sound card must support the 5.1 format. You cannot control the routing of the audio streams to individual output ports corresponding to different channels of the 5.1 system: This is done automatically. However, for automatic routing to be successful, the sound card drivers must support the Microsoft DirectX 8.0 specification or later. In other words, just select your 5.1 sound card with the latest drivers as a sound output device and pan your tracks to the surround format without taking care of anything else.

The **Preview Volume** slider (Fig. 12.3) controls the level of the signal being listened to. The **Master Level** slider controls the signal levels in all the channels of the 5.1 system simultaneously.

The procedure for working with the **Multichannel Encoder** dialog box can be described as follows:

1. Edit the surround pan automation and listen to individual or all selected tracks.
2. Save the ready mix in six-channel (5.1) audio files.

We've already discussed the first step. To proceed to the second step, click the **Export** button. The **Multichannel Export Options** dialog box will open (Fig. 12.7).

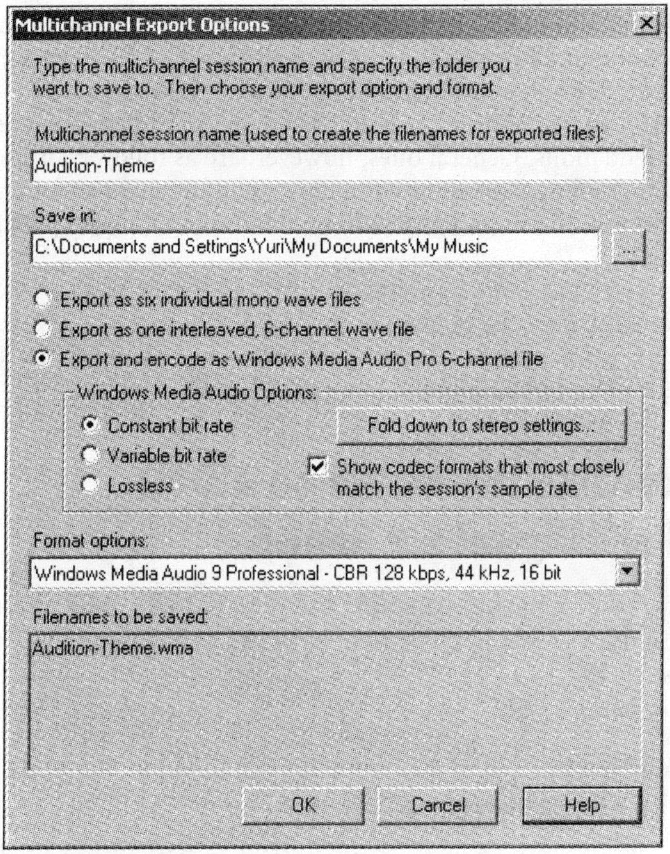

Fig. 12.7. Multichannel Export Options dialog box

The fields located at the top of the dialog box allow you to specify a name for the file and select a folder for it. The radio buttons located below make it possible to select how the mix should be saved.

- **Export as six individual mono wave files** — saves the project audio data as six mono tracks.
- **Export as one interleaved, 6-channel wave file** — saves the project audio data as one six-channel track.
- **Export and encode as Windows Media Audio Pro 6-channel file** — saves the project audio data as a Windows Media Audio Pro file.

In the last case, the parameters of the file being saved should be defined more precisely using the controls of the **Windows Media Audio Options** group.

We'd like to add just a few words. When using the panning tools, don't forget the traditional ones that allow you to convey the features of the environment: the volume and timbre of the sound source and those of reverberation.

Surround panning is more of an art than a science. Therefore, there can be no specific recommendations. General ones, however, are as follows: Listen frequently to recordings from leading recording companies in multichannel formats, use surround panning with care, and listen to the advice of more experienced people and study their experience.

We completed surround panning of our project. The result is available on the CD-ROM that accompanies the book (the file ALIST.SES in the SAMPLES\CH_11 folder). This multichannel project is related to the previous chapter, but also contains information about surround panning.

12.3. Recording the Movie on a DVD with Dolby® Digital 5.1 Sound

Several years ago, amateur computer musicians could only dream about Dolby® Digital 5.1 and DVD in a home studio. Now this is a reality that can be reached with a few mouse clicks.

You now have:

- The sound track mixed to the 5.1 format using Adobe Audition
- The video whose montage was done using Adobe Premiere

The task now is to combine them in one movie and record it on a DVD.

First, you should export the sound track of the 5.1 format to one WAV file without using any compression.

In the **Multichannel Export Options** dialog box (Fig. 12.7), select the **Export as one interleaved, 6-channel wave file** radio button and click the **OK** button. The sound track will be exported to one six-channel WAV file. Our file is called PREMIERE_51.WAV and located in the EXAMPLES\CH_12 folder.

It is interesting that if you open this file in Adobe Audition in the **Edit Waveform View** mode, it will be treated as six independent mono files.

Adobe Audition 1.0 doesn't fully support multichannel files. As for Adobe Premiere Pro 7.0, it handles the 5.1 format properly.

From now on, we'll talk only about working with the movie project in Adobe Premiere Pro.

Select the **Add Tracks** command in the pop-up menu of the main sequence tab of the **Timeline** dialog box (where you did the montage of the movie). A dialog box with the same name will open (Fig. 12.8). Using this dialog box, you can simultaneously create several tracks of different types. You don't need **Video Tracks** and **Audio Submix Tracks**, so enter zeroes into the **Add** fields of the corresponding group.

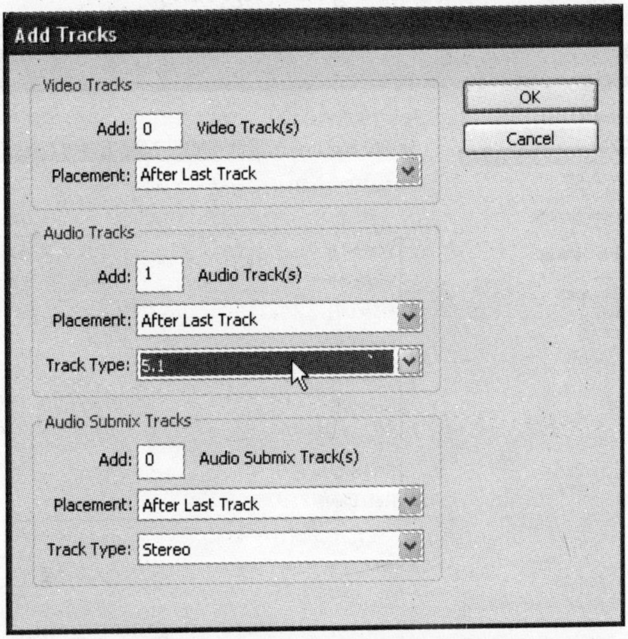

Fig. 12.8. Add Tracks dialog box (Adobe Premiere Pro)

You need just one audio track, so enter **1** into the **Add** field of the **Audio Tracks** group. Leave the **After Last Track** variant in the **Placement** drop-down list, and the created track will be the last of the tracks. In the **Track Type** drop-down list, select **5.1**. After you click the **OK** button, a new track in the 5.1 format will appear in your project. Using a standard Adobe Premiere Pro procedure, import the previously obtained six-channel WAV file into the project and place it on the newly created audio track synchronously with the video. That is, the beginning of the clip corresponding to the WAV file must coincide with the beginning of the first clip on any video track of the main sequence. Adobe Premiere Pro users should know the sequence in this application. If you don't use Adobe Premiere Pro and are reading this section just for curiosity, we'll explain it: A *sequence* is a video submix, a video assembled of a series of clips that can be put into any other sequence as a single clip.

The 5.1 audio track is now imported. The rest audio tracks of the project should be muted. Now you can write the ready movie on a DVD. However, before you give an appropriate command, you might want to listen to your movie played in Adobe

Premiere Pro. Here you are likely to be disappointed: Your movie might have stereo sound, rather than surround. The reason is in the settings of the Adobe Premiere Pro interface. Select the **Edit > Preferences > Audio Hardware** command in the main menu to open the **Preferences** dialog box (Fig. 12.9).

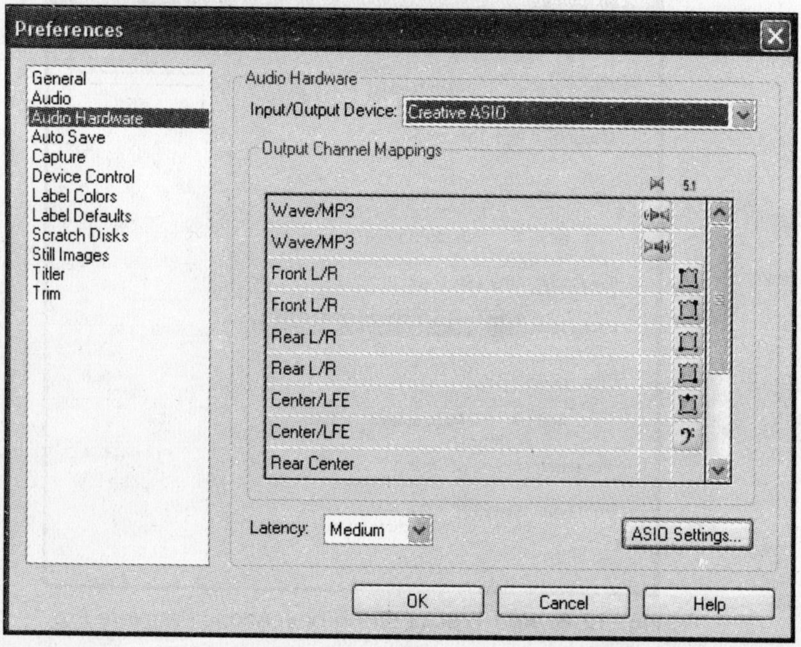

Fig. 12.9. Preferences dialog box (Adobe Premiere Pro)

Select the ASIO driver of your sound card in the **Input/Output Device** list. If ASIO isn't supported, you won't hear surround sound in Adobe Premiere Pro. In the **Output Channel Mappings** list, map the sound card channels to the surround audio channels. This should be done in an original way. The icons , , , , , and denote the channels of the 5.1 system. They should be dragged to appropriate positions in the list, taking into consideration the names of the channels. In the **Latency** drop-down list, specify the size of the buffer used for sound output. However, it must be specified not in bytes and time units, but in words meaning the latency length, from **Short** to **Long**. The **ASIO Settings** button opens a panel for setting the ASIO interface of the sound card. The appearance of this panel will depend on the sound card model and the version of its driver. If everything is all right, click the **OK** button and try to play the movie again. If any channels are heard from wrong speakers, you'll have to set the Adobe Premiere Pro interface more carefully.

Sooner or later, you may decide to record your movie on a DVD. This is done as follows. Select the **File > Export > Export to DVD** command to open the **Export to DVD** dialog box, and select the **General** section (Fig. 12.10).

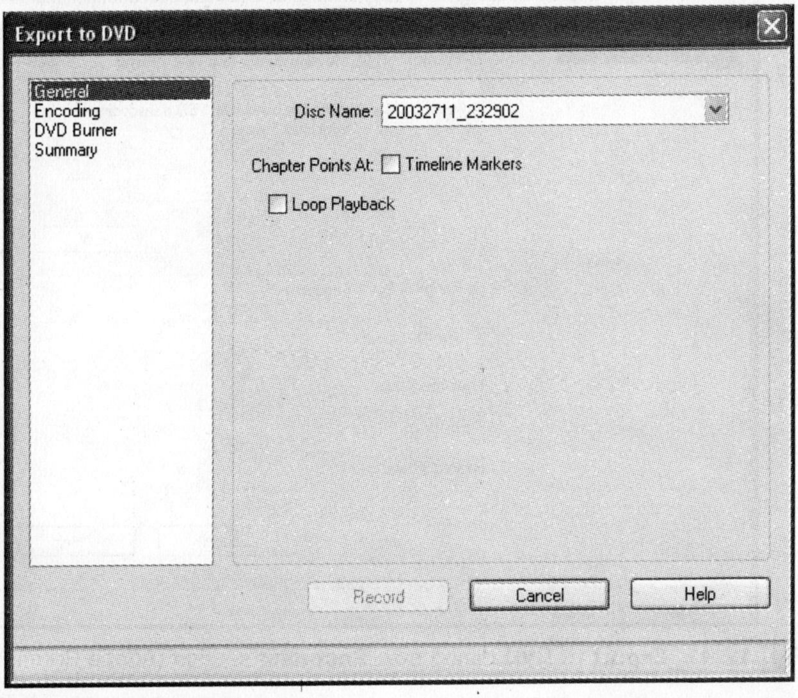

Fig. 12.10. Export to DVD dialog box, **General** section (Adobe Premiere Pro)

In the **Disc Name** list, specify the disc name: the serial number suggested by the application or any name you like. The **Chapter Points At: ... Timeline Markers** checkbox enables creation of the table of contents of the disc at markers. The **Loop Playback** checkbox enables loop playback of the movie.

Let's look at the **Encoding** section of the **Export to DVD** dialog box (Fig. 12.11).

In the **Preset** drop-down list, you can select a ready-made preset corresponding to a certain video format (NTSC/PAL), degree of compression (High/Low quality), video image scanning, and video and audio encoding method. In the **Export Range** drop-down list, select the **Work Area** item (meaning that only the project work area should be exported to a DVD).

The **Maximize Bitrate** checkbox enables the maximum bit rate of the video stream, taking into account the length of the movie and the amount of free space on the DVD. The settings of the preset will be ignored. The **Force Variable Bitrate** checkbox is used to enable a video encoding mode with a variable bit rate, regardless of the settings of the preset selected.

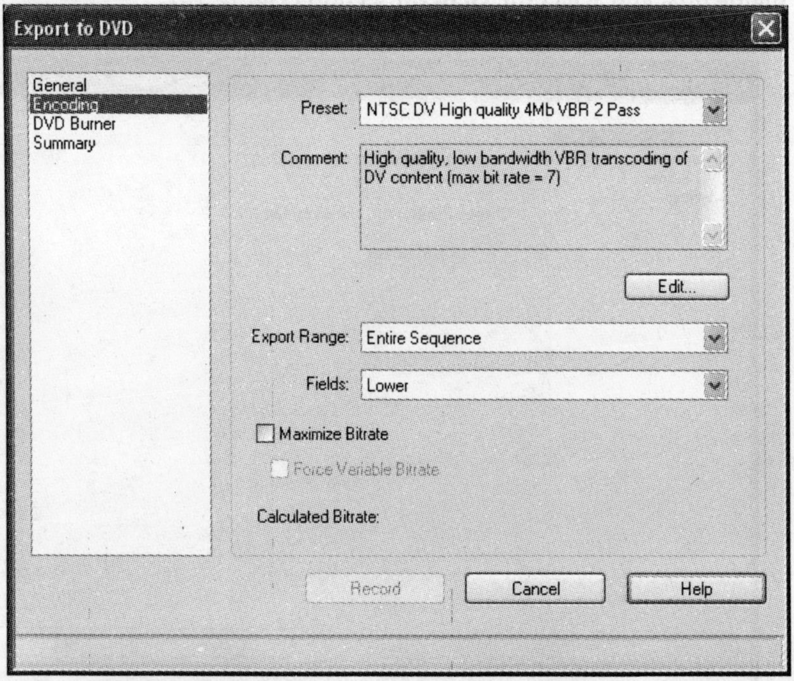

Fig. 12.11. Export to DVD dialog box, **Encoding** section (Adobe Premiere Pro)

We are primarily interested in the settings of the audio component of the movie. To obtain the sound in the Dolby Digital 5.1 format on the DVD, select the presets in the **Preset** drop-down list whose names include the words "SurCode for Dolby Digital 5.1." For finer adjustment of the audio stream parameters, click the **Edit** button. The **Transcode Settings** dialog box will open, in which you should select the **Audio** section (Fig. 12.12).

Here are just the main parameters that affect the properties and quality of the sound track of your movie:

- **Codec** — you should select **SurCode Dolby Digital.**
- **Audio Coding Mode** — determines which channels will be coded (to code all the channels of the 5.1 system, select **3/2**).
- **Data Rate (kb/s)** — is the audio stream bit rate.
- **Bitstream Mode** — you should specify the type of the sound track (for example, **Music and Effects**).

- **Dialog Normalization** — leave the default setting.
- **Dynamic Compression Preset** — type and degree of the dynamic range compression.
- **Center Downmix Level** and **Surround Downmix Level** — levels of the signal mixes in the center and rear channels when the spectator/listener turns on the stereo mode.
- **LFE On** — enables filtration of the LFE channel signal with the low-pass filter before encoding (this checkbox must be checked).

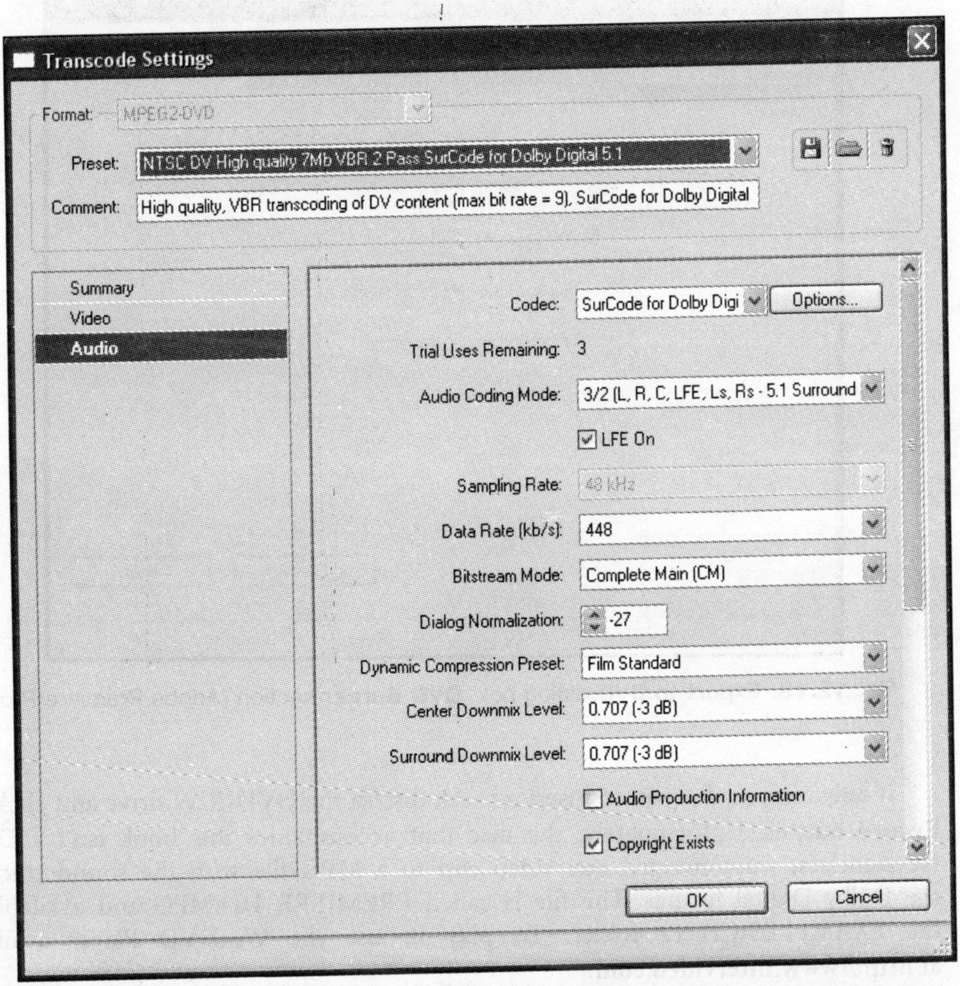

Fig. 12.12. Transcoding Settings dialog box, **Audio** section (Adobe Premiere Pro)

There is the **Options** button to the right of the **Codec** drop-down list. A click on it opens the codec setting panel. Most of the settings are duplicated by the options of the **Transcode Settings** dialog box. However, the codec panel includes the **Help** button that opens a comprehensive online manual on using the Dolby Digital codec.

Let's return to the **Export to DVD** dialog box, to the **DVD Burner** section (Fig. 12.13). Here, you can specify the **Number of Copies** and select a DVD-R/W drive (**DVD Burner**) (if you have more than one).

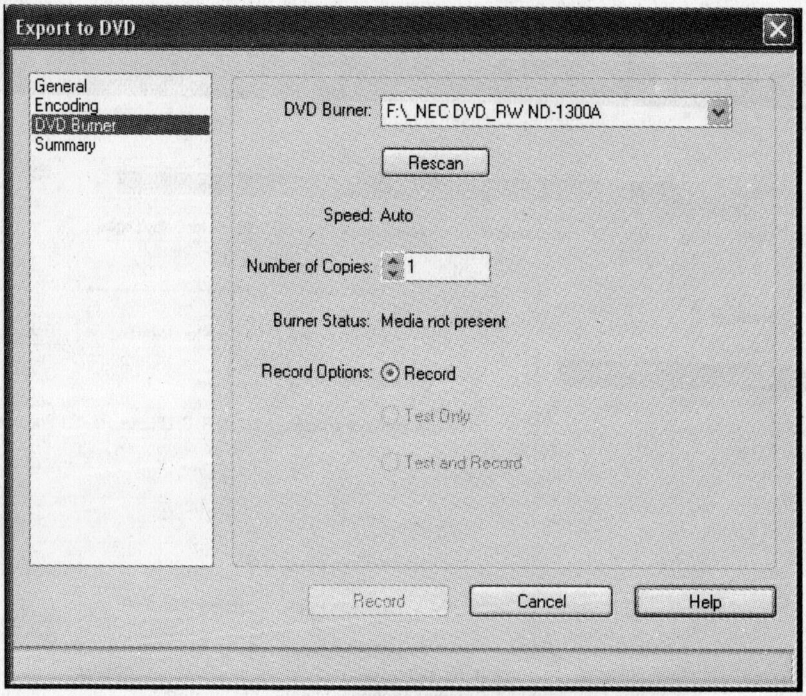

Fig. 12.13. Export to DVD dialog box, **DVD Burner** section (Adobe Premiere Pro)

It only remains for you to insert a blank disc in the DVD-R/W drive and click the **Record** button. Unfortunately, the disc that accompanies this book isn't a DVD. Nevertheless, we converted our video clip to a MPG file with the sound track in the Dolby Digital format. The file is called PREMIERE_DD.MPG and available in the EXAMPLES\CH_12 folder. To play it, use the WinDVD Player available at **http://www.intervideo.com**.

And that's all there is to it!

Appendix 1

CD Contents

A special feature of this disc is that it is in CD Extra format. In other words, it can be both played with a CD player and read with a computer:

- Its *CD-ROM* partition contains example projects, files with intermediate and final results of processing, and a few articles.
- The *CD Digital Audio* partition contains our musical compositions mixed down with Adobe Audition.

System Requirements

To work with the application, a computer with the following specification is required:

- Windows 98/ME/2000/XP
- Intel Pentium III, 800 MHz (recommended Pentium 4 2 GHz)
- 128 MB RAM (recommended 512 MB)
- PCI/AGP bus, video mode 600 × 800 (recommended 1024 × 768), High Color or True Color
- 16-bit sound card
- CD-ROM drive supporting CD Extra

CD-ROM Contents

- The *EXAMPLES* folder contains the examples referred to in the book.
- The *SRC* folder is auxiliary.
- The *WWW* folder is an off-line version of our site **http://musicalpc.com/**.

Audio CD Contents

The CD Digital Audio partition contains the following compositions:

- "Sunrise above Cydonia" (music, arrangement, recording, mixing by Roman Petelin)
- "I Hate the Time" (music, arrangement, recording, mixing by Roman Petelin)
- "Amber Sea" (music, arrangement, recording, mixing by Roman Petelin)
- "Fading to the Darkness" (music, arrangement, recording, mixing by Roman Petelin)
- "Aelita" (music, arrangement by Yury Petelin; recording, mixing by Roman Petelin)
- "In the Life Bygone" (music, arrangement, recording, mixing by Roman Petelin)

Appendix 2

CD Description

Files with examples are stored on the accompanying CD in the EXAMPLES folder, which includes 12 folders (CH_01 to CH_12), corresponding to the chapters of the book.

Example for Chapter 1

- EX_01_01.WAV — a musical composition "Aelita" (by Yury Petelin, arrangement by Roman Petelin).

Examples for Chapter 2

- EX_02_01.WAV — the first fragment of "Aelita". It is intended for illustrating how to load, save, and play files (*Sections 2.2* and *2.3*).
- EX_02_02.WAV — the second fragment of "Aelita". In combination with the EX_02_01.WAV file, it is intended to illustrate how to collect a waveform sequence on one track (*Section 2.4*).

Examples for Chapter 3

- EX_03_01.WAV to EX_03_05.WAV — are the original audio material recorded with a microphone. The material is used in the subsequent chapters. By processing the files EX03_01.WAV, EX03_03.WAV, and EX03_05.WAV in turn, we obtained a track of speech synchronous with the video image. The files EX03_02.WAV and EX03_04.WAV are source files for creating audio accompaniment asynchronous with the video image.

Examples for Chapter 4

- EX04_01.WAV — a fragment of the EX_03_02.WAV file that contains the fifth take of the recording with asynchronous speech of the narrator. It is used to explain the histogram (*Section 4.2.2*). Based on the spectral analysis of the signal stored in the file, we elaborated a plan for frequency filtration (*Section 4.3.3*).
- EX04_02.WAV — an example of an audio material whose instantaneous spectrum contains an anomaly (*Section 4.3.2*).

Examples for Chapter 5

- EX_05_01.WAV — takes No. 4 and No. 5 with the asynchronous speech of the narrator cut from the EX03_02.WAV file. It is intended to illustrate editing (*Section 5.1.5*).
- EX_05_02.WAV — a take with the asynchronous speech of the narrator chosen as a back-up. It was obtained from take No. 4 stored in the file EX03_02.WAV (*Section 5.2.3*).
- EX_05_03.WAV — a take with the asynchronous speech of the narrator chosen for processing. It was obtained from take No. 5 stored in the file EX03_02.WAV (*Section 5.1.5*).
- EX_05_04.WAV — the result of noise reduction in the signal stored in the EX_05_03.WAV file. The fragment at the beginning that contained only noise is removed (*Section 5.3*).

Examples for Chapter 6

- EX06_01.WAV — the result of filtration of the signal stored in the EX_05_04.WAV file *(Section 6.2.8)*.
- EX06_02.WAV — an example of a recording with a high level of background noise of 60 Hz *(Section 6.2.8)*.
- EX06_03.WAV — the result of attenuation of the background noise of 60 Hz by using filtration *(Section 6.2.8)*.

Examples for Chapter 7

- EX07_01.WAV — the result of removing irrelevant sounds from the signal stored in the EX06_01.WAV.
- EX07_02.WAV — the result of dynamic processing of the signal stored in the EX07_01.WAV file *(Section 7.3)*.
- NSINC1.WAV — the result of normalization of the signal stored in the EX07_02.WAV file to a level of –1 dB.
- NSINC2.WAV — the result of sequential processing of the EX03_02.WAV file (the best take was chosen; it was separated as an individual file; the signal in this file was subjected to noise reduction, filtration, and dynamic processing; short fragments with unwanted sounds between the narrator's words were removed).
- SINC1.WAV — the result of sequential processing of the EX03_01.WAV file (the best take was chosen; it was separated as an individual file; the signal in this file was subjected to noise reduction, filtration, and dynamic processing).
- SINC2.WAV — the result of sequential processing of the EX03_03.WAV file.
- SINC3.WAV — the result of sequential processing of the EX03_05.WAV file.

Examples for Chapter 8

- EX08_01.WAV — the signal obtained as a result of processing the NSINC1.WAV file with the Echo effect *(Section 8.1.2)*.
- EX08_02.WAV — the signal obtained as a result of processing the NSINC1.WAV file with the Multitap Delay effect *(Section 8.1.4)*.
- EX08_03.WAV — the signal obtained as a result of processing the NSINC1.WAV file with the Echo Chamber effect *(Section 8.2.3)*.

Example for Chapter 9

- EX09_01.WAV — the result of dynamic processing of the signal in the EX07_01.WAV file with the RVox plug-in from the Waves Platinum Native Bundle 4 package *(Section 9.2)*.

Examples for Chapter 10

- ANALOGUE_JUMPER_C_140BPM.WAV and BREAK_LOOP_A_132BPM.WAV (EXAMPLES\CH_10\LOOPS folder) — loops.
- LOOPS.SES (EXAMPLES\CH_10\LOOPS folder) — project containing the loops.

- FX-AUTOMATION.SES (EXAMPLES\CH_10\LOOPS\FX-AUTOMATION folder) — an example of automation envelopes.

Examples for Chapter 11

- PREMIERE.AVI — a movie exported from Adobe Premiere Pro (EXAMPLES\CH_11 folder).
- ALIST.SES — a multitrack project of the sound track for the movie (EXAMPLES\CH_11 folder).
- SINC1.WAV, SINC2.WAV, SINC3.WAV, NSINC1.WAV, and NSINC2.WAV — files with speech (EXAMPLES\CH_11\SPEECH folder).
- ALIST-AUDIO FOR PREMIERE.WAV — a file with sound imported from the PREMIERE.AVI movie (EXAMPLES\CH_11\SPEECH folder).
- 1.WAV, 2.WAV, and 4.WAV — files with background music (EXAMPLES\CH_11\MUSIC folder).
- PREMIERE_STEREO.AVI — a movie with a stereo sound track mixed down in Adobe Audition (EXAMPLES\CH_11 folder).

To watch the AVI files, install Standard DivX Codec(FREE) from **http://www.divx.com/divx/**.

Examples for Chapter 12

- PREMIERE_51.WAV — a six-channel WAV file.
- PREMIERE_DD.MPG — a movie with a Dolby Digital sound track.

To watch the movie, use the WinDVD Player (**http://www.intervideo.com**).

Index